PROBLEM-ORIENTED POLICING

Volume II

PROBLEM-ORIENTED POLICING: CRIME-SPECIFIC PROBLEMS, CRITICAL ISSUES AND MAKING POP WORK

Volume II

Edited by
Corina Solé Brito
and Tracy Allan
Police Executive Research Forum

POLICE EXECUTIVE
RESEARCH FORUM

Copyright © 1999, Police Executive Research Forum

Printed in the United States of America

Library of Congress Number 99-75127

ISBN 1-878734-70-9

Cover by Marnie Deacon Kenney

CONTENTS

Foreword ix

Acknowledgments xi

Introduction xiii

Part I: Crime-Specific Problems

Chapter 1: Finding and Addressing Repeat Burglaries ... 3
John Stedman
Deborah Lamm Weisel, Ph.D.
Police Executive Research Forum

Chapter 2: Theft, Stolen Goods and the Market-
Reduction Approach: Operation Radium
and Operation Heat 29
Michael Sutton, Ph.D.
Policing and Reducing Crime Unit,
British Home Office
Jacqueline L. Schneider, Ph.D.
Hudson Institute

Chapter 3: Race, Ethnicity and Gender Issues in
Gangs: Reconciling Police Data 63
David Curry, Ph.D.
University of Missouri at St. Louis

Chapter 4: Drug Market Places: How They Form
and How They Can Be Prevented 91
John E. Eck, Ph.D.
University of Cincinnati

Chapter 5:   Responding to Domestic Violence:
             A Collaboration Between the Police
             and the Medical Community 113
             Daniel Brookoff, M.D.
             Methodist Hospital, Memphis
             Walter Crews
             Memphis Police Department
             Charles S. Cook
             Memphis Police Department
             Terry Thompson
             Memphis Police Department

Part II: Critical Issues

Chapter 6:   Investigations in the Community
             Policing Context 151
             Colleen Cosgrove, Ph.D.
             Mary Ann Wycoff
             Police Executive Research Forum

Chapter 7:   Citizens in the POP Process:
             How Much Is Too Much? 177
             Samuel Walker, Ph.D.
             University of Nebraska at Omaha
             Andy Mills
             San Diego Police Department

Chapter 8:   Restorative Policing:
             The Canberra, Australia Experiment 195
             Larry Sherman, Ph.D.
             University of Maryland

Chapter 9:   Policing the New America:
             Immigration and Its Challenge 209
             William McDonald, Ph.D.
             Georgetown University

Part III: Making POP Work

Chapter 10: The Relationship Between
Crime Prevention and
Problem-Oriented Policing 253
Nick Tilley, Ph.D.
Nottingham Trent University

Chapter 11: Using Urban Design to Help
Eradicate Crime Places 281
Gregory Saville, Ph.D.
Florida State University

Chapter 12: Crime Mapping for Problem Solving 297
Nancy LaVigne, Ph.D.
Crime Mapping Research Center,
National Institute of Justice
Julie Wartell
Institute of Law and Justice

Chapter 13: Herman Goldstein Award for
Excellence in Problem-Oriented Policing ...323
Commentary by Ronald Clarke, Ph.D.
Rutgers University

Appendix: 1998 Herman Goldstein Award Winner,
Honorable Mentions 327

About the Authors 395

About PERF 405

Related Titles 407

FOREWORD

Many law enforcement agencies are currently undergoing a dramatic shift in the way they approach policing, from a traditional approach to a more problem-oriented approach. The transition can be challenging for political, organizational and financial reasons, yet when implemented throughout an agency, problem-oriented policing (or POP) often leads to greater job satisfaction for officers and better quality of life for the communities they serve.

The Police Executive Research Forum (PERF) has long recognized that the key to advancing POP is bringing together practitioners who are implementing POP efforts, allowing them to share information regarding their efforts. In this spirit, PERF has already convened its ninth annual International Problem-Oriented Policing Conference. In attendance were more than 1,000 police practitioners and researchers representing numerous law enforcement agencies, academic institutions and organizations from all over the world.

PERF is proud to offer this book as the second of an annual publication series. The book provides an opportunity for those who attended the conference, as well as those who were unable to attend, to more fully explore the concepts presented during the conference. We hope that this book, like Volume I, will stimulate discussion about the direction of problem-oriented policing and encourage the sharing of ideas and knowledge among police agencies around the world.

Chuck Wexler
Executive Director, Police Executive Research Forum
Washington, D.C.

ACKNOWLEDGMENTS

The contributing authors are leading experts in policing and represent a variety of disciplines. They deserve immense credit for providing innovative ideas on the use of problem-oriented policing to address crime-specific problems and critical issues. We thank the authors for their contributions and continued commitment to enhancing the field.

Dr. Dennis Jay Kenney, PERF's former research director, spearheaded the idea of creating a "POP Book" as a finale to the 1997 (Eighth Annual) International Problem-Oriented Policing Conference. Without his vision and dedication to enhancing policing, this book would not exist.

We thank Ellen Dollar for her extensive review and helpful editorial comments during the book's development. PERF's publications staff, Martha Plotkin and Eugenia Gratto Gravely, were extremely helpful in the process as well. Special thanks go to Jason Cheney for his last-minute help, Elliot Grant for designing the book's layout and Marnie Deacon Kenney for designing yet another beautiful cover. The final product was greatly enhanced and polished as a result of their efforts.

As the editors, we would also like to express our appreciation for the opportunity to be involved in the continuation of this series and the evolution of this volume. Not only has this book been valuable for its contribution to our professional development, but it has brought us together in friendship. It is with some regret that we complete this project as it signals the end of our collaboration.

Final thanks go to the men and women who serve and protect our communities.

Corina Solé Brito
Tracy Allan
Police Executive Research Forum

INTRODUCTION

In an era of policing defined by an increased openness to critical analysis, research and debate within the field, law enforcement agencies are inundated with an array of new concepts, theories and practices. Often, however, a new approach is abandoned in favor of the next approach that comes along within a relatively short period of time. Yet, as we move toward the new millennium, the concept of problem-oriented policing (POP) maintains its role as a powerful tool in the policing arsenal. In the late 1970s, Herman Goldstein began to formulate the concept of problem-oriented policing (POP) in an attempt to meet some of the long-term needs of the police and communities.

Recognizing the potential and value of POP, the Police Executive Research Forum (PERF) has made continued efforts to promote and support problem-oriented policing efforts around the country. In 1998, for the ninth consecutive year, PERF, in partnership with the San Diego Police Department, hosted the International Problem-Oriented Policing Conference in San Diego, Calif. This conference provides a forum for practitioners and researchers to share their knowledge of community problems as well as their experiences in responding to them. At the 1998 conference, approximately 170 people from the United States and around the world delivered presentations addressing a diverse array of POP-related topics. From this exciting pool of topics, we have selected several presentations that addressed issues we believe are the most pervasive and of the greatest interest to law enforcement agencies and criminal justice researchers alike. This book, by highlighting these presentations, will serve as a valuable reference. The contributions to this book have been divided into the following three categories: Crime-Specific Problems, Critical Issues and Making POP Work.

Crime-Specific Problems

Although communities are, to a certain extent, unique in the type and extent of crime they experience, common crimes and problems bridge geographic and/or social boundaries. This section of the book focuses on a range of crime problems that plague many of our communities—from theft and burglary to gangs, drugs and domestic violence. Chapter 1 tackles the challenge of *Finding and Addressing Repeat Burglaries.* John Stedman and Deborah Lamm Weisel explore the theory that there is an increased risk of burglary at a residence if it has been previously burgled. The authors present a synthesis of related research and their preliminary findings on the effect of an education and prevention program aimed at first-time burglary victims.

In Chapter 2, *Theft, Stolen Goods and the Market-Reduction Approach: Operation Radium and Operation Heat,* Michael Sutton and Jacqueline Schneider present the British approach to reducing theft. Instead of targeting prevention efforts at the victims, the market-reduction approach targets the buyers and sellers of stolen merchandise. With the rise in burglary and automobile theft rates in Britain over the past 15 years, British law enforcement personnel have begun to look for new theft-reduction methods. The authors contend that by tackling the markets where stolen goods are sold, the police gain a greater capacity to deal with theft.

The remaining three chapters in this section of the book focus on illegal drugs and street gangs. Once thought to be primarily urban afflictions, the problems of gangs and drugs have permeated even the most rural and suburban communities. David Curry, in his chapter on *Race, Ethnicity, and Gender Issues and Gangs: Reconciling Police Data,* believes that one of the impediments to successful gang enforcement is the disparity between law enforcement data on race, ethnicity and gender in gangs, and the same type of data gathered by others. Consequently, the author stresses the need to combine law enforcement data and other sources of intelligence to accomplish a thorough analysis and pave the way for an effective response to gang-related crime and delinquency.

In Chapter 4, John Eck details the spatial organization of retail drug dealing in *Drug Market Places: How They Form and How They Can Be Prevented*. In describing how illicit drug markets are organized, the author provides knowledge problem solvers can use to develop more effective approaches to deter and prevent such markets. Eck contends that participants in retail markets use two fundamental strategies to balance rewards and risks: restrict dealing to people they know (which restricts sales and buying opportunities) or deal with strangers (which provides greater access to both buyers and sellers but increased risk of arrest). By understanding these marketing strategies and the resulting geographic patterns, the police can develop more effective responses to retail drug problems.

The final chapter in this section describes the prevalence and role of alcohol and other drugs in domestic violence. Based on the presentation by Daniel Brookoff and Walter Crews, Chapter 5 explores *Responding to Domestic Violence: A Collaboration Between the Police and the Medical Community*. Following a brief overview of the dangers of drug use and the high rate of drug involvement in domestic violence incidents, the authors describe the powerful collaboration of the police and medical community in Memphis, Tenn. Because of the dangerous nexus between drug use and domestic violence, the Memphis project pairs an officer with a medical professional to respond to domestic violence calls.

Critical Issues

The Critical Issues section of this book introduces the reader to a sampling of issues PERF anticipates will challenge the law enforcement community as we enter the 21st century. The implementation of new policing concepts and practices has produced a new set of concerns for police managers, executives and administrators. Community policing, for example, has brought a new set of considerations to law enforcement agencies around the country. In Chapter 6, Colleen Cosgrove and Mary Ann Wycoff present their research findings on *Investigations in the*

Community Policing Context. The authors tackle administrative concerns about investigations and the role of detectives in departments that embrace community policing. To provide some guidance to managers on how the investigative function should be performed in a community policing context and how to manage the change without causing organizational turmoil, Cosgrove and Wycoff address three fundamental questions: (1) What should the investigative function encompass? (2) Who should perform the investigative function? and (3) What is its relationship to citizens and other police personnel?

With the increasing emphasis on citizen involvement in police matters through community policing and problem-oriented policing, agencies are beginning to recognize the potential for citizen manipulation of and by the police. To prompt departments to think proactively, Sam Walker and Andy Mills explore these issues and potential problems in their chapter, *Citizens in the POP Process: How Much Is Too Much?* The authors' intent is not necessarily to present solutions, but rather to open the issue to debate. By initiating a dialogue to address these issues, Walker and Mills hope that some of the potential for manipulation may be avoided.

Despite recent changes in police agencies' expectations of officers due to the adoption of practices such as community policing, there is still an emphasis on the bottom line—apprehending suspects. However, officers often find themselves frustrated with the judicial system's response once a suspect is arrested. In response to these concerns, Chapter 8 introduces the reader to *Restorative Policing,* an alternative means of justice. Lawrence Sherman provides an overview of restorative justice and explains how, by stressing the harm that the crime has caused to both the people directly involved and the community, the process is successful. The author maintains that through a conference meeting of affected individuals, a mediator is able to establish a punishment that is satisfactory to both the victim and the offender. Sherman concludes the chapter by focusing specifically on restorative justice efforts in Canberra, Australia.

The final chapter in the Critical Issues section explores the burgeoning issues associated with the changing ethnic composition of the American population due to sharply climbing immigration rates. In Chapter 9, *Policing the New America: Immigration and Its Challenge,* William McDonald explores the changes in America's ethnic composition and identifies the resulting challenges. The author stresses that, to successfully serve and protect in communities around the country, police must be prepared to cross both cultural and jurisdictional boundaries. In addition, McDonald presents contrasting examples of both promising efforts to bridge these immigration differences, and flawed enforcement efforts.

Making POP Work

One of the biggest challenges facing POP practitioners is the implementation of theory into practice. This section of the book provides insight and presents practical examples of Making POP Work. The authors of Chapters 10 and 11 explore the POP process and its potential for crime prevention. In Chapter 10, Nick Tilley discusses *The Relationship Between Crime Prevention and Problem-Oriented Policing* from a British perspective. After introducing the reader to the historical and conceptual relationship between crime prevention and problem-oriented policing, the author then describes recent British developments. From his experiences with the Home Office in Britain, Tilley provides an insider's perspective on a recent report's conclusions on potential police contributions to crime prevention, and the research findings of efforts to introduce POP in Britain. The author concludes with a discussion of efforts to direct British police into a prevention-oriented, problem-focused approach, and of the inclusion of other agencies in this process.

Gregory Saville, in Chapter 11, explores crime prevention from the perspective of *Using Urban Design to Help Eradicate Crime Places.* Saville cites the increasing prominence of CPTED (crime prevention through environmental design) as an indication of its universal appeal. He introduces the basic principles of CPTED and provides an overview of its implementation. Using practical examples, the author concludes with illustrations of how CPTED can be used to modify physical environments, thus decreasing vulnerability to crime and removing environmental characteristics that criminals prefer.

Chapter 12 explores the role technology can play in supporting POP efforts. As the 21st century approaches, the law enforcement community is encountering an array of available technology that provides timely access to information for all levels of the organization. In *Crime Mapping for Problem Solving,* Nancy LaVigne and Julie Wartell provide an introduction to crime mapping as a means of managing this information. This chapter provides an overview of crime mapping and the types of mapping available. By highlighting examples of computerized crime mapping in support of problem-oriented policing, the authors provide a national perspective on the extent to which agencies are utilizing computerized crime mapping and how the information is being applied.

Chapter 13, the book's final chapter, provides examples of problem-oriented policing projects from agencies across the United States. The Police Executive Research Forum (PERF), in an effort to promote and support problem-oriented policing, annually presents the Herman Goldstein Award for Excellence in Problem-Oriented Policing. The award was developed to recognize innovative and effective POP projects that have achieved measurable success in reducing specific crime, disorder or public safety problems. In 1998, the Herman Goldstein Award was presented to the Boston Police Department for their Operation Cease-Fire project. In addition, the selection committee recognized six projects for honorable mention: (1) Fraud Schemes Targeted at Senior Citizens (Nassau County, N.Y., Police Department); (2) Mission Valley Preserve—Restoration of a Region of the San Diego River Bed (San Diego, Calif., Police Department); (3) Police Response to Incidents of Domestic Emergencies [PRIDE] (Newport News, Va., Police Department); (4) San Ysidro International Border (San Diego, Calif., Police Department); (5) Operation Hot Pipe/Smoky Haze/Rehab (San Diego, Calif., Police Department); and (6) Transient Enrichment Network (Fontana, Calif., Police Department). These top seven projects serve as practical illustrations of how POP theory has been translated into successful practice, and are outlined following the opening commentary by Ronald Clarke, chair of the award selection committee.

Conclusion

As society changes, so must police practices. Problem-oriented policing strategies offer law enforcement personnel the opportunity to tailor their responses to crime and quality-of-life issues to the communities they protect and serve. The chapters of this book illustrate how society is changing, how crime and responses to its occurrence are changing, and how successful implementations of POP are addressing these changes. We expect that this publication will serve as a valuable resource to law enforcement agencies, academics and others committed to problem solving.

PART I

CRIME-SPECIFIC PROBLEMS

2

CHAPTER I

FINDING AND ADDRESSING REPEAT BURGLARIES[1]

John Stedman and Deborah Lamm Weisel

American police departments have employed problem solving for more than 15 years (Goldstein 1979; Eck and Spelman 1987), and much has been learned about what happens when agencies attempt its implementation (Eck and Spelman 1987; Goldstein 1990; BJA 1997). A problem-solving approach emphasizes careful analysis of problems, development of responses based on that analysis, and an evaluation of the response's impact on the problem (Goldstein 1979; Goldstein and Susmilch 1982; Eck and Spelman 1987; Goldstein 1990; BJA 1997; Cosgrove, Reuland, and Huneycutt 1998). The broad objective of problem solving is to get police to look at crime and disorder problems in new ways and develop specific responses to reduce those problems.

One promising problem-solving approach to understanding and controlling crime has emerged from repeat victimization studies. These studies illuminate the disproportionate contribution to overall crime rates of people and places that are repeatedly victimized. This phenomenon of repeat victimization builds on "hotspots" research, or studies of the clustering of crime. Although the concept of repeat victimization is relatively new in this country, it is widely recognized in the United Kingdom. In fact, British police and researchers have studied and responded to the phenomenon with considerable success for several years. Repeat victimization is

[1] This research was supported by grant # 96-IJ-CX-0042 from the National Institute of Justice. Points of view are those of the authors and do not necessarily represent the position of the U.S. Department of Justice.

now so widely recognized that police in the United Kingdom are held accountable for the incidence of repeat victimization as one measure of police performance (Tilley 1995).

Recognition of the repeat victimization phenomenon is only now increasing in the United States. In 1996, the National Institute of Justice (NIJ) published an article on repeat victimization by two respected British criminologists (Pease and Laycock 1996). In the same year, the Police Executive Research Forum (PERF) highlighted repeat victimization research at its annual Problem-Oriented Policing Conference. In addition, in 1997, PERF began an NIJ-funded study of repeat victimization for residential burglary in three cities—Baltimore, Dallas and San Diego. This research was undertaken to learn more about repeat victimization and to test the ability of police problem solving to intervene and reduce the problem's occurrence. If successful, citywide residential burglary rates would be reduced.

While the broad-based focus on repeat victimization is new, interest in the subject is not. Beginning in the 1970s, research began to demonstrate that some people were disproportionately harmed by crime (Johnson et al. 1973; Zeigenhagen 1976; Hindelang, Gottfredson, and Garofalo 1978; Fienberg 1980; Reiss 1980; Nelson 1980; Sparks 1981). Since those studies, researchers and police have learned even more about the phenomenon.

- Recent victimization surveys support the earlier research that there is a concentration of incidents among a small number of victims (Ellingworth, Farrell, and Pease 1995; Spelman 1995a). In some cases, up to 70 percent of crimes affect 14 percent of respondents (Farrell 1992). Hakkert and Oppenhuis (1996) report that 17 percent of robbery victims are repeat victims.

- Consistently across crime types, being a victim once is a good predictor of being a victim again. For example, once a residence has been burgled, it is four times more likely to be burgled again than is a house that has not been burgled at all (Forrester et al. 1988). Sampson and Phillips (1992) report that, for racial attacks, 67 percent of the victims suffer subsequent victimizations. For school crimes, Burquest, Farrell, and Pease (1992) report that 98 percent of all the crimes at 33 schools in one British community were repeats at the same location. Bennett (1995) reports that "as many as 35% of all burglaries recorded in the area [are] one of a repeat series of burglaries."

- Rates of repeat victimization vary by city. Repeat burglaries accounted for 11.5 percent of single family burglaries in Baltimore, 10 percent in Dallas and 4 percent in San Diego. These variations were related to differences in types of housing in each city (Weisel and Stedman 1998).
- Repeat victimization varies by crime type: 90 percent of domestic violence cases are repeats, 61 percent of burgled small businesses are repeats, and 8 percent of motor vehicle theft victims account for 22 percent of incidents (Bridgeman and Hobbs 1997).
- Repeat victimization is clustered in high-crime areas or hotspots (Sherman 1989, 1995; Bennett 1995; Spelman 1995a; Pease 1996, 1998; Pease and Laycock 1996; Bennett and Durie 1996; Guidi, Homel, and Townsley 1997). Personal crime is even more concentrated than property crime (Trickett et al. 1992; Pease 1993, 1998; Trickett, Osborn, and Ellingworth 1995; Farrell 1992).
- Even the best estimates of repeat victimization are undercounts. Data sources of reported crime, such as the Uniform Crime Reports and police offense reports, significantly undercount crime victims (Shover 1991; BJS 1995; Mukherjee, Carcach, and Higgins 1997), a phenomenon that is exacerbated in areas where reporting rates are low and crime is high (National Board for Crime Prevention 1994; Farrell and Pease 1995). People who are repeatedly victimized are even less likely to report subsequent victimizations to police (Mukherjee, Carcach, and Higgins 1997). Even direct victim surveys in the United States and the United Kingdom may also undercount repeat victimization (Genn 1988; Farrell and Pease 1993).

- The occurrence of repeat victimization is rapid for all crime types (Forrester, Chatterton, and Pease 1988, 1990; Pease 1991, 1998; Polvi et al. 1990; Farrell 1992; Farrell and Pease 1993; Spelman 1995b; Guidi, Homel, and Townsley 1997). Studies found that half of burglary revictimization occurred within seven days of the first incident (Polvi et al. 1990), repeat victimization for racial attacks was most frequent within the first week of the initial attack (Sampson and Phillips 1992), half of second offenses against businesses occurred within six weeks (Tilley 1993), and 79 percent of repeats against schools occurred within one month (Burquest, Farrell, and Pease 1992).
- Repeat victimization can be targeted by the police and reduced, resulting in lower crime rates (Chenery, Holt, and Pease 1997; Pease 1998). Residential burglaries in one city were reduced by 24 percent and other burglaries by 5 percent; in another city, a 27 percent drop was obtained. In a third city that focused on repeat victimization, a 72 percent reduction in burglaries was achieved over three years (Bridgeman and Hobbs 1997). By focusing on repeat victimization, police efforts reduced racial attacks in East London by 12 percent, and the percentage of students who said they were the victim of school bullying declined from 62 percent to 47 percent in one school, and 72 percent to 48 percent in another.

Barriers to Success

The use of problem-solving techniques to develop responses to repeat victimization seems to be a crime fighter's dream—it helps focus limited resources on likely victims in an effort to deter and/or apprehend offenders. The most victimized are protected and the incidence of crime is reduced (Pease 1991, 1998; Farrell and Pease 1993; Bennett and Durie 1996). In practice, however, it can be quite difficult to successfully identify repeat victimization and apply problem-solving efforts.

The Problem Analysis Barrier. Problem analysis is a key step in problem solving, although it is often the most difficult step for the police to accomplish. Often, analysis is omitted completely (Goldstein 1990; Reuland, Cosgrove and Oettmeier 1998; BJA forthcoming). In fact, most officers have little experience or training in analysis, and many get lost in the process or make their analysis efforts too cumbersome to succeed. The objective of analyzing problems is to uncover information about a problem that suggests a unique response. Successful analysis creates a cognitive "aha!" for problem solvers, presenting them with new information that helps them to see the problem in a new light.

Unfortunately, problem-solving groups all too often gather only one or two types of information, and even that is usually information with which group members are most familiar, such as data available from police records. Real analysis requires problem solvers to gather problem information from numerous other sources; residents who live near problem locations, business owners, landlords, recreation directors, social service providers, offenders, and numerous other sources may have important information about problems.

While studies of repeat victimization have provided much information about the prevalence and concentration of crime, certain research complexities have obscured the importance of the phenomenon for American police. For example, despite the international focus on repeat victimization, little research on the subject has been carried out in the United States. Among American studies, Sorenson, Siegel, and Golding (1991) looked at repeated sexual victimization, and Lauritsen and Quinet (1995) examined repeat victimization among teens and young adults. PERF's current study looks at repeat residential burglary in three cities. Other studies have examined hotspots of crime (see, for example, Sherman 1989, 1995; Block and Block 1995; Spelman 1995a), but there has been scant attention paid to the "hot dots" within those hotspots.

Despite considerable research on repeat victimization abroad, those studies have not made cross-sectional comparisons across crime types. Instead, the focus has been limited to specific crimes, such as burglary (Forrester, Chatterton, and Pease 1988; Forrester et al. 1990; Polvi et al. 1990; Pease 1991; Bennett 1995; Tseloni and Pease 1998; Osborn, Ellingsworth, and Hope 1996; Bennett and Durie 1996; Guidi, Homel, and Townsley 1997; Mukherjee, Carcach, and Higgins 1997). Other studies have been parochial, focusing on single locations (Forrester, Chatterton, and Pease 1988; Polvi et al. 1990; Anderson, Chenery, and Pease 1995), while several have examined aggregate national crime survey data (Trickett et al. 1992, 1993; Chenery et al. 1995; Ellingworth, Farrell, and Pease 1995; Osborn, Ellingsworth, and Hope 1996; Mukherjee, Carcach, and Higgins 1997), and observed variations in repeat victimization rates in different places.

There are also barriers to *doing* something about repeat victimization. Police officers at all levels are often skeptical about the existence of repeat victimization, largely because of inadequate crime data and computer systems, and the working practices of their departments (Pease 1996). Most police data systems record and report incidents as independent events (Pease and Laycock 1996; Bridgeman and Hobbs 1997; Pease 1998). Because the police work in shifts, it is unlikely that individual officers will link repeat incidents easily. Crime analysts, on the other hand, typically look for weekly or monthly trends in crime so that they can assist officers in responding quickly to emerging problems. A longer time window, however, is necessary to identify repeat victimizations. In fact, most researchers studying the phenomenon recommend that analysis include at least six months to one year of data to successfully document its occurrence (Farrell and Pease 1993; Pease 1995, 1996; Bridgeman and Hobbs 1997; Pease 1998).

Police are not alone in overlooking the repeat victimization phenomenon. Even when data are available, the presence of a repeat problem may be missed, as it was by researchers in one U.S. city who reported that "burglary is primarily a single-address phenomenon since 81.52% of all the victimized addresses and 61.1% of all the burglaries involve just one call to a single address" (LeBeau and Vincent 1997). According to this study's data, one-time victimizations occurred at 6,616 addresses—about 61 percent of the jurisdiction's 10,828 burglaries in 1990. But the remaining 39 percent of burglaries—4,212—occurred at addresses with two or more burglaries during the calendar year. This is a significant amount of repeat victimization.

Recognition of repeat victimization is often clouded by the way in which one defines a repeat victim (Pease 1996, 1998). There are three critical elements to the definition of repeat victimization—specifying a period of time during which a repeat may occur; selecting a person, place or object as the unit of analysis; and determining whether any crimes suffered by the same victim are counted as repeats or if only crimes of the same type count (National Board for Crime Prevention 1994; Pease 1995, 1996, 1998; Bridgeman and Hobbs 1997).

The lack of a standardized time frame for analyzing repeat offenses is a serious weakness. Anderson, Chenery and Pease (1995), for example, examined 11 months of data; Forrester, Chatterton and Pease (1988), Lauritsen and Quinet (1995), and Hakkert and Oppenhuis (1996) looked at one year; Bennett (1995) and Guidi, Homel and Townsley (1997) analyzed 18 months; and Hope (1995) and Sampson and Phillips (1995) used a period of three years. Polvi et al. (1990) based their research on four years, while Sorenson, Siegel and Golding (1991) included any sexual assault that occurred in a victim's lifetime. Because the time frame used to determine repeat victimization significantly alters the findings, this inconsistency across studies complicates comparisons (Farrell and Pease 1993; Pease 1995, 1996, 1998).

Specifying the victim is the next element in defining repeat victimization. For burglaries (commercial and residential), the place (specific street address) is typically considered the victim (Forrester, Chatterton, and Pease 1988; Anderson, Chenery, and Pease 1995; Pease 1995, 1996; Guidi, Homel, and Townsley 1997). For robberies, the victim may be considered as either the place (addresses in commercial robberies) or the person (street robberies) (Pease 1995; Hakkert and Oppenhuis 1996). For motor vehicle thefts, the person (owner), the object (motor vehicle) or the place (parking lot) may be considered as the victim (Anderson, Chenery, and Pease 1995; Pease 1995). Bridgeman and Hobbs (1997) report that "most forces are defining a repeat victim as a person or place that experiences a similar offense, for example a burglary followed by another burglary or attempted burglary." Pease (1996, 1998) goes on to recommend that when defining repeat victims the police should focus on offenses of the same type, use a time period of six months or one year, and count attempted offenses as repeats.

The third element of the definition concerns whether to include more than one crime type. For example, if a person's home is burgled and they are also the victim of a street robbery, are they to be considered a repeat victim? Pease (1998) recommends only considering crimes of the same type when defining repeat victimization.

Once a definition of repeat victimization has been determined, data collection can begin. This is often a difficult and time consuming process, and presents more hurdles (Anderson, Chenery, and Pease 1995). Hough and Tilley (1997) provide the following list of common data problems:

- *Poor data quality*—Often there are errors in the recording of data on police reports and/or the entry of that data into the automated system.
- *An inability to manipulate the data*—It is often difficult for police data systems to identify repeat victimization of the same address or same person (Farrell and Pease 1993; Ellingworth et al. 1995).
- *Difficulty assigning a specific location to an incident*—Many offenses occur in open spaces, rather than a specific address, making it difficult to assign a specific location to the offense for analysis purposes.
- *Data-sharing problems*—Often a good analysis, in addition to using crime data, involves land use, street or road, or demographic data, but the formats of these files are often incompatible with each other.

- *Failure to integrate crime analysis and crime intelligence data*—Often police agencies maintain numerous, yet separate, calls-for-service, crime, and intelligence database systems that have no linkage among them.
- *Inadequate data classifications*—Crime data may be grouped into aggregate categories for statistical reporting, obscuring important differences in types of offenses, or information on victim places (for example, apartment number) may not be captured as a separate field, if at all.

What to Do?

Despite the numerous difficulties in understanding repeat victimization, it shows great promise for the police as an analytical tool to develop effective interventions to reduce crime (Forrester, Chatterton, and Pease 1988; Anderson, Chenery, and Pease 1995; Bennett and Durie 1996; Weisel and Stedman 1998). Offense analysis to identify the incidence and prevalence of repeat victimization provides guidance for further analysis. Repeat victimization also offers a mechanism for using crime prevention as a specific rather than a general deterrence model, and suggests the need to integrate crime prevention and investigations functions.

Concerns about prior repeat victimization studies demonstrate the pressing need to develop a standardized definition of repeat victimization, collect solid data about the incidence of repeat victimization across diverse jurisdictions and crimes, and build American-based research on this important criminological phenomenon. In 1997, PERF began a repeat victimization project to meet these goals.

PERF's Repeat Residential Burglary Study

PERF is conducting a two-year study of repeat victimization, focused on understanding the nature of residential burglary and developing effective interventions using problem-solving approaches. The study, funded by the National Institute of Justice (NIJ), is being undertaken with police departments in Baltimore, San Diego and Dallas.

During the two-year study, PERF and the police agencies will document both the citywide nature and time course of repeat victimization, analyzing its contribution to total burglary rates, and develop and implement a 12-month "treatment package" specifically designed to address and prevent repeat burglaries in a targeted area of each city. The "treatment package" will be developed following a careful analysis of burglaries in the target area, and will likely include methods such as target hardening, access control, and formal and informal surveillance of premises.

For this study, PERF collected data on residential burglaries reported to the police for the calendar year 1996. The address burgled was considered the victim. Any burglary occurring at an address that had already been burgled once during the calendar year of 1996 was considered a repeat burglary. The burglaries in each city were separated into two groups—those occurring at single-family addresses and those occurring at multifamily addresses. In each city, the police database for each burglary included a code identifying whether an address was single-family or multifamily.

Incidence of Repeat Burglaries

There were 8,112 burglaries at 7,176 single-family addresses in Baltimore in 1996. Repeat burglaries accounted for 11.5 percent of all single-family burglaries in Baltimore. The repeat rate was higher (27.8%) for burglaries at multifamily addresses. In 1996, 1,361 multifamily addresses were burgled, for a total of 1,884 burglaries.

In Dallas in 1996, 7,881 single-family addresses were burgled for a total of 8,762 burglaries; the repeat rate was 10.1 percent. There were 2,700 multifamily addresses hit for a total of 5,839 burglaries, and a repeat rate of 53.8 percent.

San Diego had the lowest repeat rates of the three cities. In 1996 there were 1,512 burglaries reported at 1,450 single-family addresses—a repeat rate of 4.1 percent. There were 3,055 burglaries at 2,721 multifamily addresses in 1996, for a repeat rate of 10.9 percent.

Police Actions Prior to the Project

In San Diego and Baltimore, when a citizen called the police to report a burglary, an officer was sent to the residence to investigate and take an offense report. In both cities, officers were also supposed to conduct a neighborhood canvass to locate possible witnesses, etc. In San Diego, patrol officers carried basic evidence collection equipment (fingerprint powder, tape, Polaroid camera, etc.), allowing them to process the scene. In Baltimore, the officer examined the scene to determine if there was a need to have an evidence collection expert respond. In Dallas, when a victim called in a burglary, it was handled in one of two ways. If the burglary was not in progress (patrol cars were sent out immediately for these), the report could be taken over the telephone by a nonsworn member of the department. In about 50 percent of the cold burglaries, patrol officers were dispatched to the scene to take a report because the telephone report takers were too busy and the time the victim would have to wait to report the offense was considered too long. As in the other two cities, officers in Dallas were supposed to conduct a neighborhood canvass. As in Baltimore, the officer then decided if an evidence technician should respond to collect evidence.

In all three cities, after the preliminary report was taken, the offense report was reviewed by a supervisor and then either suspended for lack of leads, or sent to an officer or investigator for a follow-up investigation.

Site visits confirmed that the offering of target hardening or other crime prevention advice to the victim was a very hit-or-miss proposition, depending on the knowledge, interest and motivation of the officer taking the report. No one in any of the cities notified the victims of their increased likelihood of subsequent victimization.

Teams of officers in each city focused on three goals:

- Conduct better preliminary investigations by urging officers to include more detail in their reports, examining scenes for possible evidence, and ensuring that officers conduct neighborhood canvasses.

- Make officers, victims and neighbors aware of the victims' increased vulnerability after a burglary.
- Provide more direct target hardening and crime prevention advice and/or services to victims of residential burglaries.

Each of the three cities approached these goals in different ways.

Baltimore Treatment Program

Patrol officers and investigators played more of a role in Baltimore's treatment effort. As in the other two sites, PERF had a site coordinator assigned to Baltimore who also carried out many administrative, support and treatment tasks. The Baltimore treatment had the following elements:

- Officers assigned to the Southern District (the experimental area) received roll-call training about the project, repeat victimization, the treatment package, and the necessity of conducting better preliminary investigations.
- When officers take a residential burglary report they provide the victim with a card (see Figure 1) warning them of their increased vulnerability, providing advice on securing and protecting their residence, and urging them to have a home security check. The department also made arrangements with a local nonprofit building supply company to allow victims presenting the card to become a member of the co-op and qualify for reduced costs for such items as plywood, locks and other materials used to secure a residence.
- The officer also examines the crime scene to determine if there is a need for the evidence-collection team to respond.
- The officers taking the report then canvass the neighborhood and provide neighbors with a card alerting them that a burglary has occurred in their neighborhood. The card (see Figure 2) also provides crime prevention tips, asks them to call the police if they have any information, and urges them to get a home security check. If a neighbor is not home

Figure 1

WARNING !!

**Now that you have
been the victim of a
BURGLARY . . .**

♦

**. . .there is a 1 in 3
chance you will be a
victim again – Soon!!**

♦

**YOU CAN PROTECT
YOURSELF**

**by following the
burglary prevention
checklist on the other
side of this card.**

*Courtesy Baltimore Police Department
Southern District*

(front)

DON'T BE AN
EASY TARGET!

➤ Secure the spot where the burglar
broke in as soon as possible.*

➤ Lock your doors and windows when
you're not at home. Don't forget
second story windows!

➤ Call the police if you see suspicious
people in your neighborhood.

➤ Don't leave strangers alone in any
room, at any time.

➤ Keep cash and jewelry out of sight
from windows and doors.

➤ Install strong locks on doors and
windows.*

➤ Get a free Police Department home
security survey - call 410-354-5169.

*The Loading Dock, a non-profit company,
offers reduced price building materials.
Become a member by calling 410-728-3626.
(This card must accompany first visit.)

(back)

when the canvass is conducted, the officers leave the card
in the mailbox or under the front door.

• A copy of the offense report is sent to the Major Crimes
Unit of the Southern District—the group of investigators
who conduct all burglary follow-up investigations—and
assigned to an investigator.

Figure 2

ALERT!!!

**There was recently a burglary
in a nearby home.**

♦

**If you have any information
about this burglary or saw
anything suspicious, call the
Major Crimes Unit at
410-396-2504.**

♦

**There is a good chance the
burglar will come back.**

♦

**You can protect yourself
by following the burglary
prevention checklist on the
other side of this card.**

*Courtesy Baltimore Police Department
Southern District*

(front)

DON'T BE AN
EASY TARGET!

➢ Lock your doors and windows when
you're not at home. Don't forget
second story windows!

➢ Call the police if you see suspicious
people in your neighborhood.

➢ Don't leave strangers alone in any
room, at any time.

➢ Keep cash and jewelry out of sight
from windows and doors.

➢ Install strong locks on doors and
windows.

➢ Get a free Police Department home
security survey – call 410-354-5169.

(back)

• Investigators contact victims within 24 to 48 hours of the
burglary and ask if they would like to have officers record
the serial numbers on any property remaining in their
home. They are also asked if they have been the victim of
a burglary at the same address within the past 12 months,
and if so, whether they reported it to the police.

- If victims do want their remaining property recorded, an officer assigned to the Major Crimes Unit is sent to do so.
- Each week the Major Crimes Unit prepares a listing of the residential burglaries that have occurred in the previous four weeks and distributes this to the patrol officers. Patrol officers are expected to make special checks on these residences and record these checks on their daily activity logs. These logs are turned into the officers' sergeant each day and reviewed.
- The PERF site coordinator visits roll call and rides with officers to provide them information on the project and to get feedback.

Dallas Treatment Program

In Dallas, the deputy chief in command of the Northeastern Division assigned a crime prevention officer to work specifically on this project and do most of the tasks associated with the treatment. The treatment consisted of the following:

- Officers assigned to the Northeastern Division (the experimental area) received roll-call training about the project, repeat victimization, the treatment package, and the necessity of conducting better preliminary investigations.
- The crime prevention officer contacts every victim of a residential burglary in the treatment area (usually within 24 to 48 hours), warns victims of their increased likelihood of victimization, and offers a home security check. The victims are also asked if they have been a victim of a burglary at the same address within the previous 12 months, and if so, whether they reported it to the police.
- Also within 24 to 48 hours of the burglary, the crime prevention officer visits the location of the burglary and conducts a neighborhood canvass to locate witnesses and pass out a warning door hanger (see Figure 3).
- Because the vast majority of the burglaries in Dallas occur in large apartment complexes, the officer also con-

Figure 3

Don't be a Victim!

On _____ a nearby residence was burglarized. In this area, 2 in 5 residential burglaries occur at locations that have been burglarized before. Chances of a second burglary are greatest during the 2 months after the first crime. To help you protect yourself from becoming a victim, the Dallas Police Department offers the following suggestions:

➤   Report all suspicious activity to 911. Do NOT attempt to stop the crime yourself.

➤   Contact the Dallas Police Department for free home security surveys and crime prevention tips.

➤   The Dallas Regional Crimestoppers will pay up to $1000.00 for information that leads to the arrest AND indictment of individuals involved in the commission of a burglary (or any felony offense). Call (214)-373-TIPS (8477) with any anonymous tip.

Answers to any questions about these services can be obtained by contacting the Dallas Police Department at 214-670-7766 or visit the DPD home page at *www.airmail.net/dpd/*.

tacts the apartment management to alert them of the burglary, and to advise them and their staff (maintenance, security, etc.) of any security measures they can take. On some occasions, the crime prevention officer conducts a CPTED (crime prevention through environmental design) survey of the apartment complex and makes recommendations for improvement.
- PERF's on-site project coordinator notifies patrol and special patrol officers of the residential burglaries so that they can increase surveillance patrols of victim locations.
- The deputy chief of the Northeastern Division also sends a letter to each victim and to the managers, owners and management companies responsible for each property. These letters warn of the probability of repeat offenses and encourage participation in steps to reduce burglaries. Owners of single-family residences also receive letters that describe the probabilities of a repeat offense.
- The PERF site coordinator visits roll call and rides with officers to provide them information on the project and to get feedback.

San Diego Treatment Program

Unlike the other two departments, the San Diego Police Department uses more nonsworn and volunteer personnel in the direct delivery of certain services, and this project was no exception. In San Diego the treatment consisted of the following:
- Officers assigned to the Western Division (the experimental area) received roll-call training about the project, repeat victimization, the treatment package, and the necessity of conducting better preliminary investigations.
- Patrol officers, or in some cold cases, nonsworn community service officers (CSOs), are dispatched to take preliminary reports on all residential burglaries. The patrol sergeant on duty is also notified of the call so that he/she can monitor the quality of the investigation.

- In addition to taking the report, responding officers canvass the neighborhood and, if necessary, collect evidence from the crime scene. The officer is to inform the victim of his/her increased vulnerability to repeat burglaries.
- A copy of the report is forwarded to a sworn community relations officer (CRO) or CSO assigned to crime prevention duties for the service area in which the burglary occurred. Within one week of the burglary, the CRO/CSO contacts the victim by telephone and determines if he/she has been the victim of a burglary at the same address in the previous 12 months and, if so, if the burglary was reported to the police. The CRO/CSO also offers the victim a home security check. If the victim wants a home security check, the CSO/CRO goes to the home to conduct it.
- A copy of the report is also provided to the Retired Senior Volunteer Patrol (RSVP) for the Western Division. RSVP representatives visit each burglary location and deliver a crime prevention brochure to the victim and immediately surrounding neighbors.
- If an address is burgled more than once, a detective visits the location and conducts a CPTED evaluation.
- A biweekly report of burglaries is provided to the patrol officers, who are asked to provide increased patrol surveillance at those locations.

Victim Survey

In addition to the treatment programs described above, PERF staff conduct telephone surveys of burglary victims two months after the reported burglary. The purpose of this survey is to determine if the address has been the victim of a subsequent burglary and whether it was reported to the police, determine police compliance with the treatment program, and determine the victim's compliance with crime prevention advice given as part of the treatment.

Conclusion

PERF's study on repeat victimization is still underway in Baltimore, Dallas and San Diego as data collection continues. Preliminary findings suggest that the extent of repeat victimization varies significantly among cities and PERF staff are examining the reasons for these differences. Rates of repeat victimization also vary significantly within cities, occurring at higher rates where burglaries are more numerous. These preliminary findings, reflecting differences in the concentration and prevalence of repeat victimization, suggest that the phenomenon of repeat victimization is inherently local. Analyzing the incidence of repeat victimization at a citywide level probably tends only to minimize the extent to which a repeat phenomenon exists, because citywide data tend to dilute evidence of repeat victimization. The concentration of repeat victimization in specific areas serves to reinforce the wisdom of utilizing a problem-solving approach, rather than a citywide approach to repeat victimization. Because the nature of recurring crimes probably varies by area—because of differences in housing stock, local conditions, victim behaviors or a concentration of offenders or markets for the illegally gotten gains—responses to recurring crime problems such as residential burglary should probably be developed specifically for area-level problems.

REFERENCES

Anderson, D., S. Chenery, and K. Pease. 1995. *Biting Back: Tackling Repeat Burglary and Car Crime*. Crime Detection and Prevention Series Paper 58. London: Home Office.

Bennett, T. 1995. Identifying, Explaining, and Targeting Burglary "Hot Spots." *European Journal on Criminal Policy and Research* 3:113–123.

Bennett, T., and L. Durie. 1996. *Domestic Burglary Task Force: Cambridge*. Focus on Police Research and Development No. 8 (December). London: Home Office Police Department.

Block, R., and C. Block. 1995. Space, Place and Crime: Hot Spot Areas and Hot Places of Liquor-Related Crime. In *Crime and Place*, edited by J. Eck and D. Weisburd. Crime Prevention Studies Vol. 4. Monsey, N.Y.: Criminal Justice Press.

Bridgeman, C., and L. Hobbs. 1997. *Preventing Repeat Victimization: The Police Officer's Guide*. London: Home Office.

Burquest, R.G., G. Farrell, and K. Pease. 1992. Lessons from Schools. *Policing* 8:148–155. Summer.

Bureau of Justice Assistance. 1997. *Addressing Community Gang Problems: A Model for Problem Solving*. Washington, D.C.: Author.

Bureau of Justice Assistance. Forthcoming. *Implementing the Problem-Solving Model with Gang Problems: Lessons Learned*.

Bureau of Justice Statistics. 1995. Criminal Victimization in 1993. *Bureau of Justice Statistics Bulletin*. Washington, D.C.: Bastian.

Chenery, S., D. Ellingworth, A. Tseloni, and K. Pease. 1995. *Crimes Which Repeat: Undigested Evidence from the British Crime Survey 1992*. Unpublished article.

Chenery, S., J. Holt, and K. Pease. 1997. *Biting Back II: Reducing Repeat Victimisation in Huddersfield*. Crime Detection and Prevention Paper 82. London: Home Office.

Cosgrove, C., M. Reuland, and C. Huneycutt. 1998. *Introduction to Problem Solving*. Washington, D.C.: Police Executive Research Forum.

Eck, J.E. 1997. What Do Those Dots Mean? Mapping Theories With Data. In *Crime Mapping and Crime Prevention*, edited by D. Weisburd and T. McEwen. Crime Prevention Studies Vol. 8. Monsey, N.Y.: Criminal Justice Press.

Eck, J.E., and W. Spelman. 1987. *Problem Solving: Problem-Oriented Policing in Newport News*. Washington, D.C.: Police Executive Research Forum.

Ellingworth, D., G. Farrell, K. Pease. 1995. A Victim is a Victim is a Victim: Chronic Victimisation in Four Sweeps of the British Crime Survey. *British Journal of Criminology* 35:360–365.

Farrell, G. 1992. Multiple Victimisation: Its Extent and Significance. *International Review of Victimology*. 2:89–111.

Farrell, G., and K. Pease. 1993. *Once Bitten, Twice Bitten: Repeat Victimization and its Implication for Crime Prevention*. Crime Prevention Unit Paper 46. London: Home Office.

Farrell, G., and K. Pease. 1995. *Repeat Victim Support*. Vienna: United Nations Office.

Farrell, G., C. Phillips, and K. Pease. 1995. Like Taking Candy: Why Does Repeat Victimisation Occur? *British Journal of Criminology* 35:3.

Fienberg, S.E. 1980. Statistical Modeling in the Analysis of Repeat Victimization. In *Indicators of Crime and Criminal Justice: Quantitative Studies*, edited by S. Fienberg and A. Reiss. Washington, D.C.: Bureau of Justice Statistics.

Forrester, D., M. Chatterton, and K. Pease. 1988. *The Kirkholt Burglary Project, Rochdale*. Crime Prevention Unit Paper 13. London: Home Office.

Forrester, D., S. Frenz, M. O'Connell, and K. Pease. 1990. *The Kirkholt Burglary Prevention Project: Phase II*. Crime Prevention Unit Paper 23. London: Home Office.

Genn, H. 1988. Multiple Victimisation. In *Victims of Crime: A New Deal?*, edited by M. Maguire and J. Pointing. Milton Keynes, U.K.: Open University Press.

Goldstein, H. 1979. Improving Policing: A Problem-Oriented Approach. *Crime and Delinquency* 25.

Goldstein, H. 1990. *Problem-Oriented Policing*. New York: McGraw-Hill.

Goldstein, H., and C. Susmilch. 1982. *Experimenting with the Problem-Oriented Approach to Improving Police Service: A Report and Some Reflections on Two Case Studies*. Madison, Wis.: University of Wisconsin Law School.

Guidi, S., R. Homel, and M. Townsley. 1997. *Hot Spots and Repeat Break and Enter Crimes: An Analysis of Police Calls for Service Data*. Brisbane: Criminal Justice Commission, Research and Coordination Division.

Hakkert, A., and E. Oppenhuis. 1996. *Herhaald slachtofferschap* (Repeat Victimization). The Hague: Ministry of Justice.

Hindelang, M., M. Gottfredson, and J. Garofalo. 1978. *Victims of Personal Crime: An Empirical Foundation for a Theory of Personal Victimization*. Cambridge, Mass.: Ballinger.

Hope, T. 1995. The Flux of Victimization. *British Journal of Criminology* 35:3.

Hough, M., and N. Tilley. 1997. *Getting the Grease to the Squeak: Research Lessons for Crime Prevention*. Crime Detection and Prevention Series Paper 85. London: Home Office.

Johnson, J.H., H.B. Kerper, D.D. Hayes, and G.G. Killenger. 1973. *The Recidivist Victim: A Descriptive Study*. Criminal Justice Monograph Vol. 4.1. Huntsville, Texas: Sam Houston State University, Institute of Contemporary Corrections and the Behavioral Sciences.

Lauritsen, J.L., and K.F. Davis Quinet. 1995. Repeat Victimization among Adolescents and Young Adults. *Journal of Quantitative Criminology* 11(2):143–166.

LeBeau, J.L., and K.L. Vincent. 1997. Mapping It Out: Repeat-Address Burglary Alarms and Burglaries. In *Crime Mapping and Crime Prevention*, edited by D. Weisburd and T. McEwen. Monsey, N.Y.: Criminal Justice Press.

Mukherjee, S., C. Carcach, and K. Higgins. 1997. *A Statistical Profile of Crime in Australia*. Canberra: Australian Institute of Criminology.

National Board for Crime Prevention. 1994. *Wise After the Event: Tackling Repeat Victimisation*. London: Home Office.

Nelson, J. F. 1980. Multiple Victimisation in American Cities: A

Statistical Analysis of Rare Events. *American Journal of Sociology* 85:870–891.

Osborn, D.R., D. Ellingsworth, and T. Hope. 1996. Are Repeatedly Victimized Households Different? *Journal of Quantitative Criminology* 12(2):223–245.

Pease, K. 1991. The Kirkholt Project: Preventing Burglary on a British Public Housing Estate. *Security Journal* 2:73–77.

Pease, K. 1993. Individual and Community Influences on Victimisation and Their Implications for Crime Prevention. In *Integrating Individual and Ecological Aspects of Crime*, edited by D.P. Farrington, R.J. Sampson, and P.H. Wikstrom. BRA report 1993:1.

Pease, K. 1995. *The Definition of Repeat Victimization*. Unpublished paper.

Pease, K. 1996. *Repeat Victimization and Policing*. Unpublished paper.

Pease, K. 1998. *Repeat Victimisation: Taking Stock*. Crime Detection and Prevention Series Paper 90. London: Home Office.

Pease, K., and G. Laycock. 1996. *Revictimization: Reducing the Heat on Hot Victims*. Research in Action. Washington, D.C.: National Institute of Justice.

Polvi, N., T. Looman, C. Humphries, and K. Pease. 1990. Repeat Break-and-Enter Victimization: Time Course and Crime Prevention Opportunity. *Journal of Police Science and Administration* 17(1):8–11.

Reiss, A.J. 1980. Victim Proneness in Repeat Victimization by Type of Crime. In *Indicators of Crime and Criminal Justice*, edited by S.E. Feinberg and A.J. Reiss. Washington, D.C.: Bureau of Justice Statistics.

Reuland, M.M., C.A. Cosgrove, and T. Oettmeier. 1998. *Impediments to Problem Solving*. Washington, D.C.: Community Policing Consortium.

Sampson, A., and C. Phillips. 1992. *Multiple Victimisation: Racial Attacks on an East London Estate*. Crime Prevention Unit Paper 36. London: Home Office.

Sherman, L. 1989. Repeat Calls for Service: Policing the "Hot Spots." In *Police and Policing: Contemporary Issues*, edited by D.J. Kenney. New York: Praeger.

Sherman, L. 1995. Hot Spots of Crime and Criminal Careers of Places. In *Crime and Place,* edited by J. Eck and D. Weisburd. Crime Prevention Studies Vol. 4. Monsey, N.Y.: Criminal Justice Press.

Shover, N. 1991. Burglary. In *Crime and Justice: A Review of Research,* Vol. 14, edited by M. Tonry. Chicago: University of Chicago Press.

Sorenson, S.B., J.M. Siegel, and J.M. Golding. 1991. Repeated Sexual Victimization. *Violence and Victims* 6(4):299–308.

Sparks, R. 1981. Multiple Victimisations: Evidence, Theory and Future Research. *Journal of Criminal Law and Criminology* 72.

Spelman, W. 1995a. Criminal Careers of Public Places. In *Crime and Place,* edited by J. Eck and D. Weisburd. Crime Prevention Studies Vol. 4. Monsey, N.Y.: Criminal Justice Press.

Spelman, W. 1995b. Once Bitten, Then What? *British Journal of Criminology,* 35:3.

Tilley, N. 1993. *After Kirkhold—Theory, Method and Results of Replication Evaluations.* Crime Prevention Unit Series Paper 47. London: Home Office.

Tilley, N. 1995. *Thinking About Crime Prevention Performance Indicators.* Crime Detection and Prevention Paper 57. London: Home Office.

Trickett, A., D.R. Osborn, J. Seymore, and K. Pease. 1992. What Is Different About High Crime Areas? *British Journal of Criminology* 32:81–90.

Trickett, A., D.R. Osborn, and D. Ellingworth. 1993. *Simple and Repeat Victimisation: The Influences of Individual and Area Characteristics.* Manchester, England: Department of Econometrics and Social Statistics, University of Manchester.

Trickett, A., D.R. Osborn, and D. Ellingworth. 1995. Property Crime Victimisation: The Roles of Individual and Area Influences. *International Review of Victimology* 3(4):273–295.

Tseloni, A., and K. Pease. 1998. Repeat Victimisation and Policing: Whose Home Gets Victimised, Where and How Often? In *Problem-Oriented Policing and Crime Prevention,* edited by P.O. Wikstrom, W. Skogan, and L Sherman. New York: Wadsworth.

Weisel, D.L., and J. Stedman. 1998. *Repeat Burglary Victimization.* Panel presentation at the Police Executive Research Forum's Annual International Problem-Oriented Policing Conference. San Diego.

Zeigenhagen, E. 1976. The Recidivist Victim of Violent Crime. *Victimology* 1:538–550.

CHAPTER 2

THEFT, STOLEN GOODS AND THE
MARKET-REDUCTION APPROACH:
OPERATION RADIUM AND OPERATION HEAT

Michael Sutton and Jacqueline L. Schneider

The market-reduction approach (MRA) is quite simply designed
to reduce theft by tackling the markets where stolen goods are
sold, thereby improving police capacity to deal with theft. The
MRA is very much part of the POP model; it is about prevention
and in many cases relies on decision making at the lowest levels
of the police organization. It is born out of earlier research into
stolen goods markets, which sought to develop knowledge about
common problems such as burglary, shoplifting, car theft, and
street robbery. Markets for stolen goods have been found to be
contributing factors to theft. If markets can be dealt with directly,
we can at least reduce theft problems. The MRA relies on systematic inquiry and analysis to identify where particular types
of stolen goods are being sold and who is dealing in them. It
relies on multiagency partnerships to identify "fences" and to
deal with them in a number of ways, including prosecution, civil
proceedings and administrative regulations. It also includes educational efforts to inform young people and the general public
of the consequences of buying stolen goods. Reducing the market for stolen goods is tackling the motivation to steal, because
most thieves steal what they know they can easily sell. The MRA
tackles the *business of crime*. Overall, the MRA is all about reducing theft by dealing with the problem in its earliest stages.

In what appears to be a remarkable turnaround in national
fortunes, a recent report, based on national victim surveys and
official police statistics, shows that burglary and automobile theft
rates in England are running at nearly twice the level of those in

the United States (Farrington and Langan 1998). Previously, it was generally accepted that Americans had higher rates of these offenses than the English. Whatever the reasons for this change, observers are quick to note that American crime rates have fallen against a backdrop of programs and practices that rely heavily on the criminal justice community for responses to crime—programs such as "zero tolerance" and "three strikes and you're out." These schemes are particularly tough on offenders and use long custodial sentences to deter offenders and keep those who have been convicted away from potential victims.

The academic community is still debating the precise influence of "three strikes" and other measures on the national decline in crime figures (Fagan, Zimring, and Une 1998; Bowling forthcoming). For example, critics of the famed three strikes laws state that the high cost of implementation and the inconsistent application of the policy illustrate its ineffectiveness. Additionally, analysts claim that the policy is actually targeting the wrong population of offenders, stating that offenders incarcerated under its auspice are already reaching the age at which they mature out of criminality (Litvan 1998). However, at the same time, it cannot be denied that cracking down on prolific offenders and spending vast resources on targeting and locking up repeat offenders will undoubtedly reduce crime. If imprisonment is increased, either by imprisoning more offenders, increasing the time convicted offenders spend in prison, or some combination of the two, the level of crime will be reduced (Tarling 1993). However, this a costly venture. A large number of offenders must be incarcerated to reduce crime by a significant amount (Tarling 1993), and dealing with an aging prison population poses additional problems. It seems unlikely that the three strikes policy is solely responsible for such dramatic falling crime rates in the United States. In 1994, Home Office[1] researchers estimated that a 25 percent increase in the prison population was needed in England and Wales

---

[1] The Home Office is the British government department with responsibility for crime and criminal justice issues relating to England and Wales.

to achieve a 1 percent reduction in crime. In the United States, estimates suggest a stronger effect, as high as 0.16 percent reduction in crime for every 1 percent increase in the prison population. However, adding 25 percent to the U.S. prison population would mean an extra 400,000 inmates (Goldblatt 1998). It is hardly surprising, therefore, that a recent study in California found that the three strikes policy had no significant impact on crime rates (Goldblatt 1998; Litvan 1998; Clark, Austin, and Henry 1997).

It should also be remembered that other factors may affect falling national crime figures: declining levels of unemployment, fewer males aged between 15 and 24, increased expenditure on social programs and on policing, increased security, and crime prevention programs.

Ordinarily, custody is the most expensive sentence. However, it is no more successful at preventing offenders from obtaining further convictions than other disposals (Goldblatt 1998). It makes sense, therefore, to aim to reduce the constant flow of new prison inmates by identifying and reducing the underlying causes of crime. We know that locking up offenders does not tackle the root causes of crime. Harsh sentencing may deter potential offenders, but other factors counter this deterrence and offer immediate rewards that outweigh the risk of going to prison. These are the factors that, in neighborhoods where fences operate from their own homes or where problem drug users sell stolen goods door-to-door, encourage offending and supply a continuous stream of new inmates for our prisons. There are also businesses that, though apparently legitimate, actually encourage theft because thieves know that the business will buy stolen goods.

Home Office researchers work within the Research, Development and Statistics Directorate. This is an integral part of the Home Office, serving ministers and the department itself, its services, Parliament, and the public through research, development and statistics information, and knowledge to inform policy development and program management.

Underlying Problems

One of the main elements of problem-oriented policing (POP) is to accurately define *underlying* crime problems. Outlets for stolen goods clearly represent an underlying problem for policing, because it is difficult and expensive to obtain evidence and convict those who are guilty of handling stolen goods. The main problem, however, is that stolen goods markets play a key role in causing burglary and theft problems. Yet remarkably little has been done to tackle them. It is all the more remarkable because the role of stolen goods markets in motivating thieves has been known for hundreds of years. As early as 1796, the London Magistrate Patrick Calquhoun wrote that a thief would be "undone" if he were deprived of a sale and a ready market for stolen goods. These words must have seemed as obvious then as they do now, and yet 200 years after Calquhoun wrote them, we are only just beginning to gather valuable information about markets for stolen goods, the factors that influence demand for them, and the best ways to tackle them to reduce theft.

The first systematic research in this area began with the Home Office Handling Study (Sutton 1998), which set out to find out more about who buys stolen goods and how stolen goods markets operate.

The Home Office Handling Study

Deliberately buying or selling stolen goods is an offense in Great Britain under the Theft Act of 1968. Estimates (based on official crime statistics and figures from the British Crime Survey) suggest that in 1995, thieves selling stolen property cleared between £900 million and £1.68 billion (net), and fences cleared between £450 million and £870 million (net) selling stolen property.

The 1994 British Crime Survey (BCS)[2] revealed that a large number of people are offered, and many buy, stolen goods. Although the majority (82%) said they had not been offered them

---

[2] Core sample used for this analysis N=8,753.

in the past year and never bought them over a five-year period, the remaining 18 percent had either been offered stolen goods, bought them, or both. While most people in Britain generally agree that stealing is wrong, at least 11 percent admitted to having bought stolen goods in the past five years.

Burglars and other thieves most often live in poorer housing areas (Bennett and Wright 1984; Baldwin and Bottoms 1976). Because the opportunity to knowingly buy stolen goods depends on meeting or knowing someone willing to sell (rather than buying unwittingly from a shop), people living in these areas are correspondingly more likely than people living in more affluent areas to knowingly own stolen goods. Therefore, people living in poorer areas, where there is a more plentiful supply of stolen goods, will also have quite a few neighbors who know they have stolen goods in their homes. Because buying stolen goods is frequently done through friendship and neighborhood networks, "word of mouth" plays an important part in the distribution process (Foster 1990). Therefore, people who buy stolen goods generally know when their neighbors also buy them. Thus it is not surprising that the BCS found that a large proportion of respondents (70%) thought that some of their neighbors owned stolen goods, and 21 percent thought that at least quite a few of their neighbors did. The statistically significant difference in the numbers of respondents admitting ownership in affluent and thriving areas, compared with those living in deprived areas, indicates that stolen goods are more likely to reside in the homes of the less wealthy. In addition, four times more respondents living in the poorest housing areas believed that at least a few of their neighbors own stolen goods, such as television sets and video recorders.

Sex, Age and Opportunity. In comparing males with females, the study found that more than twice as many males are offered stolen goods and nearly twice as many buy them. Only 7 percent of those who admitted buying stolen goods in the past five years said they had not been offered them in the last 12 months. The odds that 16 to 24 year olds will buy stolen goods are more than four times those for individuals aged 36 to 60.

To better understand the reasons why some people are more likely to be offered and to buy stolen goods, it is important to consider the relative influence of particular demographic and social variables. A statistical technique, logistic regression, was used to look at these factors in more depth. The analysis is conceptually quite straightforward. It involves building a mathematical model in which each variable makes a significant contribution to explaining the likelihood of buying stolen goods among different groups of people.[3] The study found that, at a national level, buying stolen goods was significantly and independently correlated with being young and poor. It could be argued that people who fall into this category and buy stolen goods have less to lose if they are caught breaking the law. As with most other crimes, young males are most likely to buy stolen goods. However, the effect of age on the odds of buying stolen goods is virtually the same for males and females after reaching 21 years of age. Disregarding age, lack of personal wealth remains closely associated with buying stolen goods, particularly among men.

Stolen Goods Markets. To complement the BCS data, in-depth interviews were conducted with a sample of 45 burglars, other thieves and handlers of stolen goods who had been involved in buying and selling stolen goods at different levels and to various degrees. Interviewees included 14 respondents who were followed up from the Home Office Youth Lifestyle Survey (YLS) (Graham and Bowling 1995), 10 from a Young Offender Institution (YOI), four from adult male prisons, seven from the probation service, and 10 heroin addicts (or ex-addicts) from two methadone treatment clinics in the London area.

The interviews revealed that different types of stolen goods are sold in particular ways. For instance, jewelry is usually sold to jewelers' shops. Car stereos are frequently sold through networks of friends. Stolen checkbooks and credit cards are often sold to drug users who use them to buy goods to sell for cash to

---

[3] For a more complete discussion of analysis, see Sutton 1998.

buy drugs. Shoplifters sell clothes and food door-to-door or around pubs. Stolen cars, even those only a few years old, are frequently sold to car breakers' yards. In sum, stolen goods markets support not only thieves. They also provide illegal gain for a whole stratum of people supplying "criminal services," and of course, for consumers. Like other illegal markets, they are localized, fragmented, ephemeral, and undiversified enterprises (Reuter 1985, 1990).

The distribution and consumption of stolen goods fall within at least five distinct markets:

- **Commercial Fence Supplies Markets.** Stolen goods are sold by thieves to commercial fences (e.g. jewelers) operating out of shops.
- **Commercial Sales Markets.** Stolen goods are sold by commercial fences, either directly to the consumer or, more rarely, to another distributor, for profit.
- **Residential Fence Supplies Markets.** Stolen goods are sold by thieves to fences, usually at the fence's home.
- **Network Sales Markets.** This market often involves a residential fence. The buyer may be the final consumer or he/she may sell the goods through friendship networks. Stolen goods are passed on and on, with each participant adding a little extra to the price until a final consumer is found.
- **Hawking Markets.** Thieves sell merchandise directly to consumers in places like pubs and clubs, or door-to-door.

This topology of stolen goods markets reveals where the markets are likely to be located and who will be dealing in them. These markets, and the people who run them or use them to buy stolen goods, are clearly an important underlying cause of crime.

Demand and Supply. Occasionally, burglaries and other serious thefts stem from nonacquisitive motivational forces, such as thrill seeking or peer status, but these are probably few in number (Sutton 1995). Thieves may also steal items to keep for themselves (Leitch 1969; Shover 1996). Primarily, however, a potential thief is likely to know or believe that his or her intended target is, or contains, something someone else will buy. The item is stolen for the money it will bring.

In the following account, one interviewee explained how he came to be arrested and fined for stealing Victorian roofing slates. He lived in an area where extensive housing refurbishment led to shortages of legitimate Victorian building materials. Derelict properties were being "cannibalized" illegally to refurbish others from the same period. Roofing slate thieves were selling in a commercial fence supplies market. The slates were being sold on again to builders through a commercial sales market:

> I got into stealing the slates by seeing other people doing it and asking friends who they were selling the slates to. So they said how much they was making. Fifty pence a slate. So that's how I started doing it. I was selling the slates to one buyer, who knew they were stolen. There was kids taking the slates to his place. He was buying them cheap at 50 pence each and selling them for £1 each to builders.

Research in Canada (Tremblay, Clermont, and Cusson 1994) also found that demand and prices in legitimate markets play an important role in influencing illegitimate markets. The Canadian research found that changes in rates of unrecovered stolen vehicles were highly responsive to many factors that increased the price of cars and car parts. In effect, people were more likely to buy stolen cars for their own use and garages were more likely to use stolen car parts in repairs when market regulations made legitimate cars and parts more expensive.

It seems that this principle applies also to all electrical goods. When new products come on the market, such as video cassette recorders, mobile telephones, personal computers, or camcorders, they are frequently targeted by thieves because they are desirable and expensive. Products like these fetch high prices in illicit

sales when the retail price is high, but when retail prices fall, the
illicit demand also falls as stolen goods markets become satu-
rated with equipment. Once retail prices become affordable for
those with low incomes, legitimate electrical goods become more
desirable than stolen ones (Sutton 1998; Clarke forthcoming).
Some of the older thieves who were interviewed were aware of
this situation. One person dealt as a residential fence for stolen
VCRs on commission for inexperienced burglars. The peak period
was four to five years after they first appeared on the market:

> I mean you used to be able to get £70 or £80 for a
> video player seven years ago—and now you
> would be lucky to get £15 or £20 for it, because
> you can buy a video for £70 to £80 brand new.
> You've got to look at the end of the scale there.
> They [the buyers] say, "Well look I can get a video
> from a shop brand new no problems, and I'm not
> going to get no trouble about it."

As another interviewee explained, more recently the same
has happened to mobile phones:

> I used to be well into mobile phones when they
> first came out. I used to get £100, £150 a mobile
> phone. But now you can pick 'em up in the shops
> for like 10 or 15 quid. So they're not worth [any-
> thing] now. It's all gone, completely gone.

Arguments about whether demand for stolen goods causes
supply through theft (Sutton 1993) or whether supply fuels demand seem futile when the whole stolen property system is in a
state of perpetual motion. Inexperienced thieves generally rely
on preexisting markets, particularly a single residential fence who
is usually either a relative or neighbor. Active and ambitious
fences encourage thieves to increase their offending. Experienced
and prolific thieves, particularly problem drug users, are also

proactive in finding new buyers and sell to a variety of people. In this way, thieves overcome local fluctuations in stolen goods markets and sell more goods. They also sell quickly, even if they are not close to their usual buyers, thus reducing risk of arrest by only transporting stolen goods short distances. Some of those interviewed failed to sell items they had stolen in their first burglaries and gave up stealing after two or three attempts. However, burglars who successfully converted stolen property into cash at their first attempts continued with the crime. A criminal "career" choice of this kind could be explained simply as rewards-based behavior, but is probably more complex. The existence of established markets and provision of guidance from experienced offenders are likely to be almost essential local conditions for inexperienced thieves to make successful sales. Markets for stolen goods should be seen as both a consequence of theft and an underlying motivational force for acquisitive offending. This is an important area for criminality prevention because the reduction of markets for stolen goods might curtail many criminal careers before they "take off."

Stealing-to-Order. Stealing-to-order is particularly common in shoplifting, car stereo theft, and school, factory, warehouse, and office burglaries. Generally, domestic burglars do not steal-to-order because they usually don't know what items a house contains without first breaking in. When stolen goods are in short supply, thieves may be asked to steal-to-order. Interviewees mentioned receiving orders for camcorders, car stereos, computers, and other state-of-the-art electrical equipment. From the moment that a price is agreed upon, the required item represents hard cash to a thief:

> At the age of 15, we used to sort of hang around in the park, mostly the same age, a few older. People would stop in their cars and say, "Oh, can you get me [this]." Well obviously you like to get as much as you can so you'd say like you want so much for it and you'd come to some arrangement.

Sometimes you'd say like you want £100 and
they'd say, "Yeah fine." Sometimes they'd say that
would be too much. Then we'd go out and look
in every car park. Park up on the estate when it
gets dark—going out at 8 o'clock and not coming
back home 'till 5 o'clock.

Bad Business. Sutton (1998) found that small business owners are frequently offered stolen goods by strangers. One of the
heroin users said, "You can go into your local shop where you go
and buy your paper and milk, have a word with them in the
back and be guaranteed, nine times out of ten, that he will buy it
off you."

Many businesses do buy. The BCS found a significant association between living in a household where the head of the household was self-employed and the buying of stolen goods (Sutton
1998). One of the most likely explanations for this is that business
people frequently carry cash. Anyone who regularly carried more
than £200 in cash was one-and-a-half times more likely to buy stolen goods than someone who did not do so. Although the BCS did
not ask for further details about specific self-employed professions,
a number of self-employed occupations such as market trader, scrap
metal dealer, taxidriver, and small shop owner provide common
outlets for stolen goods. Particular types of shop owners and other
business people have been heavily implicated in fencing stolen
goods for more than 150 years (Ferrier 1928; Gregory 1932; Benney
1936; Hall 1952; Munro 1972; Tobias 1974; Walsh 1977; Smithies 1984;
Steffensmeir 1986; Parker, Bakx, and Newcombe 1988; Ward 1989;
Foster 1990; Tremblay, Clermont, and Cusson 1994). This has not
gone unnoticed and, in an attempt to reduce burglaries by making
it harder to sell stolen jewelry, the Metropolitan Police specifically
targeted gold shops and jewelers as part of Operation Bumblebee,
a particularly well publicized burglary-reduction campaign in the
United Kingdom. Some jewelry shops in London were "staked out"
by police officers, and suspected burglars arrested as they were about
to enter and sell stolen property (Stockdale and Gresham 1995).

Distinguishing Characteristics of Stolen Goods Markets.
While sharing many of the characteristics of legitimate markets, stolen goods markets are fundamentally different because they are
illegal. This means that fences are constrained in many ways and
need to adopt clandestine solutions to operational problems, such
as storing and transporting goods. Understanding more about such
concerns and the coping strategies of thieves and consumers will
facilitate and improve the identification of those involved in stolen
goods markets, and we hope, inform future initiatives aimed at reducing theft and the handling of stolen goods.

It would be wrong to think in terms of a single market for
stolen goods (Walsh 1977; Maguire 1982; Reuter 1985, 1990). A
thief selling to a fence constitutes one market, a thief selling directly to final consumers represents another market, and a fence
selling to consumers is yet another market. Although he did not
specifically look at stolen goods markets, Reuter (1985, 1990) examined the characteristics of various other illegal market structures, drawing useful conclusions about the structure and
organization of U.S. drug markets, numbers rackets, bootlegging
and gambling markets. Of particular interest are his findings on
the limited size of these markets. Reasons for the limited size of
illicit markets include the need to be inconspicuous; inability to
obtain legitimate credit; lack of an integrated system for transporting, warehousing and retailing the goods; and the market
operators' inability to expand their workforce. These characteristics of the various markets examined by Reuter can be readily
compared with the various markets for stolen goods.

The Market-Reduction Approach
The market-reduction approach (MRA) is a broad-based strategy designed to reduce the motivation to steal, and to lower theft
rates. The aim is to reduce demand for stolen goods and also
make it more difficult and risky for thieves to sell them. In addition, this approach is designed to increase the risks for thieves at
the point of sale to make them equal or greater than risks faced
when stealing. This should, at the very least, slow offenders

down. Ideally, it will deter some from stealing in the first place and might eventually help to convince existing prolific thieves to give up their trade.

Situational Crime Prevention. The MRA utilizes situational crime prevention techniques. Situational crime prevention has been at the center of crime prevention activity in Europe for many years and was first proposed in the Home Office publication *Crime as Opportunity* (Mayhew et al. 1976). Addressing crime from the perspectives of human situations and opportunities, situational crime prevention is particularly useful for designing solutions to prevent specific crime problems in the places where they usually happen.

Initiatives to reduce stolen goods markets might employ one or more of the four broad categories of situational crime prevention efforts (Clarke 1983, 1997): those that (1) increase the effort of offending, (2) increase the risk of offending, (3) reduce the rewards of offending, and/or (4) make it less excusable to offend. These methods can make it more difficult for thieves and fences to sell and for others to buy, and increase the real or perceived likelihood that all those involved will be apprehended and convicted. Stimulating this increased risk for sellers should reduce their rewards by either lowering the price of stolen goods or reducing the volume of sales.

Efforts to make dealing in stolen goods less excusable are best directed at buyers by stimulating their conscience at the point of contemplating purchasing stolen goods. As Henry (1978) points out, "criminals behave in a predatory way, ordinary people, in contrast, need only accept things that come their way." However, research suggests that people may be prepared to accept some things more than others. Overall, the public find it easier to tolerate the idea of buying new goods stolen from businesses rather than used goods stolen from homes and cars (Sutton 1995). Therefore, schemes aimed at pricking the consumers' conscience will be more likely to succeed if they highlight the personal suffering and misery associated with buying goods stolen from households and motorists.

Clarke (1997) points out that "measures must be carefully tailored to the settings in which they are applied, with due regard to the motives and methods of the individuals involved. Where the stakes are high, offenders must be expected to test the limits of the new defences." Bearing this in mind, market-reduction measures will need to be tailored to suit particular markets. Looking, for example, at commercial fence supplies markets, investigative and preventive strategies should focus on the crime promoters, such as business people, who buy stolen goods. In this way, crime promoters and the thieves who supply them will need to invest more effort and face greater risks if they want to convert stolen property into cash. This could be achieved by adopting the following measures:

- using local criminal intelligence information to investigate which shops thieves visit to sell stolen goods;
- establishing surveillance, including use of CCTV cameras, to monitor thieves entering these shops to gain evidence for prosecuting both the thief and the fence;
- encouraging voluntary commitments from shopkeepers and other types of business people to ensure that all sellers of second-hand goods are photographed, a scheme that can be monitored using test sales by undercover police officers; and
- promoting stricter requirements of proof of ownership.

Residential fence supplies markets might be reduced through the identification and arrest of residential fences. Multiagency partnerships can be utilized to stop fences from running illegitimate businesses from their homes. Some residential fences also deal in drugs, which is not surprising as theft is a common way to fund drug abuse. Therefore, it might be worthwhile to combine efforts to reduce local illicit drug markets with schemes aimed at reducing stolen goods markets. The following approach would tackle these two components of serious theft:

- gathering and analyzing local criminal intelligence information to identify residential fences, who they deal with, and how they operate;

- questioning recent burglary victims living in high-crime neighborhoods to determine if they know of anyone locally who might be trading in drugs or stolen goods; and
- reducing the demand for cut-price second-hand electrical goods in high-crime areas by recycling recovered stolen, yet unclaimed, goods to uninsured burglary victims (particularly repeat victims) and other potential customers of residential fences.

Network sales might be reduced by

- arresting residential fences; and
- implementing local "rule setting" publicity campaigns to discourage people from buying stolen goods and encourage them to report those who do buy, thereby tackling illegal trading subcultures in the areas where they currently thrive.

In commercial sales markets, members of the public are usually innocent buyers. Therefore, it will be necessary to concentrate on reducing the profits commercial fences make from selling stolen goods and increasing the risks they face by

- encouraging or requiring shops that buy and sell second-hand goods to display signs stating that they are part of a crime prevention program to reduce theft and handling;
- promoting property-marking schemes that involve engraving goods with the owner's name and address as well as "NOT FOR RESALE" in very large letters, along with a telephone hotline number for reporting suspected stolen goods; and
- encouraging thieves and paid informants to reveal the identities of commercial fences and then making it known to all second-hand outlets that this will be a routine and systematic police strategy.

Consumers may be considered innocent when they buy in commercial supplies markets, but they are not so innocent when they buy cheap goods in pubs or at their doorstep. In these hawking markets, surveillance measures can be combined with schemes to increase awareness of the consequences of buying stolen goods. Recent "don't drink and drive" public information campaigns have been credited with considerable success in reducing alcohol-related car crashes. Something similar could emphasise the deleterious effects of buying stolen goods. Additional measures might include

- analyzing local intelligence information to identify the housing areas, pubs and bars where hawkers frequently sell stolen goods;
- closely monitoring hawkers, usually carrying sports bags to hold stolen goods such as cigarettes and designer clothes, on the streets, in licensed premises or when they use taxis and public transportation; and
- arresting the hawker as well as the hawker's customers if there is sufficient evidence to show that customers knew or believed the goods were stolen.

Taken alone, it is unlikely that these measures will have any significant impact, as transactions may become more secretive. However, it makes sense to tackle various markets at the same time to reduce crime and to limit opportunities for displacement from one market to another. As part of a wider and coordinated operation aimed at tackling these different markets simultaneously, the market-reduction approach should send a clear message to thieves, fences and other handlers that their activities are becoming hazardous and perhaps, for many, no longer worth the risk. This perception of risk can be amplified, as Sherman (1990) suggests and Clarke (1997) reaffirms, through operational rotation of police crackdowns across different times and places to cause offenders to overestimate the real level of risk at any given place or time—a kind of "policing by paranoia." Targeting markets in this way should also make it difficult for offenders to change their method of offending. Otherwise, they might simply choose different markets and targets (e.g., stealing or dealing in cash and credit cards rather than goods). Police operations against markets would work best, in terms of reducing demand among the buying public, with an ongoing media campaign to highlight the number of people arrested and convicted. This could include the naming and shaming of offenders (Braithwaite 1989, 1993). In all cases, offenders should be made aware of the increased risks they face in continuing to offend (Kennedy 1997).

Operation Radium

Prior to the Home Office Handling Study, markets were not treated as a principle cause of acquisitive crime, but rather were simply considered a downstream consequence of theft. An earlier study, which set out to devise strategies to disrupt networks for stolen goods (Kock, Temp, and Rix 1996), found that almost all the officers and citizens interviewed felt that the key police role in this area was to investigate the original theft or burglary, rather than to worry about why goods were stolen and where they had been or were going to be sold. To address this imbalance, the Home Office Policing and Reducing Crime Unit (PRCU)[4], in collaboration with Kent County Constabulary, set about reducing burglaries and other thefts by tackling local markets for stolen goods in Kent's Medway Towns. The aim is to make the transportation and sale of stolen goods, by thieves and other handlers, as dangerous an enterprise as the actual act of stealing. A strategic initiative has been designed to develop, implement and monitor a number of strategies to disrupt and reduce local markets for stolen goods. The initiative, named Operation Radium, includes a program of market intervention strategies specifically tailored to undermine local markets for stolen goods. The operation began in October 1998 and will be evaluated in terms of both implementation and impact over the next 12 months. If successful, it will be extended.

Operation Radium forms part of the Medway policing area business plan, which means that the MRA is being utilized across all possible areas of policing activity. By disrupting existing trade in stolen property and reducing thieves' ability to cultivate new

---

[4] Formally known as the Police Research Group.

markets, Operation Radium seeks to deal with the underlying causes of criminal motivation as well as the vulnerability of victims' possessions. The force will use information gained from routine and systematic gathering and analysis of data about markets for stolen property gained from interviews with all arrested thieves, fences, other handlers, and drug dealers admitting guilt. In addition, the Kent Police Prison Liaison Team visits convicted offenders in prison to establish information about the location of fences and markets. All burglary victims are asked if they can identify local fences and burglars. Local taxi firms have agreed to set up a CabWatch scheme to provide the police with details of suspicious passengers and where they are taking stolen goods. Special Operation Radium Crime Stoppers anonymous telephone hotlines have also been set up. In addition, crime mapping has been used to identify places most in need of crime-reduction strategies. Crime pattern analysis, using geographic information systems (GIS) has played a key part in this. Additionally, police informants have been paid to identify market locations and fences.

Several early design decisions and steps were taken to ensure that Operation Radium would be as effective as possible:

- The operation was founded on prudent initial research into stolen good markets.
- The operation was based on thorough planning and collaboration with various community and social agencies, including those of the justice system.
- Resources are concentrated in areas where crimes are most concentrated, making it easier and more cost effective to achieve measurable reductions in crime (Ekblom, Law, and Sutton 1996).
- Hotspots of domestic burglary and car crime are identified using pinpoint analysis rather than by looking at crime levels within administrative boundaries such as police beats.
- Unless part of a thoroughly worked out tactical operation, attempts to identify stolen goods, establish owner-

ship and obtain evidence are avoided. This practice can take a long time, and projects that invest resources in such a tactic always find that it is "surprisingly" costly and unproductive (Whitehead and Gray forthcoming).

- Sting operations are avoided, as these may lead to an influx of crime into the area of the sting (Langworthy and LeBeau 1992) and might also induce people to begin stealing.
- Local partnerships and, where necessary, multiagency strategies are adopted to tackle the markets.

Evaluation Strategy. Operation Radium is an action research program that includes an evaluation of both process and impact. The implementation process is being monitored to ensure that important factors are discovered as soon as possible and fed back to the project team as the operation develops.

It is important to understand that monitoring is not an option; it is essential to determine whether those with responsibilities for actions carry them out. It allows participants to learn from, adapt and supplement the various market-reduction strategies as appropriate. For example,

- monitoring the impact on crime will facilitate early identification of failure to impact on the problem;
- monitoring the target problem will assist quick identification of failure to impact, or recognition of changes in the nature of the problem; and
- monitoring the MRA action taken will help trace weaknesses in implementation, which may then be adjusted. Recognizing lack of impact and redeploying effort should be seen positively as a sign of good management.

The process evaluation will also examine the implementation of the strategic programs. Several different sources are being used to provide both qualitative and quantitative accounts of Operation Radium implementation. A particularly important component will comprise a series of interviews to be conducted with police officers and other members of the problem-solving team to ascertain their perceptions of the project's value, implementation and effectiveness. Interviews will address the following questions:

- What was done and why?
- What worked and why?
- In what circumstances is the good practice likely to be transferable to another or similar problem?

Measuring Impact. In looking for reductions in domestic burglaries and car theft, a wide range of easily communicable measures of program impact can be adopted: dose response analysis (Ekblom, Law and Sutton 1996), quasi-experimental design with interforce and external matched control areas, and mechanism-based evaluation (Pawson and Tilley 1997).

Particular attention is being paid to the *mechanism* by which the various MRA operations affect the decision-making process of thieves and buyers of stolen goods. This began before the first tactical operations were implemented. In-depth anonymous interviews were conducted with a sample of 25 imprisoned offenders from the Medway Towns. The aim was to discover exactly what it was like to steal and deal in stolen goods in the Medway area before Operation Radium was launched. Convicted thieves were asked about their frequency of offending, how easy it was to transport and sell stolen goods, and their perception of risks and strategies for evading arrest and finding buyers. These initial interviews will be followed by another 25 interviews with thieves arrested after the launch of Operation Radium, some time after the project has had "time to bite," to see what effect MRA has on thieves' stealing and dealing behavior.

Overall, measures of success will include the following:

- changes in the next offender (follow-up) interviews, regarding fear, ease and time taken to sell stolen goods;
- a significant decrease in theft at the small area (hotspot) level;
- a decrease in theft in areas surrounding hotspots due to diffusion of benefits (Barr and Pease 1990);
- a decrease in theft across the whole Medway area;
- findings from intelligence information suggesting that thieves find it harder to dispose of stolen goods and consequently steal less;

- an increase in arrests and successful prosecution of thieves, prolific thieves, fences, and handlers;
- a decrease in the overall value of property stolen;
- an increase in levels of property recovered by the police;
- an increase in levels of property returned to owners;
- an increase in reports to Crime Stoppers anonymous telephone hotline; and
- a decrease in theft of certain expensive items such as jewelry and electrical goods.

Most important, the evaluation will include a Treasury-approved cost-benefit analysis to determine whether the operation was cost effective in reducing levels of theft.

Making a Case For Operation Heat: A Cross-National Replication of the MRA in Columbus, Ohio

At a national level, most serious crimes are declining in the United States. There are, however, regional differences that need to be addressed. The city of Columbus, Ohio, experienced a decrease in violent crimes from 1987 to 1997. Yet larceny and vehicle theft increased by 25.46 percent and 114.23 percent respectively, during the same period (see Figure 1).

Police officials in Columbus will develop a sister project to Operation Radium in England's Medway Towns. Columbus offers an excellent site for this project, given the level of commitment from key law enforcement officials. Researchers at the Hudson Institute and officials with the Columbus Division of Police have developed a strong working relationship with the Home Office Policing and Reducing Crime Unit. Through this affiliation, cooperation has been secured with the Kent County Constabulary in England. This collaboration of agencies, researchers and practitioners provides an excellent opportunity to conduct innovative cross-national work in law enforcement and policy development.

Like Operation Radium, Operation Heat will use situational crime prevention measures to reduce stolen goods markets. The European community has embraced the concept of situational

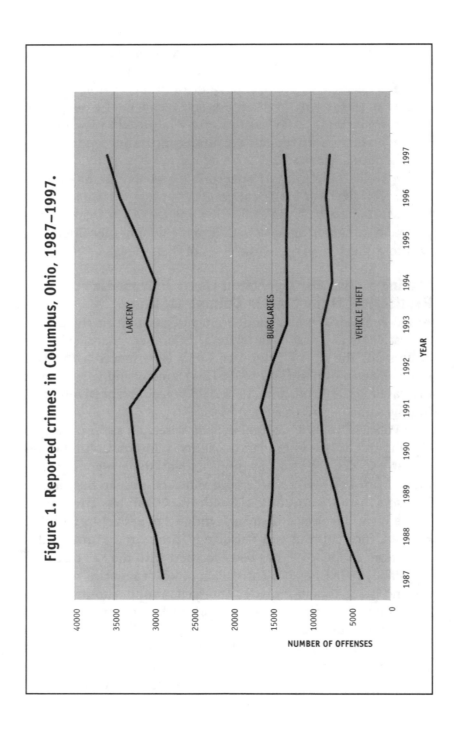

Figure 1. Reported crimes in Columbus, Ohio, 1987–1997.

crime prevention more readily than their American counterparts who, until recently, have shown relatively little interest in situational prevention programs. As Clarke (1997:2) points out, "situational [crime] prevention has rarely been accorded attention in policy debates about crime control, especially those in the United States." Americans appear to concentrate their efforts on conviction-based programs and research projects.

Researchers have identified several reasons why situational crime prevention initiatives have been overlooked in the United States. Researchers have spent decades trying to explain criminal behavior (Gottfredson and Hirschi 1990) or identify the social conditions that, when imposed on an individual, cause him or her to deviate from society's norms and mores. (Shaw and McKay 1942; Merton 1957; Miller 1958; Cohen 1955; Cloward and Ohlin 1960). Arguably, American criminologists have neglected to utilize situational measures because they have combined efforts to control crime with those aimed at dealing with the criminal (Wilkins 1990).

Americans have consistently relied on regulatory responses to criminal events. Detection, apprehension, conviction, and sentencing appear to be the normal criminal justice responses to crime. In tackling acquisitive crimes, "sting operations" have been commonly used to disrupt stolen property activity (Langworthy and LeBeau 1992; Freiberg 1997; Marx 1998). Although jurisdictions might have seen a large number of arrests and convictions resulting from these types of interventions, the costs often outweighed the benefits, especially considering that nothing was done to address the reduction of opportunity to steal. This approach has been heavily criticized by Felson (1998: 38) who notes from the findings of Langworthy and LeBeau that

> the police set up a fake storefront for auto thieves, later arresting them. Although their efforts were popular with the public, what they really did was to drive up the local theft rates. The police, in creating a fencing operation, had done a terrible

thing to the local people who were cheering them, making it easier for offenders to get rid of stolen goods.

Absent in the traditional American approach is the investigation of how situational factors such as environmental design, target hardening and opportunity reduction facilitate the commission of crimes (Ekblom 1994). Clarke (1997) indicates that reducing criminal opportunities by manipulating the environment leads to significant reductions in net crime.

Situational crime prevention tackles the causes of crime from a diametrically different viewpoint than traditional American techniques. First, rather than investigating why individuals engage in criminal activities or identifying the presence of criminal or delinquent tendencies in individuals, situational crime prevention seeks simply to make crime less attractive to potential offenders (Clarke 1997). Second, traditional American programs tend to rely heavily on the criminal justice community for answers and responses to the crime problem, whereas situational crime prevention frequently relies on private and public organizations, agencies and businesses to assist in the fight against crime.

Jurisdictions employing the MRA should design programs that meet the community's social, economic and political needs. This customization of responses will add an important dimension to replication studies, not only in American jurisdictions, but also across national borders. The MRA uses situational crime prevention techniques to reduce opportunities to deal in stolen goods and thereby reduce motivation to steal. Preventing the sale of stolen property in one place may reduce the incidence of theft in other places.

The MRA provides a new way to use the effectiveness of situational crime prevention and problem-oriented policing. It addresses an important underlying "social cause" of theft while employing existing approaches that are proven to reduce crimes in the places where they usually happen.

Displacement Issues

One of the criticisms of situational prevention programs, such as the MRA, is that crime is displaced elsewhere (Clarke 1997). Offenders may change their methods of offending or choose different targets (e.g., stealing cash or credit cards rather than goods), or new offenders may emerge who are not deterred (Bennett and Wright 1984; Barr and Pease 1990; Wright and Decker 1994). Critics of situational crime prevention methods argue that displacement can occur in several ways once the intervention is activated:

- the offender continues to commit the same type of offenses, in the same locations, targeting the same victims, but at a different time;
- the offender continues to commit the same type of offense, at the same location, at the same time, targeting the same people, but using different techniques;
- the offender simply switches the target of victimization;
- the offender maintains the same pattern of offending, but simply moves to a new location; or
- the offender begins committing a different type of offense (Reppetto 1976).

Operation Radium and Operation Heat will seek to limit displacement from one market type to another by tackling each of the different market types—sometimes simultaneously and at other times through a process of revolving crackdowns.

Some researchers now see the displacement issue as less important than originally thought. Recent research by Hesseling (1994) suggests that displacement is never total and that there always seems to be a net gain in crime reduction. Pease (1998: 21–22) notes that "often the opposite to displacement occurs, where crime reductions extend beyond the boundaries of the project area." This is known as diffusion of benefits.

Policy Considerations

The existence of markets for stolen goods undoubtedly provides temptation for young people to become involved in burglary, shoplifting and other kinds of theft. This temptation is even greater when the markets are local, with relatives and neighbors openly buying and selling stolen goods. Reducing these markets will be difficult, as they clearly exist in areas where people are less well-off but not immune to the desires promoted by the power of advertising in an increasingly consumer-oriented world. Indeed, Parker, Bakx and Newcombe (1988) argue that without the opportunity to purchase stolen goods, many poor and "respectable" families would be unable to cope.

Those living in the most economically hard-pressed areas buy and use stolen goods to a much greater extent than those living in better-off areas. Therefore, programs aimed at reducing inequality and deprivation may go some way toward reducing theft and demand for stolen goods. However, Felson and Clarke (1997: 210, 212) argue for a quicker and more pragmatic approach, to reduce temptation for local youths so that they will not get into trouble:

> We owe it to our neighbors not to assist their children in becoming burglars. If crime opportunities are extremely enticing and open, society will tend to produce new offenders and offenses. By inviting crime, society will make it more difficult for the law enforcement system to prosecute and punish those who accept the invitation.

More police resources should be directed toward tackling shoplifting, because research in the Medway Towns has revealed that shoplifting, one of the easiest offenses to commit, provides a route into other offending by initiating young thieves into fencing networks. Once in the networks, young offenders learn what it is best to steal to get the most money. This leads them into stealing-to-order, which often instigates the escalation of offending to include car crime and burglary. With more money to spend, drugs like heroin become an affordable recreational option and their use frequently increases the spiral of offending. Therefore, reducing drug markets is also likely to reduce the overall incidence of crime.

Parker, Bakx and Newcombe (1998) see the interface between legitimate and alternative economies in England as an explanation for the resilience of heroin networks and illegal trading mechanisms (Parker and Bottomley 1996). Developing a strategy that combines efforts to tackle geographically located illegal drug markets with those aimed at reducing stolen goods markets would tackle two of the principal causes of serious theft.

Conclusions

The Home Office Handling Study shows that stolen goods markets play a considerable part in creating demand for stolen goods, motivating offenders and increasing theft rates (Sutton 1998). When someone offers to sell stolen goods, they create an opportunity to buy. Likewise, when someone is known to be a likely buyer, they create an opportunity to cash in on theft. If fences and consumers do not seek out stolen goods, then accepting offers is the only way they can knowingly buy them. Operation Radium and Operation Heat will aim to reduce the number of offers made to buyers and increase resistance to offers when they do occur. This approach is designed to increase the risks for thieves at the point of sale to make them equal to or greater than the risks faced when stealing. This should, at the very least, slow offenders down and reduce crime. It may deter some from stealing in the first place and convince other existing prolific thieves to give up. The most desirable outcome would be for offenders to begin to explore noncriminal alternatives, rather than just alternative crimes.

Linking public awareness campaigns and community action with problem-oriented policing and situational crime prevention methods, the MRA aims to reduce thieves' ability to cultivate new market outlets, while reducing trade in established stolen goods markets. The main objective is to reduce theft levels by addressing offender motivation as well as the vulnerability of victims' possessions. The key new principle is that the MRA does not focus merely on specific theft situations or specific thieves. It is a broad strategy to squeeze offenders out of the market using a number of proven methods. Tackling theft in this way should also go further toward satisfying the demands of those crime prevention practitioners dealing with particular underlying causes of crime such as inequality, discrimination and offender motivation (Sutton 1996).

REFERENCES

Baldwin, J., and A. Bottoms. 1976. *The Urban Criminal: A Study in Sheffreed.* London: Tavistock.

Barr, R., and K. Pease. 1990. Crime Placement, Displacement, and Deflection. In *Crime and Justice: A Review of Research* Vol 12, edited by M. Tonry and N. Morris. Chicago: University of Chicago Press.

Bennett, T., and R. Wright. 1984. *Burglars on Burglary Prevention and the Offender.* Aldershot, U.K.: Gower.

Benney, M. 1936. *Low Company: Describing the Evolution of a Burglar.* London: Peter Davies.

Bowling, B. Forthcoming. The Rise and Fall of New York Murder. *British Journal of Criminology.*

Braithwaite, J. 1989. *Crime, Shame and Reintegration.* Cambridge: Cambridge University Press.

Braithwaite, J. 1993. Shame and Modernity. *British Journal of Criminology* 33:1–18.

Clark, J., J. Austin, and D. A. Henry. 1997. *"Three Strikes and You're Out": A Review of State Legislation.* Washington, D.C.: National Institute of Justice.

Clarke, R.V. 1983. Situational Crime Prevention: Its Theoretical Basis and Practical Scope. In *Crime and Justice: An Annual Review of Research* Vol 4, edited by M. Tonry and N. Morris. Chicago: University of Chicago Press.

Clarke, R.V. (ed.) 1997. *Situational Crime Prevention: Successful Case Studies.* 2d ed. New York: Harrow & Heston.

Clarke, R. V. Forthcoming. *Hot Products.* London: Policing and Reducing Crime Unit, Home Office.

Cloward, R. A., and L. E. Ohlin. 1960. *Delinquency and Opportunity: A Theory of Delinquent Gangs.* New York: The Free Press.

Cohen, A. K. 1955. *Delinquent Boys: The Culture of the Gang.* Glencoe, Ill.: The Free Press.

Colquhoun, P. 1796. *A Treatise on the Police of the Metropolis; Containing a Detail of the Various Crimes and Misdemeanours by Public and Private Security.* 3d ed. London: C. Dilly.

Ekblom, P. 1994. Proximal Circumstances: A Mechanism-Based Classification of Crime Prevention. In *Crime Prevention Studies* Vol 2, edited by R. V. Clarke. Monsey, N.Y.: Criminal Justice Press.

Ekblom, P., H. Law, and M. Sutton. 1996. *Domestic Burglary Schemes in·the Safer Cities Programme.* Police Research Study 145. London: Home Office.

Fagan, J., F. E. Zimring, and K. Une. 1998. Declining Homicide in New York City: A Tale of Two Trends. *Journal of Criminal Law and Criminology* 88(4):1277–1324.

Farrington, D., and P. Langan. 1998. *Crime and Justice in the US and in England & Wales, 1981–1996.* Washington, D.C.: U.S. Department of Justice.

Felson, M. 1998. *Crime and Everyday Life.* 2d ed. Thousand Oaks, Calif.: Pine Forge Press.

Felson, M., and R. V. Clarke. 1997. The Ethics of Situational Crime Prevention. In *Rational Choice and Situational Crime Prevention: Theoretical Foundations,* edited by G. Newman, R. V. Clarke, and S. G. Shoham. Aldershot, U.K.: Ashgate.

Ferrier, J. K. 1928. *Crooks and Crime.* London: Seeley, Service and Co. Ltd.

Foster, J. 1990. *Villains: Crime and Community in the Inner City.* London: Routledge.

Freiberg, A. 1997. Regulating Markets for Stolen Property. *The Australian and New Zealand Journal of Criminology* 30:237–258.

Goldblatt, P. 1998. Comparative Effectiveness of Different Approaches. In *Reducing Offending: An Assessment of Research on Ways of Dealing With Offending Behaviour,* edited by P. Goldblatt and C. Lewis. Police Research Study 187. London: Home Office.

Gottfredson, M., and T. Hirschi. 1990. *A General Theory of Crime.* Stanford, Calif.: Stanford University Press.

Graham, J., and B. Bowling. 1995. *Young People and Crime.* Police Research Study 145. London: Home Office.

Gregory, J. 1932. *Crime From the Inside: Revelations And Confessions of a Warder, Confidence Trickster And "Fence."* London: John Long Ltd.

Hall, J. 1952. *Theft, Law and Society.* 2d ed. Indianapolis: Bobbs-Merrill.

Henry, S. 1978. *The Hidden Economy: The Context and Control of Borderline Crime.* London: Martin Robertson and Co.

Hesseling, R. B. P. 1994. Displacement: A Review of the Empirical Literature. *Crime Prevention* 3:197–230.

Kennedy, D. M. 1997. Pulling Levers: Chronic Offenders, High-Crime Settings, and a Theory of Prevention. *Valparasio University Law Review* 31(2):449–482.

Kock, E., T. Kemp, and B. Rix. 1996. *Disrupting the Distribution of Stolen Electrical Goods.* Crime Prevention and Detection Series Paper 69. London: Home Office Police Research Group.

Langworthy, R. H., and J. L. LeBeau. 1992. Spatial Evolution of a Sting Clientele. *Journal of Criminal Justice* 20:135–45.

Leitch, D. 1969. *The Discriminating Thief.* London: Hodder and Stoughton.

Litvan, L. M. 1998. Can Three Strikes Reduce Crime? *The Investor's Business Daily* 15(163):1. 30 November.

Maguire, M. In collaboration with T. Bennett. 1982. *Burglary in a Dwelling: The Offence, the Offender and the Victim.* London: Heinemann.

Marx, G. T. 1998. *Undercover: Police Surveillance in America.* Berkeley, Calif.: University of California Press.

Mayhew, P., R. V. Clarke, A. Sturmann, and J. M. Hough. 1976. *Crime as Opportunity.* Police Research Study 34. London: Home Office.

Merton, R. 1957. *Social Theory and Social Structures.* Revised ed. Glencoe, Ill.: The Free Press.

Miller, W. B. 1958. Lower Class Culture as a Generating Milieu of Gang Delinquency. *Journal of Social Issues* 14(3):5–19.

Munro, A. K. 1972. *Autobiography of a Thief.* London: Michael Joseph.

Parker, H., K. Bakx, and R. Newcombe. 1998. *Living With Heroin: The Impact of a Drug 'Epidemic' on an English Community.* Milton Keynes: Open University Press.

Parker, H., and T. Bottomley. 1996. *Crack Cocaine and Drugs-Crime Careers.* London: Home Office.

Pawson, R., and N. Tilley. 1997. *Realistic Evaluation.* London: Sage.

Pease, K. 1998. *Repeat Victimisation: Taking Stock.* Crime Detection and Prevention Series Paper 90. London: Home Office Police Research Group.

Reppetto, T. A. 1976. Crime Prevention and the Displacement Phenomenon. *Crime and Delinquency* 22(2):166–177.

Reuter, P. 1985. *The Organization of Illegal Markets: An Economic Analysis.* Washington, D.C.: National Institute of Justice.

Reuter, P. 1990. *Money From Crime: A Study of the Economics of Drug Dealing in Washington DC.* Santa Monica, Calif.: RAND.

Shaw, C. R., and H. McKay. 1942. *Juvenile Delinquency and Urban Areas.* Chicago: University of Chicago Press.

Sherman, L. 1990. Police Crackdowns: Initial and Residual Deterrence. In *Crime and Justice: A Review of Research* Vol 12, edited by M. Tonry and N. Morris. Chicago: University of Chicago Press.

Shover, N. 1996. *The Great Pretenders: Pursuits and Careers of Persistent Thieves.* Boulder, Colo.: Westview.

Smithies, E. 1984. *The Black Economy in England Since 1914.* Dublin: Gill and Macmillan Humanities Press, Goldenbridge.

Steffensmeier, D. J. 1986. *The Fence: In the Shadow of Two Worlds.* Totowa, N.J.: Rowman and Littlefield.

Stockdale, J. E., and P. J. Gresham. 1995. *Combating Burglary: An Evaluation of Three Strategies.* Crime Detection and Prevention Series Paper 59. London: Home Office Police Research Group.

Sutton, M. 1993. *From Receiving to Thieving: The Market for Stolen Goods and the Incidence of Theft.* Home Office Research Bulletin No. 34. London: Home Office.

Sutton, M. 1995. Supply by Theft: Does the Market for Secondhand Goods Play a Role in Keeping Crime Figures High. *British Journal of Criminology* 38(3):400–416.

Sutton, M. 1996. *Implementing Crime Prevention Schemes in a Multiagency Setting: Aspects of Process in the Safer Cities Programme.* Police Research Study 160. London: Home Office.

Sutton, M. 1998. *Handling Stolen Goods and Theft: A Market Reduction Approach.* Police Research Study 178. London: Home Office.

Tarling, R. 1993. *Analysing Offending: Data, Models and Interpretations.* London: HMSO.

Tobias, J. 1974. *Prince of Fences.* London: Valentine Mitchell.

Tremblay, P., Y. Clermont, and M. Cusson. 1994. Jockeys and Joy-riders: Changing Patterns in Car Theft Opportunity Structures. *British Journal of Criminology* 34(3):307–321.

Walsh, M. 1977. *The Fence: A New Look at the World of Property Theft.* Westport, Conn.: Greenwood.

Ward, D. 1989. *King of the Lags: The Story of Charles Peace.* London: Souvenir.

Whitehead, P., and P. Gray. Forthcoming. *Pulling the Plug on Computer Theft.* Police Research Series. London: Home Office.

Wilkins, L. 1990. Retrospect and Prospect: Fashions in Criminal Justice Theory and Practice. In *Policy and Theory in Criminal Justice,* edited by D. Gottfredson and R.V. Clarke. Aldershot, U.K.: Avebury.

Wright, T., and S. H. Decker. 1994. *Burglars on the Job: Street Life and Residential Break-ins.* Boston: Northeastern University Press.

CHAPTER 3

RACE, ETHNICITY AND GENDER ISSUES IN GANGS: RECONCILING POLICE DATA

G. David Curry

Effective responses to gang-related crime and delinquency require accurate assessments of the nature of gang problems at the
community level. Field studies before the 1960s identified most
U.S. gang members as white ethnic males. Studies of law enforcement data in the early 1990s revealed disproportionate numbers
of Hispanics or African Americans among police-identified gang
members. Police have always estimated that gang members are
predominantly male. More recent field studies and survey research have suggested that law enforcement data do not accurately measure either ethnicity or gender among gang members.
This chapter suggests how law enforcement data can be combined with other sources of data to produce assessments of community problems from which effective gang response programs
can be developed.

In the early 1980s, most law enforcement agencies were not
concerned with gang crime problems. With the exception of Los
Angeles and Chicago, gangs were a problem of the past—an
antiquated image of white ethnic youths in leather jackets or the
romantic images of West Side Story. As the 1980s continued, gang
crimes took on a resurgence in Los Angeles and Chicago. By the
end of the 1980s, law enforcement officials, policy makers and
researchers were focused on the "proliferation" of gangs in
America. Gangs re-emerged in communities where they had long
been absent, and emerged for the first time in smaller and suburban locales. As a problem that has always been linked to specific communities, gang crime is especially suited to
problem-oriented policing responses.

The most promising contemporary model for responding to gang crime problems is a community mobilization approach built around links between law enforcement agencies and other community groups (Spergel 1995). It is especially important that effective gang response efforts be based on accurate analysis and understanding of the nature of gang problems in specific community contexts. Whether program goals are suppression, intervention, prevention, or some combination of the three, the gender and ethnic (or racial) composition of the youth population to be served must be assessed and incorporated into program design and development. Here, the focus will be on how law enforcement information fits into the response effort and how such information relates to other sources of information on gangs.

Sources of Information About Gangs

There are three ways of learning about gangs: field studies, surveys and law enforcement data. Each has provided important lessons about the nature of gang problems. Of the three approaches, field research has the longest history. Frederic Thrasher (1927), by studying a diversity of gangs in several Chicago communities, stressed the degree to which each gang emerges from its own specific community context. By conducting an in-depth study of an Italian-American gang in Boston more than a decade later, William F. Whyte (1943) demonstrated how the group dynamics of gangs can change over time with variations in specific members' participation. Both Thrasher and Whyte left their readers with an enduring perception of gang members as adolescent white ethnic males.

The next generation of gang researchers included Irving Spergel (1964), who studied the variations in delinquency in three different New York communities. Walter Miller (1958, 1962) provided multiple studies of white ethnic and African-American gangs in Boston. Gerald Suttles (1968) documented the ordered segmentation of white, Hispanic and African-American gangs in the same Chicago community. James Short and Fred Strodtbeck (1965) tested a variety of theories of delinquency on the white and African-American gang members whom they studied in Chicago. Malcolm Klein (1971) drew attention to the impact of response strategies on gang structure. In every case, scholars drew attention to greater numbers of minority gang members. Just as universally, they continued to confirm the link between community context and the nature of gang problems.

In the 1980s and 1990s, as field studies continued, John Hagedorn (1988, 1998) in Milwaukee, and Scott Decker and Barrick Van Winkle (1996) in St. Louis drew attention to differences and similarities in the "new" gangs that were appearing in emerging gang cities. They observed greater proportions of gang members representing minority groups. Individual gang members were increasingly involved in drug sales, but gangs were rarely involved as organizations. Increased availability of firearms and automobiles exacerbated levels of gang violence. Incarceration became part of the gang involvement process, as young adults increasingly continued their involvement in gangs. Joan Moore (1978, 1991), Ruth Horowitz (1983), Anne Campbell (1984), Karen Joe and Meda Chesney-Lind (1993), and Jody Miller (1996) brought attention to the roles of females in gangs. Carl Taylor (1990), James Diego Vigil (1988) and Ko-lin Chin (1990) revealed the unique contributions of community history and culture in shaping the structure of gang involvement. In these last two decades of field studies, members of minority groups were predominant among gang members studied.

In the late 1980s and early 1990s, field studies were complemented by a series of surveys of at-risk youths. The most important finding of these surveys was the relationship between self-reported gang membership and self-reported delinquency. From surveys of youths in three different cities, Jeffrey Fagan (1990) found that gang members—regardless of gender—reported greater levels of delinquency than nonmembers. In fact, in Fagan's study, female gang members reported higher levels of delinquency than male nonmembers. For minority males from Chicago middle schools, Curry and Spergel (1992) found that multiple measures of gang involvement other than self-reported membership were significantly related to multiple measures of delinquency. From their study, Curry and Spergel developed different causal models for gang involvement and delinquency for African-American and Hispanic youths. This emphasized the importance of ethnicity in gang involvement, even for youths from the same community.

Especially important among the survey findings was the work of Terrence Thornberry and his colleagues (Thornberry et al. 1993), who conducted a longitudinal survey of Rochester, N.Y., youths. By using measures taken at different times, Thornberry et al. compared levels of self-reported delinquency for the same youths before becoming gang members, during gang membership, and after leaving the gang (see Figure 1). By doing so, they addressed what had long been two alternative possibilities for the relationship between gang involvement and delinquency. One possibility had been that youths who were already involved in higher levels of delinquency were recruited or drawn to gangs. The other possibility was that belonging to a gang enhanced its members' involvement in delinquency. This study showed that youths who subsequently became gang members had significantly lower levels of delinquency before joining a gang. In addition, levels of delinquency for youths who left gangs declined significantly. This discovery that gangs in some way enhance or increase members' levels of delinquency is crucial for developing effective responses to gang problems.

The Evolution of Law Enforcement Data on Gangs

The third source of information on gangs is law enforcement data. Several problems can affect the quality of these data. The first is that, in the United States, policing is for the most part the responsibility of local political units. While this feature of law enforcement is regarded by many as an essential feature of democracy, it can certainly create problems for compiling and comparing data. Two primary problems, denial and exaggeration, have been identified by John Hagedorn (1988) and Ronald Huff (1989). In the case of denial, local political leaders ignore the pres-

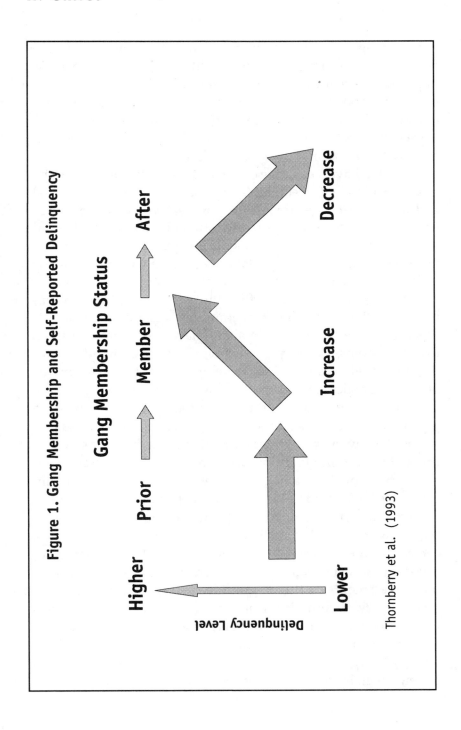

Figure 1. Gang Membership and Self-Reported Delinquency

Thornberry et al. (1993)

ence or magnitude of a gang problem. Denial can undermine citizen attitudes in neighborhoods with gang problems by making residents feel that the police simply "don't care." Besides making it impossible to organize any assessment-based response to gang problems, denial, according to Hagedorn, can lead to an overreaction when gang problems are admitted. Exaggeration can involve the unnecessary use of law enforcement resources in ways that have a negative effect on both communities and the mission of law enforcement. Such reactions have the potential of draining needed police resources to deal with imagined problems. When increased suppressive strategies are directed at minority communities, police-community relations can be negatively affected in ways that undermine a wide range of law enforcement goals (Zatz 1985; Miethe and McCorkle 1997).

Another problem that affects the usefulness of local law enforcement data in developing community response programs is that most law enforcement databases have been created as intelligence systems. These systems, designed to apprehend offenders, are not always useful for developing accurate assessments or effective policies. For example, if gangs predominantly involve adolescents, prevention and intervention programs alone have a good potential for success. If gangs involve adult leadership and heavy involvement in gang-related crime by young adults, prevention and intervention programs must be supplemented by suppression programs to work effectively. A strictly intelligence-focused database does not need to distinguish between former and current gang members. Information stemming from past gang membership, such as tattoos and personal associates, can contribute to successful apprehensions. On the other hand, reporting former members as active members can distort up-to-date assessments of the magnitude of community-level gang problems. Two methods for dealing with these kinds of distortions are (1) making distinctions between gang-motivated crimes and crimes involving gang members (Maxson and Klein 1990), and (2) "purging" aggregated statistics of gang members who haven't been involved in gang-related crimes for several years.

Surveys of local law enforcement data on gangs have been used to make national-level assessments to help refine federal agency policies for responding to gang problems. Walter Miller (1982, 1990) has been most adamant that only a national-level response can effectively reduce the nation's gang problem. To assess the quality of available national-level data on gang problems, it is useful to contrast such data with the Uniform Crime Reports (UCR). The UCR applies uniform definitions of specific crimes in gathering information from local jurisdictions. Uniform definitions of what constitutes a gang, gang member or gang-related crime have never been applied in a national compilation of gang statistics. It has been estimated that more than 16,000 law enforcement agencies provide data to the UCR, compiled annually since 1930 by the Federal Bureau of Investigation (FBI). At least 30 state laws, 15 with penalties for noncompliance, provide legitimacy for the UCR. Less than a dozen national gang surveys of law enforcement agencies have been conducted since the first one in 1975; most have been conducted by university professors and each has used a different sampling design. Legitimacy has most frequently been provided by cover letters from staff of the Office of Juvenile Justice and Delinquency Prevention (OJJDP) or the National Institute of Justice (NIJ). Until 1995 and 1996, no two national gang surveys had been conducted under the same funding agreement.

Conducted by Walter Miller, the first National Gang Survey results published in 1975 covered data from only 12 sites. Multiple agencies were contacted at each site to create triangulation of data. Six sites were identified as having gang problems, and six were not. Miller produced an empirically derived definition of what constituted a gang. Between 1975 and 1982, Miller produced a much more comprehensive report covering a broader range of cities and offering a national estimate of 97,940 gang members. Both of Miller's studies were supported by OJJDP.

OJJDP also funded a survey of a random sample of police departments in municipalities with populations of 100,000 or more (Needle and Stapleton 1983). Of 60 responding cities, 27

(45%) reported the presence of local gang problems. Five criteria abstracted from Miller's empirical definition and a sixth criterion added by the authors were used to measure commonality of definitions across jurisdictions. Of the six criteria, violence was the one most frequently reported. The other four from Miller's definition were group organization, leadership, recurrent interaction, and territory. The added criterion was symbols or distinctive dress. Only a small percentage of the agencies reporting gang problems reported using all six definitional criteria.

In late 1980s, OJJDP initiated the National Youth Gang Suppression and Intervention Program. The project used a purposive survey to identify a national sample of "promising" gang response efforts. A byproduct of the search for promising programs was an updated estimate of the national gang problem. Spergel and Curry (1993) reported 120,636 gang members in 35 jurisdictions. With NIJ support, Curry and his colleagues (Curry, Ball, and Fox 1994; Curry, Ball, and Decker 1996) conducted two national surveys of law enforcement agencies. For 1994, Curry et al. provided a "reasonable" national estimate of 555,181 gang members.

In 1994, OJJDP established the National Youth Gang Center (NYGC) in Tallahassee, Fla. The center's establishment marked the U.S. government's first continuing commitment to generating and compiling national-level statistics on gang problems. The NYGC has conducted three national surveys since its founding. In the first survey in 1995, the center attempted to validate and update prior samples. They used lists of localities obtained from Miller, Spergel, Curry, and Klein; lists of gang problem cities identified by the National Drug Intelligence Center and the Bureau of Alcohol, Tobacco and Firearms; and member agencies in the Regional Information Sharing Systems (RISS) to produce a purposive sample of 4,120 law enforcement agencies (representing 2,820 cities and 1,300 counties). With an 83 percent response rate to their survey, the resulting database of 3,440 jurisdictions made it possible to update specific information on most jurisdictions surveyed in earlier studies.

The second and third NYGC surveys administered for the
years 1996 and 1997 had a very different purpose, and employed
different and statistically representative sampling strategies.
These surveys included all cities with populations of more than
25,000, a representative random sample of cities with populations between 1,000 and 25,000, all counties identified as suburban by the U.S. Census, and a representative random sample of
rural counties.

Since Miller's first studies in the 1970s, few would disagree
that national and local awareness of gangs as a crime problem
has increased. Figure 2 shows the pattern of estimates for the
number of gang members identified by the series of federally
funded studies. Whether the quality of law enforcement data
has similarly advanced over the same period is open to question. With the development of the annual NYGC surveys, the
national data collection effort for law enforcement gang statistics has evolved into an institutionalized process capable of producing consistent annual estimates.

Analyses of the specific gang databases maintained by Chicago, Los Angeles and Los Angeles County have demonstrated
their utility (Spergel 1984; Maxson, Gordon, and Klein 1985; Curry
and Spergel 1988; Klein and Maxson 1989; Maxson and Klein
1990; Block and Block 1993). The question remains whether useful information on the social demographics of gang problems
can be derived from law enforcement agencies.

Race, Ethnicity, Gender, and Gangs

As noted above, the gang members described by early field studies were primarily of white European heritage. In his study of
African-American gangs in Chicago, Useemi Perkins (1987) was
able to find numerous references in Chicago history to gangs of
white ethnic youths dating back to 1860. Perkins noted that the
first reports of African-American gangs did not appear until after 1900. Frederic Thrasher (1927: 130) estimated that only 7.16
percent of Chicago's gangs consisted entirely of African-American members. Another 2.84 percent were estimated to be com-

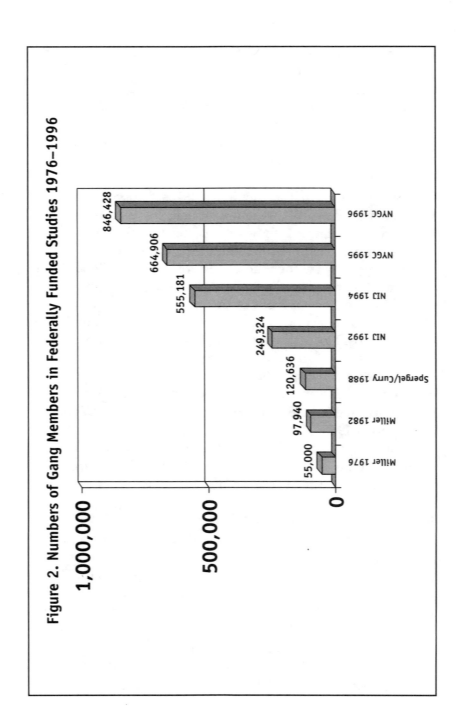

Figure 2. Numbers of Gang Members in Federally Funded Studies 1976–1996

posed of both African Americans and whites. The majority of gangs identified by Thrasher were composed of ethnic white immigrant youths. Mexican-American gangs did not appear in Los Angeles until the 1940s (Moore 1978). While some white ethnic gang members were still the subject of research into the 1960s (Short and Strodtbeck 1965; Spergel 1964; Suttles 1968), their numbers were already beginning to give way to youths of African-American, Puerto Rican and Mexican-American descent. Researchers such as John Hagedorn, Joan Moore and Scott Decker attributed increased gang problems to the growth of the predominantly minority inner-city underclass first identified by William Julius Wilson (1987).

The development and expansion of Mexican-American gangs in Los Angeles continued through the 1960s, conditioned by increased immigration, the spread of heroin and repression efforts (Moore 1978). By the 1970s, Mexican-American barrio gangs in California spanned three generations (Vigil 1988), and Mexican-American gangs were being studied in Chicago's near West side (Horowitz 1983). In the early 1980s, the highest gang homicide rates in Chicago were found in Mexican-American and Puerto Rican communities (Curry and Spergel 1988). In the 1960s, the Black Gangster Disciples, the Vicelords and the Blackstone Rangers emerged in Chicago. Such large African-American gangs would play a central role in the Chicago gang environment in prisons (Jacobs 1977) and on the streets (Block and Block 1993) for the remainder of the 20th century. A national gang survey of law enforcement agencies (Curry, Ball, and Fox 1994) reported that in 1992, law enforcement information systems on gang members identified 48 percent of all gang members as African Americans and 43 percent as Hispanics.

From his first national survey of gang problems, Walter Miller (1975) estimated that females constituted approximately 10 percent of the U.S. gang problem. As noted above, such an estimate did not differ from the male gang member image that had been portrayed by earlier field studies. The 1992 NIJ national survey of law enforcement agencies (Curry et al. 1994) explicitly sought local statistics on female gang members and their criminal activity. A number of jurisdictions did not, as a matter of policy, identify females as gang members. In others, females were relegated to the status of gang "associate" members. Not surprisingly, the number of female gang members reported to the study amounted to only 3.65 percent of the total number of gang members reported nationally.

Other sources of information provided larger estimates of the proportion of gang members who were females. Joan Moore (1991) selected a random sample of gang members whom she had identified in her earlier ethnographic research. One-third of the sample was female. Using the longitudinal Denver Youth Survey to study gang members in a general population survey, Finn-Aage Esbensen and David Huizinga (1993) found that approximately 25 percent of gang members identified over the four years of the study were females. From their analysis of the Rochester Youth Survey, Beth Bjerrgaard and Carolyn Smith (1993) concluded that 31 percent of the self-reported gang members in that study were females. One unavoidable conclusion is that law enforcement data and general survey data have produced substantially differing estimates of the proportions of gang members who are female.

Making Sense of Youth Surveys and Law Enforcement Data on Gangs

The most recent and geographically comprehensive survey of youths by Esbensen and Winfree (1998) has produced statistics on the social demographics of gang members that diverge from law enforcement data on ethnicity, race and gender. The survey was part of the broad national evaluation of the Gang Resistance Education and Training (GREAT) program. GREAT is a school-based gang prevention program developed and supported by the Bureau of Alcohol, Tobacco, and Firearms, and coordinated with local law enforcement agencies whose officers conduct the program. Survey information was obtained from 5,935 eighth graders in 315 classrooms in 42 different schools, in 11 very diverse law enforcement jurisdictions across the nation. The GREAT survey supported the finding noted above from previous surveys that self-reported gang membership is significantly related to higher levels of self-reported delinquency. The survey also revealed larger proportions of females and white youths among gang members. Among the respondents to the survey, 38 percent of gang members were females, and 25 percent of gang members were white.

The data from the 1996 National Youth Gang Center (NYGC) survey of law enforcement agencies provide the most recent, comprehensive and statistically representative information about gangs from the point of view of local law enforcement agencies. At first glance, the results of the 1996 NYGC survey with respect to gang members' gender, race and ethnicity conflict with the results of the GREAT survey. Based on estimates computed from the NYGC data, approximately 10 percent of gang members reported by law enforcement agencies in 1996 were females. This is almost three times the estimate of 3.65 percent produced by the 1992 NIJ national survey, but significantly lower than the GREAT survey estimate of nearly 40 percent. Similarly, the percentage of white gang members reported by law enforcement for 1996 was 13.9 percent. This estimate is also three times as large as the 1992 NIJ national survey of 4.4 percent white, but less than the 25 percent figure from the GREAT survey.

The differences between the GREAT youth survey estimates and the 1996 NYGC survey estimates can be easily explained and understood within the context of what is already known about gang involvement and response. The explanation of these disparities also helps explain the differences between the 1996 law enforcement estimates and the 1992 law enforcement estimates. First, how can the differences in law enforcement estimates across the four-year period be explained? It might be tempting to conclude that gang involvement among females and whites increased between 1992 and 1996. Two conditions make such a conclusion extremely risky: (1) the difference in sampling methodologies between the 1992 and the 1996 surveys, and (2) the patterns of distributions in gender and ethnic variables for the 1996 survey data.

The selection method for the 1992 National Gang Survey was significantly biased in the direction of the largest metropolitan jurisdictions. The survey specifically included the 79 largest U.S. cities. This included all cities with a population more than 195,000 in the 1990 census. The other 43 cities included in the survey represented the 1988 screening survey conducted by Spergel and Curry (1993). That survey was neither systematic nor random. It represented a purposive effort to identify all jurisdictions that had at that time developed a community-level response to gang crime problems. Only a fraction of cities with populations between 150,000 and 195,000 were included in the 1992 survey. The 1996 NYGC survey included all cities with populations of more than 25,000. Cities and towns with populations of less than 25,000 were represented by a systematic random sample.

If gang problems were equally distributed across the range of cities in terms of population, gender and ethnicity, the bias in favor of larger jurisdictions in the 1992 study would not affect the development of national-level estimates for the gender and ethnicity of gang members from that data. Figures 3 and 4 display 1996 NYGC survey data on the proportions of female gang members and white gang members across jurisdictions on the basis of population. There is no question that female gang members and white gang members are concentrated in cities and towns with smaller populations. In the largest U.S. cities with populations of more than 100,000, law enforcement reported that 7.3 percent of the gang members were females. In smaller cities and towns with populations between 1,000 and 25,000, law enforcement identified 19.7 percent of gang members as females. In the largest cities, the percent of gang members identified as white was only 8.8 percent. The comparable statistic for the smallest cities and towns was 29.6 percent white. The differences between the 1996 and the 1992 National Gang Surveys in the gender and ethnicity of gang members can be attributed to the inclusion of a representative portion of jurisdictions with smaller populations in the latter sample.

Figures 5 and 6 compare law enforcement statistics from the 1996 NYGC survey and the GREAT survey statistics for gender and ethnic distributions among gang members. At first glance, it appears that law enforcement data grossly underestimate the numbers of females and whites among active gang members. When law enforcement statistics and the GREAT survey results are compared on the basis of age, a possible explanation emerges. As Figure 7 shows, the GREAT survey statistics represent a much younger population than that represented by law enforcement data. Only 14.7 percent of the gang members reported by police in 1996 were under 15. By comparison, 77.2 percent of the GREAT survey respondents were under 15. The GREAT survey estimates for gender and ethnicity were therefore based on a significantly younger population than the law enforcement estimates.

If age is the source of the differences between gender and ethnicity estimates, it would be expected that more younger gang members would be found in the same settings as greater numbers of female and white gang members. That this finding holds for city size is demonstrated in Figure 8, which shows that younger gang members are more likely to be found in the same smaller jurisdictions as female and white gang members.

The three measures—gender, ethnicity and age—are not perfectly correlated. The biggest distinction by age is between the largest U.S. cities (those of more than 100,000 population), where juveniles make up 38.9 percent of reported gang members, and all smaller cities. In all three of the smaller city categories, the proportion of gang members reported to be juveniles was greater than 65 percent. As reported by police, female and white gang members are also more likely to be found in smaller jurisdictions. It is not surprising, therefore, that surveys of younger gang members, who may not necessarily be officially recognized as involved in delinquent behavior, would produce larger estimates of the numbers of female and white gang members.

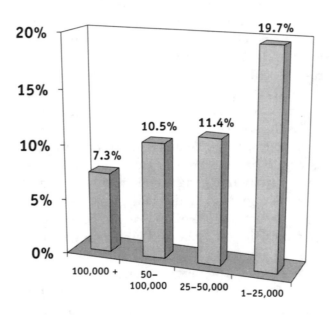

Figure 3. Female Gang Membership and City Size

% Gang Members Female by City Size

1996 National Youth Gang Survey,
National Youth Gang Center

Figure 4. White Gang Membership and City Size

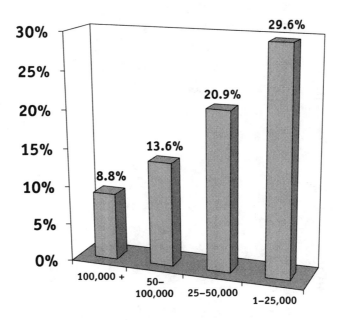

% Gang Members White by City Size

**1996 National Youth Gang Survey,
National Youth Gang Center**

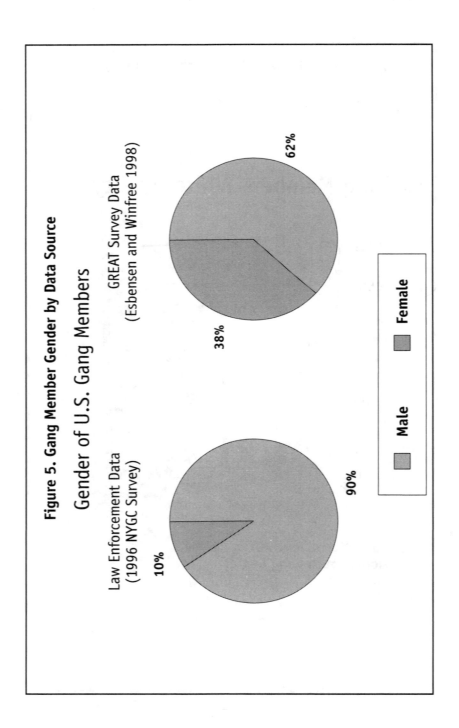

Figure 5. Gang Member Gender by Data Source

Gender of U.S. Gang Members

Law Enforcement Data
(1996 NYGC Survey)

GREAT Survey Data
(Esbensen and Winfree 1998)

10%

90%

38%

62%

Male   Female

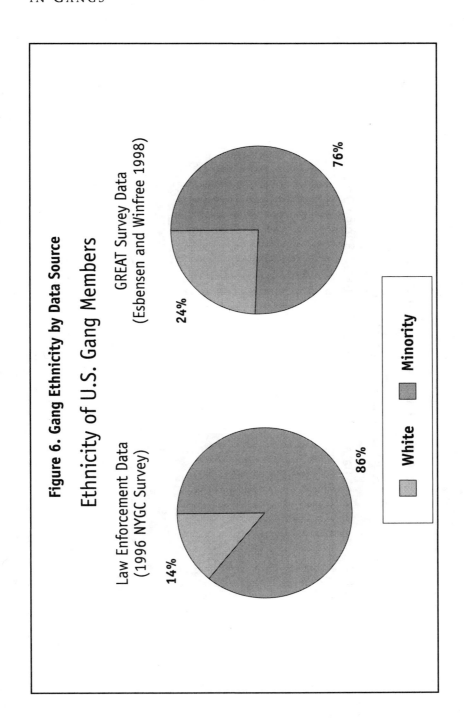

Figure 6. Gang Ethnicity by Data Source

Ethnicity of U.S. Gang Members

GREAT Survey Data
(Esbensen and Winfree 1998)

76%

24%

Law Enforcement Data
(1996 NYGC Survey)

86%

14%

White   Minority

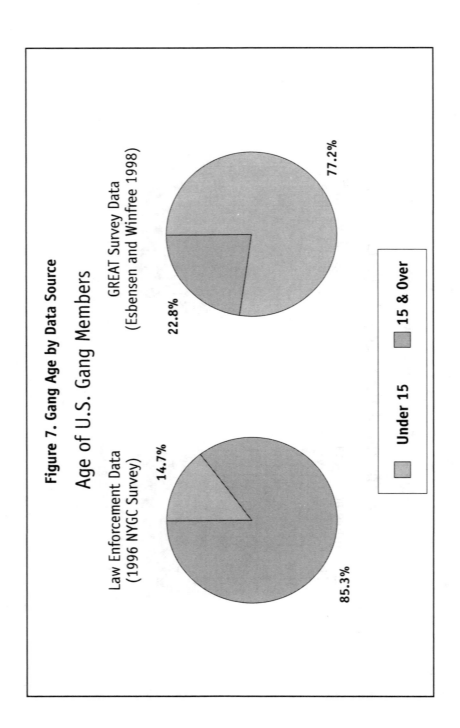

Figure 7. Gang Age by Data Source

Age of U.S. Gang Members

Law Enforcement Data
(1996 NYGC Survey)

GREAT Survey Data
(Esbensen and Winfree 1998)

14.7%

85.3%

22.8%

77.2%

Under 15

15 & Over

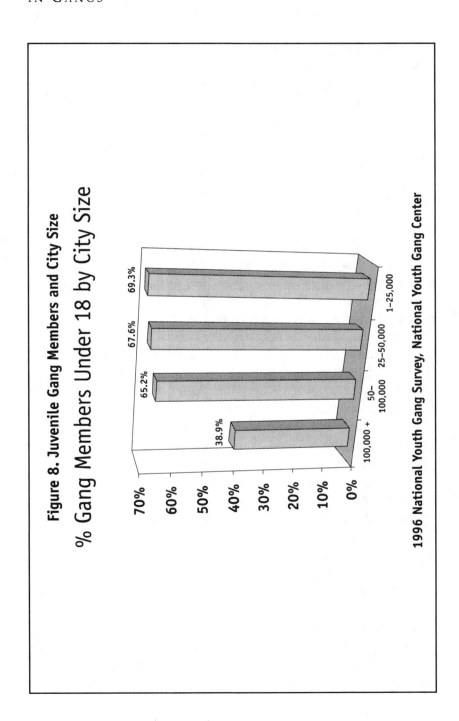

Figure 8. Juvenile Gang Members and City Size

% Gang Members Under 18 by City Size

1996 National Youth Gang Survey, National Youth Gang Center

Race, Ethnicity and Gender:
Implications for Policy and Practice

One additional statistic about the distribution of the nation's gang problems has implications for interpreting the interaction of ethnicity and gender with gang involvement. Gang-related homicide has long been considered the strongest available indicator of the severity of gang crime problems. Figure 9 shows the distribution of gang homicides by city size.

Greater numbers of potential offenders and victims result in more homicides. Additionally, gang-related homicide is greatest in the same settings where gang members are more likely to be identified as males and members of minority groups.

All of this is very important for policy and problem solving. Gang crime problems, wherever they occur, are anchored in youth populations. That these young gang member populations may differ in terms of race and gender from the older populations most at risk of being offenders or victims must be taken into consideration. For quite a while, researchers (Thrasher 1927; Moore and Hagedorn 1996) have known that females desist from gang behavior at younger ages than their male counterparts. This finding has usually been tempered by the finding that females may suffer more long-term harm from gang involvement than males (Moore 1991). These findings underscore the need for programs aimed at reducing gang involvement among adolescents to reach out to females. There is evidence that females may need different kinds of programs than males (Curry forthcoming). On the other hand, a case can be made that special programs for minority males are also needed. These programs must be designed to offer disincentives and alternatives to potential careers in criminal activity.

Finally, these findings support policy recommendations that local responses be based on assessments of available data, including data from law enforcement agencies. As illustrated here, some contradictions between law enforcement agency information and findings from other sources can be empirically explained. Effective local responses to community gang problems require

assessments of a broad range of available information, including
what has been compiled by law enforcement. Likewise, law enforcement strategies can benefit from other sources of information that may prove useful in producing the broadest possible,
in-depth understanding of local gang problems.

Figure 9. Gang-Related Homicides and City Size

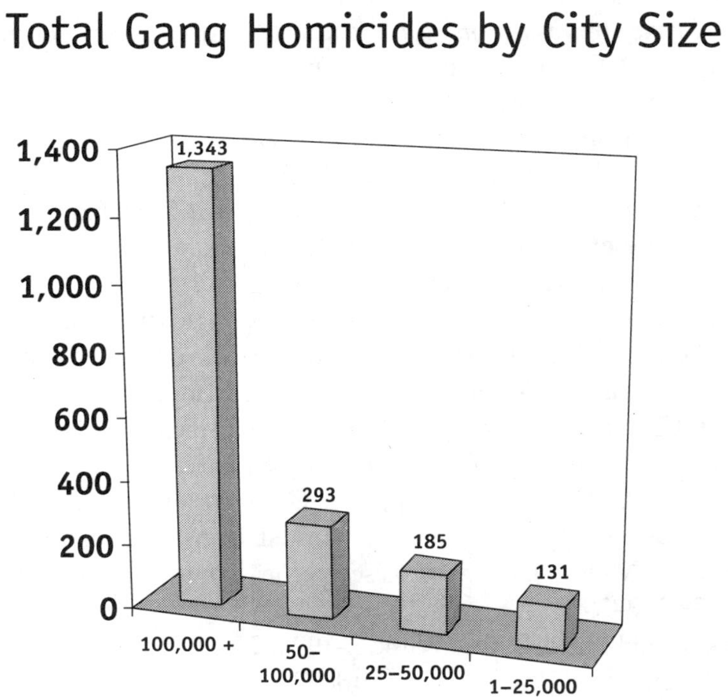

Total Gang Homicides by City Size

**1996 National Youth Gang Survey,
National Youth Gang Center**

REFERENCES

Block, C.R., and R. Block. 1993. *Street Gang Crime in Chicago*. National Institute of Justice Research in Brief. Washington, D.C.: U.S. Department of Justice.

Bjerregaard, B., and C. Smith. 1993. Gender Differences in Gang Participation, Delinquency, and Substance Use. *Journal of Quantitative Criminology* 4:329–355.

Campbell, A. 1984. *The Girls in the Gang*. Cambridge, Mass.: Basil Blackwood.

Chin, K. 1990. *Chinese Subculture and Criminality: Non-traditional Crime Groups in America*. Westport, Conn.: Greenwood.

Curry, G. D. Forthcoming. Responding to Female Gang Involvement. In *Female Gang Involvement*, edited by J. Hagedorn and M. Chesney-Lind. Chicago: Lakeview.

Curry, G.D., R. Ball, and S. Decker. 1996. *Estimating the National Scope of Gang Crime from Law Enforcement Data*. National Institute of Justice Research in Brief. Washington, D.C.: U.S. Department of Justice.

Curry, G.D., R. Ball, and R. J. Fox. 1994. *Gang Crime and Law Enforcement Recordkeeping*. National Institute of Justice Research in Brief. Washington, D.C.: U.S. Department of Justice.

Curry, G.D., and I.A. Spergel. 1988. Gang Homicide, Delinquency, and Community. *Criminology* 26:381–405.

Curry, G.D., and I.A. Spergel. 1992. Gang Involvement and Delinquency among Hispanic and African-American Adolescent Males. *Journal of Research on Crime and Delinquency* 29:273–291.

Decker, S.H., and B.Van Winkle. 1996. *Life in the Gang: Family, Friends, and Violence*. New York: Cambridge University Press.

Esbensen, F., and D. Huizinga. 1993. Gangs, Drugs, and Delinquency in a Survey of Urban Youth. *Criminology* 31:565–587.

Esbensen, F., and L. T. Winfree. 1998. Race and Gender Differences Between Gang and Nongang Youths: Results from a Multisite Survey. *Justice Quarterly* 15:505–526.

Fagan, J. 1990. The Social Processes of Delinquency and Drugs Among Urban Gangs. In *Gangs in America*, edited by R. Huff. Newbury Park, Calif.: Sage.

Hagedorn, J.M. 1988. *People and Folks: Gangs, Crime and the Underclass in a Rustbelt City*. Chicago: Lakeview. (2nd Edition, 1998).

Horowitz, R. 1983. *Honor and the American Dream*. New Brunswick, N.J.: Rutgers University Press.

Huff, R.C. 1989. Youth Gangs and Public Policy. *Crime and Delinquency* 35:524–537.

Jacobs, J.B. 1977. *Stateville: The Penitentiary in Mass Society*. Chicago: University of Chicago Press.

Joe, K., and M. Chesney-Lind. 1995. Just Every Mother's Angel: An Analysis of Gender and Ethnic Variations in Youth Gang Membership. *Gender and Society* 9:408–430.

Klein, M.W. 1971. *Street Gangs and Street Workers*. Englewood Cliffs, N.J.: Prentice-Hall.

Klein, M.W., and C. Maxson. 1989. Street Gang Violence. In *Violent Crimes, Violent Criminals*, edited by N. Weiner. Beverly Hills, Calif.: Sage.

Maxson, C.L., M.A. Gordon, and M.W. Klein. 1985. Differences Between Gang and Nongang Homicides. *Criminology* 23:209–222.

Maxson, C.L., and M.W. Klein. 1990. Street Gang Violence: Twice as Great, or Half as Great. In *Gangs in America*, edited by R. Huff. Newbury Park, Calif.: Sage.

Miethe, T.D., and R. C. McCorkle. 1997. Gang Membership and Criminal Processing: A Test of the "Master Status" Concept. *Justice Quarterly* 14(4):407–427.

Miller, J. 1996. Gender and Victimization Risk among Young Women in Gangs. Paper presented at the Annual Meeting of the American Society of Criminology, Chicago, 21 November.

Miller, W.B. 1958. Lower Class Culture as a Generating Milieu of Gang Delinquency. *Journal of Social Issues* 14:5–19.

Miller, W.B. 1962. The Impact of a "Total Community" Delinquency Control Project. *Social Problems* 19: 168–192.

Miller, W.B. 1975. *Violence by Youth Gangs and Youth Groups as a Crime Problem in Major American Cities.* Washington, D.C.: U.S. Government Printing Office.

Miller, W.B. 1982. *Crime by Youth Gangs and Groups in the United States.* Washington, D.C.: National Institute of Juvenile Justice and Delinquency Prevention.

Miller, W.B. 1990. Why the United States Has Failed to Solve Its Youth Gang Problem. In *Gangs in America,* edited by R. Huff. Newbury Park, Calif.: Sage.

Moore, J.W. 1978. *Homeboys: Gangs, Drugs, and Prison in the Barrios of Los Angeles.* Philadelphia: Temple University Press.

Moore, J.W. 1991. *Going Down to the Barrio: Homeboys and Homegirls in Change.* Philadelphia: Temple University Press.

Moore, J.W., and J.M. Hagedorn. 1996. What Happens to Girls in the Gang? In *Gangs in America,* 2d ed., edited by R. Huff. Thousand Oaks, Calif.: Sage.

National Youth Gang Center. 1997. *1995 National Youth Gang Survey.* Washington, D.C.: Office of Juvenile Justice and Delinquency Prevention.

National Youth Gang Center. 1998. *1996 National Youth Gang Survey Program Summary.* Washington, D.C.: Office of Juvenile Justice and Delinquency Prevention.

Needle, J., and W. V. Stapleton. 1983. *Report of the National Juvenile Justice Assessment Centers, Police Handling of Youth Gangs.* Washington, D.C.: Office of Juvenile Justice and Delinquency Prevention.

Perkins, U.E. 1987. *Explosion of Chicago's Black Street Gangs.* Chicago: Third World Press.

Short, J.F., and F.L. Strodtbeck. 1965. *Group Process and Gang Delinquency.* Chicago: University of Chicago Press.

Spergel, I.A. 1964. *Racketville, Slumtown, Haulburg.* Chicago: University of Chicago Press.

Spergel, I.A. 1984. Violent Gangs in Chicago: In Search of Social Policy. *Social Service Review* 58.

Spergel, I.A. 1995. *The Youth Gang Problem: A Community Approach.* New York: Oxford University Press.

Spergel, I.A., and G.D. Curry. 1993. The National Youth Gang
    Survey: A Research and Development Process. In *Gang In-
    tervention Handbook*, edited by A. Goldstein and R. Huff.
    Champaign-Urbana: Research Press.
Suttles, G.D. 1968. *The Social Order of the Slum: Ethnicity and Terri-
    tory in the Inner City.* Chicago: University of Chicago Press.
Taylor, C.S. 1990. *Dangerous Society.* East Lansing, Mich.: Michi-
    gan State University Press.
Thornberry, T., M.D. Krohn, A.J. Lizotte, and D. Chard-
    Wierschem. 1993. The Role of Juvenile Gangs in Facilitating
    Delinquent Behavior. *Journal of Research in Crime and Delin-
    quency* 30:55–87.
Thrasher, F. 1927. *The Gang: A Study of 1,313 Gangs in Chicago.*
    Chicago: University of Chicago Press.
Vigil, J.D. 1988. *Barrio Gangs.* Austin: University of Texas Press.
Whyte, W.F. 1943. *Street Corner Society.* Chicago: University of
    Chicago Press.
Wilson, W.J. 1987. *The Truly Disadvantaged.* Chicago: University
    of Chicago Press.
Zatz, M. 1985. Los Cholos: Legal Processing of Chicano Gang
    Members. *Social Problems* 33:13–30.

CHAPTER 4

DRUG MARKET PLACES: HOW THEY FORM AND HOW THEY CAN BE PREVENTED

John E. Eck

Understanding the geography of retail drug dealing is critical to developing effective drug market problem-solving strategies. By understanding how retail drug dealing is spatially organized, problem solvers can develop approaches for its prevention.

Sellers and buyers of illicit drugs must find ways of meeting each other and making exchanges. If they can meet and complete their exchanges, they can get the drugs and money they seek. But other offenders may steal their money or drugs, or the police may arrest them. Participants in retail markets can use two strategies to balance these rewards and risks. First, sellers and buyers can restrict their dealing to people they know. This reduces the risks of being arrested or having their drugs and money stolen. But it also restricts sales and buying opportunities. Alternatively, sellers and buyers can deal with strangers. This strategy provides sellers access to more customers, and gives buyers greater access to drugs. However, it increases sellers' and buyers' risks of arrest and rip-off. To offset these increased risks, sellers and buyers of illicit drugs will meet in areas busy with legitimate public activity. In these areas, they will make exchanges at places where they can protect themselves and where place managers are not attentive.

These two strategies for retail drug markets result in two different geographic patterns of drug market places. By understanding the marketing strategy being used and its resulting geographic pattern, police can develop more effective responses to retail drug problems.

Any effective problem-solving strategy to control or prevent crime must be based on a valid theory of crime. The strategy's success or failure rests in large part on the theory's validity. Sometimes the theory is obvious. In other circumstances, the theory underlying the strategy is obscure. In the absence of a theory, the police can apply a variety of tactics, but cannot develop a coherent strategy. Such is the case with current attempts to curb retail drug dealing. In the United States, police have used a wide array of tactics to combat retail drug dealing (Weisel 1994). The reason for this is obvious. Retail drug dealing became very common as crack cocaine became widely available. Before the advent of crack, drug enforcement was handled by specialized units that conducted covert investigations using undercover officers or informants. With the arrival of crack, these units became overwhelmed by the volume of street drug dealing and police departments found themselves without a coherent strategy.

The theory of retail drug dealing outlined in this chapter explains where drug dealing locations will be found, and suggests possible control and prevention measures. The theory was developed as part of a large-scale problem analysis undertaken in collaboration with the San Diego Police Department. The research sought to answer the question, "Why can drug dealing be found at one location but not at other nearby places?" Many of the ideas that led to this theory were originally expressed by San Diego patrol officers and narcotics investigators during observations of drug places. The San Diego Police Department's Crime Analysis Unit collected much of the data from which the theory was developed (Eck 1994, 1995). Police expertise was critical to the theory's development, but there were other important sources of knowledge as well.

Several well-established theories of crime and criminal behavior contributed to this theory, most notably rational choice theory (Cornish and Clarke 1986), situational crime prevention (Clarke 1997), routine activity theory (Cohen and Felson 1979; Felson 1998), and offender search theory (Brantingham and Brantingham 1981). Collectively, these theories are part of a larger body of knowledge and research known as environmental criminology. To develop effective prevention programs, environmental criminology describes how offenders make decisions based on what they learn from the physical and social environment.

Research

While the description of the geography of drug market places owes much to the theories just mentioned, it owes little to previous research on drug dealing and drug abuse. Most drug research examines such questions as:

- Who uses drugs, what kinds, and how often?
- How is illicit drug use associated with predatory crime?
- How does illicit drug use affect health and mortality?
- How do drug users associate with each other and with the rest of society?

In contrast, the following questions relate to drug places:

- Where do drug sales take place and where is drug dealing absent?
- What is the geographic pattern of retail drug dealing?
- What are the characteristics of drug sales locations?

There is considerable police lore on these subjects, much of it quite useful. Nevertheless, these insights are often mixed in with much speculation. Consequently, there was a need for a logically consistent explanation of drug places that can be applied to the prevention and control of illicit retail drug dealing.

Terms and Definitions

This chapter's explanation of drug places uses a number of terms in very specific ways. A "place" or "location" is a building, business, street corner, street address, or other small parcel of land. Places are smaller than blocks. A "drug place" is a location where drug buyers and sellers meet to exchange money for drugs. "Areas" are large regions consisting of many places, such as neighborhoods, communities and other sections of cities. An "arterial route" is a heavily used street that carries more than local traffic. "Buyers" are people interested in purchasing illicit drugs. This theory assumes that all buyers are primarily interested in consuming the illicit drugs. "Sellers" are dealers. They want to exchange their drugs for money. We will assume that sellers are more interested in making money than in consuming the drugs they have. Buyers and sellers use "strategies" to find each other. A "strategy" is a process. There are only two strategies, and we will examine them both. A "market" is a combination of sellers who use a specific strategy to sell a particular drug type, and buyers who use a compatible strategy to buy this type of drug. Note that a market is not defined by the places, areas or any other geographic territory where drugs are sold. Instead, the market is defined by the preferences of the sellers and buyers. The locations where people in the market meet to exchange money for drugs are "market places." Buyers' and sellers' preferences give rise to the geographic patterns of drug market places that we observe. Because the buyers are the final consumers of the drugs, the markets we are interested in are "retail" market places.

Problems of Drug Sellers and Buyers

To understand retail drug markets, we must recall two obvious but important facts. First, illicit drug sales and purchases are voluntary exchanges made for personal gain. The user wants the feelings associated with drug consumption. The seller wants the cash. Unlike predatory crimes, both parties willingly seek each other out to exchange money and drugs. The processes that buyers and sellers use to find each other are important for understanding retail drug markets.

Second, to sell or possess the drugs in question is *illegal*. If the police catch the parties involved holding or exchanging drugs and money, the buyer and seller can be punished by courts. In other words, the police are a credible threat. This second point is critical. If the police are not a threat to users and sellers, because of policies, budget priorities, legal restrictions, or corruption, then the theory that follows is not applicable.

Several important consequences flow from the basic facts that the actions of buyers and sellers are voluntary and illegal. The first is that drug sellers have restricted means for advertising. Advertising can attract police attention so it must be done

covertly through information channels that are not easily pen-
etrated by the police. Sellers' presence (or the presence of an associate) on a street corner is often the only advertising they have.
Therefore, they must be consistent in where they hang out, or
their customers will not be able to find them. Further, they must
look like they belong there or they will attract the attention of
the police, or people who will call the police. Because their public image must comply with legitimate activities, drug sellers will
always have some superficially plausible explanation of why they
are hanging out on the corner. Only when law enforcement is
absent, lax or unprepared will sellers overtly advertise.[1] Consequently, sellers have difficulty communicating with their potential customers.

Second, drug sellers cannot call on government for help. If
someone steals a seller's merchandise, calling the police is not
only of little help, but it also alerts the police to the seller's illicit
activities. Drug sellers must provide their own security against
both police intrusion and thefts or robberies by others.

The third consequence of these voluntary and illegal actions
is that drug buyers cannot be too overt in expressing their desires. Though most police efforts target sellers, buyers also face
risks from the police. Consequently, drug buyers must use discreet signals to tell possible sellers of their interests. These signals can be easily misinterpreted, so some sellers will miss sales
opportunities.

Finally, like sellers, drug buyers cannot call on government to
help. If the drugs purchased are of low quality, the seller provides
bogus drugs, or the seller steals the buyer's money, then calling the
police will do little to redress the grievance. Unless the buyer is
seriously injured, the police are unlikely to do much for the victim.

---

[1] Adler (1995) gives a good example of overt advertising for crack in
Detroit at a time when the local police were unprepared for this drug,
and the drug sellers were particularly aggressive at expanding their
markets.

Because sellers cannot overtly advertise and buyers cannot be too blatant in expressing their desires, buyers and sellers have difficulty meeting. They must engage in time-consuming and risky searches to locate each other. Because neither buyers nor sellers can rely on government to assist them, they face risks from both the police and criminal offenders. If fact, a recent study of armed robbers in St. Louis found that some robbers specifically target dealers because victims are less likely to call the police (Wright and Decker 1997). This increases distrust between buyers and sellers. If buyers and sellers have difficulty meeting and they distrust each other, how do drug sales occur?

How Sellers and Buyers Overcome Their Problems

To understand how drug sales occur, despite the problems described, we need to examine the preferences of risk-averse sellers and buyers—sellers and customers who want to minimize their chances of arrest and theft.

Sellers who want to minimize their risks might prefer to sell from isolated locations. Such places are hidden from police scrutiny. Further, these ideal places give sellers control over access, so potential threats can be kept out. We would expect such places to allow sellers to watch the surrounding areas so that they see police and other threats in time to destroy evidence of drug sales or to escape. Finally, these hypothetical sellers would prefer to get their money from buyers before giving them the drugs. In summary, we would expect sellers to establish business locations on side streets, far from main thoroughfares, in fortified houses or flats, and with clear lines of sight along access routes; to have barriers between themselves and customers; and to require buyers to pay cash before receiving drugs. Indeed, at the height of the crack epidemic, such fortified crack houses were common in some cities.

However, there are several problems with these isolated locations. First, selling from hidden places makes it even more difficult for buyers to find sellers. Second, many buyers might fear putting themselves at risk of being robbed on the way to the sale, or of sellers' taking their money without giving them the drugs. Consequently, only buyers who know the sellers well would frequent such places. Thus, the number of sales would be limited.

Buyers who want to minimize their risks may adopt the following strategy. To protect themselves from robbery, they might prefer the sales to take place in public areas where there are many people whose mere presence could protect them. These buyers would prefer to observe sellers before making their interests known. In addition, buyers would like to be able to escape with relative ease. These last two preferences allow buyers to leave an area without approaching sellers if they feel that a situation is too risky. And finally, these buyers would like to receive their drugs before handing over their money. In summary, these risk-averse buyers prefer to conduct business in open busy areas, such as the parking lots of busy shopping centers during peak shopping times, or at entrances to transit stations at rush hour. And some drug transactions do take place in such places.

This risk-averse buyer strategy also has major limitations. Sellers would have trouble distinguishing buyers from numerous nonbuyers also using the locations. If sellers made themselves obvious as drug dealers, so the buyers could find them, sellers would place themselves at greater risk of arrest or robbery. Consequently, highly risk-averse buyers may find they can make relatively few purchases because most sellers are unwilling to take all of the risks.

Neither of these strategies work well because the ideal situation for one group shifts most of the risk to the other group. There are two compromise solutions, or strategies. These strategies give rise to different geographic patterns in drug dealing. And as we will see, they require different prevention and control strategies.

Solution I: The Network Approach
Drug sellers can choose to make exchanges only with people they know, or with people who have been vetted (investigated and vouched for) by people they know. Similarly, drug buyers can

choose to purchase drugs only from people they know, or from people known to people they know. Buyers and sellers who act in this way are taking a "network approach," so named because buyers and sellers are connected by a web of acquaintances. People outside this network of acquaintances will have a difficult time becoming part of the drug market until they convince a member of the network that they are reasonably trustworthy (i.e., not a police official, police informer or thief).

Participants in network markets receive several benefits. First, sellers do not need to overtly advertise. News of who has drugs and how they can be found is disseminated through the network. Consequently, buyers need only make a few inquiries among their acquaintances to find willing sellers.

Because participants in a network have repeated contacts with each other, they develop reputations. One seller may be known for selling particularly high-quality drugs, while another may get a reputation for cheating customers. Some customers may be known to be good credit risks, while others may be known as bad risks. Buyers and sellers may also be known for their willingness to use violence, while others are known to be fairly peaceful. So another advantage of network markets is that reputations provide assurances of drug quality and personal safety.

The third advantage is also linked to the flow of information. To find a seller, willing buyers need only contact someone who knows the seller and who can provide directions to him or her. Thus, sellers can be located anywhere, as long as buyers can find them and transportation costs are not too high. Under some conditions, sellers may even deliver to buyers, particularly regular and reliable customers.

There are two related disadvantages to network market participants. For sellers, the number of customers is limited by the network's size because new participants are screened before coming into the market. This limits the rate of market expansion. Further, because screening is imperfect, many potentially trustworthy customers may be kept out. For buyers, the disadvantage of a network market is that they have relatively few shopping opportunities. If they cannot find the seller they normally buy from, they may have difficulty locating another seller. Additionally, the opportunities for buyers to find sellers with lower prices or higher quality drugs are restricted because the network stifles competition.

So while the network approach has several important advantages, it also has two important disadvantages. As a consequence, there are incentives for participants in a network to try another approach.

Solution 2: The Routine Activity Approach

The second approach is to buy and sell to strangers as well as acquaintances. Such an approach makes a retail drug market very like any licit retail market. Buyers need only approach sellers, whether acquaintances or not, and strike a deal. Sellers may assess the risks of making sales to new customers, and buyers may be cautious about approaching strange sellers. Nevertheless, these markets are open to anyone. We will call this a routine activity market, because buyers and sellers use the normal legitimate routines of everyday life as cover for their illegitimate behaviors, as predicted by routine activity theory (Felson 1998).

The two advantages of this approach to marketing drugs are obvious. First, drug sellers can have many more buyers, because their customer base is not restricted to a network of acquaintances. Instead, anyone who approaches the seller is a possible customer, and if the potential buyer passes some basic tests (e.g., does not look or act like a police officer or informant), a sale can be made. Sellers operating in such markets can make more sales and gain greater profits than if they operated in a network.

Second, buyers can shop for drugs. If they cannot find their primary source of drugs, they can easily find an alternative source. If they do not like the price or quality of drugs from one seller, they can go to another. If one seller appears dangerous or is untrustworthy, they can find another seller.

The disadvantages of the routine activity approach mirror the advantages of the network approach. The first disadvantage is that reputations will be harder to develop, so buyers or sellers can persist in devious activities longer. Thus, sellers can sell poor-quality drugs, short change buyers, and steal from buyers for a relatively long time before a sufficient number of customers learn of these activities and refrain from buying from the seller. Unscrupulous buyers can steal from a number of sellers before the sellers learn to avoid these buyers. Because product quality and risk are more uncertain in routine activity markets than in network markets, we would expect the participants to use several methods to reduce this uncertainty. Sellers are less likely to offer drugs on credit, and then only to regular customers proven to be credit worthy. Buyers and sellers are more likely to use threats of violence to deter others from stealing from them. Because some of these threats will not work, there is a greater chance of violence among participants in routine activity markets than in network markets.

Sellers, and to a lesser degree buyers, face a higher risk of police intervention in routine activity markets than in network markets. Though buyers and sellers will take some precautions to limit this increased risk, by deciding to participate in routine activity markets, they recognize that the increased risk is worth the increased revenues (Reuter, MacCoun and Murphy 1990). Police will be able to arrest more participants in routine activity markets than in network markets.

The third disadvantage is that unfamiliar buyers will have difficulty finding unfamiliar sellers. How do buyers make contact with sellers they do not know? In a network, searching buyers can ask acquaintances to direct them to sellers. Though in a routine activity market, this search strategy is available to some customers, it is not available to all customers. Routine activity sellers can advertise but this raises their risk of police intervention. Without advertisement, sellers and buyers must find ways to communicate with each other. The simplest approach is for sellers to establish fixed points of sale so buyers can find them.

Consequently, unlike their counterparts in network markets, sellers in routine activity markets will invest in places. Because some places will be easier for buyers to find than others, and buyers as well as sellers will feel safer in some places rather than others, we would expect routine activity drug dealing to be found in some places but not in others.

What are the characteristics of places we would expect to find drug dealing? Because buyers and sellers will distrust each other, the places that will be best for routine activity drug sales will be in areas where both buyers and sellers feel the most comfortable. These will be areas that buyers and sellers normally frequent as part of their everyday legitimate routine activities—near shopping centers, transportation hubs, schools, recreation centers, and other areas where many people come together for legitimate purposes. The places suitable for drug dealing in these areas will have characteristics that help sellers protect themselves. These characteristics can include access barriers (such as fences, to control approaches to sellers), lighting (so sellers can see who is approaching, and buyers can see that someone is at the sales place who may be willing to sell drugs), hiding places, and escape routes. Finally, the places are likely to have weak place managers. That is, the people who own these locations do little to control the behavior of people using the site. The owners may not have the resources, be ignorant of what is going on, have legal or political constraints on their actions, or be corrupted. Whatever the reason for their lack of control at these places, locations with weak place management will be attractive to drug sellers.

Where will such places be? *First, they will be disproportionately located in economically depressed areas.* The low return on investment to rental property owners in these areas means that many of them do not have the economic resources needed to control behavior of people on their property. And many of the landlords will not know what legal powers they have or how to exercise them to control behavior. Though not a requirement for the concentration of drug market places, if an economically depressed area has a relatively high proportion of people who are willing to engage in deviant behavior, this will make it even more difficult for property owners to control behavior on their sites.

Second, within these economically depressed areas the drug dealing places will be located along and near concentrations of everyday legitimate routine activities. That is, they will be located within a short distance of arterial streets and centers of activity. These areas will have many potential buyers and will be familiar to buyers and sellers.

Finally, within economically depressed areas and around the arterial routes and centers of activity, places with appropriate security features and weak place management will be more attractive to drug sellers than places with few security features and strong place management.

This prediction is shown on a map of a hypothetical region of a fictitious city (Figure 1). This city has a typical grid layout of small streets with arterial routes cutting across them. At the top is a major highway. The map also shows a park for recreation. The shaded area represents an economically depressed area. Two types of drug places are shown on the map. Stars (*) represent routine activity (R.A.) drug dealing places. The Xs represent network drug dealing places. The stars are along the arterial routes within the economically depressed area. The Xs are scattered near and far from the arterial routes and throughout the entire area shown on the map. Note also that although the routine activity drug dealing places are all in the economically depressed area, there are many blocks in this area without drug dealing. It is not the arterials or the economically depressed area that create situations ripe for the formation of routine activity drug market places. It is the combination of these two conditions.

If we could show on the map the places with security features and weak place management, we would see that those located off the arterial routes would have no routine activity dealing (though they may have some network dealing). Places located along the arterial routes within the shaded area, but without the necessary characteristics (i.e., lacking security or having good place management) have no drug dealing either. Network deal-

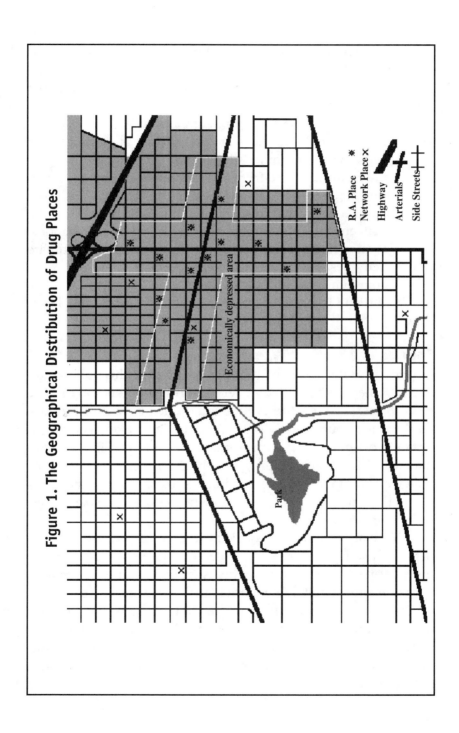

Figure 1. The Geographical Distribution of Drug Places

ing sites, however, can locate anywhere because they only need
weak place management.

We can summarize the spatial characteristics of these two
types of markets. Network markets are

- spread out in a variety of neighborhoods,
- inclusive of locations near and far from busy streets,
- seldom in outdoor locations, and
- are easily displaced from one location to another and from
  one neighborhood to another.

Routine activity markets, on the other hand, are

- concentrated in economically depressed neighborhoods,
- located near busy streets and concentrations of legitimate
  activities within these neighborhoods,
- sometimes at outdoor locations, and
- difficult to displace to other locations in other neighborhoods.

Policies and Market Types

Routine activity markets are more harmful to the public than
network markets because they serve more customers and involve
more buyers. Given the Hobbesian choice between network
markets and routine activity markets, policy makers should select network markets. If one assumes that it is impossible to eliminate drug sales and illicit drug use, then this is exactly the choice
policy makers face. The basic strategy is to convert routine activity markets into network markets, and reduce the size of network markets.

Network markets are difficult to control because the participants protect themselves from police intervention by screening new participants. Covert investigations using informants
(who are almost inevitably participants in the market) or undercover police officials (who have to pretend to be trustworthy
market participants) are the primary method for controlling these
markets. These investigations may create a credible threat and
increase the protective actions drug buyers and sellers use, with
two results. First, as the network becomes more restrictive, it is

more difficult for new participants to enter. Second, as the network becomes more restrictive, it becomes more difficult for the police to increase risks. Consequently, managing network markets is a more realistic objective than eliminating them. The cardinal objective should be to keep these markets from growing and evolving into routine activity markets. However, as these markets become smaller, enforcement costs increase so the police cannot drive them out of business without astronomically high enforcement budgets.

Routine activity markets are, in theory, more serious problems but are easier to control. Eliminating routine activity markets by forcing participants to use a network strategy is a feasible objective. There are many more options available to the police and other government agencies to control these markets. Though covert investigations can still be used, this may not be the most effective tactic. There are several alternative tactics, beginning with the areas susceptible to drug dealing and moving down to the specific locations.

Routine activity markets are found in areas where there is a concentration of weak place management. Economically depressed areas have concentrations of places with weak management. Consequently, one way of attacking routine activity drug markets is to encourage economic reinvestment in an area. The more money that owners can make from their property, the greater their capability of controlling drug dealing on their property. Because many legitimate users of the property—apartment renters, shoppers, park users, and others—will avoid areas known for drug dealing, getting rid of the obvious drug dealing can increase the number of people willing to use the area. This can increase property owners' revenues. Property owners will have an incentive to reduce drug dealing on their sites if they expect that this will increase their profits.

Within an economically depressed area, the drug sales sites will be concentrated around streets and locations that attract large numbers of people. Careful examination of the flow of people through an area may suggest methods for altering traffic flow to make it more difficult for drug sellers and buyers to meet. For example, if buyers circle around an area to find sellers, then changing the flow of traffic to make it difficult and time-consuming to circle through the area may make it more difficult for a routine activity market to function (Matthews 1993).

At the site level, changing the characteristics of places attractive to buyers and sellers may also help curb drug dealing. For example, reducing the number of entrances and exits to an apartment complex may reduce customers' ability to drive up to purchase drugs. Removing public telephones, or changing them so that calls can be made but not received, may make it more difficult for drug buyers to contact sellers.

There are a number of methods for improving the management of places in high-risk areas. If property managers and owners are ignorant of the characteristics of drug dealing, their legal authority, or specific techniques they can use to curb drug sales, then training programs for property managers may be worthwhile. Another approach is to identify specific locations that have a past history of drug dealing activities and work directly with owners to eliminate drug problems. In the United States, various laws provide local governments with the power to seize property that is persistently used for illegal purposes if an owner does nothing to control the problem (Cadwalder, Wichersham and Taft 1993). Such laws have been used as implied or explicit threats to gain property owners' compliance in controlling drug problems. While landlord training programs have not been scientifically evaluated, there have been a number of rigorous evaluations of the use of nuisance abatement. Collectively, these evaluations strongly suggest that this is a powerful tactic for reducing drug dealing, disorder and predatory crime (Eck 1997).

Finally, high-visibility patrols, particularly foot patrols, of small areas with persistent drug problems can be used to deter drug buyers and sellers. This may be particularly effective when the police officers are provided with lists of locations with histories of drug dealing, or with lists of place features that attract drug sellers.

Regardless of the tactics used to control routine activity drug markets, there is a possibility of displacing the drug sales to other places. Though sellers in network markets can move their sales to a wide variety of locations over a large area, sellers in routine activity markets have a more restrictive range of places to which they can move. The new dealing places must be in economically depressed areas, be near streets and locations that draw many people, have weak property management, and have features that provide the sellers with security. Not only will displacement be limited, but it may also be possible to make educated guesses about the most likely locations to which routine activity drug dealing will be displaced. With this knowledge, it may be possible to prevent the most obvious forms of displacement. But for a market place to displace, both the seller and the buyers must shift locations. Police can reduce the chances of displacement in routine activity markets by careful examination of how sellers and buyers communicate. Disruption of this communications process could delay, if not thwart, any displacement.

Conclusions

The theory of retail drug dealing explained here predicts that as buyers and sellers attempt to engage in the drug trade while controlling the risks associated with these behaviors, they will choose between two market strategies. The network strategy keeps risks relatively low but limits market size. The routine activity strategy has more risks for the participants, but sellers have more customers and buyers have more sources of drugs.

These two strategies create very different geographic distributions of drug dealing places. Network markets are spread over large areas and in a wide variety of places. Routine activity markets are concentrated in economically depressed areas, around busy streets and places where people congregate. Within these areas, routine activity drug places are found at locations with features that enhance seller security and have property managers who do little to regulate the behavior of place users.

Network markets are difficult to control because buyers and sellers protect themselves by restricting their exchanges to people they know. Successful covert operations against network markets can make these markets more restrictive. This may reduce the number of buyers who can participate in the market, but it also makes subsequent enforcement more difficult. Thus, there will be decreasing additional benefits from increasing enforcement efforts against such markets. At some point, the costs of additional enforcement are not worth the additional benefits. Because network sellers do not need specific types of places or areas to sell their drugs, network market places can displace over large areas. Though difficult to control, they are less harmful than routine activity markets because they involve fewer people.

Routine activity markets cater to many more people. Fortunately, there are many more prevention and control strategies that can be used against them. Strategies aimed at improving economic conditions in an area, and changing the flow of people along arterial routes and where people congregate, may prevent or control routine activity markets. Strategies aimed at the specific sites of drug dealing, or places at risk of becoming dealing locations, may also be useful. Routine activity drug places are less likely to displace and it is possible to make reasonable guesses about the most likely locations to which dealing will displace. Thus, these markets are more susceptible to control and prevention than network markets.

This theory suggests that police need to know the type of drug markets they are confronting before designing strategies to control them. The strategies that work against one type of market are less useful against the other type. It also suggests that the police need to involve other agencies in the prevention and control of routine activity markets.

This theory describes two pure market strategies that arise from simple cost-benefit decisions by drug buyers and sellers. In practice, drug markets are likely to be more complex than this theory suggests. For example, two different markets can operate in the same area, and while many people only participate in one of them, some people could participate in both. Network markets could evolve into routine activity markets or vice versa. Therefore, careful analysis of drug markets needs to accompany the development of prevention and control strategies. As important, additional research needs to be conducted to test this theory in a variety of settings.

REFERENCES

Adler, W.M. 1995. *Land of Opportunity: One Family's Quest for the American Dream in the Age of Crack.* New York: Atlantic Monthly Press.

Brantingham, P.L., and P.J. Brantingham. 1981. Notes on the Geometry of Crime. In *Environmental Criminology,* edited by P.J. Brantingham and P.L. Brantingham. Beverly Hills, Calif.: Sage.

Cadwalder, Wichersham, and Taft, Attorneys at Law. 1993. *A Civil War: A Community Legal Guide to Fighting Street Drug Markets.* New York: Cadwalder, Wichersham, and Taft.

Clarke, R.V. 1997. *Situational Crime Prevention: Successful Case Studies.* New York: Harrow and Heston.

Cohen, L.E., and M. Felson. 1979. Social Change and Crime Rate Trends: A Routine Activity Approach. *American Sociological Review* 44:588–605.

Cornish, D., and R. Clarke. 1986. *The Reasoning Criminal: Rational Choice Perspectives on Offending.* New York: Springer-Verlag.

Eck, J.E. 1994. *Drug Markets and Drug Places: A Case-Control Study of the Spatial Structure of Illicit Drug Dealing.* Unpublished dissertation, University of Maryland, College Park.

Eck, J.E. 1995. A General Model of the Geography of Illicit Retail Marketplaces. In *Crime and Place,* edited by J. E. Eck and D. Weisburd. Monsey, N.Y.: Criminal Justice Press.

Eck, J.E. 1997. Preventing Crime at Places. In *Preventing Crime: What Works, What Doesn't, What's Promising—A Report to the Attorney General of the United States,* edited by L.W. Sherman, D.Gottfredson, D. MacKenzie, J. Eck, P. Reuter and S. Bushway. College Park, Md.: Department of Criminology and Criminal Justice, University of Maryland.

Felson, M. 1998. *Crime and Everyday Life.* 2d ed. Thousand Oaks, Calif.: Pine Forge.

Matthews, R. 1993. *Kerb-crawling, Prostitution and Multi-agency Policing.* Crime Prevention Unit Series Paper 43. London: Home Office Police Department.

Reuter, P.H., R.J. MacCoun, and P. Murphy. 1990. *Money From Drugs: A Study of the Economics of Drug Dealing in Washington, DC.* Santa Monica, Calif.: RAND Corporation.

Weisel, D. 1994. *Emerging Drug Enforcement Tactics: A Comprehensive Assessment.* Unpublished report to the National Institute of Justice. Washington, D.C.: Police Executive Research Forum.

Wright, R.T., and S.H.Decker. 1997. *Armed Robbers in Action: Stickups and Street Culture.* Boston: Northeastern University Press.

CHAPTER 5

RESPONDING TO DOMESTIC VIOLENCE: A COLLABORATION BETWEEN THE POLICE AND THE MEDICAL COMMUNITY

Daniel Brookoff, Walter Crews, Charles S. Cook, and Terry Thompson

In April 1995, a group of Memphis police officers, led by Inspector Charles Cook, and a group of doctors got together to discuss their mutual frustrations about how they were getting "nowhere" with victims and perpetrators of domestic assault. Repeat 911 calls were mounting, emergency room visits for battering were skyrocketing and the batterers kept on battering. This collaboration led to a plan to have health care workers accompany police officers to scenes of domestic assault calls to help assess batterers and their victims. One predisposing factor to domestic assault that was identified was intoxication with alcohol or drugs. Building on a previous police-medical collaboration to conduct on-scene rapid drug testing of intoxicated drivers, a plan was developed to test batterers for intoxication at the scene.

The Problem: Domestic Violence

The following text is an excerpt from an internal police memo written by Inspector Cook of the Memphis Police Department:

More than 4 million people in the United States are victims of domestic violence every year. Twenty percent of women seen in hospital emergency departments have symptoms relating to physical abuse. Domestic violence accounts for 30 percent of all female trauma cases in hospitals. This is three times the number of women injured in motor vehicle accidents. In addition to its impact on the criminal justice system, the impact of domestic violence on the health care system is enormous. However, the fact remains that 90 percent of women who experience domestic violence will never bring it to medical attention.

Despite citizens' fear of death or injury from street crime, in this country, a person is more likely to be assaulted, beaten or killed at home by a "loved one" than anyplace else or by anyone else. Women in the United States are more likely to be assaulted or killed by male partners or ex-partners than by all other types of assailants combined.

While street crime deserves to be a prominent concern in our community, domestic assaults are generally more dangerous than street assaults. While 54 percent of street assaults result in injury, more than 80 percent of assaults against spouses result in injuries.

In contrast to violent street crime, which tends to occur in isolated episodes, victims of domestic violence are typically subject to a progressive stream of injury. Twenty percent of battered women who go to hospitals have a history of at least 11 prior visits for injuries; another 23 percent have had six to 10 prior visits. Domestic violence is usually continual, and tends to escalate over time. Women are not even protected by the presence of children or pregnancy. Up to 23 percent of pregnant women are battered during their pregnancy.

Domestic violence is associated with increases in violent behavior by children. Children who witness domestic violence are at increased risk for becoming abusers themselves. One of the most important determinants of whether a person will become a batterer or child abuser is a history of having witnessed domestic violence as a child.

Most people who are killed or suffer severe injury due to domestic violence had been brought to the attention of the police or health care agencies during prior episodes of domestic violence. Preventive efforts need to be incorporated into police calls and health visits. In more than 85 percent of domestic homicides, the police had been called to the home on a previous domestic violence call. In 50 percent of cases of domestic homicide, the police had responded more than five times to domestic violence calls at that home in the previous two years.

Studies have shown that the most important variable differentiating abused from nonabused women is the husband's or boyfriend's use of illegal drugs. Having a partner who is a drug user or alcoholic substantially increases the risk of being the victim of domestic violence. Most victims of domestic violence report that their partners were intoxicated at the time of the assault.

Among people who carry out domestic assaults, those with the more violent offenses are more likely to have a drug problem or a dual drug and alcohol problem than those charged with less violent offenses.

Between 50 and 85 percent of men are intoxicated when they batter their wives. Most studies implicate alcohol as the most common intoxicant. These findings may be skewed by the fact that these studies are usually surveys of battered women who might not know about their abusers' drug use.

Illegal drugs are involved in at least one-third of abuse cases, and these cases tend to result in the most severe injuries. The drugs involved include cocaine, amphetamines, barbiturates, marijuana, opiates, and phencyclidine, often used in combination with alcohol or with each other. In a recent San Francisco study of assailants in domestic violence cases who killed their victims, 30 percent tested positive for cocaine, and 20 percent had used a combination of cocaine and alcohol.

More than half of the homicides in this country involve drugs or alcohol. Substance abuse is implicated in an even larger proportion of nonfatal violence. U.S. homicide rates rose sharply after the widespread appearance of crack in 1985. In Memphis, there was a marked increase in homicides that coincided with the marked increase in the use of cocaine in this city, especially "crack" cocaine.

Most people associate drug-related violence with activities surrounding the buying and selling of drugs. But most drug-related violence is not due to drug selling; it is due to drug use. Drug selling does incite violence, but this violence is usually highly localized. Domestic violence due to drug use is more widespread.

Alcohol, cocaine, barbiturates, phencyclidine, amphetamines, and anabolic steroids have psychopharmacologic properties that can motivate violence. Some people consume alcohol or drugs to achieve emotional states that facilitate violence; this is especially true for crack cocaine. Crack smoking can cause paranoia, irritability and depression—emotional states that often precede violence. Thirty-six percent of crack smokers in emergency departments have recently made threats to others, and 19 percent have recently caused injuries to others.

Involvement with drugs not only increases some people's propensity to assault others, it can also increase others' susceptibility to violent victimization. Drug use can lead to "victim-precipitated" homicides or assaults—assaults in which the victim was the initial aggressor. Therefore, it is important to assess the drug use of both the assailants and the victims in cases of domestic violence.

Most people who carry out domestic assaults are never arrested. Most people charged with battering manage to avoid counseling. For convicted batterers with drug problems, drug treatment is rarely mandated.

Researchers have repeatedly pointed out the need to establish assessment instruments to identify high-risk, chemically dependent batterers and develop well-coordinated intra-agency treatment programs. Some researchers have even suggested having the police measure a batterer's blood alcohol level at the scene, as is done with people suspected of DUI, and collecting samples for drug tests.

Domestic Violence and the Medical Community

Domestic violence is a leading cause of injury (Flitcraft 1992), and a growing cause of chronic medical and mental illness (Flitcraft 1995; Randal 1990). In North America, which has one of the highest rates of battering in the world (Wolfe and Korsch 1994), the health consequences of domestic violence are expected to affect nearly all medical caregivers (Alpert 1995). The true impact of domestic violence on the use of medical resources cannot be known because medical facilities do not collect sufficient information to quantify the extent of the problem (Davidson 1996). Although medical organizations and government officials have called on physicians to increase their role in domestic violence prevention and treatment (Marwick 1994), the medical setting may not be the best place to initiate this care.

Victims of battering generally do not use medical facilities as a resource for problems related to domestic violence (Appleton 1980) and most medical facilities are not prepared to deal with these problems (Skolnick 1995). Few physicians ask patients about domestic violence (Parson et al. 1995; Friedman et al. 1992) and victims of battering rarely volunteer a history of abuse when they see a caregiver in a medical setting (Friedman et al. 1992). Most physicians feel that domestic violence is not a problem in their practices (Isaac and Sanchez 1994) and many express frustration with victims' behavior (Parson et al. 1995). When confronted with domestic violence, physicians commonly feel helpless and fail to arrange appropriate follow-up care (Sugg and Inui 1992), leaving the victims feeling isolated and confused (Wolfe and Korsch 1994).

Medical care for domestic violence may have to be initiated outside the medical setting. In many situations, house calls have proven useful in getting reluctant patients into treatment, conducting comprehensive assessments and strengthening support networks (Keenan et al. 1992; Kates, Webb, and LePage 1991). Many families affected by domestic violence are already receiving frequent "house calls" from police (Slade, Daniel, and Heisler 1991). Police visits for domestic violence are seldom therapeutic; the legal interventions initiated during police calls often do not protect victims of domestic violence (Alpert 1995; Hyman, Schillinger, and Lo 1995). More than 30 percent of batterers inflict additional assault during prosecution (Hart 1993). Until recently, very few police calls to scenes of domestic violence resulted in arrests or even in reports of domestic violence (Hyman, Schillinger, and Lo 1995).

In July 1995, the Tennessee legislature enacted a new domestic violence law encouraging arrests and mandating the filing of reports and development of domestic violence databases to "communicate the attitude that violent behavior is not excused or tolerated" (Tennessee Annotated Code 1995a). The passage of this new law was followed by a significant reduction in domestic violence-related homicides throughout the state (Downing 1996). In response to the new law, the Memphis Police Department asked medical personnel to accompany them on calls to see whether bringing the "caregiver approach" (e.g., trained interviewers using a nonthreatening, private and caring manner) to domestic violence scenes could help identify ways to improve victims' treatment and identify prevention opportunities.

The Memphis Program

The Survey Team. This study was carried out in the North Precinct of Memphis, a city of 690,000. The North Precinct encompasses 74 square miles and has a population of 190,000. This area is mostly residential with a diverse population, including upper-income neighborhoods and public housing projects. A survey team, which included a physician and a paramedic, monitored the police radio channel and went to calls regarding disturbances or assaults at residential addresses. When there was more than one call at a given time, the survey team went to the nearest call. Once the surveyors were finished at a scene, the team went to the next call that came up on the radio. The survey team was in operation for 23 consecutive seven-hour night shifts, Tuesdays through Saturdays from 7 p.m. to 2 a.m..

After police officers on patrol had responded and stabilized the scene, the survey team entered the home and interviewed the officers about the circumstances of the call and their decision concerning arrest. If the incident fit the legal criteria for domestic violence, the participants (victims and assailants) and adult family members who were in the house when the police arrived were asked to participate in a survey.

Definition of Domestic Violence. According to Tennessee law, domestic assault has occurred when one family or household member causes, or attempts to cause, bodily injury to another family or household member. The legal definition of "family or household member" includes people living as spouses, people related by blood or marriage, people who have a child in common, people whose sexual relationship has resulted in a current pregnancy, people jointly residing in the same dwelling unit who are 18 or older or who are emancipated, and people who have, or have had, a dating relationship (Tennessee Annotated Code 1995c). The Memphis program included only cases in which the primary assailant was positively identified as a family or household member of the victim. It also included cases in which the complaint involved specific threats of bodily harm or intimidation (e.g., holding the victim at knifepoint or gunpoint).

    Decision to Arrest. According to Tennessee code (1995b), if a police officer responding to a domestic violence call has probable cause to believe that a person has committed a crime involving domestic abuse, the preferred response is arrest. The decision to make an arrest is not contingent on the victim's request or consent. In the Memphis program, officers made the decision whether or not to arrest without any input from the survey team.

    Identifying Assailants and Victims. If two or more people made a complaint to the responding officer, then he or she had to determine who was the primary aggressor. To do this and comply with Tennessee code, the officer considered the history of domestic abuse between the parties, the relative severity of the injuries inflicted on those involved, the likelihood of future injury to each person, whether one of the people acted in self-defense, and evidence from witnesses. The survey team made an independent assessment of who was the victim and who was the assailant based on the same criteria.

    Police Services for the Victims. If the assailant was not present when the police arrived, the victim was encouraged to obtain a warrant for arrest the next day. As mandated by law, the police offered all victims at the scene transportation to a shelter or hospital. Those who refused were advised about the availability of shelter and other community services, and were given immediate notice of their legal rights and the legal remedies available to them.

Survey. Participants and adult household members at the scene were asked to participate in a survey as part of a research project about domestic violence. The subjects were informed that their responses would be confidential and that individual responses would not be reported to police officers or other law enforcement officials. The subjects were interviewed in a room away from police officers or household members. Subjects who were under arrest or posed a threat of violence were interviewed in a secured police car without the police or other family members present. When the assailant was not present at the scene, the victim and adult family members provided information about the assailant.

Surveyors used a printed questionnaire that included questions about the present incident, previous history of domestic violence and other arrests, participants' use of antipsychotic medications, children's involvement in domestic violence, and victims' previous use of health care facilities and shelters. Because witnessing domestic violence as a child is one of the most important risk factors for future participation in domestic violence (Widom 1989), the team asked subjects to identify and give the ages of children in the household who had witnessed the assault but were not direct participants. They specifically inquired about children who had seen a physical assault (as opposed to witnessing threats or displays of weapons, or hearing the assault through a closed door).

Assessment of Drug Use. All interviewees were questioned about assailants' and victims' use of drugs and alcohol. These questions were taken from the standard survey instrument used by the Tennessee Department of Health to assess the performance of alcohol and drug abuse services (Williams and Hepler 1995). Participants were questioned about their own drug use in the 12 hours preceding the assault. In addition, they were specifically asked if they had seen or had specific knowledge of drug or alcohol use by any of the participants in the 12 hours preceding the incident. Interviewees were also asked whether they considered any of the participants to be alcoholics or drug addicts. For the purpose of the survey, the interviewees were specifically told that the term "addiction" denoted daily use of alcohol or drugs to the point of intoxication for the previous month.

Toxicological Testing. After the interview, subjects who denied using alcohol and/or other drugs were asked to submit a urine specimen for drug testing. The subjects were informed that drug testing was being done for research purposes only and that they had the right to refuse to submit a specimen without any prejudice from the surveyors. The subjects' decision about submitting a specimen and the test results were not communicated to the officers on the scene. No incentive was offered for participation in testing. The Memphis Police Department reviewed and approved this procedure.

Participants provided urine specimens in the bathroom of the house at which the incident occurred, without direct observation. Subjects who were under arrest provided unwitnessed samples in a secure private toilet in the police department's mobile drug testing laboratory (Brookoff et al. 1994). Surveyors immediately tested the temperature of the sample using an electronic thermometer to ensure the sample's integrity. Measured aliquots of 200 microliters of urine were tested for cocaine metabolites, marijuana metabolites, opiates, benzodiazepenes, barbiturates, and phencyclidine using a rapid one-step qualitative immunoassay kit (Microline Drug Screen, Drug Screening Systems, Blackwood, N.J.). Subjects who submitted urine specimens were privately informed of their test results and questioned about drug use that day.

Review of Arrest Records and Court Proceedings. Records of previous arrests and convictions were reviewed for all victims and assailants using the Memphis Police Department database. Eight weeks after the police call, records of arrest, active warrants, bond hearings, preliminary hearings, and court records were reviewed for each assailant.

Program Results

The survey team went to the scenes of 182 disturbance calls and surveyed subjects at the scenes of the 62 calls that fit the criteria for domestic violence. The remaining calls included complaints of assault by unknown assailants, calls for subjects arguing with no violence or threats of physical harm, and calls to the police for disturbances involving people with mental illness or intoxication that did not involve domestic violence.

Surveyors obtained information on 136 subjects, 72 victims and 64 assailants. All of the victims and all of the 42 assailants who were at the scene when police arrived (66 percent of all assailants) consented to be interviewed. The 22 assailants who had left the scene before the police arrived were not interviewed. Adult family members of the assailants or victims were interviewed at 49 (79%) of the scenes. Information about absent assailants was obtained from the victims and family members who had witnessed the assault, and through subsequent review of police records.

In 45 (73%) of the cases, the initial assault or episode of intimidation was carried out by an adult male on an adult female who was or had been a sexual partner. Nine (20%) of the assailants in these cases were cohabiting husbands, 18 (40%) were cohabiting boyfriends, 13 (29%) were noncohabiting boyfriends and five (11%) were estranged or divorced husbands or ex-boyfriends. Four of the female victims in these cases were pregnant and their assailants were aware of the pregnancy. Two cases involved a wife's assault of her husband. Six cases involved assault on a parent or child and nine cases were assaults upon a sibling or in-law. Table 1 shows some other characteristics of those involved.

In 10 cases, there were two victims. In nine of these cases, the primary victim was an adult female and the second victim was a child under the age of 10. In the other case, a man initially assaulted his wife and then attacked his wife's sister when she tried to intervene. In two cases, there were two assailants identified whose relationship to the victim fit the criteria for domestic violence. In 39 (63%) of the cases, the victim made the call to the police.

Table 1. Characteristics of Participants in Domestic Violence

	Victims		Assailants	
Gender				
Male	20	(28%)	50	(78%)
Female	52	(72%)	14	(22%)
Age (years)				
0–12	8	(11%)	0	
13–17	3	(4%)	4	(6%)
18–25	18	(25%)	17	(27%)
26–35	21	(29%)	23	(36%)
36–45	14	(19%)	15	(23%)
46–55	6	(8%)	2	(3%)
>55	2	(3%)	3	(5%)
Reported Occupation				
Student*	13	(18%)	4	(6%)
Employed	30	(42%)	16	(25%)
Retired	2	(3%)	3	(5%)
Unemployed	21	(29%)	31	(48%)
Drug Trade**	5	(7%)	16	(25%)
No Report or Unknown	6	(8%)	10	(16%)

* Includes all subjects under age 16.
** Subjects who were unemployed and either reported that they made most of their income selling drugs or had at least two family members report that they made most of their income selling drugs.

Injuries. Eleven (15%) victims suffered injuries that, in the opinion of the physician or paramedic on the scene, required emergency medical attention (e.g., stab wound, gunshot wound, probable fractures, lacerations requiring stitches). Police at the scene called for ambulances for five victims and for two assailants (both of whom suffered stab wounds). The other six victims who needed emergency treatment refused ambulance transport and were advised to get family members to take them to the nearest hospital. Fifty-five victims (76%) suffered apparent injuries that did not require an emergency room visit. These included being punched, kicked, slapped, choked, or shaken. Six of the victims were not physically assaulted but had been subject to threats or intimidation without physical assault.

Use of Weapons. In 42 (68%) of the cases, the assailant had used or displayed a weapon. These included six guns (five handguns and one shotgun), 17 knives and 19 blunt instruments (e.g., hammers, baseball bats). The five assailants who displayed or used handguns were all adult males, three of whom were on parole or probation for felonies. The assailant with the shotgun was a male juvenile who was on probation for theft.

History of Previous Assault. Fifty-five primary victims (89%) reported that the current assailant had previously assaulted them. Fifty (91%) of these victims reported that they had previously had a police visit for assault by the same assailant, 40 (73%) within the previous month. When questioned about the average frequency of assault in the past month, 19 (35%) of victims with a history of previous assault reported daily beatings, 30 (55%) reported that they were assaulted at least once per week, and six (11%) reported that the frequency of assault averaged less than once per week. Of the women who were assaulted by a male sexual partner, 20 (44%) reported a previous assault by that man during pregnancy.

Victims' Previous Use of Medical Facilities and Shelters. Of the 55 victims who reported previous assault by their current assailant, 43 (78%) reported that they had never sought medical treatment, counseling or shelter because of domestic assault. Of the remainder, seven (13%) reported that they had sought medical treatment related to domestic assault and five (9%) had sought counseling. Three victims reported that they had sought shelter in the past, and all of them reported that they were told shelter was not available when they called for admission.

Use of Antipsychotic Medications. As an indicator of chronic mental illness, the surveyors asked about the use of preparations of haloperidol or fluphenazine (antipsychotic medications) under the supervision of a psychiatrist or community mental health center. At the time of the assault, six assailants (10%) and one victim were being prescribed these medications. Five of these assailants were interviewed at the scene, and they all reported noncompliance with their medication regimen.

Previous Arrests for Violence. Fifty-two (91%) of the 57 assailants for whom police records were obtained had prior records of arrests or convictions on charges that were not specifically related to drugs or alcohol. Twenty-eight (49%) had arrests or convictions for violent crimes. Most of these assailants had been charged with assault or aggravated assault. Two assailants had previous arrests or convictions for murder and two for kidnapping. Twenty-six assailants (41%) had been in jail within the previous month. Forty-three assailants (67%) were on parole or probation at the time of the assault. Of the 69 victims for whom a complete arrest record was obtained, 43 (63%) had no history of arrests or convictions. Six victims (9%) had a history of prior arrest or conviction for violence-related charges including assault or aggravated assault, robbery of an individual and kidnapping.

Assailants' Alcohol and Drug Use. Thirty-six (86%) of the 42 assailants who were interviewed reported that they had used alcohol on the day of the assault. Six of these assailants (14%) also reported using cocaine, four reported using marijuana and one reported using narcotics. None of the assailants reported using a drug without alcohol. Victims and family members reported that 59 assailants (92%) used drugs or alcohol during the day of the assault. Table 2 shows that victims and family members reported that 43 (67%) of the assailants had used cocaine; in all of these cases, cocaine was used in combination with alcohol.

Eleven (17%) of the assailants were reported to have used alcohol without other drugs. The use of drugs or alcohol to the point of intoxication on a daily basis for the past month was reported for 29 assailants (45%) by victims or family members. Eight assailants (12%) were reported to be drug addicts, 12 (19%) were alcoholic and nine (14%) were classified as both.

Victims' Alcohol and Drug Use. Thirty-one (42%) of the victims reported themselves or were reported by family members to have used alcohol or drugs on the day of the assault. Use of cocaine was reported for 11 (15%) of the victims (see Table 2). Six of the victims self-reported the use of cocaine and five said that their assailant had gotten them to use it. One of the victims was reported to be a drug addict, seven (13%) were considered to be alcoholics and one was reported to be both a drug addict and an alcoholic.

Previous Arrests or Convictions Related to Alcohol or Drug Use. As an index of past substance abuse, victims' and assailants' arrest records were searched for charges related to alcohol ("driving under the influence of alcohol," "public intoxication," and "drunk and disorderly") or drug use ("possession of a controlled substance"). A complete record was obtained on 57 assailants and 68 victims. Forty-six (79%) of these assailants and 23 (34%) of the victims had a record of arrest or conviction on an alcohol- or drug-related charge.

Previous Rehabilitative Treatment. Of the 38 subjects whose families reported they were alcoholics or drug addicts, 14 (29%) had undergone treatment for drug or alcohol abuse. One assailant was actively involved in a drug rehabilitation program at the time of the assault. He was a ninth grader who had been released from court-ordered inpatient treatment one month before the assault and reported compliance with daily outpatient therapy. He admitted to using cocaine and marijuana in the past but reported that he had not used any drugs since starting treatment. This was corroborated by the victim and other family members at the scene. This assailant voluntarily submitted to a urine test, which was positive for cocaine and marijuana. This assailant was not subject to drug testing as part of his current treatment program.

Table 2. Reports of Alcohol and Drug Use on the Day of the Assault (self-reports combined with reports of family members)

	Victim		Assailants	
No alcohol or drugs used	41	(57%)	4	(6%)
Alcohol only	10	(14%)	11	(17%)
Cocaine only	0		0	
Marijuana only	5	(7%)	0	
Cocaine and alcohol	6	(8%)	30	(47%)
Cocaine and marijuana	0		0	
Marijuana and alcohol	4	(6%)	5	(8%)
Cocaine, alcohol and marijuana	5	(7%)	13	(20%)
Other (LSD, opiates)	1	(1%)	1	(2%)

Toxicological Testing. Fifty-nine subjects who denied using cocaine were asked to voluntarily submit a urine sample for drug testing and 26 (43%) complied. Nine subjects who submitted to drug testing were assailants and 17 were victims. Drug testing was not offered if the subject was seriously injured or when the subject's hostility, general lack of cooperation or threat of escape would not allow the team to safely obtain an unwitnessed urine specimen according to the protocol.

Six (67%) of the nine assailants and three (17%) of the 17 victims tested positive for cocaine. Table 3 shows that there was a discordance between the subject's initial self-report or the family's report of drug use, and the test results. None of the six assailants who tested positive for cocaine reported cocaine use, though five of them did report alcohol use. For 11 (73%) of the 15 subjects who tested positive for drugs that they had denied using, both the subject and family members initially reported that there had been no drug use.

Table 3. Subjects' and Families' Report of Alcohol and Drug Use in Subjects with a Positive Toxicology Screen

Case #	Subject's Report	Family's Report	Test Result
Assailants			
23	none	none	cocaine, marijuana
51	beer, no drugs	beer, ?drugs	cocaine
56	alcohol, no drugs	alcohol, no drugs	cocaine
58	beer	alcohol, cocaine	cocaine
60	beer, marijuana	beer, marijuana	cocaine, marijuana
61	alcohol, no drugs	cocaine	cocaine
Victims			
1	one can of beer	beer	cocaine, marijuana
2	none	none	marijuana
4	none	one drink	marijuana
24	beer, marijuana	beer, marijuana	cocaine, marijuana
52	whiskey	no report	marijuana
54	none	no report	marijuana
55	none	no report	marijuana
56	none	alcohol	opiates, marijuana
60	alcohol	alcohol	cocaine

Eight of the nine subjects who were positive for cocaine admitted to using the drug when informed of their test results. One was a 40-year-old mother of three who had assaulted her husband because he had verbally abused her. All of the family members present, including the assailant and her husband, denied that she had used any drugs. In the initial interview, she denied any drug use but provided a urine sample, which tested positive at the scene for cocaine. When informed of her test results, the woman reported that she had begun smoking cocaine six months before the assault because of her increasing frustration with her husband's abuse. In the past two months she had been smoking cocaine on a daily basis, unknown to her family.

Direct Involvement of Children in Domestic Assault.
Eleven victims (15%) and four assailants (6%) were under age
18. Nine of these victims were children who were assaulted or
threatened after witnessing their mothers being beaten. All victims under age 18 were left in the household, one with the assailant remaining in the house. None of these victims was referred
to child protective services at the scene. Of the assailants under
age 18, three were transported to a mental health facility (two of
them while under arrest) and one was left at home.

Children Who Witnessed a Physical Assault. In 53 cases (85%),
children between the ages of two and 17 directly witnessed a physical assault. A total of 90 children who had seen assaults were identified; 43 (48%) were aged two to six, 32 (36%) were seven to 12
years old, and 15 (17%) were 12 to 17 years old. Seven (11%) of the
911 calls for police help were made by children, including two calls
made by seven-year-old children and one made by a six-year-old.
In many cases, the survey team and police saw small children emulating violent behavior. For example, when surveyors alerted one
of the victims that her three-year-old son was punching and stran-
gling the family cat, the victim replied that the child "always does
things like that when he sees the way his daddy beats me."

Signs of the "Stockholm Syndrome." The "Stockholm syndrome" has been defined as a situation in which a batterer uses
exaggerated forms of coercion and manipulation in addition to
threats and physical abuse to keep the victim dependent on the
batterer (Jones 1994). This may be a feature of relationships that
involve repeated domestic assault in which there is a high risk
for injury or death (Jones 1994). In 17 cases (27%) in which the
victim was a female sexual partner of a male assailant, the victim
fit at least four of the eight Stockholm syndrome characteristics.
Features of the Stockholm syndrome include the following:
- **Isolation:** The batterer deprives the victim of social supports, and separates the victim from friends or family.
- **Monopolization:** The batterer stops the victim's displays
  of attention to children, family and pets, and blocks initiatives of other family members or friends.

- **Induced Debility:** The batterer won't allow the victim to seek medical care, awakens the victim from sleep to start fights, and won't let the victim sleep.
- **Threats:** The batterer threatens to kill or harm the victim's children, pets or family members.
- **Indulgences:** After episodes of abuse, the batterer gives the victim gifts.
- **Omnipotence:** The abuser follows the victim when she leaves the house, accuses her of having relationships with men with whom she comes in contact, and may beat the victim for denying his accusations.
- **Degradation:** The batterer engages in inappropriate sexual touching in public, public insults, and makes the cost of resistance more damaging to the victim's self-esteem than capitulation.
- **Triviality:** The batterer obsesses over minute details, e.g., in cooking, cleaning.

All of these women had been previously assaulted by their current assailant, with beatings reported daily by seven and at least weekly by the other 10 victims. All of these couples had been the subjects of previous police visits. Thirteen of the women (76%) reported having been beaten by their current assailant during pregnancy. In 16 of the 17 cases, the victims reported that their boyfriends or husbands prevented them from associating with family or friends. Nine reported that their assailant did not allow them to hold a job outside the home. All of the women reported that the assailant had made explicit threats of violence against their children or family members. They all also reported that their assailant had been verbally abusive to or degrading of them in public (e.g., inappropriate sexual touching or exposure). Thirteen of these women (76%) reported that, on previous occasions, they had sustained injuries during a beating that warranted emergency medical care and that their batterer had specifically prevented them from seeking this care. When asked about the future of their relationship with their assailant, five of the victims reported that the relationship was in the process of being severed (e.g., divorce being sought) and the remainder (71%) reported that they planned to maintain the relationship.

Of the 17 assailants in cases that fit the Stockholm syndrome profile, six had previous arrests for domestic violence (one as recently as two weeks before) and eleven (65%) had previous arrests or convictions for other violent offenses. Eleven assailants (65%) had used cocaine on the day of the assault and 15 (88%) had used alcohol. Five were described by their victim as drug addicts and eight as alcoholics. In two cases, the assailant had made the 911 call. One assailant told his victim that he was "going to beat her at her own game" and initially reported that he was the victim. In the other case, the assailant husband called the police after his wife had placed a call for help to show her that "nobody was going to come." When the police arrived, the victim initially denied that she had been assaulted and reported that her husband had left. The police found the husband hiding in another room, pistol in hand.

Disposition of Victims. Fifty-five victims (78%) remained at home after the police left, seven went to the hospital and nine went to the homes of relatives or friends. Police offered all victims transportation to a shelter; all refused. One additional subject who was classified as a victim by the survey team was arrested for assault. This woman was punched by her husband while she slept with her child. She awoke and scratched or stabbed her husband, drawing a considerable amount of blood. Both were intoxicated with alcohol, and the husband had previous arrests for assault on his wife. Police officers at the scene reported that they did not want to arrest both participants because there was a two-year-old child in the house and no other family members available to care for him, and that the husband bore more signs of assault.

All victims reported that police gave them instructions on how to obtain protective orders and how to make contact with a shelter for battering victims. When the assailant was arrested at the scene, police informed victims that the assailant could be released within 12 hours.

Disposition of the Assailants. Of the 42 assailants who were present when police arrived, 28 (67%) were arrested at the scene, 24 for domestic assault and four for other charges (stalking, public intoxication, disorderly conduct, and driving while intoxicated). Four of the arrested assailants were transported directly to a mental health facility, and two to hospitals for treatment of stab wounds. Eight of the unarrested assailants remained in the home and five were ordered to leave the premises. Police transported one assailant to a mental health facility. He was a juvenile male with a history of violent assault against family members, and had threatened his family with a loaded shotgun and a knife, but did not have a prior arrest for violent crime.

The police officers estimated that, in the year before the new domestic violence law was passed, arrests were made in 5 to 25 percent of calls for domestic assault where the assailant was at the scene. Before the current law went into effect in July 1995, police did not make reports in domestic violence cases that did not involve an arrest, so the true proportion of calls that resulted in arrest could not be determined.

Arrests and Court Action After the Survey Visit. The survey team reviewed court records of the 24 subjects who were arrested at the scene for domestic assault eight weeks after the arrest. Eight assailants entered guilty pleas, two had the charges dismissed and 14 were released and awaiting disposition of charges (half of them with no bond). Eighteen of the arrested assailants spent less than 18 hours in jail. The remainder spent one to five days in jail because their arrests occurred on weekends or holidays.

All of the assailants who entered a guilty plea to domestic assault received suspended sentences of 30 to 90 days with a year's probation. Two of these assailants were ordered to perform three days of community service, and four were ordered to participate in an anger management program. One of the assailants who was ordered to undergo anger management was also ordered to undergo drug abuse treatment.

Eight weeks after the study's termination, the team reviewed warrant and arrest records for 20 of the 22 assailants who had fled the scene of the assault. Two records were not obtained, probably because victims or family members gave a false name. Five (23%) of the victims in these cases had sworn out warrants for assault. At the time the records were reviewed, three of these assailants had been arrested: one for the assault investigated in the study (by the time of the review he already had an active warrant for a subsequent assault against the same victim, which he carried out after he had been released on his own recognizance), one for a subsequent domestic assault on the initial victim, and one for a subsequent murder that did not involve the initial victim. Four additional assailants had active warrants issued for assaults that occurred after the study. Thirteen had no active warrants.

Discussion of Program Results

By accompanying the police on emergency calls, health caregivers made detailed assessments of families affected by domestic violence. Their experience suggests that linking medical care to emergency police services can be a useful approach to initiating care for families affected by domestic violence. Most of the families had suffered repeated episodes of assault. In nearly every case, the survey team was able to delineate risk factors for future assault that could be ameliorated by treatment. They also identified young children who were apparently traumatized due to witnessing the assault, and in need of help. The study was limited to families whose involvement with domestic violence was signaled by an emergency call to the police. For most of these families, a call to the police was the only call for help that they would ever make.

While calls to the police yielded immediate results, these results were rarely lasting. Even when arrests were made, they only separated the victims from their assailants for several hours or days. In contrast to their frequent use of police services, very few of the victims (less than one out of four) ever sought care for problems related to domestic violence from medical facilities, counselors or shelters, despite the fact that many had suffered injuries and most had experienced frequent assaults. This was not due to a lack of service availability. In Memphis, counseling, health care and shelter services are available to all victims of domestic violence around the clock. If a victim is in need of shelter and the shelters are full, the Abused Women's Service of the Memphis YWCA will arrange emergency housing and counseling without charge.

The deficiency in the care of families affected by domestic violence was not a lack of caring resources, but rather the lack of an organized approach to initiating and delivering care. To be effective, any approach to delivering care to domestic violence victims and their families must overcome the social and psychological barriers that stand between them and the help that they need. Interviewing the participants in a family context at home brought many of these barriers to light, more so than in a specialized victim-oriented medical setting, which is where most of the medical research on battered women is carried out (McCauley et al. 1995). One well-known barrier to care is the prospect that seeking help will escalate the abuse (Hyman, Schillinger, and Lo 1995). Another barrier is the strong bond that many of the victims maintain with their batterers, and their reluctance to expose their batterer to punishment.

Many victims asked that the police remove or frighten their assailants without arresting them. Many victims changed their story and even denied being beaten (despite obvious physical signs) once they became aware that their assailant was going to jail. In many cases, the victims cited their economic dependence on their assailant as the reason that they didn't want him arrested. In some cases, there were signs of a psychological state among victims characterized by progressive loss of social relationships and exaggerated dependence on their batterers for social and emotional support (Jones 1994). Some victims reported that their assailants had forced them into criminal activities or drug abuse as leverage against them should they try to find outside employment or leave the relationship. This behavior has been reported in previous studies of domestic violence (Statman

1995). The pathological bonds that exist between some victims and their batterers will have to be considered if interventions into domestic violence are to be effective. For some victims, a crisis due to domestic violence may have to be regarded as a psychiatric emergency warranting compelled care (Alpert 1995).

Bringing the caregiver approach to scenes of domestic violence expanded police ability to assess families for risk factors for future abuse. The team focused specifically on assailants' drug abuse. Surveys of battering victims in medical settings often will not reveal assailants' drug abuse (McCauley et al. 1995). This study found evidence that two-thirds of the abusers had used cocaine and alcohol on the day of the assault, and that many were using alcohol or cocaine habitually.

The relationship between alcohol and family violence is well established, but there is little research into combined alcohol and cocaine abuse and its relationship to domestic violence (Miller 1990; Roberts 1988). Cocaine use can cause paranoia, irritability and depression—emotional states that are often the antecedents of violence (Fagan 1993; Honer, Gewirtz, and Turey 1987). Most people who use cocaine use it in conjunction with alcohol (Grant and Harford 1990). This may lead to the formation of cocaethylene, an active metabolite of the two drugs that is more intoxicating and has a longer half-life than cocaine (Randle 1992). The effects of this mixture may kindle violent behavior (Hearn, Flynn, and Hime 1991).

The presence of drugs in violent events does not imply that these substances caused the violence. Nonetheless, drug abuse is a common characteristic of men who batter (Fitch and Papantonio 1983; Kelleher et al. 1994). Several studies have shown that one of the most important variables for discriminating between battered and nonbattered wives is their husbands' drug use (McCauley et al. 1995; Kantor and Straus 1989; Rath, Jarrat, and Leonardson 1989). There have been calls to evaluate domestic assailants for substance abuse and initiate immediate treatment to prevent drug abuse and family violence from becoming linked as legacies that are passed on to future generations

(Kelleher et al. 1994; Gorney 1989). While many associate violence with the buying and selling of drugs, most of the violence due to cocaine occurs in the home and is carried out by drug consumers rather than drug traffickers (Fagan 1993; Tardiff et al. 1994). In Memphis, for example, a marked increase in the use of cocaine in 1986 was accompanied by a marked increase in domestic homicides (Harruff et al. 1988).

The association between drugs and family violence highlights the need to establish strategies to identify high-risk chemically dependent batterers (Roberts 1988). While interviewing family members revealed drug use in many cases, toxicologic testing added to the ability to detect drug users. This bears out previous observations on the utility of screening for drug use in selected medical (McNagny and Parker 1992; Brookoff, Campbell, and Shaw 1993), law enforcement (Brookoff et al. 1994; Feucht, Stephens, and Walker 1994; National Institute of Justice 1994) and workplace settings (Wish, Hoffman, and Nemes 1996). Other investigators have already suggested that police handling of domestic violence cases will be improved through training to note whether alcohol or drugs are present (Slade, Daniel, and Heisler 1991), and that specimens for toxicologic testing ought to be collected from all suspected domestic assailants (Slade, Daniel, and Heisler 1991; Roberts 1988). The U.S. Supreme Court has ruled that blood sampling for drug testing in a criminal case, obtained without consent, does not represent an invasion of privacy and that the test results can be used as evidence at trial (U.S. Reporters 1996).

Assessing family violence in the home highlights the fact that there are children who witness assault and are in need of care. Children who witness family violence far outnumber the direct victims of domestic assault (Wolfe and Korsch 1994). Exposure to family violence has observable detrimental effects on children. Children's reactions to violence are most pronounced during the immediate aftermath of the incident (Wolfe and Korsch 1994). These reactions contribute to long-term developmental and psychological problems that turn domestic violence into a legacy (Fitch and Papantonio 1983; Cappell and Heiner 1990). Without timely identification and intervention, children who witness repeated episodes of family violence can come to see such behavior as usual or acceptable (Wolfe and Korsch 1994). As the team observed, male children often exhibit aggressive behavior when they witness violence against their mothers (Wolfe et al. 1985), and many girls will begin to model the victim's role (Sternberg, Lamb, and Greenbaum 1993). Children who witness family violence feel unsafe and cannot commit to higher goals such as social development and academic achievement (Wolfe and Korsch 1994). There is a lack of support services for children who witness violence because, technically, they have not been abused (Wolfe and Korsch 1994). After participating in this study, law enforcement officials in Memphis have initiated efforts to expand the definition of child abuse to include children who are exposed to assault on their mothers.

This was an uncontrolled study; the group studied may not be representative of all people who are involved in domestic assault in Memphis. An important limitation of this study is that it did not examine many of the factors that are known to contribute to domestic violence, such as socioeconomic status (Centerwall 1995). One conclusion that we do draw from this study is that to adequately care for some families in crisis due to domestic violence, the delivery of medical and counseling services must be integrally linked to the delivery of emergency (i.e., police) services. In a domestic violence crisis, health caregivers have to participate actively, in a role that can be likened to that played when faced with a suicidal patient or a patient with a cardiac crisis (Flitcraft 1995; Alpert 1995). To participate capably, both the police and health caregivers may have to adopt a family-focused perspective (Dubowitz and King 1995), which, like domestic violence itself, begins in the home.

At PERF's 1998 Problem-Oriented Policing conference, the team showed videotapes of some cases they participated in. The following is an excerpt from an article based on one of the videotapes and written by one of the doctors who participated in this project:

The Faces of the Children

"Send a policeman fast! Daddy's got a big knife and he's gonna cut Mommy's head off into the kitchen sink." The voice on the radio was the voice of a child. Approximately 10 percent of the 911 calls for help for domestic violence in our city are made by children, some of them as young as six.

The dispatcher tried to ask the boy more questions but he started crying so hard that he couldn't give her any answers. By the time the police arrived 10 minutes later, Daddy was gone. He must have heard the sirens. Mommy was pretty shook up but she wasn't too badly hurt. The police found her sitting at the kitchen table with her 14-year-old daughter. They weren't touching and they weren't talking. They just sat there looking shocked. The 11-year-old boy was found crying in a corner of the back bedroom. He had a large welt on the side of his face where his father had hit him when he had tried to intervene in the beating of his mother.

I got to spend an hour in the kitchen with the mother and her two children that night. I was part of a group of primary care physicians trying to gain a better understanding of domestic violence by participating in a project sponsored by my hospital and the Memphis Police Department. The police were bringing us, with our interns and residents, on emergency calls for domestic violence. An intern and I interviewed the mother and her children at the kitchen table. The police videotaped the interview. The mother did almost all the talking while the children stood silently at her side.

By the time I got there, 20 minutes after the first patrol car, the mother's composure was coming back and so was her sense of denial.

"What happened here tonight?"

"Oh, it was the same old thing. He just slapped me a few times. He threatened to kill me."

The daughter put her hand on her mother's shoulder. "Tell them about the knife," she said.

"Oh yeah, he had this big hunting knife and grabbed me by the hair and pushed my head over the sink. And he started putting that knife on my neck and rubbing it there and saying, 'I'll kill you, I'll kill you.' But he was laughing."

As she described the action she pulled her son to her and used him demonstrate where on her throat her husband had laid the hunting knife. The boy didn't say anything.

"Did the children see this?"

"Yes they saw it. But this one got scared and ran off into the back." She pointed to her son.

"Was your husband drinking tonight?"

"Yes he was."

"Does he have an alcohol problem?"

"Yes, he's got an alcohol problem."

"Was he taking any drugs tonight?"

"No, he didn't do any drugs tonight."

"Does he ever take any drugs?"

"Cocaine."

"How does he take cocaine—does he snort it, does he smoke it?"

"He smokes crack."

"How often would you say he smokes it—once a month, once a week, once a day?"

"He's smoking it every day."

"But he wasn't doing any tonight?"

"No, because he was in the house all day and he wouldn't smoke it in the house."

"So he wouldn't smoke crack in the house?"

"Yeah, he smokes it the house." She waved her hands at her children. "I can't hide it from them. Children are smart. They know. He was smoking crack tonight."

In a study of 70 families who called the police for emergency help for battering, we found that the use of alcohol and drugs by the assailant was very common. Two-thirds of the assailants were using a combination of cocaine and alcohol, just like the man in the incident above. There is an epidemic of dual addiction to cocaine and alcohol sweeping the country and it is going largely unnoticed. When used in combination, alcohol and cocaine can form a third active drug, cocaethylene, which is more intoxicating, longer lasting and more potent in its ability to kindle violent behavior than either alcohol or cocaine alone.

One of the rules of our project was that the doctors had to interview everyone at the scene of the crime and do so in a private and caring way. In two-thirds of the cases, that meant interviewing the assailants. Sometimes we had to do it in the back seat of a police car. Sometimes it was hard to be caring after seeing the pain and destruction of family violence. Many of the assailants told us about their drug abuse. Many had prior arrests relating to violent behavior and drug abuse but very few had received treatment.

While it is widely known that alcohol and drug use are related to family violence, there are very few interventions aimed at drug abuse among batterers. Law enforcement officials are aware that domestic assault is one of the most dangerous crimes and that assaults carried out under the influence of drugs and alcohol are much more likely to result in severe injury and death. In Memphis, the police now investigate drug use by domestic assailants and bring it to the attention of prosecutors and judges. This has resulted in stiffer sentences and higher rates of compelled treatment. It used to be the dogma that a drug abuser had to have the insight to seek treatment on his own if he was to have any chance of success. Recent studies have proven this wrong and have shown that drug abusers who are forced into treatment have success rates that are comparable to those who enter the same programs voluntarily.

Our study also pointed out that there are victims of drug abuse that go uncounted. There are the women who get battered. There are children who are exposed to the beating of their mothers and are often direct victims of the violence themselves. Seeing the children turned out to be the hardest part of the project for me. Children were direct witnesses to the battering of their mothers in more than half the families we visited. Much of the time we would find them cowering under beds or in corners, or emulating violent behavior in front of the doctors and the police. I remember one case where we were leaving a home and found a three-year-old boy who had just seen his mother badly beaten. The boy was sitting in the corner and holding the family's kitten by the throat and punching it.

One of the police officers called out to the mother, "Your boy is about to kill your cat."

"Oh don't worry about that," she called back. "He always does things like that when he sees the way his daddy beats me."

After completing the project, a group of police officers and physicians approached our state legislators and asked them to make beating a woman in front of her children a felony, raising it from simple assault (which carries penalties like those imposed on reckless drivers) to aggravated assault. This would have mandated criminal investigations and exposed these batterers to the risk of state prison. Similar laws have been passed in other states, such as Florida. Our legislators brought this idea to a state senate committee, where it was rejected as being "too expensive." One senator asked us if we were trying put a third of the male population of Tennessee in state prison.

Drug abuse plays a major role in many cases of family violence. Many people sincerely think that most drug-related violence arises from the commerce in drugs. This has given rise to calls for drug legalization as a means of reducing violence. I am convinced that most of the violence due to drug abuse is related to the consumption of drugs. The victims include people who don't use drugs. Thousands of battered women and despairing children have to be counted among the victims of drug violence.

In a joint report prepared by police officers and physicians, we called for

- testing assailants for drugs and alcohol,
- detoxifying arrested assailants prior to release from jail (of those who had been arrested, the majority were released within eight hours),

- making assault under the influence of drugs a felony because it carries a higher risk of severe injury or death, and
- compelling drug treatment and periodic monitoring for drugs for people convicted of assault under the influence of drugs.

AUTHORS' NOTE:

An article describing the domestic violence project appeared in the *Journal of the American Medical Association* in 1997 (277:1369–1373). A portion of this article ("Faces of the Children") is reprinted here with permission. A videotape titled *Drug Use and Domestic Violence* (which includes part of the interview described above) was produced by the U.S. Department of Justice and is available from the National Criminal Justice Reference Service by calling 800-851-3420 or 301-251-5500 and ordering tape NCJ 163056.

REFERENCES

Alpert, E.J. 1995. Violence in Intimate Relationships and the Practicing Internist: New "Disease" or New Agenda? *Annals of Internal Medicine* 123:774–781.

Appleton, W. 1980. The Battered Woman Syndrome. *Annals of Emergency Medicine* 9:84– 91.

Brookoff, D. 1996. *Drug Use and Domestic Violence.* NIJ Research in Progress video. Washington, D.C.: National Institute of Justice.

Brookoff, D., E.A. Campbell, and L.M. Shaw. 1993. The Underreporting of Cocaine-Related Trauma: Drug Abuse Warning Network Reports vs. Hospital Toxicology Tests. *American Journal of Public Health* 83:369–371.

Brookoff, D., C.S. Cook, C. Williams, and C.S. Mann. 1994. Testing Reckless Drivers for Cocaine and Marijuana. *New England Journal of Medicine* 331:518–522.

Brookoff, D., K.K. O'Brien, C.S. Cook, T.D. Thompson and C. Williams. 1997. Characteristics of Participants in Domestic Violence: Assessment at the Scene of Domestic Assault. *Journal of the American Medical Association* 277: 1369–1373.

Cappell, C., and R.N. Heiner. 1990. The Intergenerational Transmission of Family Aggression. *Journal of Family Violence* 52:135–152.

Centerwall, B.S. 1995. Race, Socioeconomic Status and Domestic Homicide. *Journal of the American Medical Association* 273:1755–1758.

Davidson, L.L. 1996. Preventing Injuries from Violence Towards Women. *American Journal of Public Health* 86:12–14.

Downing, S. 1996. New Law Cited as Domestic Violence Deaths Plummet. *The Memphis Commercial Appeal.* 19 January.

Dubowitz, H., and H. King. 1995. Family Violence: A Child-Centered, Family-Focused Approach. *Pediatric Clinics of North America* 42:153–163.

Fagan, J. 1993. Interactions Among Drugs, Alcohol and Violence. *Health Affairs* 4:65–79.

Feucht, T.E., R.C. Stephens, and M.L. Walker. 1994. Drug Use Among Juvenile Arrestees: A Comparison of Self Report, Urinalysis and Hair Assay. *Journal of Drug Issues* 24:99–116.

Fitch, F.J., and A. Papantonio. 1983. Men who Batter: Some Pertinent Characteristics. *Journal of Nervous and Mental Disease* 171:190–192.

Flitcraft, A.H. 1992. Violence, Values and Gender. *Journal of the American Medical Association* 267:3194–3195.

Flitcraft, A.H. 1995. From Public Health to Personal Health: Violence Against Women Across the Life Span. *Annals of Internal Medicine* 123:800–801.

Friedman, L.S., J.H. Samet, M.S. Roberts, M. Hudlin, and P. Hans. 1992. Inquiry About Victimization Experiences. A Survey of Patient Preferences and Physician Practices. *Archives of Internal Medicine* 152:1186–1190.

Gorney, B. 1989. Domestic Violence and Chemical Dependency: Dual Problems, Dual Interventions. *Journal of Psychoactive Drugs* 21:229–238.

Grant, B.F., and T.C. Harford. 1990. Concurrent and Simultaneous Use of Alcohol with Cocaine: Results of a National Survey. *Drug and Alcohol Dependence* 25:97–104.

Harruff, R.C., J.T. Francisco, S.K. Elkins, A.M. Phillips, and G.S. Fernandez. 1988. Cocaine and Homicide in Memphis and Shelby County: An Epidemic of Violence. *Journal of Forensic Sciences* 33:1231–1237.

Hart, B.J. 1993. Battered Women and the Criminal Justice System. *American Behavioral Scientist* 36:624–638.

Hearn, W.L., D.D. Flynn, and G.W. Hime. 1991. Cocaethylene: Unique Cocaine Metabolite Displays High Affinity for the Dopamine Transporter. *Journal of Neurochemistry* 56:698–701.

Honer, W., G. Gewirtz, and M. Turey. 1987. Pyschosis and Violence in Cocaine Smokers. *Lancet* 8556:451.

Hyman, A., D. Schillinger, and B. Lo. 1995. Laws Mandating Reporting of Domestic Violence. Do They Promote Patient Well-being? *Journal of the American Medical Association* 273:1781–1787.

Isaac, N.E., and R.L. Sanchez. 1994. Emergency Department Response to Battered Women in Massachusetts. *Annals of Emergency Medicine* 23:855–858.

Jones, A. 1994. *Next Time She'll be Dead: Battering and How to Stop It.* Boston: Beacon.

Kantor, G.K., and M.A Straus. 1989. Substance Abuse as a Precipitant of Wife Abuse Victimizations. *American Journal of Drug and Alcohol Abuse* 15:173–189.

Kates, N., S. Webb, and P. LePage. 1991. Therapy Begins at Home: The Psychiatric House Call. *Canadian Journal of Psychiatry* 36:673–676.

Keenan, J.M., P.E. Boling, J.G. Schwartzenberg, L. Olson, M.. Schneiderman, D.J. McCaffrey, and C.M. Ripsin. 1992. A National Survey of the Home Visiting Practice and Attitudes of Family Physicians and Internists. *Archives of Internal Medicine* 152:2025–2032.

Kelleher, K., M. Chaffin, J. Hollenberg, and E. Fischer. 1994. Alcohol and Drug Disorders Among Physically Abusive and Neglectful Parents in a Community-Based Sample. *American Journal of Public Health* 84:1586–1590.

Marwick, C. 1994. Health and Justice Professionals Set Goals to Lessen Domestic Violence. *Journal of the American Medical Association* 271:1147–1148.

McCauley, J., D.E. Kern, K. Kolodner, L. Dill, A.F. Schroeder, H.K. DeChant, J. Ryden, E.B. Bass, and L.R. DeRogatis. 1995. The "Battering Syndrome": Prevalence and Clinical Characteristics of Domestic Violence in Primary Care Internal Medicine Practices. *Annals of Internal Medicine* 123:737–746.

McNagny, S.E., and R.M. Parker. 1992. High Prevalence of Recent Cocaine Use and the Unreliability of Patient Self-Report in an Inner-City Walk-In Clinic. *Journal of the American Medical Association* 267:1106–1108.

Miller, B. 1990. The Interrelationships Between Alcohol and Drugs and Family Violence. In *Drugs and Violence: Causes, Correlates and Consequences,* edited by M. De La Rosa, E. Lambert and B. Gropper. Washington, D.C.: U.S. Department of Justice.

National Institute of Justice. 1994. *Drug Use Forecasting: 1994 Annual Report on Adult and Juvenile Arrestees.* Washington, D.C.: U.S. Department of Justice.

Parson, L.H., D. Zaccaro, B. Wells, and T.G. Stovall. 1995. Methods of and Attitudes Toward Screening Obstetrics and Gynecology Patients for Domestic Violence. *American Journal of Obstetrics and Gynecology* 173:381–387.

Randal, T. 1990. Domestic Violence Intervention Calls for More than Just Treating Injuries. *Journal of the American Medical Association* 264:939–944.

Randle, T. 1992. Cocaine, Alcohol Mix in Body to Form Even Longer Lasting, More Lethal Drug. *Journal of the American Medical Association* 267:1043–1044.

Rath, G.D., L.G. Jarrat, and G. Leonardson. 1989. Rates of Domestic Violence Against Adult Women by Men Partners. *Journal of the American Board of Family Practitioners* 2:227–233.

Roberts, A.R. 1988. Substance Abuse Among Men Who Batter Their Wives. *Journal of Substance Abuse Treatment* 5:83–87.

Skolnick, A.A. 1995. Physician, Heal Thyself—Then Aid Abused Women. *Journal of the American Medical Association* 273:1744–1745.

Slade, M., L.J. Daniel, and C.J. Heisler. 1991. Application of Forensic Toxicology to the Problem of Domestic Violence. *Journal of Forensic Sciences* 36:708–713.

Statman, J.B. 1995. *The Battered Woman's Survival Guide.* Dallas: Taylor.

Sternberg, K.J., M.E. Lamb, and C. Greenbaum. 1993. Effects of Domestic Violence on Children's Behavior Problems and Depression. *Child Development* 29:44–52.

Sugg, N.K., and T. Inui. 1992. Primary Care Physicians' Response to Domestic Violence: Opening Pandora's Box. *Journal of the American Medical Association* 267:3157–3160.

Tardiff, K., P.M. Marzuk, A.C. Leon, C.S. Hirsch, M. Stajic, L. Portera, and N. Hartwell. 1994. Homicide in New York City: Cocaine Use and Firearms. *Journal of the American Medical Association* 272:43–46.

Tennessee Code Annotated Sec 36-3-618. 1995a.

Tennessee Code Annotated Sec 36-3-619. 1995b.

Tennessee Code Annotated Sec 36-3-601. 1995c.

U.S. Reporters 1996. *Schmerber vs. California*. 384:757–760.

Widom, C.S. 1989. The Cycle of Violence. *Science* 244:160–166.

Williams, C., and N. Hepler. 1995. *Tennessee Outcomes for Alcohol and Drug Services (TOADS)*. Nashville: Tennessee Department of Health, Bureau of Alcohol and Drug Abuse Services.

Wish, E.D., J.A. Hoffman, and S. Nemes. 1996. The Validity of Self-Reports of Drug Use at Treatment Admission and at Follow-Up: Comparison with Urinalysis and Hair Assays. In *The Validity of Self Reports: The Implications for Survey Research*, edited by L. Harrison. Rockville, Md.: U.S. Department of Health and Human Services.

Wolfe, D.A., P. Jaffe, S. Wilson, and L. Zak. 1985. Children of Battered Women: The Relation of Child Behavior to Family Violence and Maternal Stress. *Journal of Consulting and Clinical Psychology* 53:657–665.

Wolfe, D.A., and B. Korsch. 1994. Witnessing Domestic Violence During Childhood and Adolescence: Implication for Pediatric Practice. *Pediatrics* 94:594–599.

PART II

CRITICAL ISSUES

CHAPTER 6

INVESTIGATIONS IN THE
COMMUNITY POLICING CONTEXT[1]

Colleen A. Cosgrove and Mary Ann Wycoff[2]

As with many current issues in community policing, concerns about the investigative function and detectives are not new, not simply generated by the adoption of the community policing philosophy. Rather, they represent old issues brought back into focus by current rethinking about police service delivery.

Questions about the nature and structure of the investigative function constitute a central concern for administrators who are implementing community policing. The concerns are both substantive and political. Substantive questions address what the investigative function should encompass, who should perform it, and its relationship to citizens and other police personnel.

[1]This project was supported by grant #96-IJ-CX-0081 awarded to the Police Executive Research Forum (PERF) by the U.S. Department of Justice, National Institute of Justice. Points of view or opinions expressed in this document are those of the authors and do not necessarily represent the official position or policies of the U.S. Department of Justice or the Police Executive Research Forum.

[2]We wish to thank the following individuals who served as our advisory board and provided vital assistance in innumerable ways: George Kelling, professor, Rutgers University; Wesley Skogan, professor, Northwestern University; Timothy Oettmeier, assistant chief, Houston Police Department; Donald Quire, major (Ret.), St. Petersburg, Fla., Police Department; Craig Honeycutt, captain, Charlotte-Mecklenburg, N.C., Police Department; Roderick Beard, lieutenant, Portland, Ore., Police Bureau; and Alexandra Olson, detective, Madison, Wis., Police Department. We also thank Lois Felson Mock, our NIJ grant monitor, who played both supportive and substantive roles in the project's design and implementation.

Political questions pertain to redefining the roles for detectives and other personnel who may be involved in the investigative process. Detectives are commonly a highly organized workgroup—often perceived as conservative, insular and elitist—and consequently, administrators who attempt to change investigators' roles often encounter substantial resistance to change, no matter how minor or practical.

When agencies consider new models of police service, questions pertaining to the role and function of detectives or investigators always arise. Because there are no easy answers, managers of change are looking for guidance on how the investigative function should be performed in a community policing context, and how to manage the change in a way that will not cause organizational turmoil.

Mike Masterson (1995), previously a detective bureau manager, has written:

> While there has been a considerable amount of literature written on community policing, most of it has overlooked the important goal of getting everyone in an organization working together to create safer living environments and improved service to our citizens. For the most part, emphasis on the investigative functions and its contribution to those goals has been largely ignored. Has it been done deliberately to avoid the resistance of a deeply ingrained culture and the intolerance to change by vociferous, fiercely independent, and highly talented individuals?

Detective recalcitrance notwithstanding, there is a larger question of what the investigative function should be in a community policing context. Does the largely reactive role that detectives traditionally play represent the full nature of the investigative function? Or is a proactive approach, in which police anticipate crimes and work to prevent them or to intercept the criminals, more appropriate? Then there are coactive operations in which police, citizens and other agencies work together to prevent crime and control criminogenic conditions in the community. Is this a better model? It is evident that a primarily reactive investigative function supports only one element of community policing. What might the investigative function look like if it were designed to support the full range of community policing efforts?

The research reported here was designed to address these issues and fill an important gap in our knowledge about community policing implementation. This project considered three main questions:

1. How are community policing agencies in this country structuring the investigative function?
2. How are they integrating the investigative function with other police services?
3. How have they managed/are they managing the change process within this function?

Research Methods

This research was divided into two parts. The first portion consisted of a national mail survey of municipal police departments and sheriffs' offices in all jurisdictions with populations of more than 50,000 *and* 100 or more sworn officers.[3] These selection criteria were based on the assumption that agencies with these characteristics would be large enough to have an investigative unit consisting of more than a handful of staff. The survey collected descriptive information about both community policing and non-community policing departments, the organization of the inves-

---

[3]While it was easy to identify sheriffs' offices that met the initial selection criteria, PERF anticipated that several of these agencies had neither patrol nor investigative functions. Rather, in some jurisdictions, the responsibilities of the sheriff's office are limited to certain court functions, maintaining the jail and executing warrants. Unfortunately, we were not able to identify these agencies in advance. Therefore, in the survey packet

tigative function, and the ways in which the investigative organizational structure or function had been modified to accommodate a community policing approach. Based on the survey results, seven sites were selected for site visits. At the time of this writing, PERF staff have completed six site visits.[4] The site visits confirmed that departments have adopted innovative methods for integrating investigative and patrol operations. The visits also provided considerable insight into the organizational, administrative and logistical problems confronted by detectives. Substantial data were collected as part of this project, and this chapter presents highlights of the major findings from the national survey and the site visits.

Survey Findings

Surveys were sent to 483 municipal departments and 405 were completed, a response rate of 83.9 percent. Completed surveys were received from 197 sheriff's offices, a response rate of 64.6 percent.

Community policing implementation. Almost all (95.8%) of the responding municipal agencies reported that they have implemented community policing, compared with 80.7 percent of the sheriffs' offices.

---

sent to the sheriffs, we included a postcard asking the respondents to return the postcard if their agency does not have patrol and/or investigation functions. Questionnaires were sent to 355 sheriffs' offices, and 26 agencies returned postcards indicating that they were ineligible for the survey. Twenty-four other agencies were excluded as we obtained additional information. This reduced the sample population to 305 agencies, of which 197 (64.6%) completed the survey. Although this response rate is high, we would likely have obtained a higher rate if we had been able to identify eligible agencies with greater accuracy.

[4] The six sites that have been visited at this time are the municipal police departments in Boston, Mass.; San Diego, Calif.; Sacramento, Calif.; Mesa, Ariz.; and the sheriffs' offices of Spokane County, Wash., and Arapahoe County, Colo. The site visit for Arlington, Texas, has not been completed.

Table 1. Extent of Implementation of Community Policing (N=547)

	Municipal		Sheriffs		Total	
	N	%	N	%	N	%
Planning	4	1.0	4	2.5	8	1.5
Early Phase	29	7.5	30	18.9	59	10.8
One Quarter	47	12.1	23	14.5	70	12.8
Half Way	83	21.4	38	23.9	121	22.1
Three Quarters	75	19.3	16	10.0	91	16.6
Most Objectives Accomplished	128	33.0	38	23.9	166	30.4
Other	22	5.7	6	3.8	28	5.1
Missing	0	0.0	4	2.5	4	0.7
Total	388	100.0	159	100.0	547	100.0

Note: This table provides data only for departments that indicated that they had implemented community policing.

Table 2. Department Status Regarding Redefining Role of Detectives/Investigators (N=547)

	Municipal		Sheriffs		Total	
	N	%	N	%	N	%
(1) This matter has not yet been considered.	87	22.4	40	25.2	127	23.2
(2) We currently are considering this matter.	67	17.3	38	23.9	105	19.2
(3) We are in the process of actively planning the redefinition or restructuring.	27	7.0	10	6.3	37	6.8
(4) We have implemented some initial changes in the definition or structure of the function.	78	20.1	22	13.8	100	18.3
(5) We have implemented some major changes in the definition or structure of the function.	56	14.4	12	7.5	68	12.4
(6) We have considered this issue and concluded that the investigative function as currently defined and structured supports the organization's community policing goal.	69	17.8	30	18.9	99	18.1
Missing	4	1.0	7	4.4	11	2.0
Total	388	100.0	159	100.0	547	100.0

Extent of implementation. There was substantial variation in the extent to which survey agencies have implemented community policing, and the differences between the municipal agencies and sheriffs' offices were marked. In contrast to the municipal agencies, sheriffs' offices were not only somewhat less likely to have implemented community policing, but also, once engaged in the community policing process, were still in the planning or early implementation phases. Specifically, as Table 1 indicates, 8.5 percent of the municipal agencies indicated that they were in the beginning stages, compared with 21.4 percent of the sheriffs' offices. Conversely, 52.3 percent of the municipal agencies reported that they were "three-quarters of the way" or "most objectives have been accomplished," compared with 33.9 percent of the sheriff respondents.

Redefining the role of detectives/investigators. Table 2 illustrates that, for agencies that have implemented community policing, about one out of four municipal agencies and sheriffs' offices indicated that their organization had not considered redefining the role of detectives/investigators. Approximately 17 percent (17.3%) of the municipal agencies and 23.9 percent of sheriffs' offices reported that this matter was currently under consideration. A small proportion of the municipal agencies (7%) and sheriffs' offices (6.3%) stated that they were actively planning the redefinition and restructuring. Among municipal agencies, 20.1 percent reported that they had made some initial changes, while an additional 14.4 percent indicated that they had made some major changes. Thus, more than a third of these agencies (34.5%) had implemented changes. Among sheriffs' offices, 21.3 percent reported making either initial changes (13.8%) or major changes (7.5%).

It is interesting to note that comparable proportions of the municipal agencies and sheriffs' offices (17.8% and 18.9%, respectively) agreed with the statement, "We have considered this issue and concluded that the investigative function as currently defined and structured supports the organization's community policing goals." Many of these departments already had in place

---

Figure 1. Structural Models for Seven Selected Sites

Physical centralization of detectives who have citywide responsibilities:
- No site selected.

Physical centralization of detectives; assignment to specific geographic areas:
- Arapahoe County, Colo., Sheriff's Office

Physical decentralization of detectives who report through an investigative chain of command:
- Mesa, Ariz., Police Department
- Sacramento, Calif., Police Department
- Spokane County, Wash., Sheriff's Office

Physical decentralization of detectives who report through area command:
- Arlington, Texas, Police Department
- Boston, Mass., Police Department
- San Diego, Calif., Police Department

---

the types of arrangements that other departments reported having made to support community policing.

Model Development and Site Selection

Sixty-eight (12.4%) of the departments reported having implemented community policing *and* instituting some major changes in the definition or structure of the investigative function. To aid site selection, this grouping of 68 departments was reduced to 41 by restricting eligibility to agencies with at least 30 investigators, and that had implemented major changes at least two years prior to the survey. The two-year time frame was necessary to ensure that the agencies had sufficient experience with changes in the investigative function to understand the process' strengths, weaknesses and results.

Data for these agencies were then used to identify "models" or clusters of changes and to bring implementation issues associated with these changes to the surface. Four models were empirically derived from the data, and Figure 1 briefly describes each model and the corresponding sites that were selected for visits. It must be emphasized that these models are not necessarily mutually exclusive. Additionally, the structure of the entire investigative unit/bureau may not conform to the model. In many jurisdictions, particularly those with large investigative units, various combinations of centralization/decentralization, geographic assignment and chain of command may be used. These types of organizational structures are "mixed models." For example, the Mesa, Ariz. Police Department divides investigators into four divisions, only one of which has physically decentralized detectives. The other detectives are physically centralized and many are responsible for specific geographic areas.

Procedural Changes or Developments

The site visits revealed that several agencies had not only made structural changes, but had also modified procedures, performing investigations differently. These changes or modifications were grouped into seven categories: (1) area responsibility, (2) generalization, (3) teamwork, (4) case prioritization/self-assignment of cases, (5) citizen volunteer involvement in investigations, (6) interagency linkages, and (7) technology. The following section highlights examples of these changes, without including all of the sites that may use these procedures.

     Area Responsibility/Geographic Assignment. Whether working in a centralized or decentralized setting, *some* detectives in an agency may have investigative responsibility for specific geographic areas. Twenty-three percent of respondents in community policing departments agreed with the statement, "Most investigators are *physically centralized,* but they may work *specific geographic areas.*" Fifteen percent agreed with the statement, "Certain investigative functions are *physically decentralized* and investigators are assigned *specific geographic areas.*" Geographic assignment was used in every site visited. In most cases, investigators with area responsibility are property detectives. Nevertheless, in some sites, assaults and street robberies may be assigned to area investigators, and in some sites, street drug units have area responsibility.

Generalization. Some detectives, often those with geographic assignments, may be crime generalists who investigate all types of crimes that occur in their area of responsibility. Nearly half of all respondents (47.5%) agreed with the statement, "A core of investigators is *physically centralized*, and is responsible for *specific types of crime* of a *citywide nature*." Twenty-three percent of respondents agreed with the statement, "Certain investigative functions are *physically decentralized*, and investigators are assigned *specific geographic areas* and *specific types of crimes*." Proponents of generalization contend that criminals tend not to specialize in specific crime types and therefore detectives should not. The Arapahoe County Sheriff's Office in Colorado was the only site visited in which most investigators have area responsibility *and* all detectives are generalists. This agency has invested substantial time and financial resources in investigator training. The investigative personnel interviewed by PERF staff report that the emphasis on generalization coupled with geographic assignments has been very successful. For example, Arapahoe County detectives believed that fewer criminals are "slipping through the cracks" now that detectives are focusing on area crime patterns rather than crime types.

Teamwork (Officers, Citizens and Agencies). In several agencies, detectives work in either formal or informal teams with officers, citizens or other agencies. In Boston, San Diego and Arapahoe County, for example, the teams are formal. Officers and detectives on the "team" may or may not have the same supervisor (i.e., participants may report through different chains of command), but members know who "their" patrol officer or "their" detective is. In Spokane County, Wash., informal groups of detectives and citizen volunteers have become teams because they work in the same small neighborhood office.

Case Prioritization and Self-assignment of Cases. The Spokane County Sheriff's Office was the only site visited where detectives are changing their system for prioritizing cases. Property detectives are assigned to neighborhood storefront offices staffed and managed by neighborhood citizen volunteers. The detectives' goal is to become community-oriented and problem-oriented rather than case-driven. Rather than prioritizing cases based solely on solvability factors, they are attempting to identify neighborhood problems and to give priority to cases related to the underlying problems and community concerns. These detectives read all property crime incident reports for their area and self-assign their own cases. In this way, the detectives develop a more in-depth understanding of crime patterns and trends than if the sergeant screened and assigned cases. Additionally, in some instances, citizen associates in the storefronts also read the cases and provide second opinions about the problem-relevance of particular complaints.

In this jurisdiction, centralized homicide, sex crime and drug/gang detectives also self-assign cases. Self-assignment allows for a problem orientation that is difficult to achieve when cases are assigned according to solvability factors alone, or by a supervisor who may not be familiar with a neighborhood's particular problems and crime patterns. It must be noted that when the self-assignment system began, property crime detectives tended to take on too many cases and become overloaded—a tendency common to officers assigned to neighborhood stations or storefronts. As they became more familiar with this procedure, however, they were better able to manage their caseload.

Citizen Volunteer Involvement in Investigations. In both Spokane County and San Diego, citizen volunteers assist detectives in investigations. For example, these community members may lift prints from stolen/abandoned automobiles that previously may not have been processed. They may also photograph graffiti or make follow-up calls to victims to inform them of the status of their case or to seek additional information. Additionally, they may attend community meetings and work on citizen surveys. In Spokane County, citizen volunteers assist some detectives in establishing investigative priorities.

Interagency Linkages. Interagency drug task forces and other collaborative efforts designed to address drug problems are now common in many departments and the sites we visited. However, certain sites have applied this strategy to other crimes. The Mesa Police Department provides an excellent example. Two detectives from this department were instrumental in researching and obtaining city council and grant funding for what became the Center Against Family Violence (CAFV). This unit, operated by the police department, provides an aggressive, proactive, multipronged approach to handling cases involving physical and sexual abuse, domestic violence and, in some instances, elder abuse. Several detectives with expertise in domestic violence investigations and related matters are assigned to this unit. These detectives work closely with civilian victim services personnel who provide immediate, on-site intervention and long-term counseling. As part of this program, the detectives have established strong links with both the city and county prosecutors' offices, private therapeutic programs, area doctors and hospitals, and the state Child Protective Services. Anecdotal and interview data gathered during the site visit suggest that CAFV provides a systematic, humane and effective method for handling these very difficult situations. The cooperative efforts between the police department and the prosecutors have enabled these agencies to develop strong cases resulting in high conviction rates and, in certain cases, substantial prison sentences.

Technology. All of the departments visited are on the brink of major technological advances, many of which were funded by grants from the Office of Community Oriented Policing Services (COPS) of the U.S. Department of Justice. Within the next year, detectives and officers in recipient agencies will have crime analysis capabilities that were previously not available to cash-strapped crime analysis units. In San Diego, for example, all officers and detectives will have laptop computers that facilitate automated field reporting. They will also have access to geographic information systems (GIS) capabilities that will allow them to conduct their own analysis of the data for their area.

Additionally, many of the problems often associated with decen-tralization—being outside the information/communications loop, having to file reports at headquarters, not having access to crime analysis data—will be solved. Detectives will be able to retrieve the information they need through the computer, and e-mail will provide for fast and easy communication. Other departments are upgrading their computer-aided dispatch (CAD) systems and reconciling and integrating disparate manual and automated databases. The Mesa Police Department is acquiring Laboratory Information Management System (LIMS) software for tracking evidence as it is processed through the crime laboratory, the iden-tification unit, and into evidence storage. Spokane County and Arapahoe County are also introducing highly sophisticated data entry and retrieval systems.

In the interim, some agencies have made effective use of available technology. In Arapahoe County, voice mail, pagers and cell phones have greatly enhanced communication both between officers and detectives, and among detectives. Both groups indi-cated that they were more likely to share the "small" pieces of information when they could simply leave a message, rather than having to search out the person they needed to contact.

Functional Changes and Developments

In contrast to procedural developments—detectives conducting investigations in a new or different manner—the term "functional developments" refers to detectives assuming tasks that they may not have undertaken in the past. These functions were grouped into six often interrelated areas: (1) problem solving, (2) crime prevention, (3) alternatives to arrest, (4) community outreach, (5) community education, and (6) training and cross-training. It must be emphasized that these functional areas may not be new to a police department or a sheriff's office, but they may be new to detectives. Moreover, in some instances, detectives may have assumed responsibilities that had previously been assigned to another specialized unit. While several of the visited sites have implemented one or more of these functional changes, three sites were particularly noteworthy: the Arapahoe County Sheriff's Office, the Mesa Police Department, and the Spokane County Sheriff's Office.

Problem Solving. In many jurisdictions, the problem-solving function is assigned to the patrol division. Yet, in all of the sites that project staff visited, detectives are expected to assist in problem solving. The Spokane County Sheriff's Office, however, was the only site visited in which detectives have been given the primary organizational responsibility for problem solving. Detectives were assigned this function because the administration believed that the detectives had the most flexible schedules, and the most complete and readily accessible information (all the case reports) about crime problems in any given area. As noted previously, property detectives have been decentralized to neighborhood storefronts and are attempting to self-assign cases using priorities that reflect the problems of greatest concern to the neighborhoods in which they are working.

In contrast, while detectives in the Arapahoe County Sheriff's Office are encouraged to engage in problem solving, they do not have the primary organizational responsibility. Yet, this office has adopted an innovative approach to problem solving called "45 Day Plans." As part of this option, detectives are freed from their regular caseload for up to 45 days to conduct research, investigate an unsolved case or focus on an identified problem. If the plan is approved by the captain, the other detectives assigned to that geographic area will assume the problem solver's caseload for the requisite period of time.

Crime Prevention. Many detectives in the sites visited are participating in a broad range of crime prevention activities. The following example is only a brief review of the most innovative projects. Detectives in the Mesa Police Department have assumed responsibility for a number of "crime free" projects. As part of the Crime Free Housing program, the detectives organize property owners/managers or residents in multi-unit housing and educate them about their roles in preventing crime and quality-of-life problems. Additionally, the detectives provide program participants with training in the principles of crime prevention through environmental design (CPTED). Interviewees stated that this project's success is reflected in the 70 to 80 percent reduction in calls for service from certain properties. The "crime free" approach provided the framework for the Crime Free Mini-Storage program, designed to address burglary and drug manufacturing problems in mini-storage units. This program was designed by detectives and signaled the introduction of community-oriented policing principles into the Criminal Investigation Division. Again, detectives trained owners and managers of mini-storage facilities in CPTED principles, and in the first year of the program, burglaries dropped 86 percent. This approach is also reflected in the department's Crime Free Mini-Warehouse program and the Crime Free Hotel/Motel program.

Alternatives to Arrest. The Arapahoe County Home Check program is an example of a crime prevention program that focuses on interventions other than arrest, and provides an alternative to placing young offenders in the juvenile justice system. Specifically, the detective deputies have received court authorization to implement the Home Check program for juvenile offenders who are "at risk," including youths who are suspects in active cases, have active warrants, or are identified as repeat runaways, habitually truant, or "wanna be" gang associates. Detectives make "cold calls" during the evening to the youths' homes to discuss the situation with them and their families. The detectives may provide referrals to counseling or other social service agencies, or may require that the youth perform community service or make restitution. The detectives also identify the associates of the at-risk youths and visit them as well, informing them that they are known to the sheriff's office and making them aware of the probable consequences of their behavior. This program is designed as a form of "caring intervention," and interviewees indicated that many parents and the targeted youths have been grateful for the contacts and the alternatives. Arapahoe County Social Services, the county probation office and the district attorney's office participate with the sheriff's office in this collaborative effort. PERF interviewees believe that the program's success as a prevention and intervention effort is reflected in department data on the reduction in juvenile criminal activity and the number of juveniles arrested. Currently, detectives are considering ways of measuring their performance other than by the number of arrests and cases closed.

Community Outreach. Many police departments and sheriffs' offices throughout the country have detectives actively engaged in community outreach, often through attendance at community meetings. The sites visited were no exception. The most dramatic example of this change is the pairing of detectives with citizens in Spokane County's storefront offices, as discussed previously.

Community Education. Community education efforts are often part of crime prevention and community outreach programs. An Arapahoe County detective assigned to a specific neighborhood launched an initiative that combined all of these elements. This neighborhood had school-related traffic problems, and the residents formed a council to lobby for greater assistance from local authorities. The detective attended a council meeting and taught participants the SARA (scanning, analysis, response, assessment) model of problem solving. As a result of this training, citizens scanned, analyzed, responded to , and assessed their success in addressing the traffic problem, with some technical assistance from the sheriff's office. The detective explained, "We help people change their habits so that the [sheriff's office] is *part* of the solution, not *the* solution. We teach the citizens to do for themselves." Mesa's various Crime Free projects are another example of community education used as a central element of the problem-solving process.

Training and Cross-Training. This research suggests that in decentralized settings in which detectives have specific geographic assignments, an informal training process evolves whereby detectives and patrol officers train each other. Specifically, detectives can easily train officers about the information needs for various types of cases, while officers can describe the assortment of crime problems, suspects and victim characteristics in their area. An interesting variation on this theme is provided by Spokane County, where a neighborhood prosecutor and a neighborhood detective share the same office and exchange mutually beneficial information about evidence retrieval, evidentiary standards and case-building techniques.

As noted previously, Arapahoe County is unusual in that, since 1992, all detectives are generalists who investigate all categories of crimes. All of these detectives have been cross-trained and initially, property investigators were paired with persons investigators for on-the-job training. Moreover, all investigators receive training in community policing and problem solving.

Observations

When reviewing these preliminary observations, bear in mind that the scope of this work was narrow. The national survey collected descriptive data about the approach to community-oriented policing and the organization of the investigative function in mid- to large-sized metropolitan departments and sheriff's offices as a means of identifying ways of or models for effectively integrating detectives into the community policing process. Additionally, due to financial constraints, the researchers were able to visit and develop in-depth information on only seven sites. While it is certain that detectives in other jurisdictions are involved in many innovative programs and activities within the community policing context, this research did not document these efforts. Additionally, even in the sites visited, the researchers were not measuring success. The objective was merely to describe what appeared to be effective, and describe innovative approaches to the structural and functional aspects of the investigative process.

Detectives/Investigators Are Not (Necessarily) Dinosaurs. The kinds of changes observed are not made easily. However, it is apparent that not all detectives are resistant to change, and many may be less resistant than some police chiefs and sheriffs expect. Specifically, the research indicates that some detectives not only welcome changes in their procedures and functions, but also, in some cases, initiate changes to address perceived departmental deficiencies in addressing certain crime and quality-of-life problems. Moreover, although change in some agencies was initially met with skepticism or resistance, many detectives not only adjusted, but several agreed that they did not want to go back to the traditional approach. Thus, detectives are willing to change and, when provided with the opportunity (or forced) to modify procedures or functions, they will adapt.

Change is easier, of course, when personnel are prepared for it and are given a rationale for the new approaches. In one of the most graceful transitions in this study, Arapahoe County detectives were prepared by being given articles to read about community policing and problem solving. They were doing this reading while officers in the patrol division were actively involved in the transition. Detectives began to wonder where they would fit into the overall community policing picture. By the time organizational attention was turned to them, they were unsurprised and were intellectually prepared. This preparation was strongly reinforced with training in both community policing and problem solving.

In contrast, in another department (not one of the sites visited), several months after decentralization, detectives are still asking with genuine concern, "But what do you want us to do differently?" The change was made because department leaders believed, in general, that decentralization provided structural support for community policing. Many detectives in this department support the idea of decentralization for patrol, but have not been given a sufficient rationale for their own decentralization. As they moved into the change, they could only imagine the disadvantages but not the advantages to their job performance.

Something Lost and Something Gained. Although this study was not designed to evaluate the effectiveness of geographic assignment, the data suggest that there are advantages to this method regardless of whether detective offices are physically decentralized—that is, housed in their geographic area of responsibility—or located in headquarters. Geographic assignment not only promotes a sense of turf and proprietorship, but also an in-depth knowledge of crime patterns, local suspects and "good people" in the community who may assist in the investigative process. It contributes to a sense of shared ownership on the part of patrol officers and detectives, which should increase levels of cooperation. Detectives may feel greater satisfaction in seeing their efforts contribute to the welfare of an area with which they identify.

But these advantages are not cost-free. There are strengths and weaknesses in all models of geographic assignment; yet, in the views of the departments studied, they all present improvements over the traditional model. Still, detectives who are suspicious of physical decentralization are probably correct in believing something will be lost in the transition. Physically decentralized detectives may feel isolated at an outpost, separated from the mainstream of detective work. Insofar as they perceive their prior success as dependent on close interpersonal communication among themselves, detectives may feel some distress. They almost surely will lose some ease of within-group communication. There is good reason to expect (but no available data to demonstrate) that this loss of information will be offset by greater supplies of information to be derived from a detective's increased familiarity with an area, its problems, its residents, its resources, and its trouble makers, and from increased contact with patrol officers, community members and other service providers in the geographic area of responsibility. These new contacts do not happen overnight, however, and until they are established, the newly decentralized detectives will probably feel that their resources are diminished.

Decentralized detectives may also need to drive long distances to deliver routine reports to a central office, attend meetings or line-ups, and obtain crime analysis data that would be available if they were at headquarters. Some believe that they are out cf the "information loop," or "out of sight, out of mind." Interviewees indicated that they may miss out on training opportunities, including the opportunity to learn from more experienced colleagues. They may miss opportunities to participate in larger scale investigations that may aid their individual investigations and professional development. And they fear that citizens will suffer if detectives lose or fail to see information about perpetrators who range across district boundaries.

Technology. Technology plays a major role in the loss/gain equation for decentralization, and will play an even greater role in the near future. Almost all of the departments visited are in the process of installing powerful information and communication systems that will give all personnel—patrol officers and detectives, centralized or decentralized—astonishingly greater and faster access to information and to each other. Most detectives have not even begun to envision the potential of these systems. Information about career criminals involved in a variety of criminal activities and operating across district boundaries will not be lost. It will become easier for certain analysts to be assigned the responsibility of analyzing these criminals' movements. Until such systems are in place, however, decentralized detectives who must invest substantial travel time to do their work may feel they are wasting time they could be spending on cases, or may fear they are losing valuable information. Are these costs offset by ready access to patrol officers and local information? It probably depends on the department. But it is almost certain that new technologies will soon minimize these problems in many departments.

In the meantime, some departments are making very effective use of available technologies. The Arapahoe County department, for example, uses pagers, cell phones and e-mail for easy communication among personnel. With the personal familiarity that came with the development of geographically based work groups, detectives and officers have been willing to trade home phone numbers for quicker communication. In Madison, Wis., district stations are linked by an in-house television hookup that allows sites to share briefings. In addition, at any point during the day, Madison personnel in one station can have face-to-face video contact and share visual information (e.g., photos of suspects) with people in the other

stations. In very low-tech settings, the problem of transferring reports between sites can be addressed by assigning couriers (citizen
volunteers, perhaps) who make regular runs between department
facilities. If a department does choose to physically decentralize
before implementing the new information technology, managers
need to anticipate the burdens of physical separation and devise
ways to address these problems.

Degrees of Decentralization. In departments in which some
detectives have been physically decentralized and/or given geographic assignments, the crimes most commonly associated with
these structural arrangements are property crimes, although this
varied across the departments in the survey and site studies. A
few (e.g., Arapahoe County and Madison) have assigned all
crimes geographically; some have geographically assigned and/
or physically decentralized most crimes, and others have geographically assigned and/or physically decentralized only property crimes. The crime investigation types that are most
commonly centralized are homicides, robbery, sex crimes, juvenile crimes, and fraud.

Sex crimes seem to pose the greatest challenge for geographic assignments. One department reported that centralization of sex crime investigations is required by state statute. Since
the 1997 survey, Madison has geographically assigned all investigations, but there continues to be substantial pressure from
former sex crime investigators and some community activists to
recentralize investigation of these crimes. Juvenile crimes pose
similar issues. Jefferson County, Colo., reported decentralization
of juvenile offenses in 1997, but has just recently recentralized
these investigations on an experimental basis, at the same time
separating adult and juvenile investigations.

Degrees of Generalization. In Arapahoe County, all detectives
are generalists, but certain investigators are acknowledged and frequently called upon as the juvenile experts. In the case of both sex
crime and juvenile crimes, some investigators and their supervisors argue the need for special expertise and experience, and also
point out that these crimes require the most coordination with other

agencies. This coordination is facilitated by knowing who the contact people (including investigators) are in each organization.

Chain of Command. Among departments with geographic assignment and/or physical decentralization, some have a separate chain of command for investigators, while others have only an area-based chain of command through which both patrol and investigative personnel report. In Arapahoe County, for example, investigators are physically centralized but are given geographic responsibility. Investigators there report through an investigative chain of command. This may change when area substations are constructed. Garden Grove, Calif.; Waco, Texas; Sacramento, Calif.; Rochester, N.Y.; and Spokane County, Wash., have physically decentralized investigators who report through an investigative chain of command. A number of departments (e.g., Albuquerque, N.M.; Arlington, Texas; Baltimore County, Md.; Ft. Worth, Texas; Fresno County, Calif.; Madison, Wis.; Richmond, Va.; San Diego, Calif.; and Toledo, Ohio) have at least some (and in some cases, all) investigators who are physically decentralized and report with patrol personnel through an area commander. In this model, there may or may not be a supervisor who has specific responsibility for investigations. In Boston, decentralized detectives report to the area commander but also are accountable to the Investigations Division.

One Best Model? Probably not. The initial, exploratory research does not indicate whether one model is preferable to another. Admittedly, the model of physical decentralization or area assignment combined with reporting through an area commander seems, at least in theory, to be an especially strong one. It promotes a coordinated approach on the local level (e.g., district, precinct), investigator knowledge of the territory, consistency and continuity in priority identification, and information sharing and teamwork between and among investigators and patrol officers. The sense of identification with an area and its people may heighten a detective's motivation. Still, detectives may perceive a disadvantage to this model if they feel that not being in the investigative chain of command (assuming one exists in the agency) places them outside the information loop, and perhaps deprives them of equal consideration for choice assignments and other rewards within the investigative division.

The "detective as generalist" model has the advantage of broadening an investigator's knowledge of a geographic area and may also provide a more varied and interesting workload for many investigators. In Arapahoe County, it was also a way of equalizing the workload between persons detectives and property detectives. Nevertheless, the value of generalization may depend on the jurisdiction's volume, type and geographic distribution of crimes, and whether an agency has the financial and personnel resources for the necessary cross-training.

In general, it appears that the value of any of these models depends on the department's characteristics, its goals and the community it serves. A small community, in which physical decentralization does not seem necessary to ensure quality service, may benefit from area assignment of cases and not suffer from a bifurcated chain of command *if the separate commands are in accord*. This appears to be the case in Arapahoe County. Some cities are geographically large; therefore, physical decentralization of all basic police services may be appropriate. In these settings, decisions about the chain of command issue should probably be based on a review of the department's goals. If decentralization of investigators is done for the primary purpose of making them more effective at what they have always done (i.e., the investigation of crimes), then two chains of command may not be dysfunctional. Detectives can associate more easily with officers, citizens and others who are knowledgeable about the community, thereby expanding sources of information—all within the traditional chain of command.[5] If the primary reason for decen-

---

[5] The researchers did visit one site in which geographically decentralized detectives who reported through the investigative chain of command appeared to be confused and frustrated by lack of clear direction. They felt the need to "protect" themselves from what they considered the area commander's inappropriate expectations.

tralizing detectives is to create an area-based service team that is working together to prevent crimes, solve crimes, and provide both a better and broader police service, then it seems critical to have an area commander who has control over all of his or her resources. Unity of purpose and effort is difficult to achieve within the context of a bifurcated chain of command.

Training. Detectives and investigators need to receive training in the principles, strategies and tactics of problem solving and community policing if they are expected to incorporate these practices into the investigative process. They need information not only about the operations of detective units in other jurisdictions, but also about investigative and programmatic approaches to address specific problems such as domestic violence, gangs and quality-of-life problems.[6] Although training may be expensive, labor intensive and time consuming, the benefits derived may be substantial and greatly enhance an agency's capacity to address community concerns.

Functional Changes. The data suggest that to date most efforts to integrate investigations into a community policing approach have involved changes that are physical (decentralization) or procedural (geographic responsibility). Mesa, Spokane County, and Arapahoe County were selected for site visits largely because they reported changes in the functions of at least some detectives, but they are exceptions rather than the rule. Most other agencies have not yet explored functional changes, but it seems likely that more such innovations may result from physical and procedural changes. As detectives become more closely identified with small areas and begin to work in teams with officers who are expected to be community-oriented problem solvers, they may come to see for them-

---

[6] A substantial amount of literature containing practical information about programs in these areas is available free of charge from the National Criminal Justice Reference Service sponsored by the U.S. Department of Justice. Additionally, detectives/investigators may obtain a great deal of practical information from site visits to other agencies or through peer-exchange programs.

selves the potential for broader functions. This appears to have happened in Mesa and Arapahoe County. The nontraditional activities that detectives have undertaken resulted from detectives being in a better position to see the needs and to know the needy. A study by Wycoff and Skogan (1993), conducted several years ago, introduced us to a physically decentralized detective who was responsible for her own case assignment (as detectives in Spokane County are today). This meant she read all the reports of incidents that occurred in her area, regardless of whether they had enough solvability factors to justify further investigation. As a result, she became familiar with families and locations that had not yet crossed the line to major crime, but were clearly headed in that direction. She intervened in some of these cases in a deliberate effort to forestall greater problems. No one asked her to do it. It just seemed the logical thing to do when she knew enough (and cared enough) about "her" neighborhood to be alert to developing problems. It seems unlikely that she will be unique among detectives.

Authors' Reflections on the Project

Finally, it should be said that this has been a fun and an inspiring project. We have learned a lot while realizing that we have only scratched the surface of many important topics. The sense of having opened doors is an exciting one. We found more change in approaches to investigations than anticipated. We know from long experience that these are perceived as very difficult changes to make. The number of departments currently undertaking these changes (and the much greater number who have contacted us seeking information) confirms that there is a lot of thought and energy currently being committed to the question of how best to support community policing with investigations. That so many departments are interested in this subject tells us that many have now moved well beyond the rhetoric of community policing to embrace the hard realities of institutionalizing the philosophy. This is good and gratifying news. And we wish to thank the hundreds of departments and, specifically, our seven intensive sites, who shared it with us.

REFERENCES

Masterson, M. F. 1995. *From Polarization to Partnership: Realigning the Investigative Function to Serve Neighborhood Needs.* Unpublished manuscript.

Wycoff, M. A., and W.G. Skogan. 1993. *Community Policing in Madison: Quality From the Inside Out.* Washington, D.C.: National Institute of Justice.

CHAPTER 7

CITIZENS IN THE POP PROCESS: HOW MUCH IS TOO MUCH?

Samuel Walker and Andy Mills

The nature of community policing and problem-oriented policing (POP) leads to a variety of new issues and potential problems that are inherent in encouraging and welcoming increased citizen input and participation. Increased citizen involvement in policing efforts, while applauded by many, is an area of concern. As yet, there has not been a thorough consideration of the potential problems that may result from officer/community interaction and, therefore, there are inadequate governing policies and procedures in place. In a variety of situations, officers are being placed in ethical and moral harm's way. In this chapter, Dr. Samuel Walker will discuss several of the circumstances in which citizens may attempt to manipulate the police and, in turn, those under which the police may attempt to manipulate citizens. Sergeant Andy Mills will then discuss specific kinds of moral weaknesses, problems and issues that may arise.

Issues of Manipulation and Control: Dr. Samuel Walker

A Problem-Solving Incident. About two-and-a-half years ago, I was out in my front yard raking leaves. At one point, a car with three youths in it drove up; one youth got out and went across the street to Ryan's house. A few minutes later, he came back and the car drove off. Meanwhile, I was still raking leaves. Ten minutes later another car drove up; this time there were four youths in it. Again, one got out and went across the street to see Ryan. A few minutes later he came back and the car drove off. This went on all afternoon. As it turns out, Ryan was dealing grass. The bike patrol officer in our neighborhood at the time

responded by enlisting residents' help. He asked all of the neighbors to record the license plate numbers of the cars that stopped
in front of Ryan's house. The officer's solution was to address
the drug dealing problem by targeting the buyers. When I talked
with my neighbors down the street, I found they all loved this
approach. They were excited and impressed that a police officer
was addressing a problem in the neighborhood, had talked to
them about it, expressed his concern about the quality of life in
the area, and asked for their help.

This incident represents a classic example of problem solving. There was focus on a specific problem and citizens were involved in the problem-solving process. This incident dealt with
a relatively small problem that was occurring in a generally crime-
free neighborhood. By involving citizens, there were more eyes
and ears available for collecting useful information, thereby expanding police resources. Community relations with the police
department were improved as people were made to feel that the
department cared about their quality of life. This was a creative
and imaginative POP response.

However, when we stop and study this episode, we must
realize that the approach is filled with potential problems. For
instance, consider the following scenario. What if there was somebody on my street that I really didn't like? A program like this
one would provide an excellent opportunity to create problems
for him. In fact, there was an ongoing dispute on our block between two neighbors. One neighbor owned a truck that was used
for hauling trash. He would park it across the street in front of
an attorney's house. The attorney was very concerned about his
property values and so the two were embroiled in a dispute that
went on for years. Both neighbors had tried almost everything,
including reporting minor truck violations or garbage violations,
to harass each other. It would not be difficult to imagine one of
them trying to manipulate our neighborhood officer to get even
with the other.

The idea of involving citizens in problem solving and, in particular, asking them to perform surveillance on their neighbors to

report suspected violations, without any form of guidance, certainly opens the door for a wide variety of potential problems.

At the 1998 PERF Problem-Oriented Policing (POP) Conference, a panel was organized to address the lack of discussion concerning the potential problems of citizen involvement in problem solving. Citizen involvement is like motherhood, apple pie and the flag. There is no critical thinking about what could go wrong and what could be done to avoid potential problems. The purpose of this panel, therefore, was to initiate a dialogue about citizen involvement in the POP process. Participants hoped that the dialogue, in turn, would serve as an impetus for discussion in police agencies of ways to avoid problems from inappropriate citizen involvement.

Potential Problems. Citizen involvement is one of the core principles of both community policing and problem-oriented policing. Let us now consider some problems that could arise from citizen involvement.

Citizens may manipulate the police. The potential problem of citizens' manipulation of the police corresponds to the example just given. There was a dispute on my street, and it was entirely conceivable that one of the neighbors would use the opportunity to turn in the other for an alleged violation. If we state that problem-oriented policing and community policing *should* have citizen involvement, that police *should* listen to neighbors, residents, and so forth, and that the police *should* follow their direction, there is a potential for citizen misuse of the police. During our planning process for this session, Robert Leuci (New York Police Department, retired), Andy Mills (San Diego Police Department) and I shared some real examples that we had encountered.

   a) *Citizens may use the police to meet personal agendas.* In one example, neighbors informed the police about drug dealing that was occurring in a house across the street. In response, the officers went to the house, knocked on the door, and asked if they could look around. The residents were quite agreeable and when the officers looked around, they saw no evidence of drugs. A few weeks later the episode was repeated; the neighbors told the police there was drug dealing, but when the police investigated they found nothing. As it turns out, this house was occupied by two homosexual males who were a couple. The neighbors in this older, traditional neighborhood did not support this type of domestic arrangement. In this case, citizen involvement became a device for using the police to settle a conflict over lifestyle. Similarly, in another example, neighbors reported a series of noise problems and suspected drug activity coming from one house. In this case, the house was occupied by the first Hispanic family in the neighborhood.

b) *Groups or organizations may use involvement in the problem-solving process to disguise criminal activity.* When I did a ride-along several years ago in Brooklyn, the officers informed me that one of the problems they faced involved storefront churches that were really fronts for drug or gambling activity. As it turns out, some of these storefront churches were very active in working with the police as part of problem-solving, community policing programs. This involvement included reporting criminal activity in the neighborhood. Partnership with the police represented an attempt to deflect police attention from their own criminal activities. In some cases, these storefront churches would report their competitors to the police as a means of reducing the competition. Currently, there are no policies or procedures in place that filter out this information or guide officers in this particular process.

c) *Citizens may use political influence to get at individual police officers.* If residents dislike a particular officer working in the area, established neighborhood organizations might try to use their influence to pressure the police department to transfer him or her. There is a real potential for the community interfering with a police department's personnel process.

Police may manipulate citizens. Problem-oriented policing holds that an officer should increase citizen involvement and build a network of community organizations, with regular meetings and so on. However, what if a police officer uses this network to endorse specific candidates for political office? An officer may attempt to garner support for ballot issues or referendums. This is illegal and an abuse of police authority. There needs to be a definite distinction and specific guidelines in place to differentiate between what officers do while off-duty, what a police association representative might do as a lobbyist, and what an officer on-duty, in uniform, can do.

Police corruption. Sergeant Andy Mills will discuss the potential for police corruption later in this chapter.

Who Controls Police Policy? The real question that remains is, who controls police policy? The basic concept of citizen involvement in problem-oriented and community policing is providing citizens a voice in police policy making. The advocates of these policing philosophies view this as a positive step. However, the citizens' voice must not be permitted to be a controlling voice. Another project I'm involved with concerns a major East Coast city and one of the nearby suburban departments. The major city has significant and growing African-American and Hispanic populations. Meanwhile, the suburban community is 99.9 percent white. What do you suppose the citizens from the suburban community primarily want from their police department? "Keep those black kids out of our town." The chief's major problem is telling the citizens, "No. I'm sorry. We can't stop every car driven by an African American that crosses the city line. No. We can't stop all these kids who happen to walk into neighborhoods if there's no suspected criminal activity."

There are many situations in which the police, as professionals, know best. The minute we begin to do what the citizens request without considering proper legal standards or police priorities, we are opening the door for very serious problems. What we really need to do is strike the balance between healthy citizen involvement and a proper degree of police professional control of law enforcement.

A Practitioner's Perspective: Sergeant Andy Mills

Before I begin, I would like to make two points. First, I am not an academic. I've never written a book and I certainly don't have the credentials that some of my fellow panel presenters have. My views come from a practitioner's standpoint. I'm in the field on a daily basis, dealing with the issues that other police practitioners deal with. In addition, I'm a problem solver. This chapter is motivated by my desire to ensure that problem solving continues, and that our hopes are not dashed by some of our peers' inappropriate activities. Second, I've had the opportunity to travel around the country and visit a lot of departments. Although I haven't seen a lot of problems with the manipulation of citizen involvement, there have been some. The problems that do exist have the potential for catastrophic results if they aren't dealt with now.

Weights and Balances. In traditional policing, we get the things done that need to be done. We are given the tools and authority to perform our jobs. We can perform search and seizures, we have access to information by the virtue of our uniforms and squad cars and, if need be, we can whip our 12-gauge out of the rack and chamber a round. We get things done. However, for each form of authority that we are granted as police officers, there are coinciding counterbalances or calls for accountability.

The legislature has given police the unique authority to perform such tasks as taking people's liberty and incarcerating them, building criminal cases, and looking into people's personal lives. Having been given all of this legislative authority, it follows that there must be some means of accountability. Imagine a balancing scale. Legislative authority has put a 25-pound weight on one side of the scale. The counterbalances take the form of training and policy and procedure manuals that help to ensure that everything is conducted correctly. As an employee of my police department, I am expected to know all 1,252 pages of our policies. The policy and procedure manual provides guiding principles and expectations for the organization.

On that same scale, positional authority has placed an additional 25-pound weight alongside the legislative authority weight. In this case, the uneven distribution is counterbalanced by citizen review boards and internal affairs. In our jurisdiction, the citizen review board has access to some internal affairs documentation to determine whether the disciplinary action was appropriate. Internal affairs personnel ensure that every officer knows that he or she will be investigated for misusing positional authority.

More generally, our behavior is monitored by the court system. Civil and criminal proceedings ensure that officers are accountable for their actions. The courts serve as an omnipresent counterbalance.

Recently, there has been the addition of one more big weight to the scale: a 45-pound weight. This weight is called community policing. In my mind, this is one of the biggest weights. When you go into an impoverished neighborhood, you can see that the citizens are struggling and have no hope. A police officer can offer them some hope. Once you have provided some families with hope, you, in some sense, become their salvation. They will begin to look to you for their answers. This situation gives the officer a lot of authority; if there is no counterbalance for this weight, there will be problems. Many of the citizens we serve haven't thought through the constitutional, positional and legislative issues that officers deal with on a daily basis. One of the possible counterbalances to equalize the weight of community policing is cultural accountability. If I know that when Joe Brown and I are working together, I can't get away with punching someone, I'm not going to throw that blow. If I know that my partner will say it is inappropriate for me to tell a store owner that I can solve his problems if he hires me off-duty, and I know my partner will hold me accountable, a large counterbalance has been added opposite the community policing weight.

Problem Personality Types. The greater the power, the greater the need for control. For police officers, this is an extremely important concept. To begin, let's look at some of the reasons people do stupid things. We can separate these people by personality types.

   The moral chameleon. The moral chameleon has a commitment to accommodation (Gaffigan and McDonald 1997). He will change his colors and stripes to accommodate the ebb and tide of community opinion. The chameleon is morally weak-willed. If there is a situation that has citizens really upset, the moral chameleon will say anything to appease them and accommodate them. This is prevalent in the mid-management ranks of police agencies. In one example, when community members were upset at the tamale vendors on their streets, they marched down to the local police department and demanded that this problem be taken care of. Based on the community pressure, the moral chameleon then decided to target the tamale vendors. Meanwhile, all the patrol officers were scratching their heads saying, "We had four drive-by shootings this week at one location. Maybe we want to deal with that first." We need to consider the community's requests while ensuring public safety at the same time.

   The moral hypocrite. The moral hypocrite pretends to live by a certain set of standards, but doesn't actually do so (Gaffigan and McDonald 1997). For instance, as a chief executive officer, the moral hypocrite might promote the pretense that the department has a community policing team, while in reality, all it has is a pretty pathetic bike team. There might be a couple of DARE officers and even though there is no additional problem solving, the hypocrite will tout the department as having a good community policing program. In fact, she is going to apply for a COPS grant and secure another million dollars for additional officers to undertake community policing efforts, all the while knowing that the extra officers will be used only as rapid responders.

   The moral opportunist. The moral opportunist will sacrifice his values and dearly held principles to better his self-interests (Gaffigan and McDonald 1997). I'm sure everybody has encountered the opportunist in their agency. This is the person who will do anything to get ahead.

The morally self-deceived. The morally self-deceived view themselves as being principled individuals. Unfortunately, they are not (Gaffigan and McDonald 1997). I call this the TV Preacher Syndrome. He can talk a good religious game and act appropriately pious, but will turn around and pick up a prostitute on the street corner. The key is motivation. For instance, why is our agency a problem-solving agency? In the case of San Diego Police Department, we believe in its tenets and principles. We are not solely motivated by the $2.5 billion that President Clinton has offered to problem-solving agencies.

The morally ignorant. These individuals don't have a hard set of values or principles (Benjamin 1990). This type of officer has not considered potential problems. She hasn't really thought about the potential consequences that could arise when she goes to a community group and lies to the residents to accomplish a simple goal. Of all the categories of personalities, I see the morally ignorant as the biggest area of concern for community policing.

Hypothetical Situations. Because community policing is a relatively new phenomenon, there has not been sufficient opportunity to sit down and think through the significant issues. Try to think about what you would do in the following situations.

An officer is targeting drug dealers in a particular part of town. Before going, the officer goes home and manufactures a dime rock, puts it in a Ziploc baggie, and carries it around in his top pocket. When he stops a drug user on a traffic stop and can't immediately see the drugs he just watched being bought, the officer takes the baggie out of his pocket and dumps it in the car. Instead of working through the system, he plants drugs in the car. He can now say, "Hey, what's this?" He picks the baggie out of the car, waves it back and forth and now he has probable cause to search the car.

In another situation, community members march down to the captain's office and demand more patrol officers in their neighborhood. "We need officers on foot in our neighborhood and we want it done." The captain realizes that the sergeant is unavailable, so she takes the community members into the office and shows them the patrol plan. She opens the books and goes through the daily staffing data with them. Is this top secret information? Were the captain's actions right or wrong? Were they ethical or unethical? Again, the point is that people in leadership positions in an agency, whether at a low level or high level, need to think through these issues.

Community Policing Pitfalls

Unrealistic expectations. The information that is conveyed with community policing may create unrealistic expectations. In many cases, police convey to the community and local government that if they buy the agency mountain bikes and staff a neighborhood bike patrol, the police will take care of crime. We are raising these residents' expectations of something we may not be able to do. At the same time, the community is building unrealistic expectations of what police can do for them.

Entitlement problems. Both officers and citizens have entitlement expectations. For instance, a community member may approach an officer and say, "Officer, I was here for you when you needed me. I helped you organize this community block meeting and got 100 people to attend. All I'm asking you to do is make sure that homeless person isn't sleeping in back of my house." The citizen feels entitled to be the officer's top priority, and feels that he is owed this favor in exchange for any help he provided. At the same time, officers may feel entitled to special treatment in a neighborhood: "When nobody else would organize this community group, I took it over. Now it's promotion time and I need you to do me a favor. Could you write a letter to the chief?" Suddenly, the chief's office is flooded at promotion time with 100 letters saying how great the officer is.

Noble cause deviance. Noble cause deviance occurs when an officer feels justified in altering his actions for a "noble cause." In her opinion, others' actions are "worse" than her own. To get the job done and deal with problems, she is willing to deviate from department policies as long as her actions are *relatively* good. For instance, an officer could pressure a predominantly African-American community group to boycott an Iraqi-owned business, because the officer believes the business to be troublesome. For the sake of a "noble" cause, an officer may also manufacture probable cause for searches or stops (Delattre 1996).

In another example, an officer was given the task of dealing with false 911 payphone calls. To deal with the problem, he took bolt cutters out with him on the third shift. The officer took all the receivers that had been left hanging off the hook and tied them to his chief's door. That took care of the problem. There was no thought about the consequences of removing a payphone from somebody's neighborhood, or the penalty for destruction of property.

Corrupting influence. When officers are working shoulder to shoulder with others with a lower level of ethical behavior, problems arise. Sooner or later, others' behavior can influence an officer. Most officers who are fired or convicted for unethical behavior in a police department did not behave unethically when they joined the force. Most officers don't start out swearing like troopers, or start with the tendency toward unethical behavior that some develop 10 or 15 years later. Sometimes when you rub shoulders with enough slimy people, you become slimy. If we're going to put officers in contact with potentially corrupt people, we need to better prepare them for what they will experience.

Silence of compromise. As officers and supervisors, we are rarely willing to confront each other about areas of concern. There is a supposed blue code of silence in place among law enforcement officers. The code of silence may not be as prevalent as the media thinks, but are we, in fact, less inclined to confront our peers on minor or significant issues? Around the country, supervisors have got to step up to the plate and take a stand. Specifically, supervisors have to be willing to undertake rigorous analysis in the problem-solving process. Unfortunately, the ranks of sergeant and above are the weakest in the organization in terms of problem-solving analysis. As supervisors, we have to be prepared to ask thoughtful questions in a noncritical and noncondemning manner. "Why are you choosing this particular response when your analysis showed that the problem was something completely different?" If we want to achieve quality problem-oriented policing, we have to be willing to confront our officers.

Audience Questions and Comments

Audience Member: Do you think that the selection process can be made stricter to circumvent the potential problems with sending officers into the community?

Walker: The devil wears many disguises and temptation appears in many different forms. If the federal government provides your agency with money to do additional hiring, you may end up hiring faster than you otherwise would. If you are already dealing with a low pool of recruits, you may have to begin to dip even farther down. This creates potential problems. In the face of this money, many departments have hired too many officers too fast. To accomplish all of this hiring, they have had to lower their standards.

Mills: Generally, I think that law enforcement agencies around the country conduct hiring well. Our recruits score with a pretty high level of intelligence, they undergo extensive psychological batteries, polygraphing, etc. Instead of changing selection criteria, I think the key is the way in which we market for personnel. Applicants need to be made aware of the department's expectations. In some cities, the first letter newly selected recruits receive is from the chief saying, "We are a community-oriented police department. If you want to be Rambo, look for another department." In addition, no matter how officers are recruited, if the department does not provide them with proper guidance and support in determining what is permissible and right, good people can go bad.

Audience Member: The problem that we're having in New Jersey is that we don't have enough time in police training academy to give our new recruits all the tools that they will need to do the sophisticated things that are necessary in community policing and problem-oriented policing. To compensate, I think we need to start requiring a higher degree of sophistication from our officers so they are able to perform the duties that are required of them: computer capabilities, more sophisticated report writing and neighborhood grassroots work. I think this message needs to be coming from the top of the organization to institute these changes in recruitment.

Audience Member: What practical things is the San Diego Police Department doing to teach line staff and supervisors about these ethical issues?

Mills: This is an area that can be improved. We do have an ethics component in our advanced officer training that everybody is mandated to go through. However, we're not doing enough that specifically deals with the area of problem solving. On the command level, we are formulating ideas that we would like to implement. We would like to institute an "on-target team" to ensure that patrol officers are on target with their analyses and problem solving. There is conditional approval from my captain to form a committee of officers who will look at these cases one at a time and focus on the specific issues (such as weak analysis). After looking through a batch of cases, the committee will determine how to provide training to patrol officers and supervisors so that the department is heading in the right direction. This would facilitate ethical discussions. For instance, if community members want to boycott a business, the committee can discuss the extent to which we should be involved in this process, look at the ethical principles and provide guidance to the patrol officers. Perhaps there will be a problem-solving award in the future for officers in the department who initiate discussions about potential problems and offer suggestions.

Audience Member: At times, good people with good motives are going to ask an officer to do something that may not be proper. For instance, community groups and nonprofit organizations want to give the police department equipment such as mountain bikes. In some instances, this equipment is donated with the expectation that it will be used in a particular area. This can distort the department's priorities and present a picture of unequal policing between communities if one community cannot afford to donate the same equipment. Some agencies require the community and the department to cosign a contract of terms and conditions to remedy such problems.

Audience Member: I think an area of concern then becomes less affluent neighborhoods that don't have these resources. Are they still receiving an equal level of police protection? The basic police mission is to provide equal protection for the entire community. So, in a subtle way, are we distorting this mission by giving more protection to those who have the money to pay for it?

Audience Member: At our precinct, some neighborhoods will come forward and donate mountain bikes. When we accept the bikes, we have to be up front and honest with them. We tell the citizens, "We appreciate your donation, but you have to understand we have a big precinct and we will use these bikes to cover the entire area. They cannot be used to only police your neighborhood." If the bikes are given with the expectation that they will be used only for a certain area, we don't accept the donation. It becomes an integrity issue. We get paid by all the citizens.

Audience Member: In my department, it is impressed on officers that any actions they take in problem solving and in working closely with the community should be able to pass the media test. If their actions were in tomorrow's headlines, would it be something they would want to be associated with?

Audience Member: One of the problems I see is when citizens form a nonprofit group that becomes the police department's local fundraising arm. The group raises money to purchase things that don't necessarily get approved by either the local budget or citizen advisory boards. I see this as an enormous risk of corruption. Certain individuals will have undue influence over these nonprofit organizations and the funds that are raised. We are not in the business of raising funds and we shouldn't be. If resources are available that are not being controlled through the budget process, you can make a very few people very powerful.

Audience Member: I think you have a valid point. However, does the problem really arise from private citizens simply raising money for the police? I think that the problems arise when the police begin to compromise their budget, or when the police do not have the internal integrity to deal with these types of issues.

Conclusion

This session's purpose was to initiate a discussion of what the panelists believed was an important issue that has not received sufficient attention. It is evident from the audience responses that our assumption was correct. There is obviously a great deal of concern about this issue among law enforcement officers, and audience members provided examples of difficult questions that they have encountered in their work.

Citizen involvement is one of the basic elements of the POP process, as well as most community policing programs. As this panel discussion has demonstrated, however, there are many potential dangers from citizen involvement. The main problem is not with citizen involvement per se, or with too much involvement, but rather with the wrong kind of involvement. It is possible for people to manipulate the police or for the police to manipulate people in improper ways. We should not throw the baby out with the bath water by ending all citizen involvement. Rather, our task for the future is to identify procedures for directing and controlling citizen involvement to ensure that it achieves proper goals and avoids potential problems. In short, we should apply the problem-solving process to citizen involvement. We need to devote serious effort to identifying specific problems related to citizen involvement and developing creative solutions that are tailored to those problems.

REFERENCES

Benjamin, M. 1990. *Splitting the Difference: Compromise and Integrity in Ethics and Politics.* Lawrence, Kan.: University Press of Kansas.

Delattre, E. J. 1996. *Character and Cops: Ethics in Policing.* Washington, D.C.: American Enterprise Institute Press.

Gaffigan, S., and P. McDonald. 1997. *Police Integrity: Public Service With Honor.* A Partnership Between the National Institute of Justice and the Office of Community Oriented Policing Services. Washington, D.C.: U.S. Department of Justice.

CHAPTER 8

RESTORATIVE POLICING:
THE CANBERRA, AUSTRALIA EXPERIMENT

Lawrence Sherman

Restorative justice addresses crime by stressing the harm that crime causes to victims, communities and offenders. Victims and their families, offenders and their families, police, and community representatives all participate in defining the harm caused by the offense and determining what should be done to repair it. All affected parties attend a conference (often mediated by a police officer) and express their views about the harms caused by the crime and potential remedies. These conferences are well received by the victims, who often receive reparation and gain a certain level of empathy toward the offender.

One of the problems the police have experienced with the criminal justice system is that the prosecution is not listening to victims or defendants in a meaningful way. One way police can help to remedy a number of problems is to be more actively involved in listening to both victims and offenders. Experts in the restorative justice field believe that police have the potential to do a better job than the courts are inclined or have time to do.

Traditionally, the courts attempt to do something they rarely **can** do—that is to figure out the facts of a case. In 95 percent of court cases in New Zealand, guilt is not an issue. Instead, the issue is what is to be done about the facts of the crime. With respect to the victims, offenders and the police in general, the courts are pretty bad at figuring out what is to be done about the crime.

Rediscovered in New Zealand and Australia in the last few years, restorative justice takes all parties into consideration and is a much more practical way of dealing with crime. This method was *re*discovered in the sense that it has been around for at least 3,000 to 4,000 years. In fact, some historians are now arguing that throughout most of the world's history, restorative justice has been the far more common approach in dealing with crime. They argue that it is much more common than retributive justice, in which the sole focus is on repaying the victim.

In 1989, New Zealand adopted a legal justice system from the Maori culture. Maoris came to New Zealand 500 years ago and have a very strong family structure—crimes were considered to be committed not just against the victims, but against families as well (the New Zealand Maoris' definition of family encompasses about 100 people). For as long as anybody could remember, when a crime happened in a Maori society, the response was to have a conference of families. Everyone came together—the victim, the victim's family, the offender, and the offender's family—but not to argue about guilt. Guilt was never an issue. The discussion, instead, was about how the harm could be repaired. Currently in New Zealand, the traditional Maori family conference is the model for resolving juvenile offenses.

Within the New Zealand model of restorative justice, social workers are in charge of setting up and managing the family conferences. When the police in Sydney, Australia heard about this approach, they thought it was a great idea. So in the early 1990s, the New South Wales police developed a procedure to deal with juvenile justice cases that would normally proceed to a "slap on the wrist," or probation if the case went to court. The police officer working on the case would interview the victim and the victim's family and the offender and the offender's family. Then all parties would meet for a 90-minute conference, during which they all would sit in a circle and deal with how to repair the harm. This police-driven model was so effective, and so popular, that it was banned. The Parliament of New South Wales said, in effect, that they did not want the police having so much power. In 1994, they passed a law saying that the police could not do this anymore; the cases had to go to social workers instead.

At that point, the Australian Federal Police in Canberra adopted the model that had been banned in New South Wales. In fact, Canberra is now apparently the only jurisdiction in Australia that is using a police-run model. All the other Australian jurisdictions adopted variations on the New Zealand crime model, under which social workers run the conferences, and offenders' main contacts with the police continue to occur either in prison or when exchanging case-related facts.

Restorative justice in the United States has a strong success record. In Minnesota, a small police department is using the police-run conference model. An experiment using a similar model has been completed at the Bethlehem, Pa., Police Department, with somewhat mixed results. The Baltimore police are just starting a model in which community leaders facilitate the conferences.

This chapter focuses on a police-led restorative justice experiment in Canberra, Australia. The Canberra experiment is a controlled test, the same type that has been used to study other topics such as policing domestic violence. Following an incident that would qualify for restorative justice, the police or prosecution calls the research staff on their 24-hour telephone number. Researchers answer the phone, take the details of the incident and then choose between unmarked envelopes. The envelopes dictate the response strategies. It will either dictate that the case go to court, or that the case be diverted to the restorative justice process.

At this point, the evidence is sufficient to illustrate that this process greatly benefits victims by making them feel safer and more prepared to deal with the crime. Restorative justice gives victims more rights during the procedure, and generates many more apologies from the offender. This process also helps victims to dispel some of their fear of the offender by allowing the victim to meet the offender and see that he or she may deserve some empathy.

At the same time, the offender receives what he or she sees as fairer treatment. The process gives offenders respect for the police and the law—more so than when he or she goes to court.

The offender generally comes out of the restorative justice process less angry and closer to his or her family. In a few more years, we will be able to determine whether the offenders wind up getting less jail time as a result of this process and if they learn from the experience. Preliminary evidence suggests that people have more respect for the law when they feel that the law has treated them fairly and, in turn, these people are more likely to abide by the law.

It is vital that victims attend the conference. In contrast to the New Zealand model, where the social worker is in charge, the federal police in Canberra are much more successful in getting the victim to come to the meeting. In New Zealand, only about half of the victims attend these meetings, partly because of poor notification and partly because of lack of trust. In Canberra, police deal with both the victims who suffer the emotional consequences of the crime, and the offender or co-offenders simultaneously. So the conference focuses on the harmful effects of the crime as a whole. As standard procedure, everybody who is part of causing the harm has to be there. All of the participants—the victim, the victim's family, the offender and the offender's family—sit in a circle with the police facilitator, who asks the questions. What harm was caused? How can that harm be repaired? Sometimes there is a community representative at the meeting who discusses the harm the offense has caused the community. Many crimes not only hurt the people who were directly involved, but may also hurt community organizations (e.g., businesses, churches and law enforcement).

Once all of these people are in a room, what happens next? First, the police facilitator asks the offender to describe what happened, how the day proceeded and how the crime happened. The offender usually makes a brief, mumbling, kind of shy statement. The big, bold offenders are a little less brave when they have the spotlight shining on them with everybody focusing on the bad thing that they did. Then the officer turns to the victim and asks him or her to describe the harm that they experienced from this crime, revealing the "ripple effect" that the crime may have on others. Sometimes what matters most is that the offender did not steal the car from somebody who could afford it, but stole a car from someone who is out of work and had an appointment for a job interview that day. Because the car was stolen, he couldn't get to the interview, and because he couldn't get to the interview, he didn't get the job. In turn, because he didn't get the job, the surgery his child was supposed to have had to be postponed.

All of the circumstances described during the meeting are presented in an emotional way that is never seen in a plea bargaining process. Often, as the victim describes the harm, the offender's mother or some other key family member starts to cry. This illustrates the impact of the victim's statement of harm on the offender's family. In turn, the police officer might say, "We all realize this was a very bad thing that the offender did, but if we facilitate him getting a job in the community, it may stop his tendency to damage the community. He may try to focus on how to repay the harm."

That leads to a very deliberate discussion in which all parties express ideas and opinions about how to fix the harm. At any time in the process, the offender has the option of terminating the conference and requesting that the case proceed through the traditional court process. Alternatively, if the offender refuses to agree to a plan for repairing the harm, then the case is sent to court. None of the admissions that the offender made during the conference will be used against him or her as evidence in court. In most cases, though, from the outset, the offenders are not disputing their guilt. During a typical conference, the officer writes up the agreement and gets the offender to sign it and apologize for the crime. This often leads to good feelings all around the room. When the officer assures the group that the offender will repay the harm and make a community service agreement, these feelings are accentuated.

Restorative justice is partly based on a theory by John Braithwaite (1996), who describes the "reintegrative shaming" ceremony of family discipline. When kids do something wrong, family members still love them and tell them they did a bad thing but they are not a bad person. This requires offenders to admit what they have done and to be *sincerely* sorry about it. There needs to be a separation of what they *did* from who they *are*. Even though they did a bad thing, it doesn't mean that they're bad all the time. By doing something bad, they are required to repair the harm by paying back the debt. Once the debt is paid, they have earned the right to return to the moral community of citizens who don't commit bad deeds. The Braithwaite theory emphasizes that if you give offenders the opportunity to apologize and make retribution, they are more likely to obey the law in the future. They will not have been forced into assuming the permanent label of being a bad person (e.g., the "scarlet letter").

Of course, a theory cannot be considered valid until it is tested with an experiment. The Canberra project involves three separate experiments. One experiment examines violent offenses, including armed robbery (excluding rape or sexual assault), committed by offenders under age 30. Another experiment looks at juveniles under 18 who commit a property crime that falls under one of two categories: (1) shoplifting cases with security guards who serve the role of victim, and (2) other cases involving a victim of burglary, theft, auto theft, and the like. The third and largest experiment is in the area of impaired driving. In Australia, the maximum legal blood alcohol level is .08, and the Australian police have the power to test anybody for alcohol at any time, so there are many arrests.

Preliminary Project Results

Time is the most important difference between the standard court process and restorative policing. The average amount of time spent on court cases is 17 minutes. This is a *sum* of time across all appearances, with an average of three different court appearances for a case dealing with juvenile offenses. The average amount of time spent on conferences, however, is 70 minutes. Arie Frieburg said, "No wonder you're getting good effects! If the judge took 70 minutes for each one of these cases, they could get the same result." I said, "Arie, I doubt there is a judge in the world who wants to spend 70 minutes talking about these crimes. She doesn't want to listen to the victim telling the story about it. She doesn't want to listen to the offender talking about it." It's not just that judges don't have time. They are not particularly inclined to do it.

The legal process is polarized in that there has to be a winner and a loser, and everything is a competition or contest. The legal process attempts to hijack the democratic idea of liberation, in which there is an open discussion and a problem-solving session on what to do about the crime. That is one of the reasons that no lawyers are allowed in the Canberra restorative justice conferences. It was not surprising to that there was some opposition to this project in the legal community—especially because the court system was self-supporting and had just built a new courthouse, and because what was normally paid by the offender in fines was being donated to charitable institutions as the Salvation Army.

As you can imagine, the 70 minutes the participants spend together involve an intensive process of talking about the harm, how to fix it, and the offender's future in terms of preventing further crimes. Of course, preventing repeat offending depends a great deal on the offender having adequate social support— family and friends who will try to keep him or her straightened out. This is an especially difficult task if the family and friends are criminals themselves. However, a lot of supporting evidence shows that criminals really want to obey the law. In fact, they say things along these lines during the conferences. The evidence also shows that having family, friends or any adult figure that the offenders care about—even football coaches—present at the conference increases their potential to feel real remorse about what they did, and to commit themselves to repairing the harm. In turn, they are less likely to recidivate. Clearly, the restorative justice conference is more fair when more people participate. In fact, the police will not hold a conference unless a minimum number of supporters are present.

What about the victims? A conference will not have an emotional impact unless the victim describes the harm that the offender caused. The victim is present in only 3 percent of court cases. However, the victim is present in 86 percent of restorative justice conferences. The primary reason that victims appear in only 3 percent of court cases is that police officers do not tell them about the court appearances. For conferences, a smaller percentage of victims said they were not notified in time to attend the conference. Timely notification is a very important factor when considering the victim's attendance at either a trial or conference. When the victims come to a conference, their reward is that they get reparation. In 83 percent of the cases that go to conference, the victims get some form of payback, whereas that only happens in 8 percent of court cases. Very often, victim reparation takes the form of the offender's increased acknowledgment of the crime. Three out of four conferences are successful in getting the offender to acknowledge his role in the crime. "Getting the offender to acknowledge" does not mean that the police officer is turning to the offender, twisting his arm, and saying, "Don't you think you ought to apologize?" The conference is run in such a way that the offender often feels moved to apologize to the victim. Usually this happens because a family member is twisting the offender's arm and saying, "Don't you think you ought to apologize?"

The victims may not care about the sincerity of the apology, as much as the fact that the apology was made. Something about this process seems to drive the victim's psychological reaction to the incident. When asked if they felt the need to protect themselves more now that they had been victimized, 78 percent of the victims in cases that went to court versus only 30 percent of victims in cases handled by restorative justice felt fearful. Clearly, victims who attend a conference are less fearful of subsequent victimization.

In one case, an offender in prison heard that one of his heroin-using buddies had raped his girlfriend. As soon as he got out of prison, he went to the buddy, knocked all his teeth out, and left him lying unconscious. Because both men were members of the heroin subculture, the police were skeptical that the court would accept the case. The case was diverted into this experiment, and went to conference. Several people from the heroin-using subculture, including the woman who had allegedly been raped, attended the conference. The battered victim claimed that the girlfriend had been having consensual sex with another one of the friends in this subculture, so he figured it was his turn next. Clearly, the woman did not agree. No one disputed the fact that the victim had done something to provoke the offender, or that the offender had knocked the guy's teeth out. But when the police officer asked whether the offender would compensate the victim $6,000 for dental work, the offender said no. The victim was primarily concerned that if the offender went to jail, the offender would become even more angry and kill him upon his release. The question of how to repair the harm, therefore, centered on the victim's psychological security. When another individual from the subculture pointed out that the two men, because they bought from the same dealer, were going to keep seeing one another, a proposal was made that they keep 100 yards from each other. Therefore, to repair the harm in this case, the offender was issued a restraining order to stay 100 yards away from the victim. Now, almost two years later, neither the victim nor the offender have had any further violent incidents, nor have they been arrested.

Throughout the course of the experiment, researchers have asked the victims, before and after the conference, if they felt anger toward the offender. Of the 60 percent who were angry before the conference, only 30 percent were still angry following the conference. In fact, this study found that about 20 percent of the victims whose cases go to court want to do some harm to the offender as retribution. However, only 8 percent of victims whose cases go to conference say that they feel that way. Of the cases that go to conference, 23 percent of victims feel sympathy for the offender before the conference. This figure nearly doubles to almost 43 percent of victims feeling sympathy after the conference.

Two-thirds of victims whose cases go to court expect that offenders will repeat. Only one-third of the victims whose cases go to conference expect the offender either to repeat against them specifically, or society in general.

Only about half of the court victims say they were pleased with the way the court dealt with their case. On the other hand, 72 percent of the conference victims say they were pleased. Even if there were no difference in the offender's response, one could argue that restorative justice is preferable simply because of the benefits for the victim. But the process is likely to be better for the offender as well. Offenders do not see these conferences as being more lenient, and they are not considered a "soft option."

The study also compared the average hours of community service assigned to the offenders for each approach. The restorative justice process has a much more intensive penalty, with an average of 16 hours of community service per offender compared with two-and-a-half hours on average assigned by the court. Emotional intensity is also greater, although not substantially greater. The researchers did not want the offenders to feel what Braithwaite calls "stigmatic shaming," but they did feel more "humiliated" in the conferences, at about 34 percent versus 28 percent. Eighty-four percent of offenders in conference felt that what they did was wrong, versus 68 percent of the offenders in court.

When it comes to repaying the harms and willingness to repay, the differences are much greater. About 80 percent of the offenders who go to conference believe they are repaying the harm they have caused to the victim. Meanwhile, only about 40 percent of those going to court feel that they are repaying the harm. Approximately the same numbers appear when offenders consider repaying the harm to society. Again, offenders who go to conference are more likely to say they are making up for what they did, clearing the debt and re-entering the community. Even though they are ashamed of what they did, these offenders have cleared their conscience. The conferences have also succeeded in making the offenders more conscious of the shame and disapproval they will risk by re-offending—86 percent versus 67 percent. This may not be a big difference, but it is certainly a move in the right direction. The bottom line is that there are big differences in the offenders' perspectives. Half of the offenders who go to conference say that as a result of the process, their respect for police increased, compared with 20 percent of offenders who go to court.

Who Owns Each Crime?

In terms of criminal justice goals, there is not much consideration of victims in general. The focus is on the offender. In a broader historical context, this raises the question of who *owns* the crime. Is the crime the property of the victim? Does the community have some ownership? What about the offender's ownership, in terms of control over what is to be done, and responsibility for dealing with the harm that has been caused?

Each owner has an interest in controlling different outcomes. Victims have an interest in achieving restoration of the harm, and perhaps retribution against the offender. Perhaps the most important interest is in the prevention of future crime against the victim. The state shares that interest, but the state really doesn't have a stake in restoration, except to the extent that it helps reinforce legal legitimacy and the prevention of further offenses.

As for the offenders' stake in the crime, one can argue that the offenders' best approach is to find a way out of the box that the offense has put them into. This draws a clear contrast to retributive justice. Sentencing guidelines focus on consistency of punishment across like cases, rather than on helping victims or even on deterrence. The emphasis is on inflicting the right amount of pain on the offender, and making it identical across similar cases. The emphasis of this retributive approach differs from the restorative justice emphasis of repairing the harm. There is concern for repairing harm not only to the victim, but also to the community (those who suffer the ripple effects of the harm). Ultimately, offenders harm themselves in ways that can also harm the community. The evidence is accumulating—people with arrest records have a harder time getting and keeping a job, and barriers in the labor force increase the odds that they will commit further offenses in the future. Therefore, by preventing that future harm to the victim and community, the offender, in fact, is repairing the present harm and preventing future harm to him- or herself in the process.

The issue of community ownership versus the legal system's or the state's ownership of the crime makes us draw some important distinctions. Community justice is not necessarily restorative justice. Community retributive justice is called lynching! It is important to remember that, although we may not want the lawyers in the room during the conference, the rule of law has to remain in the background with the option to take the case to court if necessary.

All of these issues raise a question: Do we want to continue with the state monopoly ownership of each crime, or do we want to focus on a partnership among the state, the community and the victim? Many people now think the victim should own a percentage of the crime, as should the community, as should the offender and the police.

The final remaining question is, is it fair to treat similar cases alike? One's first reaction would probably be to say yes. However, if you put it in the context of restorative justice, the answer is not so clear. For instance, imagine that a little old lady's house is burglarized. She will most likely be more psychologically and economically harmed than, say, a "double income no kids" couple who took two weeks to notice anything was missing from their house. The conference, in this instance, would probably come up with a more severe restoration for the little old lady then it would for the couple. Even though this is an inconsistent way of dealing with the harm, the process is based on the general proposition that it is not just the severity, but also the quality of the penalty. A penalty is determined by listening, talking and respecting the point of view of all parties concerned: the victim, the offender and the community.

Another very interesting finding was derived from an examination of 800 domestic violence arrests. An analysis was conducted of repeat offending in relation to what the offender told the researchers right after he had been arrested. Researchers asked offenders a series of questions relating to the way the police treated them while they were being arrested: "Did they listen to your side of the story? If they talked, did they treat you with respect?" Before computing the difference in repeat offending based on police politeness, the researchers reviewed the offender's entire record to determine the likelihood of re-offending. They also considered the police officers' opinion on whether the offender was likely to recidivate. Interestingly, if the police said yes and other things being equal, the police were very likely to have guessed accurately without even having known the offender's prior record.

Controlling for the offenders' prior records, the researchers found a striking result: When the offenders said the police did not listen to them or treat them with respect, they were much more likely to repeat their violent crimes. In fact, those offenders had a 40 percent re-offending rate over six months. Offenders who said they were treated fairly and listened to and/or supported by the police only had a 25 percent re-offending rate.

This suggests that the process of listening, the process of showing respect to all parties involved in the offense, is perhaps key to building not only respect for the police but also for the law. It gives us some ideas about how we might use this research by simply getting police to listen more to offenders.

These findings suggest there are ways to improve police capacity to react to and to solve problems—perhaps solve the more basic problems—of the community, victims and offenders. Success in the style—the participation—of this type of problem solving may be key to the police earning the respect of all who are involved in crimes.

REFERENCES

Braithwaite, J.1996. Reintegrative Shaming. In *Criminological Perspectives: A Reader*, edited by J. Muncie, E. McLaughlin and M. Langan.

CHAPTER 9

POLICING THE NEW AMERICA: IMMIGRATION AND ITS CHALLENGE[1]

William F. McDonald

This chapter is dedicated to Ed Powers, a high school English teacher, whose genius should not be judged by the work of his students.

Immigration: A Nexus of Issues

The Scope of the Problem. The challenge of immigration for the police is about a lot of things: violence and crime *by* immigrants but also violence and crime *against* immigrants. It is about methamphetamine trafficking, drunk driving, massive frauds (Brimelow 1995), spouse abuse, and urinating in public. But it is also about border bandits; xenophobia and hate crime; extortion; the revival of slavery, involuntary servitude and sweatshops; transnational organized crime networks; alien smuggling; and the trafficking of women and children. It is about ethnic-based gangs, corruption, the nature of community, and the pursuit of an ideal of mutual respect, dignity and equality. It is about police agencies crossing cultural and jurisdictional barriers to serve and protect.

[1] Research for this report was supported by award #95-IJ-CX-0110 from the National Institute of Justice, Office of Justice Programs, U.S. Department of Justice and by Georgetown University. I gratefully acknowledge the stimulus of discussions with Deborah Jones in developing this paper. Points of view and opinions in this document are those of the author and do not necessarily represent the official position or policies of the U.S. Department of Justice or Georgetown University.

Immigration: A Global Perspective. Human immigration is a global historical process that began in East Africa about 1.5 million years ago (Kottak 1991), and only became problematic when nation states arose and began controlling their borders and distinguishing between citizens and noncitizens. In today's post–Cold War, high-tech and economically integrated world, borders everywhere have become very porous, and movement around the planet very easy. Seven million people a day cross international borders (Schmid 1996).

People's desire to improve their lot or to escape political or environmental disasters has been a powerful motivator of migration. That is why most of our ancestors came to America. Others arrived here by way of forced migration during the slave trade. In 1992, an estimated 100 million people (2 percent of the world's population) were living outside of their homelands (Schmid 1996). An unknown proportion of them were illegal immigrants. Virtually all countries where opportunities exist are confronting the problem of illegal immigration (McDonald forthcoming). None seems to have found a fair, humane and effective solution (Cornelius, Martin, and Hollifield 1994).

Alien Smuggling. As always, when people want something that is forbidden, a market is created for illicit activities. The smuggling of humans has become the fastest growing new business of transnational organized crime. Although the exact amount of the increase cannot be measured with precision, rough estimates suggest that alien smuggling has risen dramatically since the collapse of the Soviet Union, particularly the long-distance smuggling of people from Asia to Western Europe and America. Many smuggled aliens willingly participate. Others are duped or coerced. All are vulnerable to exploitation, abuse and violence.

People are literally being bought and sold around the world (Maxwell 1977). Sweat shops, debt bondage and indentured servitude have made a remarkable comeback (e.g., Alexander 1981; Wysocki 1981; Stevens 1980; Blake 1984; Gorsline 1989; Whitaker 1982; Christianson 1981; Pryce 1989; Federation for American Immigration Reform 1992; Chiswick 1988; Branigin 1997). As of

September 1998, the United Nations High Commissioner for Human Rights estimated that some 4 million people a year are being "trafficked" for diverse purposes including "forcing women and children into sexually or economically...exploitative situations...as well as other illegal activities" (U.N. Office of the High Commissioner for Human Rights 1998). There are no systematic estimates of the extent to which illegal migrants are abused and criminally victimized (Davis and Erez 1998). But there are plenty of gruesome reports of smugglers, employers or bandits raping, beating, extorting, degrading, and killing migrants (e.g., Rawls 1981; Asher 1994; Rojas 1996; Constable 1995; Associated Press 1998a; Pyle 1998; Chin 1997; DeStefano 1997; Lieb 1998). Three recent cases in the United States include the New York ring of Mexicans who smuggled deaf Mexicans into the country, forced them to sell trinkets and controlled them with beatings (Associated Press 1998b); the Mexican family that smuggled women and forced them to work in brothels in Florida and South Carolina (Knight Ridder News Service 1998); and the sweatshop in suburban Los Angeles where 56 illegal immigrants from Thailand were forced to work in slave-like conditions (Swaboda and Webb Pressler 1995).

Global Organized Crime. Alien smuggling has ballooned into a multibillion-dollar global enterprise operating in dozens of countries. Organized crime earns between $5 and $7 billion a year worldwide from trafficking in illegal immigrants (Schmid 1996; Smith 1997a). Suppressing the smuggling of humans has emerged as one of the international community's highest priorities. It is a key component of the developing systemic response to global crime.

A global response requires a global change. The institutions of the modern administration of criminal justice began in the 19th century, and 19th century thinking shaped them. But it is precisely that kind of thinking that needs to be changed. We are in a "culture lag" (Ogburn 1922). Our institutions are out of step with the technological realities of our time. Criminals today are operating in a borderless world, while law enforcement agencies still operate within borders (Williams 1998). Criminals think and act globally. Law enforcement thinks and acts locally. Law enforcement must learn to think globally.

Reinventing the Police. It was not too surprising when in 1984 the Los Angeles Police Department (LAPD) discovered that 100 of its 237 outstanding murder warrants were for Mexican nationals who presumably had fled to Mexico (Gates and Ross 1990). But it came as a shock in the summer of 1998 when the Washington, D. C., Metropolitan Police Department reported that two-thirds of its 37 outstanding homicide warrants were for Salvadorans believed to have fled to El Salvador (Thomas-Lester 1998). In jurisdictions across the country, there is an increasing number of serious crimes in which the suspect is believed to have fled back to Mexico or Central America.

Recently, the international community has sped up its effort to find transnational criminals (Vlassis 1998). Many countries have signed treaties regarding extradition, mutual legal assistance, prisoner transfers, the abduction of children, and the return of stolen vehicles. These legal structures are important but not enough (McDonald 1995; Nadelmann 1993) . What is needed is a transnational law enforcement network capable of matching the transnational criminal networks. In other words, "It takes a network to catch a network" (Ronfeldt 1996).

Networks are not organizations per se. They are a form of organization through which individuals, groups or traditional organizations are linked together in ways that allow them to communicate and cooperate toward a goal. Local law enforcement agencies are already embedded in larger networks of other law enforcement agencies. Community policing has enabled the police to extend those networks into the community and into other government and private organizations.

With regard to transnational and global crime, the police need to go further. In addition to identifying and analyzing problems underlying discrete incidents, they need to look for transnational/global linkages underlying local problems. The prostitution ring, the foreign trinket vendor and the sweatshop are possible links to larger and more sinister activities (Rosenberg 1998). The analysis step of the SARA model needs to include a search for transnational connections (Goldstein 1990).

Institutions are invented and reinvented as needs and interests change. The world has changed. Our culture has changed. Immigration is driving more change. It remains for us to adjust police institutions to serve the new needs and move us closer to our ideals. The police are a 19th century institution that needs to be refitted for the realities of crime in the 21st century. The police were invented to manage conflicts in a society that became more ethnically diverse due to immigration. They worked in a cultural context in which bigotry and discrimination were openly tolerated. Today, immigration is again the source of conflict, but the context has changed.

This chapter will look at the police institution in the context of those changes, concluding with an examination of community policing and some examples of police responses to immigration. In principle, community policing is the right kind of philosophy for a democratic society. But community policing can be dangerous. It can lull political leaders into thinking that their police-community relations are fine, when in reality, deep resentments are brewing and might erupt into conflict, as evidenced by the 1991 Mount Pleasant riots in Washington, D.C. And community policing can easily go awry in hands of people who lack the vision and sensitivity to choose wisely among the many conflicting interests that surface when one starts asking people what they want of the police. The $35 million lawsuit against the Chandler, Ariz., Police Department by a group of Mexican Americans asked to prove their citizenship during a round-up of illegal migrants illustrates these dangers (Associated Press 1998c).

Immigration and the American Experience

The Pluralist Ideal. For Americans, the topic "immigration and the police" has special significance. In American history, there has been a long association among immigration, crime, the police, and racial and ethnic conflict. Many of today's problems of immigration are not new, although the cultural and legal contexts are.

Figure 1 illustrates total legal immigration trends from 1820 to 1980. America is a nation of immigrants. When the nation began, its population was ethnically diverse. The diversity was regarded as both remarkable and a great opportunity to build a new kind of nation. The new nation would be not just an experiment in democracy, but an experiment in pluralism, with many different people living together as one. It was believed that a new "race" was being created out of the blending of many races. At the time, the word "race" meant nationality or ethnic group (e.g., the French "race").

The pluralist ideal is expressed in the American national motto, which Congress had engraved on the Great Seal of the United States. It reads "E Pluribus Unum" (from the many, one). It is an ideal to which the Founding Fathers subscribed. George Washington stated, "The bosom of America is open...to the oppressed and persecuted of all Nations and Religions....Let them bring their language, habits and principles (good or bad)...but let them be prepared for intermixture with our people." Then they will be "assimilated...[and would] soon become *one people*"(emphasis added by author) (Schlesinger 1992).

Criminal Immigrants and American Policy. Although America has a special tie to immigration and pluralism, it is important to recognize the distinction between ideals and realities. Cultures are complex and contradictory. Cultural symbols cannot be accepted at face value. For Americans, the symbol of immigration is, of course, the lady in New York harbor bidding a generous welcome to all comers.

> "Give me your tired, your poor,
> Your huddled masses yearning to breathe free,
> The wretched refuse of your teeming shore.
> Send these, the homeless, tempest-tost to me..."

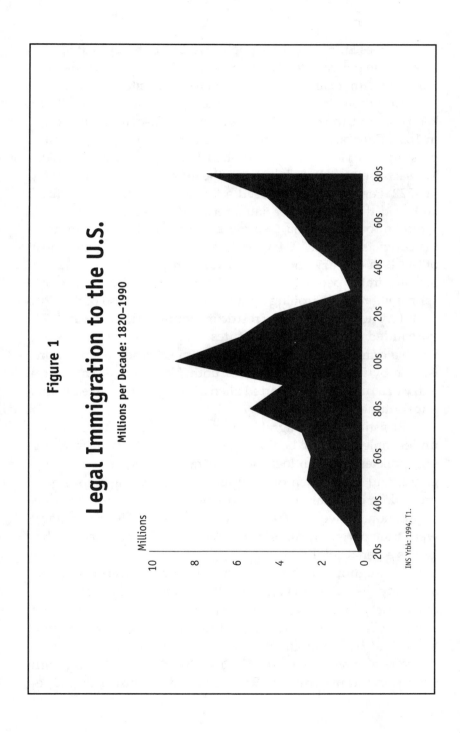

Figure 1

Legal Immigration to the U.S.

Millions per Decade: 1820–1990

INS Yrbk: 1994, T1.

So goes Emma Lazarus' poem, a noble sentiment but hardly an accurate portrayal of American immigration policy. Indeed, if anything, American policy has been the opposite.

First the colonies, and later the states tried repeatedly to keep the tired, the poor and the wretched refuse from our shores. In 1639, Plymouth, Mass., required the removal of foreign paupers; in 1676, Maryland prohibited landing convicts; in 1700, Massachusetts excluded the lame, the infirm and the dependent; in 1722, Pennsylvania imposed a tax on every criminal landed and held the ship owner liable for any damages; and in 1788, Virginia, South Carolina, Georgia, and New York penalized landing convicts (Abbott 1924; Christianson 1981). Throughout most of the 19th century, the states tried to prevent the immigration of undesirable people. The federal government did not take responsibility for controlling immigration until the end of the 19th century. The first federal law restricting immigration came in 1871. It excluded convicts and prostitutes. Illegal entry per se was not made a crime until 1929, when it became a misdemeanor punishable by fine, imprisonment or both. The same act made re-entry of a previously deported alien a felony punishable by fine, imprisonment or both.

Resisting the immigration of criminals, vagrants and other undesirables was the beginning of the struggle over immigration policies between local and central governments. First England, and then much of Europe used America as a dumping ground for criminals, vagrants, paupers, and unwanted surplus population. Between 1700 and 1800, an estimated 50,000 convicts were transported to America (Ekirch 1987). In fact, Georgia began as a penal colony.

Throughout the 19th century, European powers continued to empty their asylums and give their inmates one-way tickets to America, often to New York City. In the fall of 1854, after two ships had landed 150 paupers and 49 convicts, Mayor Fernando Wood had had enough. He protested to President Pierce that the federal government should bear the costs of dealing with such immigrants (Busey 1969). The federal government responded but not in vulgar haste. In 1994, it began releasing millions of dollars to states and local governments as reimbursements for the costs of incarcerating criminal aliens. By May 1998, the federal government had paid more than $1.1 billion to the program (PRNewswire 1998; Mittelstadt 1998).

Anti-Immigrant Violence and the Police. During the 19th century, 19 million immigrants, mostly Europeans, poured into America (U.S. Department of Justice, Immigration and Naturalization Service 1996). Differences in the immigrants' religious and ethnic character touched off xenophobic reactions, ranging from mere ridicule to bigotry, discrimination, and anti-immigrant lynchings and riots. Often the underlying issue was competition for jobs. Immigrants were often used to break strikes or lower wages (Calavita 1984). Demeaning caricatures of ethnic groups were common. Discrimination was practiced openly, without fear of public disapproval.

Immigration shaped 19th century American police institutions, and they shaped the immigrant experience. Many police departments were founded in response to anti-immigrant violence. In fact, the Boston Police Department was established in 1837 after the Broad Street riot, touched off by a confrontation between an Irish funeral procession and local firefighters (Calavita 1984). The American police made possible an ethnically and racially diverse society, but not always in ways that would be approved today. In the north and central states, police departments reduced anti-immigrant violence. They also provided immigrants with a place to sleep and often with a job. In the South a special police institution known as the slave patrol or plantation police regulated the movement of slaves, who were the forced immigrants of an earlier time (Williams and Murphy 1990).

Nowhere is cultural change more evident in our history than in our move away from bigotry and intolerance. We abolished slavery and involuntary servitude in 1865. A hundred years later, we prohibited discrimination, and a quarter of a century after that, we made crime motivated by hate eligible for enhanced sentencing.

The New Immigration

The Demographic Transformation. These developments could not have happened at a better time. Immigration has been rising sharply. The immigration laws of 1964 and 1986 have caused a momentous shift in the ethnic composition of the U.S. population. We are becoming far more diverse. This country used to be overwhelmingly white, non-Hispanic and Protestant of European descent. Majority-minority relations in the United States were thought of in bipolar terms: white vs. black. Today we are headed toward a society in which there will be no majority ethnic or racial group. We will all be minorities and will all want the kind of policing that respects minorities and diversity.

By 1996, more than half the foreign-born population in the United States was from Hispanic cultures, and more than a quarter was from Asia (U.S. Bureau of the Census 1997). Mexico is by far the largest single source country. The Census Bureau estimates that by 2050 non-Hispanic whites may be a minority in the country as a whole (United States Bureau of the Census 1997). Hispanics will surpass African Americans as the most populous minority by 2010. They have already done so in certain gateway cities (e.g., New York, Houston, Los Angeles, and Miami).

More than two-thirds of the legal immigrants live in six states: California (22%), New York (16.8%), Texas (9.1%), Florida (8.7%), New Jersey (6.9%), and Illinois (4.6%) (U.S. Department of Justice, Immigration and Naturalization Service 1998); and 60 percent of all foreign-born residents live in six cities: Los Angeles, New York, San Francisco, Chicago, Miami, Washington, D.C., and Houston (Booth 1998; Holmes 1998). In addition there are approximately 5 million illegal immigrants in the United States (Branigin 1997). About 40 percent live in California, and another 40 percent live in only five other states (Texas, New York, Florida, Illinois, and New Jersey) (Associated Press 1997a).

Xenophobic Responses to the New Immigration. As in the 19th century, the new immigration has been accompanied by xenophobia, conflict and crime motivated by the hatred of foreigners. In many incidents across the country, immigrants have been threatened, assaulted or otherwise victimized. For example, Turner, Maine, is a rural township of about 5,000 people (Maine is the second "whitest" state in the nation). In the 1980s, Mexicans began arriving—today hundreds live there, many working for the world's largest brown egg producer. In 1995, two white men harassed a group of Mexicans at the convenience store, shouting, "Go back to Mexico!" then pursued them at high speed, firing shots and injuring one of them. The assailants were subsequently convicted of federal civil rights violations (McDonnell 1998). We have not had any lynchings yet—at least none that have been proven. But in the 1980s, newspapers reported that Ku Klux Klan members in San Diego County boasted of "beheading and burying undocumented aliens" (Eisenstadt and Thorup 1994). In March 1998, the San Bernardino County District Attorney's Office, acting on information supplied by the Los Angeles Police Department's Anti-Terrorist Division, alleged that four men belonging to a militia group were plotting to massacre illegal aliens as they entered the country. The group's leader, Glenn Yee, a reserve officer with the Irwindale Police Department, said he knew nothing of the border plot, and that the LAPD had fabricated evidence to frame his multiracial group (to which some LAPD officers belong) (Lait 1998).

Immigration produces winners and losers. Among the losers are low-skilled workers and African Americans, who are losing both jobs and hard-won political power. In Los Angeles in 1977, there were 2,500 unionized African-American janitors. By 1985 the number had decreased to 600 due to the use of non-union immigrant labor (James 1991). Some African Americans resent the fact that they led the struggle for civil rights, but Latinos and others are reaping the benefits. For example, in the Watts area in Los Angeles, the Martin Luther King Hospital was a symbol of black power when it opened in 1974. Today most of its patients are Latino. Latino critics complain that the number of African-American doctors and staff is disproportionately high (Timms and Suhler 1998). The tensions have erupted in various settings—at school board meetings (Booth 1998), in gang violence and race riots. The 1992 Los Angeles riot immediately took on a racial character—Korean-owned businesses in largely African-American neighborhoods were singled out (Chang 1994). The 1991 Mount Pleasant riot in Washington, D.C., was a protest by the Salvadoran community against the primarily African-American police force and political establishment (Manning 1997).

Criminality and Victimization Among Immigrants. The new immigration has brought crime and disorder with it, although its extent cannot be measured precisely because our data do not capture immigrant status reliably, if at all. Determining immigrant status usually relies on what the arrestee claims. It was not until the prison overcrowding crisis collided with the illegal immigration crisis in the late 1970s that studies of immigrant or "noncitizen" crime began (e.g., D'Amato 1983; McDonald 1997b, 1998).

Those few studies focused mostly on the criminality of immigrants, rather than on immigrants as victims or witnesses. The picture that emerged was fragmentary, and neither very surprising nor particularly useful for police policy. It showed that states with large foreign-born populations also have large numbers of foreign-born people in their prisons. In 1994 there were approximately 21,000 illegal aliens in seven state prisons (71 percent in California, 10 percent in New York) (Clark et al. 1994). The number of foreign-born people in American prisons rose sharply after the late 1970s (e.g., D'Amato 1983; Clark et al. 1994; Scalia 1996), and noncitizens were more likely than citizens to be arrested (or incarcerated) for certain types of crime. However, the type varied among communities and over time from property offenses, to drug crime, to violent crime, to drunk driving (Texas Criminal Justice Policy Council 1995). One study reported that immigration had no effect on crime rates, and that youths born abroad were less likely than native-born youths to be criminally active.

There are no national studies of U.S. immigrants as victims, but Angelika Pitsela conducted one in Germany (Pitsela 1988). One recent study asked a national sample of criminal justice officials about difficulties immigrant victims have in dealing with the American criminal justice system. The consensus was that immigrants are less likely to report their victimizations than others are. A study of the Vietnamese community in Southern California (known as "Little Saigon") found that Vietnamese immigrants do not report crime to the police not only because of their distrust of police from their homeland experience, but because admitting to being a victim is a way to "lose face" (McLaughlin and Jesilow forthcoming). Also, Vietnamese victims believe that someone from their own culture could not help them. As one middle-aged man explained, "First, it is humiliating to admit to someone of your own culture that you are being victimized." Second, many victims believe that Vietnamese think alike and don't have solutions to their problems (McLaughlin and Jesilow forthcoming).

Police Responses to the New Immigration. The police have been responding to the new immigration for a long time. In jurisdictions where refugees from Vietnam, Cambodia, Iraq, and elsewhere have been resettled, the police received special federal funds to meet the challenges. In other places, they developed strategies on their own. The refugees appear to have gotten disproportionately better attention than mere immigrants—especially immigrants from more familiar sources such as Mexico. The availability of special federal funds to assist with the resettlement process allowed some police departments (e.g., Lincoln, Neb.) to launch creative and comprehensive outreach programs.

The range of responses is notable for its inventiveness, reach and sense of justice. Many of the challenges are the same whether the immigrants are legal or illegal. But illegal immigrants do represent an extra challenge. Their fear of deportation makes them more vulnerable and their illegal status raises questions about the police role in enforcing federal immigration law.

The police responses to the new immigration include: (1) increasing foreign language capability, (2) improving police officers' cultural competence through cultural sensitivity training, (3) increasing diversity in the police ranks, (4) educational programs for immigrants and host communities, (5) police-community coalitions, (6) immigrant community liaison officers and ministations, (7) programs to prevent or solve crime by or against immigrants, and (8) transnational law enforcement units.

Enhanced Foreign Language Capabilities. Overcoming language barriers is not new. But the scale of the problem has increased greatly, driving up costs for interpreters and putting a premium on multilingual police officers. In fact, in Lincoln, Neb., there are 65 different languages spoken as a result of the refugee resettlement programs. According to Captain Catherine Citta of the Lincoln, Neb., Police Department (in a June 1998 phone interview), the police department has between five and eight translators on call at a time. Providing foreign language assistance is the most common service to immigrants (Davis and Erez 1998). Agencies are trying to improve that service by giving officers language lessons, hiring bilingual officers (DeGeneste and Sullivan 1997) and exploiting technology. Telephone answering systems have been programmed to answer in multiple languages, and the AT&T foreign language lines, available through the 911 system, have been used to forward callers to interpreters of their language.

Additionally, some police agencies have translated into foreign languages many documents and manuals that describe everything from basic constitutional rights and how to report a crime, to driver training and any topic for which immigrant communities have special needs.

Greater Cultural Competence. In a multicultural society, the concept of community policing must include the notion of cultural competence for the police—that is, police must understand the culture of the people they are trying to serve and protect. In Lexington, Ky., a community of illegal Mexican immigrants showed up almost overnight. Hispanic involvement in serious crime rose dramatically from five (of 594) arrests for homicide in 1994 to 200 (of 1,298) in 1998. The police department is giving officers Spanish language instruction, but it is also sending officers to live in central Mexico to learn the culture (Honeycutt 1998;

Bennett 1998a, 1998b). The first two officers who returned from their immersion in Mexican culture reported that their Spanish language skills improved more in one month than they had in several years of instruction. One of those officers became the main police liaison with the Mexican community. An unanticipated benefit is a new perspective on resisting arrest. The officers noticed that the Mexican police do not routinely handcuff all arrestees, and that this seemed related to fewer problems with resisting arrest. In a telephone interview on 7 January 1999, Assistant Chief Fran Root of the Lexington, Ky. Police Department stated that the department is going to re-examine its handcuffing policy.

Increased Diversity Among Police. In a multicultural society, effective policing requires a police force that reflects that diversity. Since the Equal Employment Opportunity Act in 1972, law enforcement agencies have moved to recruit ethnic minorities (National Crime Prevention Council 1994). In localities where immigrant communities have mushroomed, the police have tried to build bridges with the new communities by recruiting officers from the cultural group. This quick fix, however, has its limitations.

Some immigrant groups do not want their family members to be associated with the police—at least not initially. The experience with some Asian groups has been instructive. In Lincoln, Neb., where a large number of Southeast Asian people were resettled in the 1980s, the police tried to recruit members of the group. They succeeded in hiring one young man, who eventually quit under tremendous pressure from family and friends. Even the interpreters from the community were pressured not to work for the police, as mentioned by Captain Citta in a 30 June 1998 telephone interview. These pressures abated as the Lincoln Police Department succeeded in its campaign to win the refugees' confidence and show that they were not the same kind of police that the refugees left behind in their homelands.

Initially, refugee and law enforcement relations had gotten off to a rough start. Refugees were arrested for fishing in the lake without fishing licenses—an unimaginable requirement for them. Then, because there were no interpreters or no probation officers who could speak their languages, they served time in jail for a violation that normally results in a minor fine. The Lincoln Police Department set about rectifying these cultural snafus. It lined up interpreters, had materials of all kinds translated into native languages and distributed, and produced and distributed free videotaped lessons and explanations about various aspects of local government, how to access city services, and certain features of American culture and normative expectations. (Many refugees owned VCRs so that they could play tapes in their own languages.) According to Captain Citta in a 25 January 1999 phone interview, the department also ran "citizen academies," where 40 or so members of the refugee community attended a class at which the police told them "everything that we do."

Educational Programs. The police have initiated a wide variety of educational programs for immigrants and refugees, alone or in cooperation with others. The programs cover topics from English language instruction to driver education; from personal safety and crime prevention to how to report a crime and how the criminal justice system works. Several programs are designed not only to help immigrants adjust to the unfamiliar environment, but also to manage tensions and prevent crimes of various kinds. Hate crime, for example, is often rooted in violent reactions to differences between people. So the Willows, Calif., Police Department's community relations officer makes presentations to community groups explaining the ways of the new immigrants, dispelling myths and stereotypes.

Domestic violence is as serious a problem in immigrant communities as elsewhere. Of course, departments with mandatory arrest policies are not changing their policies for immigrants. The Lincoln, Neb., Police Department found that spouse abuse in the Southeast Asian community often happened because the women did not want to get pregnant and resisted their husbands' advances. Physical resistance was the only means of birth control they knew. According to Captain Citta in a 1998 phone interview, the captain in charge of the refugee assimilation project, with an interpreter's help, provided birth control instruction to refugee women.

The domestic assault problem was not just over birth control. It was linked to the tensions caused by reversal of the relative power of men and women in migrating from Asian to American culture. The sudden loss of the legitimacy of male domination, and the new equality and freedom for females in the United States, has been a source of conflict and misunderstanding in immigrant communities. Captain Citta recalls two immigrant men on separate occasions telling her that they did not beat their wives anymore, not because they believed that they did not have a right to do so, but because they did not like going to jail.

Coalitions, Partnerships and Task Forces. The possibilities for coalitions or partnerships among police, immigrant groups and other organizations concerned with immigrants' well-being are endless. Youth clubs, cultural centers, mutual assistance associations, community associations, ethnic and religious organizations, human rights groups, victims' rights groups, schools and colleges, business associations, and many others are ready and willing to work with the police to help integrate foreigners, manage tensions, overcome cultural misunderstandings and xenophobia, and prosecute crime. Many partnerships could be cited as examples but the one formed between the City of Portland, Ore., and an organization of H'mong refugee leaders is particularly notable for its explicit recognition of and hence respect for the norms of the immigrant group. A letter of agreement signed by the Police Chief Tom Potter, and Paul Pia Cha, the president of the H'mong American Unity Association, reads:

> WHEREAS the City of Portland has made it a concern of priority to empower the citizenry of the City to direct the Bureau of Public Safety to work collaboratively with the various and diverse communities...We...pledge the honor of our respective offices, and the resources of our respective organizations, toward the execution of a

comprehensive partnership agreement of mutual
policies and practices conforming to the aspira-
tions of the Oregon Constitution, the expectations
of Federal, State and local law, in deepest respect
toward the ethno-cultural norms of the H'mong
customary law (where such law is not inconsistent with...Oregon law) (National Crime Prevention Council 1994).

One nontraditional partner with whom the police need to
establish ties is the consular authorities of local immigrants' countries of origin. Consular protection is a long-standing principle
of international law. Foreigners have the right to receive help
from their consulates to ensure their rights under the host
country's laws. Consulates want to be notified when their citizens have been taken into custody. In fact, the Mexican government maintains a network of 40 officers in the United States and
regards protecting the rights of Mexican immigrants as one of its
highest priorities.

Outreach: Liaisons and Ministations. Police have used
storefront operations and designated immigrant liaison officers
to establish bridges to immigrant communities. For example, the
Philadelphia Police Department and District Attorney's Office
have outreach programs directed at Southeast Asian immigrants.
The police department has two ministations, each located near
the relevant ethnic community. One is for a Vietnamese police
liaison staff person who attends meetings of Vietnamese organizations, discusses how to report crimes to the police, and explains
how the U.S. criminal justice system works. Vietnamese residents
living anywhere in the city are encouraged to contact the liaison
to report crimes or get feedback on the status of investigations.
There is a similar liaison for Cambodians (Davis and Erez 1998).
However, it has been reported that some liaison officers often
experience role conflicts. They feel that they are "working in two
camps at the same time," and expected to solve all the problems
for everyone (National Crime Prevention Council 1994).

Special Crime Prevention and Crime Solution Programs Regarding Immigrants. Virtually all of the programs mentioned so far can be considered crime prevention or crime solution measures in a general sense. Additional operations have been more directly targeted at either preventing crimes against immigrants, or solving crimes involving immigrants.

The best-known local police initiative to protect immigrants is the border banditry task force established in 1976 by the San Diego Police Department under Chief Bill Kolender. The task force was nicknamed by its team members "the Border Alien Robbery Force" (BARF) and memorialized by Joseph Wambaugh in his book, *Lines and Shadows*. The unit was created because of the high crime rate in a small strip of land just north of the international border at Tijuana (where many illegal immigrants make their nightly crossings). In 1975, there were 130 known cases of robbery (with multiple victims), three rapes, three homicides, and many other crimes believed to have gone unrecorded (Kolender 1978).

These victims were not Americans; they were entering the country illegally at a time when the people of San Diego were becoming increasingly impatient with illegal immigration. These immigrants were among the most powerless people imaginable. There was no constituency in the San Diego demanding that they be protected. There was no reason to care about them except for the fact that they were human beings. And so, San Diego's police department put one sergeant and nine patrol officers in the hills at night to stop the killing, raping and robbing. Within five months, they had charged 131 people with 203 criminal offenses, and the incidence of local youth gangs preying on immigrants ceased (Kolender 1978).

The initiative had an important ripple effect. The Mexican government followed suit and established a similar unit on its side of the border. The unit, known as Grupo Beta, has established a remarkably favorable reputation among Mexicans as well as with U.S. law enforcement agencies. It has been so successful that the Mexican government has instituted about a dozen cop-ies of it at other border locations (Freedberg 1994; Rotella 1992; Golden 1997; Romero 1991).

Rent a Cop. One of the obstacles in dealing with immigrant criminals is the problem of not being able to infiltrate ethnic groups. Physical and cultural differences serve as shields for criminal enterprises. Ethnic crime groups are well aware of this, and prefer to deal only with members of their own ethnic group. Even if the police manage to recruit a few members of that ethnic group, those officers quickly become known to the local community.

The solution is to rent a cop from somewhere else. Some law enforcement agencies have established partnerships with foreign law enforcement agencies. In an interview at the Executive Leadership Seminar on Strategic Approaches to Transnational Crime and Civil Society at Georgetown University in Washington, D.C. on 22 July 1998, a former Drug Enforcement Agency (DEA) agent indicated that the DEA arranged to have Chinese police officers flown in from Hong Kong to infiltrate Chinese gangs in New York City. The little town of Gilroy, Calif., asked its sister city in Baja California, Tecate, to whom it donates used equipment, to loan it two police officers to help break up a local drug ring that the DEA was unable to penetrate, according to Sergeant Daniel Castanedo of the Gilroy, Calif., Police Department in a 21 October 1998 interview.

Partnering with Foreign Law Enforcement. It is difficult for American law enforcement officers to imagine cooperating with law enforcement officials from countries that have an image of less than professional law enforcement, or outright corruption. In the late 1970s, globalization began forcing federal and local agencies to rethink those biases.

At the federal level, Justice Department attorneys recall that in the 1970s, when they were investigating drug trafficking by the Sicilian mafia, they never considered working together with Italian police and prosecutors because they did not trust them (Martin 1991, 1998). However, they kept bumping into the Italian officials because both sides were investigating the same Mafia groups in what became known as the "Pizza Connection" case (Blumenthal 1988; Jacobs, Panarella, and Worthington 1994). On one occasion, two Justice Department attorneys arranged to meet with two Italian magistrates. The Italians were Giovanni Falcone, the magistrate whom the Mafia has since assassinated, and Gianni DiGennero. The Americans were Richard Martin and Louis Freeh, the current director of the FBI.

Something happened at lunch. They liked each other, they trusted each other, and they realized that both countries have people of integrity working in law enforcement, that such people can be found and worked with, and that both sides would be better off working together than alone. Out of that meeting came the first binational anti-crime task force, the U.S.-Italian Task Force against the Mafia.

Crosscultural breakthroughs also happen at the local level. Along the border with Mexico, binational law enforcement relations in the past have been cautious and limited—even when friendly—but often were strained or nonexistent. In some localities, police agencies from either side of the border exchanged information and did occasional favors. But they tended to see themselves as living in separate worlds. Differences in language, law and culture, and the long history of troubles along the border reinforced that separation (Carter 1978, 1979a, 1979b).

Procedures for dealing with criminals who fled to Mexico were mostly nonexistent. The United States and Mexico have had an extradition treaty since 1861 (Malloy 1910). But extradition is subject to the politics of international relations. Mexico, like many countries, was unwilling to extradite its nationals and did not extradite anyone for years. American law enforcement agencies despaired of ever getting criminals back. In the absence of legal procedures, unsavory practices developed. Aggrieved victims hired bounty hunters to bring back wanted suspects or property. The American police themselves sometimes kidnapped suspects and brought them back, or asked Mexican police to deliver suspects to the border (Nadelmann 1993; Zagaris and Padierna Peralta 1997).

In the late 1970s, an American law enforcement officer named Ruben Landa discovered a promising legal procedure. He was working Mexican liaison duties for the California Department of Justice. While Landa was on business in Mexico, a Mexican attorney told him about Article 4 of the Mexican Penal Code, which provides for a procedure known as "foreign prosecution." Many countries in the civil law tradition have it. Mexico could prosecute criminals on behalf of a foreign government if the crime had a Mexican connection, meaning either the criminal or the victim was a Mexican national. The country requesting the prosecution had to supply the evidence and appropriate documents in Spanish. Mexico would then conduct the prosecution itself and at its own expense.

In 1981, California sent Mexico the first case. Since then, several hundred have been sent. In 1985, after the LAPD discovered all those unserved homicide warrants for Mexican nationals, it learned about the foreign prosecution procedure, established a special unit, and began filing cases (Gates and Ross 1990). In the early 1990s, Texas Attorney General Dan Morales learned about the procedure and established a foreign prosecution unit, as have all the border states and several local jurisdictions in California (Gilbreath 1995). On the other side, the Mexican Attorney General's Office has established a special unit to assist with the increasing volume of foreign prosecutions, and has located three deputy prosecutors at consulates in the United States to help local law enforcement make these cases.

The Americans and the Mexicans are satisfied with the results. Criminals who used to operate with impunity are being arrested and put away for substantial sentences (Council 1996). Foreign prosecution provides a vital alternative to the stark choice between impunity or lawlessness. In fact, the LAPD expanded operations to other Central American countries, and handles about 25 homicide cases a year (Yi 1998). It illustrates the fact that law enforcement systems with different traditions, different resources and different degrees of professionalism can nonetheless work together and do justice in individual cases.

The Limits of Community Policing. Not all police responses to immigration have been exemplary. The police are a reflection of the American people and, despite considerable progress, some Americans continue to be troubled by pluralism and immigration. Some police continue to be insensitive and unresponsive to minorities, even when the police themselves are minorities. The fact that a police department establishes a problem-oriented community policing program does not mean it truly understands the fundamentally democratic spirit of this philosophy, or its view of the police as human rights workers and agents of democracy.

The essence of community policing is not about repairing broken windows, organizing neighborhood watches, or putting the police in storefront offices. Those are the trees, not the forest! Community policing is not a program. It is a vision. It is about making *community* out of *disunity*. It is not something that can be delegated. The entire force must be involved and the entire community must be considered. Law enforcement cannot alienate some people in the community while trying to respond to the concerns of others.

Chief Ray Davis of Santa Ana, Calif., understood this, and in 1983, he challenged the INS practices of questioning people at bus stops and cruising residential neighborhoods looking for illegal aliens. His department would no longer support INS street round-ups of possible illegal immigrants. He maintained that such tactics were useless. "When you've arrested 1,000 illegal aliens and 995 of them are right back within a couple of days, then it's time to start rethinking your policies." More important, the round-ups destroyed the relationship he was trying to build with the community. He was pioneering a new philosophy that he referred to as "community policing" (New York Times 1983; Skolnick and Bayley 1986). After a round-up, his phones would ring off the hook with desperate Latinos searching for missing family members feared shipped off to Mexico, or complaining about being harassed just because they looked Mexican.

More recently the Chandler, Ariz., Police Department wanted to do good. If they had consulted Ray Davis, they might have done better. They got a federal grant to implement a problem-oriented community policing program. They went through all the steps: conducted surveys, removed the signs of crime, and held meetings to find out what residents wanted. Some people from a section of town where illegal immigrants gathered for pick-up work wanted the immigrants removed. There was a report that some immigrants were bothering the children at a nearby school.

The Chandler police invited the Border Patrol in for a joint operation. They rounded up more than 400 illegal immigrants and deported them (Associated Press 1997b; Kelley 1997; Drake 1998). But they infuriated dozens of Mexican Americans whom they stopped and asked for proof of citizenship. More than a year later, and after two lawsuits and a scathing report by the Attorney General's Office, a tidal wave of illegal immigrants continues to flow through Chandler. But at least some progress toward true community policing has been made. A human relations commission has been appointed, and a Hispanic police liaison officer has been named. Police officers and civilian employees have attended nearly 1,500 hours of classes on cultural awareness and hate crimes, and there is a proposal to teach Spanish to all officers (Magruder 1998).

The 1991 Mount Pleasant riot in Washington, D.C., was about police-community relations in a city where the police department and the political administration was predominantly African American, and the police have neighborhood advisory councils to get community input. The incident began when three Metropolitan Police Department officers stopped a 30-year-old Salvadoran immigrant who had been drinking in a park. When he drew a knife on the Hispanic female officer who was handcuffing him, her black female partner shot him, nonfatally. Word of the incident spread immediately and Hispanic youths went on a rampage.

Virtually all Hispanic neighborhood residents cited police abuse as the reason for the riot. "It's just like in Guatemala, except that what happens back home during the day happens here at night," said one immigrant (James 1991). "The same oppression that there is in my country...is here too. The police are the same as in El Salvador. For the simple pleasure of it, they harass people. The rioting is the response to years of oppression," said another (James 1991).

Mayor Dixon responded that Hispanics had not tried hard enough to integrate themselves into the community:

> I do think that in order to become a part of the community here you have to make an effort. Hispanics are not involved in ANC [Advisory Neighborhood Councils] or town meetings. They say, 'When in Rome do as the Romans do.'...It's to everyone's advantage to learn how to speak English...You cannot have people drinking in public, because that is an inappropriate and criminal activity...And you have to respond to that symbol of authority in whatever forms it takes in our culture...(James 1991).

Hispanics responded that assimilation of poorly educated, non–English-speaking, immigrants from a culture where drinking in public, urinating on the street and throwing garbage on the sidewalk is commonplace, is not easy. A Peruvian baker pointed out that town hall meetings and neighborhood councils were completely foreign to the immigrants and did nothing to integrate them into the community (James 1991).

Perhaps a more proactive approach to reducing cultural conflicts might have been taken—as many agencies have done. Whether it is spouse abuse, drinking or urinating in public, throwing garbage on the streets, or fishing without a license, the police do not have to wait for violations to happen before starting the acculturation process. Agencies can do as the Lincoln Police Department did with the Asian refugees. It assumed that the immigrants wanted to be law abiding citizens, and would be if they knew what the expectations were and how to meet them.

An educational campaign, a place to drink and visit, and a few urinals might have averted some encounters between the Salvadorans and the D.C. police, and perhaps even the riot.

The Police Response to Illegal Immigration. No account of immigration and the police would be complete without saying something about the police reaction to illegal immigration. The role of the local police in the enforcement of immigration law has been restructured. After decades of close cooperation with the INS and the Border Patrol in apprehending illegal aliens, the local police have taken themselves out of that partnership, either on their own initiative or by order of local authorities.

As the illegal immigration crisis heated up and the federal government was unable to control the borders, the local police became a key asset fought over in the larger struggle about immigration control policy. Restrictionists wanted to use the police to help solve the illegal immigration crisis. The police themselves (for the most part), as well as immigration and refugee advocates and ethnic minorities, particularly Mexican Americans, wanted the police out of the business of immigration control. The latter group has prevailed. In 1996, Congress authorized the Attorney General to deputize local police departments to enforce immigration law. So far, no department has taken on that role (Donaldson 1998).

This disconnect between local police and immigration law enforcement is remarkable for several reasons. It comes at a time when police agencies are trying to be responsive to community wishes, and one of the clear wishes of the community for the past several years is that something be done about illegal immigration. It reverses past police policies whereby the police willingly enforced immigration law. Police departments across the country have responded similarly, even though they are separate and autonomous units. And it represents the opposite development from what is happening in Europe where local police are taking on traditional immigration enforcement functions, as the European Union eliminates interior borders (European Commission 1997).

Before the civil rights revolution of the 1960s, and before immigration rates started to rise, most police agencies willingly cooperated with the INS. In the 1930s, the New York Police Department established a special unit called the Criminal Aliens Bureau, whose purpose was to round up and investigate all aliens with criminal records to determine if there were grounds for deportation. If so, they would be turned over to the INS for deportation.

The last time the United States could claim that it had control over its border with Mexico was in 1954, at the conclusion of a massive nationwide round-up of Mexican illegal immigrants known as "Operation Wetback." It was orchestrated by the INS, but state and local law enforcement agencies in the Southwestern and Central states joined in the round-up. Even radio stations supported the effort, calling on citizens to report illegal immigrants to the police. More than 50,000 Mexicans—some of them American citizens—were driven back into Mexico (European Commission 1997).

As recently as the early 1970s, some police agencies were paid monthly per capita fees for arresting illegal immigrants on behalf of the INS. In 1972, San Diego County Sheriff John Duffy issued an order to taxicab drivers to report suspected illegal aliens to the police. Drivers were given a code to notify their dispatcher to notify the police. Mexican Americans, the cab drivers and their union all objected to the order. But it was supported by Attorney General Evelle Younger, in an opinion that stated "any law enforcement officer may call upon any citizen or private company to aid in the detection and prevention of crime" (Anonymous 1973). In 1973, the San Diego Police Department had a policy of detaining and questioning illegal aliens. When the policy was challenged by Mexican Americans, Chief Ray Hoobler defended it and was supported in an opinion by Attorney General Evelle Younger (Anonymous 1973).

The parting of the ways between local police and immigration enforcement began in the 1980s with people like Chief Ray Davis and Chief Daryl Gates of the LAPD (Lopez and Connell 1996; McDonnell 1996). About the same time, local and state political authorities issued orders to their law enforcement agencies prohibiting them from cooperating with the INS (Levine 1988; Skerry 1995). By 1994, a poll of 78 cities found that more than a third of them did not inform the INS of illegal immigrants who turned up in the course of routine law enforcement activities (U.S. Conference of Mayors 1994).

While local law enforcement agencies were moving away from enforcement of immigration law, the federal government was forging a new kind of partnership with local law enforcement. It was designed to deport criminal aliens more efficiently by improving the procedures for identifying them during criminal record checks and through joint crime task forces with local police. Deportation is the centerpiece of the strategy, into which a lot of effort is being invested. The strategy's costs and benefits need to be critically evaluated. There is good reason to suspect that the deportation of criminal aliens may be the "fools gold" of immigration policy.

Deportation was a reasonably effective measure of controlling and even rehabilitating criminals in the days before steam power, when it took several months or years to get back to the host country. But in the jet age, with porous borders, deportation serves to export hardened criminals to other countries, which until now were not familiar with drive-by killings and American-style gangsterism. It undercuts American foreign policy interests, such as trying to establish law and order in Central American countries (Rohter 1997). And it provides little guarantee that the deported criminal will not be back in the country, this time connected to transnational criminal gangs (Sontag 1997; Wallace 1998). The deportation of criminal aliens is superficially appealing, but there is no evidence that it deters illegal immigration or crime by immigrants.

Conclusion

International Implications. Immigration points the police in two directions: outwardly at the burgeoning world of transnational crime and justice, and inwardly at the perennial problems of professionalism and police-community relations. At the international level, immigration requires that the police develop new forms of cooperation with foreign law enforcement agencies and more efficient forms of cooperation with domestic agencies that are often seen as rivals and competitors.

Today, nations are building transnational structures to eliminate safe havens. The police are an essential part of these networks. A few American police agencies in border locations have moved into this role. But border problems are no longer confined to the border. Police departments across the country regularly confront immigrants who are likely to flee the country if they get involved in serious crime.

National Implications. At the national level, the police leaders and national associations need to participate more fully in the setting of immigration policy, at least with regard to crime, justice and law enforcement policies. They should counterbalance mean-spirited or shortsighted immigration policies that would adversely affect crime. In fact, during discussion of the Immigration Reform Act of 1996, two of the nation's largest police organizations urged Congress to drop a provision that would have allowed states to deny public education to the children of illegal immigrants, arguing that it would lead to more crime (Schmitt 1996).

Local Implications. At the local level, police must build bridges to immigrant communities to overcome language and other cultural barriers, particularly the deep distrust of the police that many immigrants bring with them. In many of their countries of origin, corruption is rampant and the police prey on the people for bribes. The police are distrusted and despised (Huey-Long 1988). In some places, they or criminal suspects have been lynched in protest over corruption and failure to enforce the law (Associated Press 1996).

According to a Gallup poll that asked people to indicate how much confidence they have in 12 American institutions, the police came in second only to the military as the institution with the highest degree of confidence (Gallup 1997). Newly arrived immigrants from developing or Third World countries, however, are unlikely to share that confidence. If the police are to be effective in immigrant communities, they must work on making up the confidence deficit. They do this most powerfully through positive routine contacts with immigrants, and special efforts to develop cultural competence among police officers and build bridges to immigrant communities (National Crime Prevention Council 1995).

In our society the police are the key institution for integrating foreigners into the culture, managing social tensions, promoting democracy, protecting life and property without regard to immigrant status, and ultimately, helping achieve the ideals of equality, dignity and tolerance that our culture now demands. Community policing is suited to achieving these tasks, and in several places is being used to do so. But community policing has moved from its charismatic to its institutional phase, and is at risk of being trivialized.

All of the above may sound like an impossible wish list, and would be just that, if it were not for the fact that police agencies are already implementing many of these strategies. Immigration has given us diversity out of which we must make unity. To do so, we all need to improve our language skills and increase our cultural competence. We can start with Latin and with our own cultural ideals. So what is the challenge of immigration for the police? The answer is *E Pluribus Unum*. Make it happen!

REFERENCES

Abbott, E. 1924. *Immigration: Select Documents and Case Records.* Chicago, University of Chicago Press.

Abbott, E. 1969. *Historical Aspects of the Immigration Problem: Select Documents.* Chicago, University of Chicago Press.

Alexander, C. 1981. Notes from the Underground: Millions of Illegal Workers Will Not Be Celebrating Labor Day. *Time.* 7 September.

Anonymous. 1973. Police Right to Hold Suspected Aliens Affirmed. *Los Angeles Times.* 29 August.

Asher, J. 1994. Comment: How the United States Is Violating Its International Agreements to Combat Slavery. *Emory International Law Review.*

Associated Press. 1996. Another Lynching. *The (Mexico City) News.* 14 September.

Associated Press. 1997a. *Illegal Aliens State-By-State.* 7 February.

Associated Press. 1997b. Arizona to Investigate Roundup of Immigrants. *San Diego Union-Tribune.* 10 August.

Associated Press. 1998a. Thai Woman Denies Slave Charges. *Associated Press News Service.* 13 April.

Associated Press. 1998b. More Sentences on the Deaf Mexican Illegals Case. *CISNEWS.* 15 May.

Associated Press. 1998c. *City, Citizens Battle Over '97 Roundup: Chandler Incident to Be Settled in Court.* 21 July.

Bennett, B. 1998a. Officers to Spend Time in Mexico to Learn More About Immigrants. *Lexington (Kentucky) Herald-Leader.* 7 August.

Bennett, B. 1998b. Raid Strikes Fear in Illegal Aliens, Employers. *Lexington (Kentucky) Herald-Leader.* 21 May.

Blake, C.G. 1984. North Carolina's New Involuntary Servitude Statute: Inadequate Relief for Enslaved Migrant Laborers. *North Carolina Law Review* 62:1186–1193.

Blumenthal, R. 1988. *Last Days of the Sicilians: At War with the Mafia: The FBI Assault on the Pizza Connection.* New York: Times Books.

Booth, W. 1997a. Illegal Immigrant Population Grows to 5 Million. *The Washington Post*. 8 February.

Booth, W. 1997. Reaping Abuse for What They Sew: Sweatshops Once Again Commonplace in U.S. Garment Industry. *The Washington Post*. 16 February.

Booth, W. 1998a. One Nation, Indivisible: Is It History? Soon, No Single Group Will Comprise Majority. *The Washington Post*. 22 February.

Branigin, W. 1997. Illegal Immigrant Population Grows to 5 Million. *The Washington Post*. 8 February.

Brimelow, P. 1995. *Alien Nation: Common Sense About America's Immigration Disaster*. New York: Random House.

Busey, S.C. 1969. *Immigration: Its Evils and Consequences*. New York: Arno Press and The New York Times.

Butcher, K.F., and A. Morrison Piehl. 1995. *Cross-City Evidence on the Relationship Between Immigration and Crime*. Paper Presented at the Wiener Center Lunch, Kennedy School of Government.

Calavita, K. 1984. *U.S. Immigration Law and the Control of Labor: 1820–1924*. Orlando, Fla.: Academic Press.

Carter, H.M. 1978. Law Enforcement and Federalism: Bordering on Trouble. *Policy Studies Journal* 7:413–18.

Carter, H.M. 1979a. *Federalism and the Judicial Process: A Case Study and Discussion from the US-Mexico Border*. Unpublished Paper. Annual Meeting of The American Political Science Association, Washington, D.C.

Carter, H.M. 1979b. *Law, Order, and the Border: El Paso Del Norte*. Unpublished Paper. Annual Meeting of the National Council on Geographic Education.

Chang, E.R. 1994. An Emerging Minority Seeks a Role in a Changing America. *Los Angeles Times*. 31 May.

Chin, K. 1997. Safe House or Hell House? Experiences of Newly Arrived Undocumented Chinese. In *Human Smuggling,* edited by P.J.Smith. Washington, D.C.: Center for Strategic and International Studies.

Chiswick, B.R. 1986. Illegal Alien Policy Dilemma. In *Essays on Legal and Illegal Immigration*, edited by S. Pozo. Kalamazoo,

Mich.: W.E. Upjohn Institute for Employment Research.

Chiswick, B.R. 1988. *Illegal Aliens: Their Employment and Employers*. Kalamazoo, Mich.: W.E. Upjohn Institute.

Christianson, K.S. 1981. *The American Experience of Imprisonment, 1607–1776*. Ph. D. Dissertation. Albany: State University of New York.

Clark, R.L., S.J. Passel, W.N. Zimmerman, and M.E. Fix. 1994. *Fiscal Impacts of Undocumented Aliens: Selected Estimates for Seven States*. Washington, D.C.: Urban Institute.

Constable, P. 1995. Laborers Get Clout from Force of Law: Program Helps Gain Pay from Employers. *The Washington Post*. 25 November.

Constable, P., and A. Argetsinger. 86 Illegal Immigrant Suspects Caught in Coincidental Maryland Raids. *The Washington Post*. 19 July.

Cornelius, W.A., P.L. Martin, and J.F. Hollifield. 1994. *Controlling Immigration: A Global Perspective*. Stanford, Calif.: Stanford University Press.

Council, J. 1996. Bringing Them Home: Together, Texas and Mexican Officials Are Bringing More Fugitives to Justice—Even When It's Meted Out on the Opposite Side of the Border. *Texas Lawyer*. 16 September.

Crevecoeur, H. St. John de. 1994. Letters from an American Farmer. In *The Heath Anthology of American Literature*, edited by P. Lauter. Lexington, Mass.: D.C. Heath and Company.

D'Amato, A.M. 1983. Aliens in Prison—The Federal Response to a New Criminal Justice Emergency. *Detroit College of Law Review* 4:1163–1169.

Darling, J. 1998. New Migrants, Same Covert Route to U.S. *Los Angeles Times*. 15 February.

Davis, R.C., and E. Erez. 1998. *Immigrant Populations as Victims: Toward a Multicultural Criminal Justice System*. Research in Brief. Washington, D.C.: National Institute of Justice.

DeGeneste, H.I., and J.P. Sullivan. 1997. *Policing a Multicultural Community*. Fresh Perspectives. Washington, D.C.: Police Executive Research Forum.

DeStefano, A.M. 1997. Immigrant Smuggling Through Central America and the Caribbean. In *Human Smuggling*, edited by P.J. Smith. Washington, D.C.: Center for Strategic and International Studies.

Dimeglio, S. 1997. Border Chaos Shifts East. *The (Coachella, Calif.) Desert Sun*. June.

Donaldson, A. 1998. Salt Lake Crime Declined Again in 1997. *(Salt Lake City) Desert News*. 18 May.

Drake, J. 1998. INS Targeted in Claim Over Roundup of Illegal Immigrants. *The Arizona Republic*. 7 August.

Eisenstadt, T.A., and C.L. Thorup. 1994. *Caring Capacity Versus Carrying Capacity: Community Responses to Mexican Immigration in San Diego's North County*. San Diego: The Center for U.S.-Mexican Studies, University of California.

Ekirch, A.R. 1987. *Bound for America: The Transportation of British Convicts to the Colonies, 1718–1775*. Oxford: Clarendon Press.

European Commission, Justice and Home Affairs <msk@us.net>. 1997. Overseas Immigration News: European Commission Press Release. 11 July.

Federation for American Immigration Reform. 1992. *Immigration 2000: The Century of the New American Sweatshop*. Washington, D.C.: Federation for American Immigration Reform.

Freedberg, L. 1994. Mexico Slowly Getting Tougher On Illegals: Shift in Longtime Attitude Reflects New Realities. *The San Francisco Chronicle*. 12 August.

Fried, J.P. 1998. Immigrant Smuggling Case Ends in Guilty Plea. *The New York Times*. 12 March.

Gallup Organization. 1997. Police Investigation: GIDOPS' Tools to Improve Community Relations with the Cops Are Attracting Attention. *The Gallup Globe* 3(5).

Gates, D.F., and K.E. Ross. 1990. Foreign Prosecution Liaison Unit Helps Apprehend Suspects Across the Border. *The Police Chief* April:153–154.

Geller, D. 1998. Smuggling of Chinese Continues Unabated. *The (Bergen, N.J.) Record*. 9 July.

Gilbreath, J. 1995. *The Mexico-Texas Relationship: Redefining Regionalism*. Mexico City. "La Nueva Agenda de la Relacion Bilateral:" A Conference of El Programa para Analisis de las Relaciones Mexico-EU-Canada, Instituto Tecnologico Autonomo de Mexico and Centro de Investigaciones sobre American del Norte, U.S.-Mexican Policy Studies Program, Lyndon B. Johnson School of Public Affairs, University of Texas at Austin held at Mexico City.

Golden, A. 1997. Grupo Beta Seen as Law Enforcement's Shining Light. *San Diego Union-Tribune*. 10 February.

Goldstein, H. 1990. *Problem-Oriented Policing*. New York: McGraw-Hill.

Gorsline, S.J. 1989. Casenotes: Criminal Law—Involuntary Servitude—Pursuant to Section 241 and Section 1584 of the United States Code, 'Involuntary Servitude' Is Limited to Conditions in Which a Person is Forced to Work for Another Person by the Use or Threatened Use of Physical or Legal Coercion. *University of Detroit Law Review* 66:297–309.

Harris, M. 1978. *Cows, Pigs, Wars, and Witches: The Riddles of Culture*. New York: Vintage.

Holmes, S.A. 1998. Hispanic Population Moves Closer to Surpassing That of Blacks. *The New York Times*. 7 August.

Honeycutt, V. 1998. Plan Formulated for Hispanics: Mayor's Task Force Plans to Tackle Manageable Immigrant Issues. *Lexington (Kentucky) Herald-Leader*. 31 July.

Jacobs, J.B., C. Panarella, and J. Worthington. 1994. *Busting the Mob: United States v. Cosa Nostra*. New York.: New York University Press.

James, D. 1991. *Illegal Immigration—An Unfolding Crisis*. Lanham, Md.: University Press of America.

Kelley, M. 1997. Hispanics Blast Police Harassment. *Associated Press*.19 August.

Knight Ridder News Service. 1998. 16 Mexican Immigrants Charged with Sex Slavery in South Carolina. *Lexington (Kentucky) Herald-Leader*. 3 June.

Knight Ridder News Service. 1996. *Hmong Refugees in California Flee Crime and Intolerance*. 4 December.

Kolender, W.B. 1978. Remarks Regarding Illegal Aliens. In *The Police Yearbook 1978*, edited by the International Association of Chiefs of Police. Gaithersburg, Md.: International Association of Chiefs of Police.

Kottak, C.P. 1991. *Anthropology: The Exploration of Human Diversity*. 5th ed. New York: McGraw-Hill.

Lait, M. 1998. Men Accused of Plotting Massacre. *Los Angeles Times*. 12 March.

Levine, R. 1988. Koch Favors Measure to Protect Illegal Aliens. *The New York Times*. 22 December.

Lieb, D.A. 1998. Five Charged in Immigration Sex Case. *Associated Press News Service*, 8 July.

Lopez, R.J. and R. Connell. 1996. Police Told to Review Rule on Immigrants. *Los Angeles Times*. 17 December.

Magruder, J. 1998. Chandler's Tidal Wave of Illegals: Year After Roundup They're Still Coming. *The Arizona Republic*. 26 July.

Malloy, W.M. 1910. *Treaties, Conventions, International Acts, Protocols and Agreements*. Washington, D.C.: U.S. Government Printing Office.

Manning, R.D. 1997. Washington, D.C.: The Changing Social Landscape of the International Capital City. In *Origins and Destinies: Immigration, Race and Ethnicity in America*, edited by S. Pedraza and R.C. Rumbaut. New York: Wadsworth.

Martin, R.A. 1991. Problems in International Law Enforcement. *Fordham International Law Journal* 14(1990–1991):519.

Martin, R.A. 1998. *The Italian American Working Group Against the Mafia*. Presentation at the Executive Leadership Seminar: Strategic Approaches to Transnational Crime and Civil Society, Georgetown University, Washington, D.C., 20–31 July. For published version of the remarks, see Martin, R.A. 1998. *The Italian American Working Group: Why it Worked*. Working Group on Organized Crime Monograph Series. Washington, D.C.: National Strategy Information Center, Inc.

Maxwell, E. 1977. U.S.-Mexico Smuggling: The Buying and Selling of Humans: Borderlands Are A Free-Fire Zone Where Living Bodies Become the Goods in a Kind of Slave Trade. *Los Angeles Times.* 22 February.

McDonald, W.F. 1995. Globalizing Criminology: The New Frontier is the Frontier. *Transnational Organized Crime* 1:1–22.

McDonald, W.F. 1997a. Crime and Justice in the Global Village: Towards Global Criminology. In *Crime and Law Enforcement in the Global Village,* edited by W.F. McDonald. Cincinnati: Anderson.

McDonald, W.F. 1997b. Illegal Immigration: Crime, Ramifications and Control (The American Experience). In *Crime and Law Enforcement in the Global Village,* edited by W.F. McDonald. Cincinnati: Anderson Publishers.

McDonald, W.F. 1997c. Crime and Illegal Immigration: Emerging, Local, State, and Federal Partnerships. *National Institute of Justice Journal* 232:2–10.

McDonald, W.F. 1998. Criminal Aliens: Crime Control, Immigration Control, of Political Control. In *Migration and Crime,* edited by A. Schmid and I. Melup. Milan, Italy: International Scientific and Professional Advisory Council.

McDonald, W.F. Forthcoming. Los Estados Unidos, Méjico y Asuntos de Inmigración. *CRIMINALIA.*

McDonnell, P.J. 1996. Law Could Alter Role of Police on Immigration. *Los Angeles Times.* 30 September.

McDonnell, P.J. 1998. Mexican Arrivals Seek New Frontiers. *Los Angeles Times.* 1 January.

McLaughlin, C.M., and P. Jesilow. Forthcoming. Conveying a Sense of Community Along Bolsa Avenue: Little Saigon as a Model of Ethnic Commercial Belts. *International Migration.*

Mittelstadt, M. 1998. Millions Go to Jail Criminal Aliens. *Associated Press News Service.* 14 May.

Moore, M. 1996. Lynch Law The Rule in Mexican Towns. *The Washington Post.* 7 September.

Nadelmann, E.A. 1992. *Criminalization and Crime Control in International Society.* Unpublished Manuscript.

Nadelmann, E.A. 1993. *Cops Across Borders: The Internationalization of U.S. Criminal Law Enforcement*. University Park, Penn.: Pennsylvania State University Press.

National Crime Prevention Council. 1994. *Building and Crossing Bridges: Refugees and Law Enforcement Working Together*. Washington, D.C.: National Crime Prevention Council.

National Crime Prevention Council. 1995. *Lengthening the Stride: Employing Peace Officers from Newly Arrived Ethnic Groups*. Washington, D.C.: National Crime Prevention Council.

New York Department of Correctional Services. 1989. *The Impact of Foreign-Born Inmates on the New York State Department of Correctional Services*. Albany, N.Y.: New York Department of Correctional Services. November.

New York Department of Correctional Services. 1992. *The Impact of Foreign-Born Inmates on the New York State Department of Correctional Services: Executive Summary*. Albany, N.Y.: New York Department of Correctional Services.

New York Department of Correctional Services. 1996. *The Impact of Foreign-Born Inmates on the New York State Department of Correctional Services*. Albany, N.Y.: New York Department of Correctional Services. February.

New York Times. 1930. Police to Round Up Criminal Aliens Here; New Bureau to Get Evidence for Mulrooney. *The New York Times*. 29 December.

New York Times. 1983. Coast City Spurns Action on Aliens. *The New York Times*. 11 September.

Ogburn, W.F. 1922. *Social Change with Respect to Culture and Original Nature*. New York: Viking.

Pitsela, A. 1988. Criminal Victimization of Foreign Minorities in the Federal Republic of Germany. In *Crime and Criminal Justice*, edited by G. Kaiser and I. Geissler. Freiburg i. Br.: Max-Planck-Institut.

PRNewswire. 1997. *Immigration Enforcement*. 10 March

PRNewswire.1998. *Reimbursement Funds Provided to 249 Jurisdictions That Incarcerate Criminal Illegal Aliens*. 15 May.

Pryce, K. 1989. *Endless Pressure: A Study of West Indian Life-Styles in Bristol*. Bristol: Bristol Classics Press.

Public Broadcasting System. 1996. *Background Briefings: Slamming the Door*. Online NewsHour web site (www1.pbs.org/ newshour/bb/congress/may96/immigration_status_5_3.html). 2 May.

Pyle, R. 1998. First Sentencing in Mexican Deaf Case. *Associated Press News Service*. 8 May.

Rawls Jr., W. 1981. Migrant Slavery Persists on Southeast Farms. *The New York Times*. 19 November.

Reuters. 1995. 8 Arrested in L.A. on Charges They Enslaved Thai Immigrants. *The Washington Post*. 4 August.

Reuters. 1998. *U.S. Warns Mexicans About Ruthless Alien Smugglers*. 29 April.

Rohter, L. 1997. Deportees From the U.S. Unwelcome in El Salvador. *The New York Times*. 10 August.

Rojas, A. 1996. Growers Hire Illegals With Impunity: Workers Pay the Price for Lax Scrutiny of Farm Industry. *San Francisco Chronicle*. 19 March.

Romero, F. 1991. Baja and City Reach Pact on Border Justice. *San Diego Union-Tribune*. 14 November.

Ronfeldt, D. 1996. *Tribes, Institutions, Markets, Networks: A Framework About Societal Evolution*. Santa Monica, Calif.: RAND.

Rosenberg, A.S. 1998. 13 Women Arraigned in Prostitution Case: A Raid On Atlantic City Massage Parlors Netted the Women, from Korea and Thailand. *The Philadelphia Inquirer*. 9 October.

Rotella, S. 1992. Reducing the Misery at the Border: Immigration: Grupo Beta Is an Elite Mexican Multi-Agency Force with the Task of Protecting Migrants. It Has Cut Violence and Improved Relations Between U.S. and Mexico. *Los Angeles Times*. 10 March.

Scalia, J. 1996. *Noncitizens in the Federal Criminal Justice System, 1984–94*. Bureau of Justice Statistics Special Report. Washington, D.C.: Bureau of Justice Statistics.

Schlesinger Jr., A.M. 1992. *The Disuniting of America*. New York: W.W. Norton and Company.

Schmid, A.P. 1996. Migration and Crime: A Framework for Discussion. In *Migration and Crime*, edited by A.P. Schmid. Milan: International Scientific and Professional Advisory Council of the United Nations Crime Prevention and Criminal Justice Programme.

Schmid, A.P., and I. Melup. 1998. *Migration and Crime*. Milan: International Scientific and Professional Advisory Council.

Schmitt, E. 1996. Police Scorn Plan to Deny Schooling to Illegal Aliens, Groups Say Bill Will Lead to Rise in Crime. *The New York Times*. 9 April.

Skerry, P. 1995. Many Borders to Cross: Is Immigration the Exclusive Responsibility of the Federal Government? *Publius: The Journal of Federalism* 3 .

Skolnick, J.H. and D.H. Bayley. 1986. *The New Blue Line: Police Innovation in Six American Cities*. New York: The Free Press.

Smith, P.J. 1997a. Chinese Migrant Trafficking: A Global Challenge. In *Human Smuggling*, edited by P.J. Smith. Washington, D.C.: Center for Strategic and International Studies.

Smith, P.J. 1997b. *Human Smuggling: Chinese Migrant Trafficking and the Challenge to America's Immigration Tradition*. Washington, D.C.: Center for Strategic and International Studies.

Song, H.J. 1988. *No White-Feathered Crows: Chinese Immigrant's and Vietnamese Refugees' Adaptation to American Legal Institutions*. Ph.D. Dissertation. Irvine: University of California.

Sontag, D. 1997. Many Deported Felons Return to U.S. Unnoticed. *The New York Times*. 11 August.

Stevens, M. 1980. Crackdown on Sweatshops. *Christian Science Monitor*. 7 March.

Swaboda, F., and M. Webb Pressler. 1995. U.S. Targets "Slave Labor" Sweatshop: Back Wages Sought from Clothing Makers. *The Washington Post*. 16 August.

Texas Criminal Justice Policy Council. 1995. *Criminal Alien Project for the State of Texas*. Austin, Texas.: Texas Criminal Justice Policy Council.

Thomas-Lester, A. 1998. Salvadoran Fugitives Frustrate D.C. Police, Suspects Fleeing U.S., Officials Say. *The Washington Post*. 18 July.

Timms, E., and J.N. Suhler. 1998. Americans at Odds: Struggles in Dallas Between Minority Groups Mirror National Trend. *Dallas Morning News.* 4 January.

U.S. Bureau of the Census. 1996. *Population Projections of the United States by Age, Sex, Race, and Hispanic Origin: 1995–2050.* Current Population Reports. Washington, D.C.: U.S. Department of Commerce.

U.S. Bureau of the Census. 1997. *The Foreign-Born Population: 1996.* Current Population Reports. Washington, D.C.: U.S. Department of Commerce.

U.S. Bureau of the Census. 1998. *The Foreign-Born Population in the United States: March 1997 (Update).* Current Population Reports. Washington, D.C.: U.S. Department of Commerce.

U.S. Conference of Mayors. 1994. *Immigrant Policy Issues for America's Cities: A 78 City Survey.* Washington, D.C.: U.S. Conference of Mayors. June.

U.S. Congressional Research Service. 1980. *History of Immigration and Naturalization Service. A Report.* 96th Cong. 2d Sess. Washington, D.C.: U.S. Government Printing Office.

U.S. Department of Justice, Bureau of Justice Assistance. 1996. *Addressing the Criminal Alien Problem. The Interstate Criminal Alien Working Group's Report.* Tallahassee, Fla.: Institute for Intergovernmental Research.

U.S. Department of Justice, Immigration and Naturalization Service. 1996. *Statistical Yearbook of the U.S. Immigration and Naturalization Service, 1994.* Washington, D.C.: U.S. Government Printing Office.

U.S. Department of Justice, Immigration and Naturalization Service. 1998. Table 3. Immigrants Admitted By State and Metropolitan Areas. In *INS Statistics* (http://www.ins.usdoj.gov/stats/annual/fy96/997.html).

United Nations, Office of the High Commissioner for Human Rights. 1998. *Trafficking in Peoples: The Human Rights Dimension.* International Conference on Responding to the Challenges of Transnational Crime. Courmayeur, Italy. 24–27 September.

Villafranca, A. 1998. Immigrants' Role Being Seen In New Light. *Houston Chronicle*. 20 April.

Vlassis, D. 1998. *Convention on Organized Crime*. International Conference on Responding to the Challenges of Transnational Crime. Courmayeur, Italy. 24–27 September.

Wallace, B. 1998. Deported Criminals Stream Back Into the U.S. by the Thousands. *San Francisco Chronicle*. 11 May.

Weiser, B. 1998. 28 Accused of Racketeering as Members of Asian Gang. *The New York Times*. 8 July.

Whitaker, B. 1982. *Slavery*. New York: United Nations.

Williams, H., and P.V. Murphy. 1990. *The Evolving Strategy of Police: A Minority View*. Perspectives on Policing No. 13. Washington, D.C.: National Institute of Justice. January.

Williams, P. 1998. *Organizing Transnational Crime: Networks, Markets and Hierarchies*. International Conference on Responding to the Challenges of Transnational Crime. Courmayeur, Italy. 24–27 September.

Wolf, D. 1988. *Undocumented Aliens and Crime: The Case of San Diego County*. San Diego: Center for U.S.-Mexican Studies, University of California.

Wysocki, D. 1981. Sweatshops Return: Established Safeguards Don't Work: Possible Links to Crime Figures. *United Press International*.

Yi, D. 1998. Nation's Borders Don't Stop Special LAPD Unit Police: Unique Cadre of Investigators Works with Foreign Authorities to Help Prosecute Suspects for Crimes in U.S. *Los Angeles Times*. 16 March.

Zagaris, B, and J. Padierna Peralta. 1997. Mexico-United States Extradition and Alternatives: From Fugitive Slaves to Drug Traffickers—150 Years and Beyond the Rio Grande's Winding Courses. *American University Journal of International Law and Policy* 12(4):519–621.

PART III

MAKING POP WORK

CHAPTER 10

THE RELATIONSHIP BETWEEN
CRIME PREVENTION AND
PROBLEM-ORIENTED POLICING[1]

Nick Tilley

The Historical and Conceptual Relationship Between Crime Prevention and Problem-Oriented Policing

Situational crime prevention emerged in Britain in the late 1970s at much the same time that Herman Goldstein was developing his ideas on problem-oriented policing in the United States (Goldstein 1979; Clarke 1980). Situational crime prevention arose in a context where faith in the criminal justice system's ability to prevent crime was on the wane. Controlling crime by manipulating offenders'disposition to commit crime was not proving successful. The slogan "nothing works" had taken hold. Crime rates were rising. The ground was fertile for the formulation of new ideas, new policies and new practices. Ron Clarke, now at Rutgers University in New Jersey, was in the British Home Office Research and Planning Unit. Along with colleagues, he formulated an approach to crime prevention that revolved around reducing opportunities for crime, rather than reducing the disposition to commit a crime. It advocated careful and detailed analysis of individual crime problems, formulation of an opportunity-reducing response, and evaluation of the response's effectiveness. This normally involved implementing some change to the environment in which the crime problem was occurring:

[1] I am grateful to Tim Read for invaluable comments on an earlier draft of this chapter.

increasing risks, reducing rewards and/or increasing the efforts for prospective offenders. While these bare elements remain, the theory has since been substantially elaborated, and the approach has subsequently yielded extensive success across a wide range of crime types (Clarke 1997).

This new way of approaching crime prevention required the cooperation of agencies outside the criminal justice system, because relevant environmental changes to prevent crime opportunities could not, in most cases, be directly implemented by those within. The approach played a part in informing a series of British government efforts to encourage multiagency collaborations in crime prevention.

Herman Goldstein's 1979 paper advocating a problem-oriented approach for policing begins with an amusing story from an English newspaper about the failure of buses to stop and pick up passengers because doing so prevented them from keeping to their timetable. Just as the English bus service had forgotten its purpose in the drive for timetable efficiency, Goldstein contended that American police services had forgotten their purpose in their drive to accomplish quick responses to calls from the public. Goldstein was preoccupied with the failures of American police services to deal effectively with the many problems brought to them by the public. The result was inefficiency in resolving problems, which led to repeated calls for service, and ineffectiveness in providing the service the public wanted.

In problem-oriented policing (POP), Goldstein has advocated systematic identification and analysis of problems, and the formulation of creative responses in an effort to reduce calls for service and better meet public needs. He also emphasizes the need to check that the measures applied have indeed had their intended effects. When it is not within police power to directly deal with the source of a particular problem, he then has argued that other agencies need to be drawn in and persuaded to act.

There were no references to Goldstein's writings in the Home Office work of the late 1970s. Similarly, at that time, there were no references to the Home Office research in Goldstein's writings. The two developments occurred independently. There are, nevertheless, clear parallels:

- Both POP and situational crime prevention advocate evidence-based, analytic methods.
- Both approaches suggest the need for cooperation between differing agencies.
- Both approaches call for imaginative ways of addressing issues beyond the criminal justice system's control.

We should not, however, disregard some significant differences:

- POP was developed in the *United States* in late 1970s, while situational crime prevention was developed in *Britain* in the late 1970s.
- POP was developed to address criticism of prevailing *policing and enforcement methods*. Situational crime prevention addressed criticism of prevailing *efforts to control crime*.
- POP is about more effectively addressing *all issues* coming to the police. Situational crime prevention is about controlling *crimes* more effectively.
- POP advocates use of *any ethical and effective methods*. Situational crime prevention advocates *opportunity-reducing methods*.

In practice, acknowledging their differences and building on their parallels, POP and situational crime prevention may effectively complement one another. Situational crime prevention suggests some powerful ways of addressing problems, while POP provides an institutional context for delivering situational crime prevention.

The following discussion will look specifically at recent developments in Britain. These are fueling a practical convergence between crime prevention strategies that draw heavily on the situational approach, and the forms of policing inspired by Goldstein's problem-oriented approach.

The British Context for Policing and Crime Prevention

Figure 1 shows some distinctive features of the organizational and procedural structure of British policing. These features help

Figure 1. The Context for British Policing

- There is just one tier of policing, with 43 police services covering the whole of England and Wales, with a population of a little more than 50 million.
- These 43 services include a total of about 127,000 police officers.
- There is an association of chief police officers (ACPO), comprising all the chief constables, deputy chief constables and assistant chief constables. These are the approximately 200 most senior officers in England and Wales. Though the various forces remain strictly autonomous, the association formulates agreed positions about policing.
- The Home Office, a government department, has the overall responsibility for the police service. The Home Secretary sets national objectives for the police. Local accountability is through a police authority, comprising elected local authority councillors (9), representatives of the magistracy (3), and Home Office nominees (5). The chief constable has operational responsibility.
- Her Majesty's Inspectorate of Constabulary (HMIC), led by current or former senior police officers, inspects every force regularly for efficiency and effectiveness. It publishes its inspection reports and recommendations, and awards the forces' Certificate of Efficiency. HMIC also undertakes periodic thematic inspections to provide a national overview of particular areas of policing. These findings and recommendations are also published and the recommendations are followed up in individual force inspections.
- There are about 5 million recorded crimes per year in England and Wales.
- Given that only about a third of calls for service are directly crime-related, there are an estimated 20 million calls for service each year.

place current policing developments into a context.[2] They show that England and Wales have a relatively small number of forces, each covering a relatively large geographical area.[3] Responsibility is exercised through a tripartite system comprising the Home Office, the local police authority and the chief constable. The Home Office-based national inspectorate for policing (HMIC), the Association of Chief Police Officers (ACPO), and the Home Office are all significant national influences over developments in British policing.

Several current British developments are especially significant for crime prevention and POP. Those listed in Figure 2 are helping to embed attention to crime prevention in local areas, in ways that include the police, but other agencies as well. In particular, ACPO policies, an HMIC crime prevention report and a new law allocating statutory responsibilities for crime prevention to multiagency partnerships are steering police services to increased attention to prevention. Moreover, the frameworks being advocated for crime prevention have affinities with problem-oriented policing. They stress the importance of an analytic approach, wherein local problems are clearly identified and analyzed before decisions are made about response implementation. The involvement of nonpolice agencies in helping to address crime problems is deemed crucial. In addition, there is a consistent emphasis on monitoring and evaluation, as necessary for management, lesson learning and accountability.

Getting the Grease to the Squeak (Hough and Tilley 1998a) attempted to distill lessons from the research literature about how the police can best organize themselves and their relationships with others in the service of crime prevention. The main conclusions are presented here, as they help reveal, in detail, the ways

---

[2]See Morgan and Newburn (1997) for an excellent discussion of developments in British policing.

[3]The City of London Police is an exception here. It covers only a small part of London.

Figure 2. The British Context:
Recent and Current Developments

- In 1996, ACPO produced *Towards 2000* (ACPO 1996), stressing the central importance of focusing on crime prevention in partnership with other agencies.
- In 1996, HMIC asked the Police Research Group (a research unit within the Home Office, now called the Policing and Reducing Crime Unit) to compile lessons from research about how the police can best organize themselves for crime prevention. This led to the publication of *Getting the Grease to the Squeak* (Hough and Tilley 1998a).
- Influenced by *Getting the Grease to the Squeak,* HMIC undertook a thematic inspection of crime prevention work in police services. This led to the publication of *Beating Crime* (HMIC 1998), containing a review of current practice and a set of recommendations.
- In 1998, the Crime and Disorder Act was passed. This requires the formation of crime and disorder partnerships including the police, relevant local authorities, probation, and the health authority, in all district-level authorities (about 400 in England and Wales). Other locally relevant bodies, including those from the voluntary and private sectors, must also be invited to participate. The partnerships are to undertake an audit of crime and disorder, publish the results, consult the public, devise a strategy with targets, and monitor and evaluate their achievements on a three-year cycle (Home Office 1998, Hough and Tilley 1998b).
- In 1995, the Police Research Group, working with Leicestershire Constabulary, initiated a demonstration project in one of Leicestershire's policing areas (East Area), to gauge the prospects for POP in Britain. This project resulted in the production of two reports (Leigh, Read, and Tilley 1996, 1998), the second of which documented subsequent efforts to implement POP in other areas of Britain, notably in Cleveland and Merseyside.
- In 1999, the Home Office launched a substantial Crime Reduction Program. The program includes significant support for the development of a problem-oriented approach, in regard to both specific initiatives and routine use.

(continued)

Figure 2. The British Context:
Recent and Current Developments (continued)

- An audit commission report was published in early 1999 examining the work of local authority in community safety (addressing issues of crime, criminality, disorder, anti-social behavior, incivilities, and fear of crime). It complements the Crime and Disorder Act's focus on effective partnership and endorses a problem-solving approach.
- The Home Secretary's national objectives for policing are set to move away from their previous emphasis on detection and toward prevention.

---

in which a police service organized around crime prevention will be drawn into a problem-oriented approach.

Getting the Grease to the Squeak:
Research Lessons for Policing and Crime Prevention

The title of this report, *Getting the Grease to the Squeak*, adopts a phrase used by Graham Farrell and Ken Pease in a publication about repeat victimization (Farrell and Pease 1993). Farrell and Pease have shown how crime tends to be heavily concentrated on a small minority of frequently victimized targets. Victimization is a good predictor of heightened risk, most noticeably in the period immediately following an incident. Farrell and Pease argue that in the interests of efficiency, economy and equity, individuals already victimized represent squeaks to which preventive grease can be applied. It makes good sense to allocate scarce resources to those who are most vulnerable. The result may be a less uneven and more equitable distribution of victimization, even if there is some displacement. Hough and Tilley appropriated the expression "getting the grease to the squeak" to capture their concern with the ways in which police can more effectively prevent crime.

Hough and Tilley's report (1998a) drew four main conclusions, as follows.

1. What the police can (and cannot) do to prevent crime.

- Enforcement is insufficient to prevent crime. In Britain only about 0.3 percent of offenses lead to incarceration (and hence temporary incapacitation). The remaining offenses are lost through the failure to report, record, detect, prosecute, convict, and/or incarcerate.

- Beyond a minimum level, merely increasing police presence through undirected patrol does not have any significant impact on crime levels, though the presence of policing *per se* does have an impact (Clarke and Hough 1984; Homel 1994). There are rapidly diminishing marginal preventive returns from simple increases in patrol.

- There are varying types of intervention to prevent crime. They include enforcement, situational prevention, community/social/developmental work, and rehabilitation. Agencies vary in their scope for each of them. While the police can contribute to the other approaches, they are particularly well placed when it comes to enforcement (see Figure 3).

- If the police are to make prevention a real priority, commitment throughout the force will be needed. Potential effectiveness is reduced if the responsibility for prevention is relegated to specialists only. The separation of prevention and detection diminishes the scope for mobilizing targeted detection for preventive purposes.

2. The need for an effective problem-solving approach.

- A problem-solving approach appears to offer the most promise for effective crime prevention. Figure 4 shows the model presented in *Getting the Grease to the Squeak*. POP has strong roots not only in crime prevention but in many other spheres also (Hough and Tilley 1998a:8).

- The problem-solving process depends on the availability of data, and the human and technological capacity to routinely analyze crime patterns in informative and imagi-

Figure 3. Local Crime Prevention Strategies: Who Does What?

	Police	Partnership	Nonpolice
1. Enforcement	Routine patrol Zero tolerance Detective work Intelligence-led targeting	Town guards Security guards	Trading standards Noise legislation Licensing
2. Situational prevention	Targeted patrol	Public CCTV schemes Preventing repeat victimization Architectural design advance Neighborhood watch	Private CCTV Improving car security Architectural design Planning guidance Land use decisions
3. Community/social/ developmental prevention	Police-operated youth clubs	Community action groups Youth work Drug education Schools liaison	Diversion schemes "Headstart" schemes Citizenship schemes Mediation schemes
4. Rehabilitation	Cautioning Attendance centers	Caution plus Arrest referral	Probation supervison Drug treatment Mentoring scheme

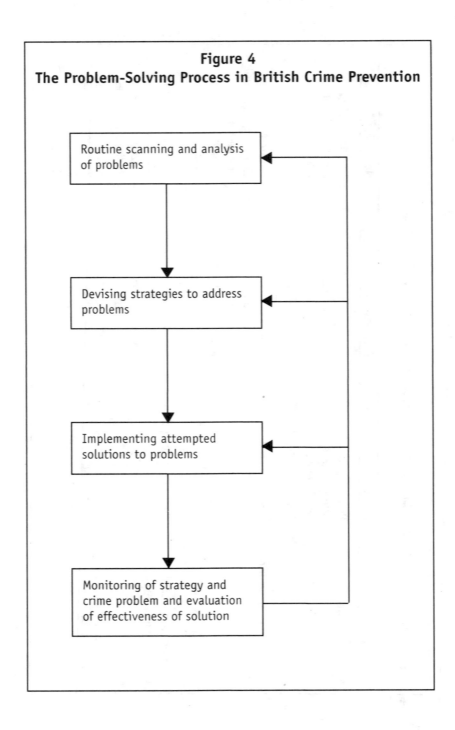

Figure 4
The Problem-Solving Process in British Crime Prevention

Routine scanning and analysis of problems

Devising strategies to address problems

Implementing attempted solutions to problems

Monitoring of strategy and crime problem and evaluation of effectiveness of solution native ways. To achieve effective results, police services need to allocate able, educated and trained staff, and make available appropriate computer hardware and software.

- Devising strategies depends on an ability to think through ways in which measures might work to prevent crime in its local settings. The same measure will not necessarily work in differing conditions. What works depends on a conducive context (see Figure 5).

- Lateral thought may be needed in order to think through relevant measures in regard to an outstanding problem (see Figure 6).

- Many measures fail because they are not implemented well.

3. The need for partnership.

- If the police are to make the problem-solving process effective, they will need cooperation from diverse partners. The police are not the only custodians of data on crime problems. They are also not the only agency with a contribution to make to understanding crime patterns or devising strategies to prevent crime. The police are not in a position, without outside contributions, to implement many of the interventions aimed at preventing crime. They will also not necessarily have all the data needed for monitoring and evaluation. To date, all research conducted on partnership efforts has suggested that an effective partnership is difficult to establish. It requires hard work and sensitivity (see Figure 7).

- Because agencies or individuals who are well-equipped to put effective crime prevention in place do not necessarily benefit from its achievements, there may be a need for leverage to persuade them to implement suggested measures (see Figure 8). While the police can exert some leverage, so too can other agencies, either on their own or in collaboration.

4. Monitoring and evaluation.

- Most in-house evaluations of crime prevention initiatives are weak. There are few police personnel with the tech-

Figure 5

**Same Measure, Different Context,
Different Mechanism, Different Outcomes**
Evaluations of the impact of mandatory arrest for domestic violence in North America have come up with contradictory findings (Sherman 1992). Three evaluations identified a deterrent effect, and three found that arrest increased the frequency of officially detected re-offending. Where data could distinguish the offender's employment status, however, findings became consistent. Among unemployed suspects, arrest increased the rate of offending. Among those employed, however, arrest resulted in a decreased rate. Arrest increases the probability of re-offending even more markedly in areas of concentrated unemployment and single-parent households. Shame is likely to be the dominant crime-inhibiting mechanism among the employed, while anger is the dominant mechanism among the unemployed. In different contexts, the same measure triggers different mechanisms, generating distinctive outcome patterns.

**The Importance of Local Conditions for
Particular Measures to Work: A Case Study**
Laycock (1985, 1997) showed how property marking could produce substantial reductions in burglary. The pattern of implementation and the conditions in the South Wales villages where the demonstration project was introduced were, however, crucial to the reductions. High rates of participation (some 70%) and extensive local publicity in the small and relatively self-contained communities in the area were crucial. Local burglars (and most of the burglars were local) were persuaded that their risks had been increased, and, correspondingly, their activity was reduced for a while. There were no increases in arrests or recovery of property. It is important to note that property marking does not "work" in an unqualified way, and cannot automatically be expected to yield falls in crime however and wherever it is introduced.

Figure 6. Thinking Laterally About Crime Prevention

Purse snatching was a big problem in Birmingham (England) markets. The police had adopted traditional detection methods in special operations, which did not lead to an overall reduction of crime. Store aisles were then widened, making it easier for shoppers to notice thefts. The risk (or perceived risk) to offenders was increased and there was a subsequent substantial decrease in theft rates (Poyner and Web, 1992).

Kerb-crawling (solicitation) was a significant nuisance in Finsbury Park, North London. Again, traditional policing methods had not improved matters. A road closure scheme to divert traffic from the area did the trick. Effort for the prostitutes to find their "tricks" and for punters (johns) to find prostitutes increased. Anticipated displacement did not occur (Matthews 1992).

Immediately cleaning graffiti off underground trains in New York deprived the "artists" of the reward of seeing their works on show. They stopped doing it (Sloan-Hewitt and Kelling 1992). Thought-provoking historical examples, where innovations have reduced crime opportunities include the following (taken from Pease 1997, see also Ekblom 1997):

- substituting indelible black for washable red franking ink (and the associated switch to the Penny Red), because the red franking ink used on the Penny Black was being wiped off and the stamps re-used;
- introducing hinged eyes around the winders of pocket watches making it impossible for cut-purses to snap the watches off; and
- casting silver in 600-pound lumps rather than small ingots in the Old West, thwarting robbers who could not carry it away.

Figure 7. Keys to Effective Partnerships

If the rhetoric of partnership is to be converted to reality, and partnerships are to deliver the promised benefits, partnerships need to be nurtured. For many agencies, ceding authority may seem threatening. Apparent additional claims on already scarce human and financial resources will be unwelcome. In many cases, the time spent on partnership work will be viewed as time spent away from the agency's "real" work. Practitioners at the sharp end will be apt to ask, "What's in it for us?" and unless there is a good answer, their enthusiasm will wane and subversion will set in. Here are some suggestions for initiating a virtuous circle of increasing reward, trust, achievement, and commitment, drawn mainly from the early experience of Britain's Safer Cities Program (Tilley 1992). Though they may sound both pious and somewhat obvious, unsuccessful partnerships are notable for ignoring these simple strategies.

1. Begin with "quick wins" from which individual workers and agencies benefit.
2. Take opportunities to bestow "gifts" on partners in the form of funds, recognition, publicity, or expressions of appreciation.
3. Avoid individual agency (mis)appropriation of credit for collective achievements.
4. Make efforts to understand the circumstances of your potential partners—their problems, aims, traditional ways of working, and the like—and try to adapt them.
5. Avoid taking umbrage.
6. Take part in joint training.
7. Show up to meetings.
8. Avoid malicious gossip about partners.
9. Recognize problems when they arise and take advantage of helpful outsiders to help sort them out.

**Figure 8. Bearers of the Costs of Crime and Control:
A Case Study**

One relatively small store on London's Oxford Street produced nearly 40 percent of the arrests at the central police station. Sleeves and boxes containing audiotapes and records were put on display at this store. By displaying them, the store avoided the expense of additional staff and storage that would be required to fill the empty cases at the point of sale. Crime control was attempted through the use of store detectives to apprehend shop thieves. The result was the "recruitment" of many young people into the criminal justice system. The costs of the sales and control methods were borne by the taxpayer and the community generally, not the store. Any additional costs of less criminogenic methods of running the shop would be borne by the shop (Ekblom 1986).

---

nical skills required for robust evaluation of crime prevention initiatives. Typical shortcomings include the use of simple before/after comparisons, use of short and arbitrary before and after periods, neglect of benchmark statistics, failure to consider possible other (nonintervention) causes of the changes observed, failure to test for displacement or diffusion of benefits, and uncritical promotion of success stories. When significant resource allocation decisions are likely to follow, investment in competent external independent evaluation is desirable. Monitoring the initiatives on a regular basis, however, is also important for dealing with very frequent implementation problems.

The HMIC Report on Policing and Crime Prevention

Making use of the framework furnished in *Getting the Grease to the Squeak*, HMIC examined in detail what police were doing by way of crime prevention. The major overall findings of the HMIC report, published as *Beating Crime* (HMIC 1998), were as follows:

- Most forces in Britain expressed a commitment to crime prevention.

- While there were examples of excellent leadership and robust systems of accountability, one or both were absent in some forces.
- Police services were committed to working in partnership with other agencies. This commitment was valued by those agencies.
- Crime prevention work involving partnership, however, sometimes lacked coordination or direction.
- The commitment to prevention found in most police services was not always matched with the manner of resource management. There was variable awareness of the financial costs and benefits of preventive activity.
- The problem-solving approach highlighted in *Getting the Grease to the Squeak* was the most effective approach for crime prevention.
- This problem-solving approach was not, however, normally adopted. This resulted in unfocused and misdirected efforts, which had an unknown impact on crime.

Additional HMIC findings revealed that only six police forces actually described a problem-solving approach to crime reduction in their crime-reduction strategy. Moreover, of the 232 initiatives that were submitted to HMIC as successes,

- 159 showed evidence of the actual existence of a problem,
- 64 showed a proper analysis of the problem,
- 47 included a monitoring process, and
- when only those initiatives that underwent any form of evaluation are considered, only 17 (5%) could be judged as having fully followed the problem-solving approach.

On the basis of these results, *Beating Crime* points to a way forward for policing and crime prevention. It advocates a framework that

- identifies crime reduction as a core policing function whose performance is managed through a clear strategy with unequivocal leadership, robust accountability and management support to enable and coordinate the total crime-reduction effort;

- uses a problem-solving approach that draws on accessible, reliable information and intelligence systems to blend innovation with tried and tested methods to produce effective solutions tailored to meet local needs;
- develops partnerships that can agree on joint priorities and broaden the range of potential solutions, ensuring that action is taken by the most appropriate partner to produce a sustainable crime reduction; and
- deploys its resources in the way best-suited to support its strategy and priorities, while retaining an awareness of the costs and expected benefits.

Beating Crime is important because it provides an authoritative HMIC judgment about what is actually happening and what else needs to happen in British police services for effective crime prevention to occur. HMIC is respected because it is led by former senior police officers, and much of its work is conducted by very capable, active officers on temporary assignment. Practitioners are also aware that HMIC recommendations will be followed up in later inspections. HMIC's endorsement of the problem-solving approach, conviction that crime prevention needs to be at the center of policing, emphasis on partnership, and acknowledgment that change is needed in police services are all highly significant and point implicitly toward problem-oriented policing.

There are clearly affinities among the conclusions in *Getting the Grease to the Squeak*, the findings and recommendations of *Beating Crime*, and problem-oriented policing.

- All specify the need for a problem-solving approach.
- All emphasize the need for the police to make prevention central to policing.
- All note the requirement for committed personnel who have the skills, resources and incentives to use data properly to identify and analyze problems as a precondition for thinking through possible solutions.
- All stress that finding and implementing solutions requires ability, imagination and the cooperation or participation of nonpolice agencies.

- All acknowledge the need (and frequent failure) to monitor and evaluate the effectiveness of preventive efforts.
- All are oriented toward maximizing the returns from finite and stretched resources.

Problem-Oriented Policing in Britain: Brit POP

There is increasing interest in problem-oriented policing in Britain, expressed in the first national conference held in October 1998. There are a number of reasons why senior officers, many of whom are taking the lead in introducing POP to their forces, are turning their attention to problem-oriented policing. First, police have seen an explosive rise in the numbers of calls for service without a commensurate increase in police resources. POP is seen as one route to managing demand by dealing with the source of problems rather than repeatedly responding to related calls. Second, many practitioners want to provide better service to the community. Many police officers, of all ranks, are unhappy about simply documenting the existence of problems that surface in calls. They would rather address the causes of these problems using a range of methods that will only sometimes include enforcement. Third, interest has grown because of the links drawn between problem-oriented policing and the conclusions of *Beating Crime*. Moreover, the provisions of the recent Crime and Disorder Act call for a problem-oriented approach that extends beyond the police service (see Figure 2).

The Police Research Group has recently completed a study of efforts to introduce problem-oriented policing in a British context (Leigh, Read, and Tilley 1996, 1998). Notwithstanding some significant achievements in addressing both crime and noncrime problems (see Figure 9 for some examples) the study found a number of implementation problems. These difficulties reveal that POP's implementation and eventual success is likely to be quite a long-term process. Several of these difficulties are outlined in the following examples.

When the initiative introducing POP began in Leicester's East Area with supportive management, training and regularly

Figure 9. Examples of POP Initiatives in Leicestershire

Complaints of Cottaging

"These toilets, on an isolated lay-by, are used by the gay fraternity. We get a couple of complaints every year from the villagers that live nearby through the parish council etc., etc. We know about them and it's year in and year out. We commenced an operation telling people who sit in their cars that within the next few weeks people will be prosecuted for any offenses that come to light. As well as that, the reason why this lay-by was used is because it's overgrown. The trees are thick, and it's very, very isolated although very near a main road. So, the Action Group decided to contact the county council to get the trees thinned, so that it's not isolated any more. The operation has been successful—we've had just one caution."

Poaching Deer

"There was evidence that the land had been driven across for the purposes of chasing deer and there was evidence of a deer carcass that had been stripped of various parts of its body, obviously for meat, in one of the fields. And this happened on several occasions. There was a lot of crop damage and what have you. We carried out observations initially but never managed to see anything. But then a vehicle that the poachers had been using got bogged down in soft soil. We kept observations on the vehicle to see if anybody would come to pick it up, but they never did. So we took it into police possession and nobody ever claimed it. We couldn't find out who the owner was. We had an idea who it was, but the person never came forward and never admitted to being the owner, so the vehicle was disposed of at a loss of about £1,000 to whoever owned it. After that the farmers, at my suggestion, dug ditches around all the accessible areas of land with low hedging or in areas where there were gaps in the hedge. They dug ditches to prevent any access onto land by vehicles and then blocked off open field entrances with large hay bales and what have you to again prevent access. And, indeed we didn't have any further problems."

(continued)

Figure 9. Examples of POP Initiatives in Leicestershire (continued)

Obstructing Vehicle Deliveries

"This small market town wasn't really built with superstores in mind. Deliveries nowadays are done by 30-ton lorries that the streets aren't built for. You would have thought they would have put the houses further apart or something, planned ahead at least! They never did. So, with narrow streets, no car parks, and things like that it was a matter of sorting out convenient parking times, or convenient delivery times. It was actually causing a lot of problems, because once the lorry came, it was capable of stopping the whole traffic flow, right through the whole town—just one lorry. And it wasn't even one main road that was blocked. Because of the tail back that came out of the high street, you could actually stop the traffic for 15 minutes. And of course you would have a lot of moaning motorists. We cracked it. Common sense strikes. First off, talking with the shop people themselves to see if there was any alternative delivery possibilities—you know, through a backyard or other access. Basically there wasn't. It would have been easy if it was once or twice a week deliveries but it is daily. There are artics going in there daily and so you couldn't block off part of the street repeatedly. So it was actually a matter of getting the deliveries brought forward to a time before the actual town got up and running, you know, came on at 9. The idea was to get them there before 9 o'clock. In fact we get earlier deliveries, at 7 or 7:30. We have had only one complaint since."

---

provided data on incident patterns, it was expected that beat officers would jump at the opportunity to take the lead in problem-oriented work. While some officers did become committed, many others remained cynical and resentful of what they often perceived as an additional burden or something they already did anyway. For problem-oriented policing to become routine in the British context, it appears that responsibility for its maintenance needs to be placed on more senior officers. Also needed are long-term efforts to address some aspects of police culture, where what is ordinarily valued above all else is operational effectiveness in dealing with crimes and crises.

Most British officers dislike completing forms. Many officers resented having to fill out SARA forms, which required completion at the scanning, analysis, response, and assessment stages of addressing problems, and were developed by the Police Research Group for East Area (reproduced in Leigh, Read, and Tilley 1996). Many completed them only when pressure was applied. The rationale for the forms was to help structure and discipline problem-oriented work and create records from which lessons could be learned. This was not sufficient incentive to establish officers' regular use of the forms. If records are to be kept in Britain, it may be unwise to depend on basic grade officers to routinely fill them in.

British police officers are not accustomed to reading and using statistical data. Although officers initially welcomed the provision of data, there was little evidence that they performed detailed analyses to better define or understand problems. It may be that capacity building for data analysis by officers, or the involvement of civilians with special expertise, is needed.

Though there were some outstanding examples of problem-oriented policing initiatives, the police tendency to emphasize detection and enforcement (which had been remarked on by William Tallack as early as 1896) was also evident. Notwithstanding the drift to enforcement methods, in Leicestershire two-fifths, and in Cleveland almost half of the problems identified led to responses targeting the victim/caller or the location of the problem.

In addition, it was rare for officers to assess their own problem-oriented initiatives as anything other than successes. Yet few hard data were collected. If POP is to include serious learning by doing, while it would not be reasonable to expect elaborate academic evaluations, somewhat greater attention to real, rather than casual impressionistic evidence, is needed. Again, some skilled and specialized civilian help might be needed here.

There are ambiguities and uncertainties in Britain over what it means to introduce problem-oriented policing. There is a wide range of conceptions of exactly what POP is and the appropriate means of implementing it. Although the basic idea of problem-oriented policing is not complex, in practice it has been construed in differing ways. In summary, POP has been understood

- as a whole-force philosophy, dealing with all issues, involving all officers, and covering all parts of a force, **OR** as a specialism, by type of officer, type of problem, and/or type of area;
- as involving a way of thinking that will inform responses to all incidents, **OR** as a way of identifying and dealing with recurrent or patterned problems;
- as a means of dealing with problems while minimizing use of law enforcement (for example, through modifying the physical environment, or addressing anti-social behavior via family group conferences), **OR** as the open-minded pursuit of problem solutions through whatever means offer prospects of success (including enforcement when needed);
- as the adoption of some specific techniques, such as the SARA process and/or the Problem Analysis Triangle (which draws on Cohen and Felson 1979) as key defining features, **OR** as the use of these techniques only as potentially useful tools;
- as involving "zero tolerance" as an element of, a tactic in, a complement to **OR** an alternative to problem-oriented policing; and/or
- as calling for a "big bang" transformation of the police service to try to effect a comprehensive and consistent new way of working, **OR** a gradual, creeping implementation of change with a variety of possible stopping points.

It is clear that POP, in the British context, is tricky to put in place, and fluid in conception. Yet, because of its timeliness, common sense and demonstrated potential when conducted well, it has substantial allure. If the various implementation problems are addressed and overcome, the more ambitious variants of POP offer a vehicle for conducting situational crime prevention and other forms of crime prevention in a systematic way, and provide a means of addressing noncrime problems as well.

Brit POP and Police Crime Prevention

In Britain, POP is taking off. It clearly has affinities with high-quality crime prevention. POP provides a context for whole-force commitment to prevention of problems, including crime. It provides a mandate for non-criminal justice preventive responses to crime, and it facilitates partnerships working across a range of issues that include crime. It also provides impetus to address crime as a product of conditions generating a variety of forms of anti-social behaviors.

The problems encountered in implementing problem-oriented policing echo those found in the HMIC review of crime prevention efforts. Though there has been some achievement, practice often falls short of the POP ideal.

Not surprisingly, in view of what has been said, both effective problem-oriented policing and effective crime prevention depend on similar contingent conditions:

- information technology systems that are adequate to routinely provide reliable incident data in a form that is open to systematic interrogation;
- appropriate skills in problem pattern/crime pattern analysis, possibly using civilian specialists;
- whole-force commitment, notably from the most senior officers;
- effective incentives with appropriate rewards and systems of accountability;
- training in problem-solving techniques relevant to local conditions;
- able, adequately trained and educated staff;
- effective ways of collaborating/involving other agencies;
- attention to implementation issues; and
- valid feedback on performance.

Future Prospects for Crime Prevention and Problem-Oriented Policing in Britain

While the implementation problems for effective crime prevention and problem-oriented policing should not be underestimated and are likely to remain as problems, the context for progress in Britain looks promising. The stimulus from *Beating Crime* has already been mentioned. The 1998 Crime and Disorder Act (discussed briefly in Figure 2) requires the police, along with other local partner agencies, to adopt a systematic problem-oriented approach to crime and disorder issues. Extensive Home Office guidance is aimed at facilitating informed implementation of these requirements. Efforts will be made to monitor achievements, elicit lessons for improved implementation and hold partnerships accountable for what they do. This will further provide incentive for effective work.

The demonstration projects reported by the Police Research Group are acting as pathfinders for other forces who are anxious to learn from mistakes as well as achievements. The stimulus provided for attention to POP at senior levels and the recognition that leadership is needed will, it is hoped, prevent problem-oriented policing from amounting only to an occasional style of policing adopted by isolated, exceptional officers. Finally, the government's crime-reduction program will likely provide funds to support major problem-oriented crime prevention initiatives and support the mainstreaming of problem-oriented work in police services. These funds will elicit lessons that will be fed back into improved practice. It is intended that problem-oriented policing in Britain will help identify and address problems beyond the level of their manifestation in particular local settings. It is clear, for example, that children missing from residential homes, crimes against service stations with convenience stores, and violence and abuse at hospital accident and emergency departments exist as problems for local officers, as significant calls on resources in local areas, and as national issues. The problems can be addressed at these varying levels.

This chapter began by pointing out that POP and situational crime prevention developed independently at much the same time. Since that time, Goldstein has paid substantial tribute to the work of Ron Clarke and others working within the framework of situational crime prevention (Goldstein 1990). In much the same way, those involved in situational crime prevention acknowledge the importance of Goldstein's work in problem-oriented policing. Indeed, Ron Clarke is currently one of the adjudicators for the Herman Goldstein Award for Excellence in Problem-Oriented Policing (see Clarke 1997). There has thus been something of an academic, as well as substantive and conceptual, rapprochement between situational crime prevention and problem-oriented policing, though they do retain some distinctive emphases. There is ample scope for improvement in problem-oriented policing through a complementary, practical rapprochement.

REFERENCES

Association of Chief Police Officers. 1996. *Towards 2000: A Crime Prevention Strategy for the Millenium.* Leicester, U.K.: Association of Chief Police Officers.

Clarke, R. 1980. Situational Crime Prevention: Theory and Practice. *British Journal of Criminology* 20:136–147.

Clarke, R. 1997. *Problem-Oriented Policing and the Potential Contribution of Criminology.* Unpublished report to U.S. Department of Justice.

Clarke, R., and M. Hough. 1984. *Crime and Police Effectiveness.* Police Research Study 79. London: Home Office.

Cohen, L., and M. Felson. 1979. Social Change and Crime Rate Trends: A Routine Activity Approach. *American Sociological Review* 44:588–608.

Ekblom, P. 1986. *The Prevention of Shop Theft: An Approach Through Crime Analysis.* Crime Prevention Unit Paper 5. London: Home Office.

Ekblom, P. 1997. Gearing Up Against Crime: A Dynamic Framework to Help Designers Keep Up with the Adaptive Criminal in a Changing World. *International Journal of Risk, Security and Crime Prevention* 2(4):249–265.

Farrell, G., and K. Pease. 1993. *Once Bitten, Twice Bitten: Repeat Victimisation and its Implications for Crime Prevention.* Crime Prevention Unit Paper 46. London: Home Office.

Goldstein, H. 1979. Improving Policing: A Problem-Oriented Approach. *Crime and Delinquency* 26:236–258.

Goldstein, H. 1990. *Problem-Oriented Policing.* New York: McGraw-Hill.

HMIC. 1998. *Beating Crime.* London: Home Office.

Home Office. 1998. *Guidance on Local Crime Prevention Partnerships.* London: Home Office.

Homel, R. 1994. Can the Police Prevent Crime? In *Unpeeling Tradition,* edited by K. Bryett and C. Lewis. Sydney, Australia: Macmillan.

Hough, M., and N. Tilley. 1998a. *Getting the Grease to the Squeak: Research Lessons for Crime Prevention*. Crime Detection and Prevention Series Paper 85. London: Home Office.

Hough, M., and N. Tilley. 1998b. *Auditing Crime and Disorder: Guidance for Local Partnerships*. Crime Detection and Prevention series Paper 85. London: Home Office.

Laycock, G. 1985. *Property Marking: A Deterrent to Domestic Burglary*. Crime Prevention Unit Paper 3. London: Home Office.

Laycock, G. 1997. Operation Identification or the Power of Publicity? In *Crime Prevention: Successful Case Studies*, edited by R. Clarke. New York: Harrow & Heston.

Leigh, A., T. Read, and N. Tilley. 1996. *Problem-Oriented Policing: Brit Pop*. Crime Detection and Prevention Series Paper 75. London: Home Office.

Leigh, A., T. Read, and N. Tilley. 1998. *Brit Pop II: Problem-Oriented Policing in Practice*. Police Research Series Paper 93. London: Home Office.

Matthews, R. 1992. Developing More Effective Strategies for Curbing Prostitution. In *Crime Prevention: Successful Case Studies*, edited by R. Clarke. New York: Harrow & Heston.

Morgan, R., and T. Newburn. 1997. *The Future of Policing*. Oxford: Clarendon Press.

Pease, K. 1997. Predicting the Future: The Role of Routine Activity and Rational Choice Theory. In *Rational Choice and Situational Crime Prevention*, edited by G. Newman, R. Clarke, and S. Shoham. Aldershot, U.K.: Dartmouth.

Poyner, B., and B. Webb. 1992. Reducing Theft from Shopping Bags in City Center Markets. In *Crime Prevention: Successful Case Studies*, edited by R. Clarke. New York: Harrow & Heston.

Sherman, L. 1992. *Policing Domestic Violence*. New York: Free Press.

Sloan-Hewitt, M., and G. Kelling. 1992. Subway Graffiti in New York City: "Getting Up" vs. Meanin It and Cleanin It. In *Crime Prevention: Successful Case Studies*, 2d ed, edited by R. Clarke. New York: Harrow & Heston.

Tallack, W. 1896. *Penological and Preventive Principles*. London: Wertheimer, Lea and Co.

Tilley, N. 1992. *Safer Cities and Community Safety Strategies*. Crime Prevention Unit Paper 38. London: Home Office.

CHAPTER II

USING URBAN DESIGN TO HELP ERADICATE CRIME PLACES

Gregory Saville

Sometimes the simplest ideas can have the biggest impact on crime. It has been said that a crowbar can move a mountain if applied to the right places. Simplicity is the force behind the concept of crime prevention through environmental design—CPTED (pronounced sep-ted). CPTED offers urban designers and neighborhood problem solvers an effective and practical tool for reducing the opportunity for crime. The premise of CPTED is simple—watch those who engage in criminal or nuisance behavior in public. If you watch carefully, you will notice that these individuals prefer some areas over others, prefer certain times of the day and week, and will focus on specific targets while ignoring others. Why? The criminals' choices are called environmental preferences. CPTED attempts to modify physical places to remove characteristics that conform to criminals' environmental preferences.

CPTED is primarily a prevention strategy that deals with the design, planning and structure of cities and neighborhoods. It recognizes that the physical environment has a great impact on the types and locations of crime problems. Therefore, CPTED has become a key ingredient for responsible planning of new housing projects, shopping malls, parks, parking lots, commercial areas, and other places in the modern city. Because the majority of crime is based in opportunity, modifying the environment can reduce or prevent further criminal acts or illicit behavior. The issues of neighborhood environmental design, land use, social diversity, and extent of local activities are of great concern to urban planners, police officers and residents alike. Preventing crime by designing it out of an area can save enormous costs and time for police, courts and prisons, it can reduce the social and psychological impact of crime in neighborhoods and, most important, CPTED improves the livability and safety of urban places.

CPTED emerged in the 1970s following a series of studies on the effect of physical environment on crime. These studies ultimately concluded that there is no replacement for proper design. This idea harkens back to Jane Jacobs' pioneering work in her book *The Death and Life of Great American Cities* (1961). Jacobs' assertion that neighborhood diversity and social mix influence the opportunities for crime was the seminal concept that instigated the work of the CPTED pioneers. The early development of this CPTED concept is generally attributed to criminologist C. Ray Jeffery in his book *Crime Prevention Through Environmental Design* (1971), and architect Oscar Newman's *Defensible Space* (1972). Other foundation work includes Schlomo Angel's doctoral dissertation on the subject in 1968 (Angel 1968) and a government-sponsored study in 1969 (Luedtke et al. 1970).

The Basic CPTED Principles

CPTED's basic principle is territorial reinforcement; physical design can create or reinforce residents' feelings of control and ownership over a specific location or territory. This involves the careful subdivision of neighborhood spaces, using landscaping, architecture and planning, into different degrees of neighborhood ownership: public, semipublic or private.

Territorial reinforcement requires the consideration of several different components of environmental design: access control, natural surveillance, neighborhood image and maintenance, and environmental land use. Access control reinforces "turf" or feelings of ownership by focusing specifically on the location and appearance of entrances to and exits from buildings, parks, parking lots, and neighborhoods. The mere relocation of entrances to more strategic positions can restrict or inhibit undesirable traffic flow through an area. When people are able to observe neigh-

bors coming and going from a common entranceway, they can
begin to identify familiar faces and, in turn, recognize who does
not belong in the building or the neighborhood. Individuals develop a sense of ownership over common areas when they are
able to challenge strangers in their building or on their street.

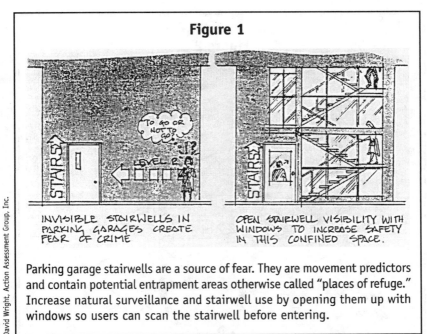

Figure 1

INVISIBLE STAIRWELLS IN PARKING GARAGES CREATE FEAR OF CRIME

OPEN STAIRWELL VISIBILITY WITH WINDOWS TO INCREASE SAFETY IN THIS CONFINED SPACE.

Parking garage stairwells are a source of fear. They are movement predictors
and contain potential entrapment areas otherwise called "places of refuge."
Increase natural surveillance and stairwell use by opening them up with
windows so users can scan the stairwell before entering.

David Wright, Action Assessment Group, Inc.

Natural surveillance, as a component of territorial reinforcement, involves placing legitimate "eyes" on the street to help
make a place unattractive to offenders. Areas that offer a clear
view from streets or nearby houses are unattractive to offenders,
and therefore, the possibility of that area becoming a criminal's
environmental preference—a place to commit crime—is reduced.
Increased natural surveillance can be achieved by improving sight
lines, strategically placing windows and lighting, and removing
obstructions. However, it is important to note that community
building—the creation of a safe neighborhood environment—

involves more than simple design. Placing eyes on the street may be insufficient if they are the "wrong" eyes (the eyes of a local drug dealer, for instance) or if those eyes are too afraid to take any action against what they are witnessing.

Figure 2

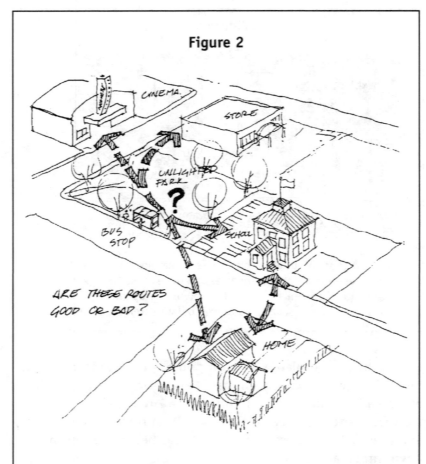

Illustration showing the relationship between land uses, movement predictors and their roles in becoming crime facilitators. Is this a good land use mix for a neighborhood village center?

Neighborhood image and maintenance impacts CPTED because the more dilapidated an area has become, the more likely it is to attract unwanted activities and become victimized. A regular program of school maintenance or street clean-ups can be an effective deterrent to offenders in an area. The "broken windows theory" (Kelling and Coles 1996) has been supported in a multitude of studies that focus on a location's image and its influence on an area's potential of becoming a crime target. The New York City Subway's 1984 Clean Car Program utilized graffiti removal to create a more positive image in the subway. "The program succeeded because it attacked the basic motives of graffitists who, above all else, wanted their work seen. The strategy of never permitting tagged trains to be used meant that graffiti would be defeated" (Kelling and Coles 1996:116).

The environmental land use component of CPTED and of territorial reinforcement aims to reduce conflicts between different user groups over a common area. For instance, a user group, such as teen skateboarders, may be legitimately using a space,

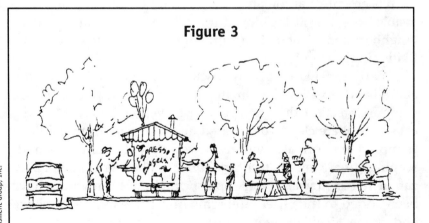

Figure 3

Street vendors on public streets become "street mayors," in that they take ownership of their turf for sales to customers. With nearby seating, informal or natural surveillance is provided.

David Wright, Action Assessment Group, Inc.

yet still conflict with other user groups, such as seniors out for a stroll. CPTED strategies are useful for redesigning public spaces to better control where and how different groups interact, and enable all groups to use the public domain safely. The environmental land use component of CPTED has been the subject of new research in the ecology of crime. Recent work has focused on such topics as the impact of abandoned buildings as magnets for crime (Spelman 1993). The ecology of crime offers problem-oriented policing practitioners many promising new approaches, including CPTED.

How Does CPTED Work?

CPTED can include both short-term and long-term design strategies. Short-term tactics address problems that already exist. This may include improving the lighting outside a store to reduce robberies, trimming the hedges around a townhouse to prevent burglaries, or removing high-risk items from easy access to shoplifters in a shopping mall. Long-term CPTED strategies, on the other hand, target potential problems. This may include the careful placement of automated bank machines in an open, easily visible and well-lit location during the planning of streets or neighborhoods aimed at encouraging legitimate downtown activities in the evenings.

Early CPTED, as briefly discussed above, utilized natural surveillance to allow legitimate users to defend public spaces, using architectural design to put more "eyes on the street." Physical spaces were clearly delineated in a hierarchy from public to semiprivate to private, with improved street lighting and landscaping enhancing the territoriality or public ownership of a location. In recent years, more sophisticated CPTED methods have been added to the repertoire: removing crime targets, effective and proper displacement of problems, reducing crime facilitators, avoiding the neighborhood crime threshold or tipping point, and the like. The renewed interest in CPTED in recent years has led to a more comprehensive, ecological approach for reducing crime niches in neighborhoods.

Second-generation CPTED, also referred to as environmental crime prevention, situational crime prevention and environmental criminology, represents the next generation of sophisticated strategies for implementing CPTED. It involves newer forms of large-scale planning strategies, such as the tipping point phenomenon and effective displacement (Saville and Cleveland 1997). Environmental modifications are implemented to set the stage for crime reduction, and additional social changes are employed to maintain the impact of those modifications. New findings that arise from these social changes are documented, reassessed and incorporated with the information already gathered to provide additional tools to prevent crime.

One example of second-generation CPTED is the concept of ecological threshold or the neighborhood tipping point (Saville 1996). Basically, the concept holds that a neighborhood has the capacity to accommodate only a certain number of adverse conditions—a certain number of abandoned buildings, taverns, drug dealers residing in an apartment complex, or the like. If you add too many, the system will exceed its carrying capacity, overrun the tipping point and collapse. Initially, the idea of tipping points was utilized primarily as a planning concept (Famelis 1970; Kozlowski, Hughes, and Brown 1972; Kozlowski 1971; Whyte 1988). Ultimately, however, the idea was expanded and incorporated into the ecology of crime (Wilson 1980; Taylor and Covington 1988). It is inherently difficult for police and other public officials to determine a specific area's tipping point as a means of establishing CPTED planning strategies. In a preliminary study of a Vancouver neighborhood's bars and taverns, a statistical model known as logged-regression was used to test for the existence of a tipping point. In this study, the accessibility of alcohol, termed alcohol-units, in a particular neighborhood was established by measuring the number of alcohol-serving establishments, the amount of alcohol sales in that area, and the number of bar seats in each bar. The number of alcohol-units was subsequently "regressed" against (compared with) the alcohol-related calls for police service, in an attempt to determine whether the resultant relationship was linear (one call per alcohol-unit) or exponential (doubling numbers of calls as alcohol-units increase). If the relationship was exponential, it was foreseeable that the number of alcohol-related calls would soon exceed the police ability to respond in a timely, effective manner. There would also be the potential for exceeding the ability of social services, ambulance services and other response units to respond due to limitations imposed by resources, politics and time availability. When the capabilities of an area's agencies have been exceeded, the area is experiencing the tipping point phenomenon. When this occurs, the implications are at once felt by crime victims, the police who respond to alcohol-related calls, and those controlling the alcohol establishments—and a crime hotspot is created.

In the Vancouver bar and tavern study, the data on five different neighborhoods did, indeed, provide preliminary evidence that tipping points are crime-generating factors in urban neighborhoods (Saville and Wong 1996). The evidence indicated that too many bars in too small an area created an excessive amount of alcohol-related crime that would be curtailed if the bars were spread out more evenly across the city. Vancouver began to address this potential for crime by scrutinizing the licensing requirements in more troubled neighborhoods. Tipping point evidence can justify imposed moratoriums on the approval of additional alcohol licenses in very troubled areas. Other cities are combating the potential problem by imposing bar distance requirements or minimum size restrictions. This work in second-generation CPTED and ecology of crime can decrease the number of crime hotspots in a city.

CPTED Implementation

There are three primary means for implementing CPTED strategies: (1) mechanical devices, (2) organizational or management practices, and (3) natural design. Mechanical devices have the advantage of enhancing security in high-risk areas without requiring the presence of an individual in that area. Devices include closed circuit television (CCTV) and security locking systems. Electronic point-of-sale scanners in department stores can reduce shop theft, and anti-theft detectors at library exits can reduce book thefts. Mechanical devices, however, have the disadvantage of requiring constant maintenance. In addition, they may also imply safety and security to the public when there is none. For example, while CCTV may help identify offenders, it has rarely been responsible for stopping an actual crime in progress. Although they may deter some offenders, mechanical devices often merely displace problems to areas just outside of camera range, thereby solving nothing.

Organizational or management practices as a means of implementing CPTED include formal police and security patrols, bouncers in late-night taverns, and citizen patrols in high-risk neighborhoods. These practices can put more eyes on the street and offer a visible deterrent to crime. However, they have the disadvantage of being reliant on extensive people-power, which can be very expensive. Because few communities can afford constant, organized surveillance, the expense can make these practices of limited use. In recent years, there has been an explosion of police CCTV on public streets aimed at enhancing organized police patrols. However, this concept of "big brother watching" has raised privacy concerns in a democratic society. Not everyone wishes to be monitored by police while they walk down the street, speak to shop owners or simply go about their daily business.

Natural design, as a means of implementing CPTED, encourages the use of space and the design of urban places to enhance the social interaction of people in the public domain in a less explicit manner. Natural methods have the advantage of being less intrusive than mechanical devices, and longer lasting than organized surveillance. Potential targets are removed from easy opportunity by proper planning, and the potential for conflicting land uses is reduced through effective landscaping. Lighting can enhance nighttime sight lines, while street clean-ups can eliminate hiding places and help residents take ownership of their neighborhood. If people live in a neighborhood they care for, effective design can help protect them and their area.

CPTED Example I:
Break-In and Vandalism Problems at a Local School

This example chronicles the efforts of a CPTED officer in Port Simpson, British Columbia, Canada to analyze break-in and vandalism problems at a local small-town school. Because they lacked other community activities, local juveniles were hanging out at the rear of the school in the evenings, causing problems. The officer's first stage of problem solving, scanning, included an initial site visit and a review of the relevant crime statistics to determine the underlying problem. Based on her findings, the officer proceeded with problem analysis, which included examining crime reports, conducting on-site interviews and attending a planning meeting with staff and parents. During this meeting, suggestions were made about how to resolve the problem and, together with parents and the school principal, the officer developed a tailor-made response that incorporated positive displacement.

The officer encouraged the school to implement design changes that included turning off the night lights. In turn, she anticipated displacement of the juveniles to a nearby recreation center, and in preparation, the officer spoke with youth workers at the center. They, in turn, planned evening activities for the youths. Once the CPTED measures were executed, the youths were, in fact, displaced to positive programming at the recreation center and, since that time, crime at the school has dropped off completely. Afterward, the CPTED officer assessed her results and noted that willful damage to the school was significantly reduced. Most of the youths started hanging out at the recreation center across town, which had the facility and programs for them. The community felt this was positive. The parents advisory council was so pleased by the results, they decided to support the students in an additional proposal for a new outdoor arena (McLea 1995).

CPTED Example 2: Time Displacement

In Delta, British Columbia, just south of Vancouver, a CPTED officer responded to noise complaints lodged from homes adjacent to a golf course. The offensive noise was becoming a recurring problem. After speaking to residents, and conducting a site visit, the officer ascertained that the noise complaints were arising from the golf course gardener's choice of mowing times and locations. This situation required some form of time displacement. Interviews with the gardener revealed that the mowing with a large motorized mowing machine began at 7 a.m. on the ninth hole, situated in close proximity to the residents lodging noise complaints. By studying the layout of the course, the CPTED officer recognized an alternative solution to reduce the problem. When informed he was committing a noise infraction, the gardener agreed to change his mowing routine, beginning at the first hole where there were no nearby residents. Consequently, by the time the gardener reached the ninth hole, it was 9:30 a.m. and residents were already awake. There were no more noise complaints.

CPTED Example 3: Crimes in a Housing Estate

As an example of a much larger scale problem-solving exercise utilizing CPTED, this case chronicles the activities of a planning and consulting firm hired to assess crime problems at a public housing estate in Vancouver. It illustrates the universal appeal of the problem-solving model and CPTED practices, not only for police officers but also for other groups interested in neighborhood safety. This effort involved a more extensive scanning and analysis phase, termed risk assessment by urban planners, that included crime mapping to examine hotspots, local surveys, a site visit, safety audits, numerous meetings and focus groups on site, and interviews with housing staff, residents, local adolescents, and gang members. A variety of mitigating factors for the problems were identified, including poor territoriality on the grounds, absence of access control, excessive numbers of unsupervised adolescents on site, poor lighting, and limited natural surveillance. The high number of unsupervised adolescents was indicative of the role that social factors were playing in the problem, and the need for a response incorporating second-generation CPTED.

At the heart of this problem were a half-dozen apartments housing active drug dealers. Legitimate renters on site were unable to exert any control of the premise—the drug dealers had taken over the estate. This loss of ownership and control resulted from the situation exceeding the community's tolerance or tipping point and serves as an example of an ecosystem that had become dysfunctional. The number of drug dealers and the amount of activity they generated tipped over the residents' capacity to effectively take control (Saville 1996). Consideration of the crime niches at this estate in an ecological or holistic way facilitated the development of CPTED strategies to reduce crime opportunities.

Initially, some, but not all, of the drug dealers were evicted. Enough dealers were evicted to return control of the site back to legitimate residents and return the neighborhood to a level below the tipping point. By displacing some of the troublemakers from the estate, legitimate renters regained control of their own building. In addition, managers took greater care in balancing the number of single-parent families on site so that fewer unsupervised youths could be influenced by the drug dealers. Physical design changes were then made to the complex that helped establish territoriality, formulate access control and improve natural surveillance. Within a few months, the reported problems decreased and far fewer police calls are now received at the estate. In addition, there has been no discernible increase in police calls to other nearby areas in the neighborhood. In other words, there was an overall reduction of crime with no significant negative displacement.

The Future of CPTED

Second-generation CPTED formulates an understanding of the context of crime through risk assessment. It utilizes an ecological framework in which to view the neighborhood as an ecosystem, taking into account that an ecosystem can become unbalanced or tip over if proper land uses and activities are not instituted. Furthermore, second-generation CPTED, as a process, recognizes the need for caution when using displacement as a potential tool. The Vancouver Bar Study, along with all the emerging research in the ecology of crime, signals the emergence of a new form of crime prevention in neighborhoods. It shows how the ecological model can explain and help reduce crime opportunities and crime niches. This emerging research suggests that second-generation CPTED, with its emphasis first on the physical environment where crime occurs and then on social community-building strategies, is the best way to deal with the complex issue of crime in its many contexts.

REFERENCES

Angel, S. 1968. *Discouraging Crime Through City Planning*. Ph.D. dissertation. Institute of Urban and Regional Development, University of California at Berkeley.

Famelis, N. 1970. On the Validity of Urban Threshold Theory: Further Comments. *Journal of the Town Planning Institute*, January.

Jacobs, J. 1961. *The Death and Life of Great American Cities*. New York: Vintage.

Jeffery, C. R. 1971. *Crime Prevention Through Environmental Design*. Beverly Hills, Calif.: Sage.

Kelling, G., and C. Coles. 1996. *Fixing Broken Windows: Restoring Order and Reducing Crime in Our Communities*. New York: Touchstone.

Kozlowski, J. 1971. The Place and Role of Threshold Analysis in the "Model" Planning Process. *Ekistics* 32:348–353.

Kozlowski, J., J. T. Hughes, and R. Brown. 1972. *Threshold Analysis: A Quantitative Planning Method*. London: Architectural Press.

Luedtke, G., et al. 1970. *Crime and the Physical City: Neighborhood Design Techniques for Crime Reduction*. Washington, D.C.: U.S. Department of Justice.

McLea, R. 1995. Port Simpson Break-Ins. *The Vanguard: The British Columbia Problem-Oriented Policing Newsletter* 2(1):3–4.

Newman, O. 1972. *Defensible Space: Crime Prevention Through Urban Design*. New York: Macmillan.

Saville, G. 1996. Searching for a Neighborhood's Crime Threshold. *Subject to Debate* 10(10):1–6.

Saville, G. 1996. *Assessing Risk and Crime Potentials in Neighborhoods*. Paper presented at 1st Annual International CPTED Association Conference, Calgary, Alberta. 30 October–1 November.

Saville, G., and G. Cleveland. 1997. *Second-Generation CPTED in Schools*. Paper presented at 2nd Annual International CPTED Association Conference, Orlando, Fla. 2–4 December.

Saville, G., and P. Wong. 1994. *Exceeding the Crime Threshold: The Carrying Capacity of Neighborhoods*. Paper presented at 46th Annual Meeting of the American Society for Criminology, Miami, Fla. 9–12 November.

Spelman, W. 1993. Abandoned Buildings: Magnets for Crime? *Journal of Criminal Justice* 21:481–495.

Taylor, R., and J. Covington. 1988. Neighborhood Changes in Ecology and Violence. *Criminology* 26(4):553–589.

Whyte, W. 1988. *City: Rediscovering the Center*. New York: Doubleday.

Wilson, S. 1980. Vandalism and Defensible Space on London Housing Estates. In *Designing Out Crime*, edited by R. V. G. Clarke and P. Mayhew. London: Home Office.

CHAPTER 12

CRIME MAPPING FOR PROBLEM SOLVING

Nancy La Vigne and Julie Wartell

Despite the limited use of computerized crime mapping, many examples exist of its utility for problem-solving efforts. Following an overview of the basic fundamentals of geographic information systems (GIS), this chapter will highlight examples of mapping in support of problem-oriented policing. In 1997, the Crime Mapping Research Center conducted a nationwide crime mapping survey of approximately 2,700 law enforcement agencies in an attempt to quantify crime mapping efforts. The survey was designed to determine the extent to which agencies are utilizing computerized crime mapping and how the information is being applied. In addition, if an agency was not using crime mapping at the time the survey was administered, the survey solicited information on whether there were future plans for instituting mapping, and the resources the agency would require to implement a mapping system. The survey responses revealed that the majority of U.S. law enforcement agencies are still in their infancy with respect to crime mapping. Only 13.5 percent of all responding agencies were performing computerized crime mapping in some form. Of the agencies with at least 100 sworn officers, 35 percent were performing mapping.

These surveys allowed the Crime Mapping Research Center to determine what agencies are doing, what they would like to be doing, and what is preventing them from reaching their goals (whether resources, training or organizational/management support). The results indicate that there is a wide range of mapping being conducted around the country, and correspondingly diverse uses for this mapping.

Geographic Information Systems (GIS)

The advent of crime mapping has allowed law enforcement agencies to accomplish five important tasks:

1. identify problems and reveal trends and patterns,
2. analyze problems by using multiple data sources,
3. assess efforts to evaluate responses,
4. show and assess resource allocations, and
5. share information with the community and other agencies.

These tasks, which will be discussed in this chapter, are achieved through the use of a geographic information system (GIS). GIS allows users to represent large quantities of diverse data in a comprehensible, informative map format. Printed maps have been produced for centuries in an attempt to represent the real world on paper in a way that can be carried and used as a guide. A GIS contains a digital model of that abstracted real world—in essence, it is the printed map in a digital form. However, this digital form consists of a relational database with multiple data fields containing a great deal of geographically referenced information. A map created by a GIS can illustrate both the spatial and temporal attributes of a crime. The beauty of this format is that it contains a wealth of information and yet can be easily displayed in a format similar in usability to a basic paper map.

With all the resources available to law enforcement personnel, why do they need digital maps? Policing is data-driven, and maps produced by a GIS integrate large quantities of accumulated data in a useful, meaningful way. In addition, the presentation of data in the visual form of a map may be a more effective way to communicate information to officers than simple oral recitation or pages of statistics. "A picture is worth a thousand words." Once a GIS database has been constructed, the data that are stored within it can be quickly accessed at any point in the future; the digital maps can serve as archives for information.

With a paper map, analysis is limited to looking at it, drawing circles on it and putting pins in it. However, unlike paper maps, GIS makes it possible to analyze data and map them in a variety of ways, enabling the user to experiment with different scenarios and data layers without the cumbersome process of placing and removing pins. The GIS software can store data in a manner that makes information accessible in any number of ways: you can analyze the data, display it on the screen and print it out. In fact, with the digital database, it is possible to query (ask questions of) the geographically referenced data to solicit specific information and produce focused maps. GIS enables individuals to produce readable maps that can show, for instance, only specified crimes at a certain time of day or week.

The maps' usefulness and relevance are generally limited only by the type of data that are input into the system. Normally, for crime mapping purposes, data will be obtained from various police systems such as records management systems (RMS) and computer-aided dispatch (CAD), including crime incidents, arrests and calls for service. In addition, some agencies will incorporate information from other criminal justice agencies, such as probation and parole, or community-related data, such as demographics and environmental characteristics. Aside from the typical crime data, there are a wealth of data that can be incorporated into a map. For instance, you may want to map street robberies in relation to the location of automatic teller machines (ATMs). In addition, when studying robberies and ATMs, you may also choose to incorporate bus lines, street lights, federally assisted housing, and high-rise apartment buildings into the digital database. It seems that no matter how often crime mapping and crime analysis classes are held, there are always new ideas coming from the students on data that can be mapped. For instance, in one class, after going through the types of city and county agencies that could provide information, a chief from a small town in New York indicated that his department maps the trash collection routes. There were a number of reasons why they wanted to know these routes: to keep updated on whether streets were closed, avoid conflict with the trash collectors when executing a search warrant, and know the best time and day to search through trash if it was necessary. The possibilities of types of information that can be mapped are endless; any data element that is address-based or has a global positioning system (GPS) location can be mapped.

A Quick Lesson in GIS

To comprehensively discuss crime mapping, it is necessary to become familiar with basic GIS concepts and terminology. There are three primary ways to plot a location on the map: points, lines, and polygons or areas. Points are positioned at a specific address and can be placed on the map to represent types of crimes, types of arrests or home addresses of offenders and parolees. The use of points is similar to using pins to mark areas on a paper map. Lines are used in GIS to communicate information that has direction. The most common use of lines for crime mapping is to highlight streets. However, they can also be used to illustrate the routes that individuals use to get to school, or bus and subway routes. Streams or other objects that normally appear on a map as a line will also be lines within a GIS. This ability to map street networks (lines) in conjunction with crime and address information (points) can prove valuable for calculating distances. Polygons are used in GIS to represent areas such as patrol districts, parks, housing complexes, shopping malls, school zones, and gang territories.

GIS analysis is accomplished by forming layers of information on a map. Whereas simple paper maps represent all the information on one layer, on one piece of paper, GIS allows users to choose the specific information or layers to display on the map. A very basic example of layering is illustrated in Figure 1. The first layer of information is a street grid, the second layer is the location of street lights on the street grid, and the third layer is the location of street robberies in the area. When all three layers are integrated, the resulting map indicates a relationship between street robbery and areas where there are no street lights.

Types of Maps

GIS maps range from simple to quite sophisticated. The choice of type of map is based primarily on the type of data that are

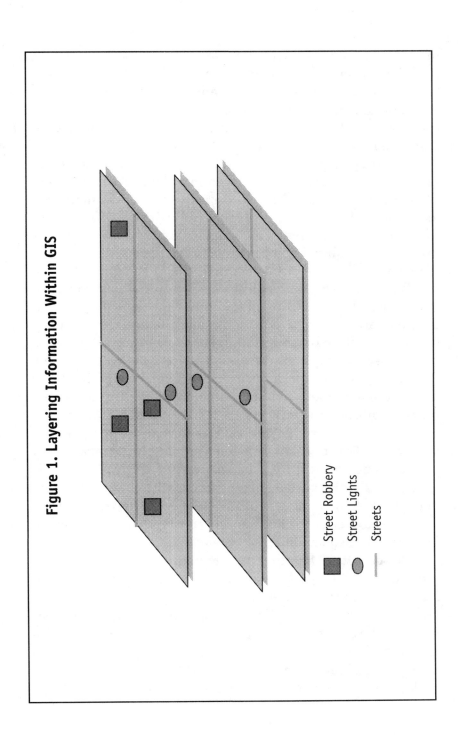

Figure 1. Layering Information Within GIS

Street Robbery

Street Lights

Streets

mapped, analysis expectations and computer software being used. More computerized mapping programs and extensions are being tailored for law enforcement applications. Some programs provide the option of mapping symbols such as guns, people, cars and so forth. The following section introduces a variety of mapping formats and provides illustrations.

Pin Mapping. People unfamiliar with computerized mapping primarily think of its application as limited to "pin mapping"—the placement of pins on a paper map to mark key locations, such as addresses of robbery incidents. GIS does produce its own variation of a pin map. Figure 2 is a map of Washington, D.C., showing homicides over a two-year period. However, by looking at this example, the exact crime situation may not be entirely clear. For instance, a cluster of dots may make it difficult to determine how many crimes have actually occurred in one location. Indeed, what looks like one dot could actually be many events happening at the very same address. With standard paper pin maps, the only way to determine whether there have been multiple incidents in one location is to go back and look through the files. GIS, on the other hand, has the data within the program, and the answers are readily accessible.

Choropleth/Area Mapping. This form of mapping is a revised form of the pin map. Point data are simply aggregated and represented in the form of a shaded polygon. Depending on the type of data and expected analysis, one might aggregate by resident population, number of businesses per census tract or number of students per school boundary. Figure 3 is a map of homicides per square mile.

Association Mapping. By integrating two or more maps representing different types of information, it is possible to analyze more than one variable at a time. In this way, visual correlations can be conducted to determine whether a relationship exists between the two variables. Figure 4 is an example of an association map. This example shows a relationship between persons per square mile and number of homicides. In other words, more homicides occur where there are more people.

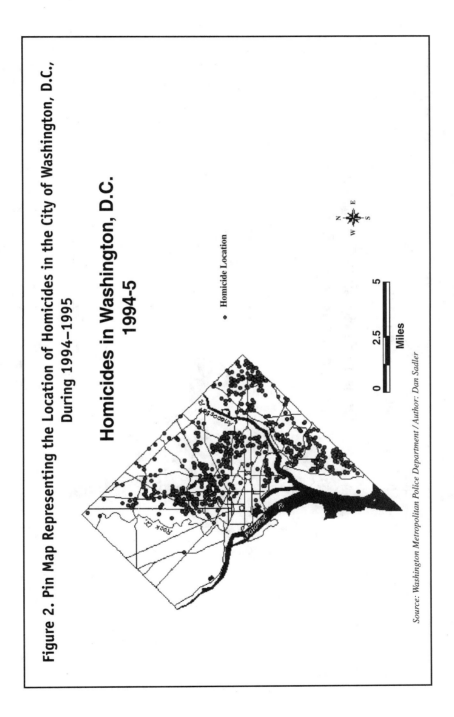

Figure 2. Pin Map Representing the Location of Homicides in the City of Washington, D.C., During 1994–1995

Homicides in Washington, D.C. 1994-5

• Homicide Location

Miles
0   2.5   5

Source: Washington Metropolitan Police Department / Author: Dan Sadler

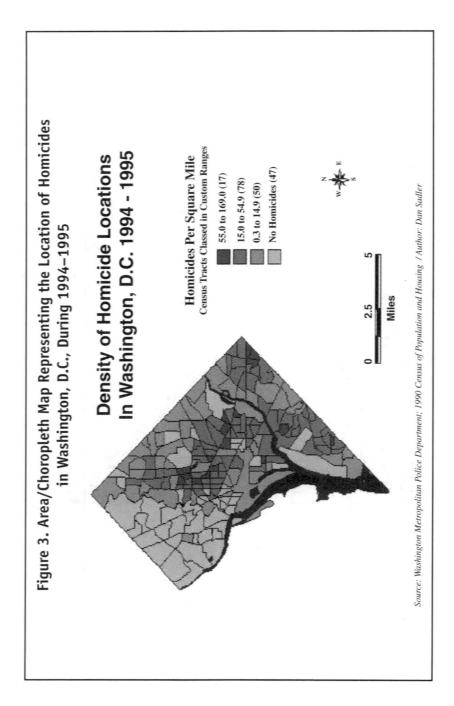

Figure 3. Area/Choropleth Map Representing the Location of Homicides in Washington, D.C., During 1994–1995

Density of Homicide Locations
In Washington, D.C. 1994 - 1995

Homicides Per Square Mile
Census Tracts Classed in Custom Ranges

55.0 to 169.0 (17)
15.0 to 54.9 (78)
0.3 to 14.9 (50)
No Homicides (47)

0   2.5   5
Miles

Source: Washington Metropolitan Police Department; 1990 Census of Population and Housing / Author: Dan Sadler

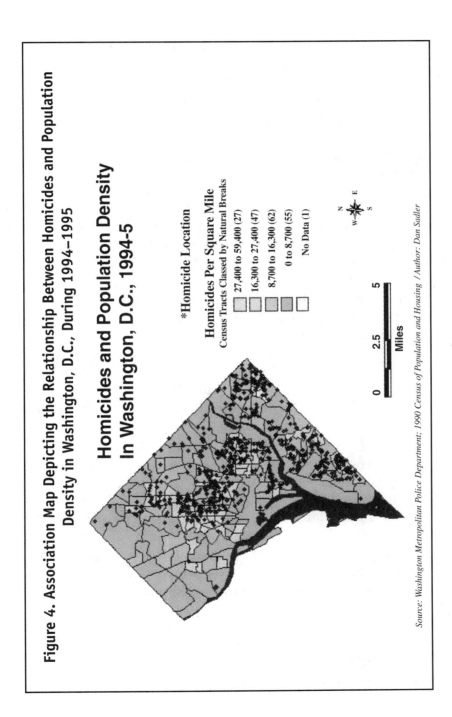

Figure 4. Association Map Depicting the Relationship Between Homicides and Population Density in Washington, D.C., During 1994–1995

Homicides and Population Density
In Washington, D.C., 1994-5

*Homicide Location

Homicides Per Square Mile
Census Tracts Classed by Natural Breaks

27,400 to 59,400 (27)
16,300 to 27,400 (47)
8,700 to 16,300 (62)
0 to 8,700 (55)
No Data (1)

0   2.5   5
Miles

Source: Washington Metropolitan Police Department; 1990 Census of Population and Housing / Author: Dan Sadler

Hotspot Mapping. Hotspot mapping is a means of identifying high-crime locations. Whereas pin mapping makes it difficult to visually discern whether one dot is on top of another, or how many dots are clustered over one location, hotspot mapping can overcome this difficulty. This type of mapping is helpful when attempting to identify and mark unusually high concentrations of crime or disorder problems in specific locations. Computer programs, such as STAC (Spatial and Temporal Analysis of Crime), can identify hotspots by looking at the dots and establishing where the clusters lie. STAC is available free of charge through the Illinois Criminal Justice Information Authority, and is used by many crime analysts to identify hotspots. While STAC uses elliptical boundaries to mark hot spots, other software extensions use various techniques to display the density of incidents through varying shades of gray or color gradations.

Radial Mapping. This form of mapping establishes distance radii around specific points of data. For instance, one might want to determine how many violent crimes are within a 500-foot radius of alcohol establishments. Figure 5 illustrates the distance relationship between home addresses of child sex offenders and schools. The circles on the map represent the buffer zone around the schools and extend out from the dot for a radius of 1,000 feet. Many of the released sex offenders live within 1,000 feet of a school. This information can be useful for investigative and notification purposes.

Grid Cell Mapping. When producing a grid cell map, the computer divides all the data into grids with very small squares. By establishing these divisions, the computer smoothes the data for the variable that is being studied. Grid cell mapping is a means of hotspot analysis, but it has the added power of enabling the user to perform mathematical calculations on the map. For example, one can subtract crimes occurring from one time period to another, to determine whether crime is increasing or decreasing in specific geographic areas. Figure 6 is a grid cell map of vehicle thefts in Baltimore County.

Figure 5. Radial Map of Registered Child Sex Offenders and School Buffer Zones in Fair County

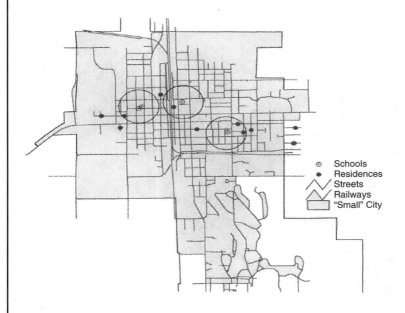

REGISTERED CHILD SEX OFFENDER
REPRESENTATION "SMALL" CITY - MARCH 1997

Schools
Residences
Streets
Railways
"Small" City

1.4   0   1.4 Miles

SOURCE: FAIR COUNTY LAW ENFORCEMENT AGENCIES-MARCH 1997
NOTE: THE BUFFER CONTAINS 1000 FT OF THE AREA.
SUBMITTED BY PRIYAMVADHA SRINIVASA. 03/20/97

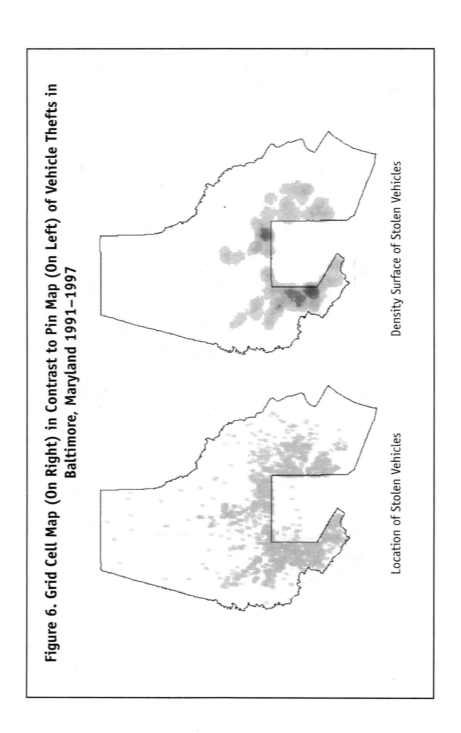

Figure 6. Grid Cell Map (On Right) in Contrast to Pin Map (On Left) of Vehicle Thefts in Baltimore, Maryland 1991–1997

Location of Stolen Vehicles

Density Surface of Stolen Vehicles

GIS in Law Enforcement: A Tale of Five Cities

Until recently, law enforcement agencies have been leading the way in crime mapping efforts. Within the last year or two, however, courts, corrections and other segments of the criminal justice system have gotten on the crime mapping bandwagon. The use of crime mapping is becoming more universal as the extent of its applicability is recognized. However, the majority of crime mapping examples are still from the law enforcement field. This section of the chapter highlights crime mapping efforts from five agencies: (1) New York City Police Department, (2) San Diego Police Department, (3) Chicago Police Department, (4) Baltimore County Police Department, and (5) Redlands, Calif., Police Department.

New York City Police Department. The New York City Police Department's CompStat is based on timely, geocoded data. Law enforcement personnel all realize the importance of timely information because when they are on patrol, officers are not particularly concerned with what occurred a month or six months ago. Primarily, they are concerned with what has happened today, yesterday or last week. CompStat allows the agency to retrieve this timely data, and geocoding allows the information to be retrieved in a map format. This access to information enables police to quickly identify emerging crime problems. In New York, the police department updates their GIS daily.

The CompStat process also helps establish and emphasize accountability. After instituting a response, police personnel can restudy the map a week or month later to see if there has been a change. The need for accountability promotes cooperation among units and across agencies. Calls for accountability in a CompStat meeting bring individuals and teams together, and the precinct commander and his or her staff are questioned on the nature of the crime problem and what they are doing to address it. For instance, if there is a narcotics problem, management will bring together code compliance enforcement, the narcotics unit and patrol officers to work together on the common problem.

San Diego Police Department. Whereas the NYPD's CompStat process presents a top-down approach to mapping, the

San Diego Police Department (SDPD) takes a line-officer approach in its use of mapping. SDPD has typically been known as a problem-solving department, and thus it seems fitting that the department uses crime mapping and GIS to facilitate all four stages of the SARA problem-solving model: scanning, analysis, response, and assessment. Analysts produce the maps every two weeks or month and distribute them not only to patrol officers, but to the community and the council districts as well. These maps prompt the initial scanning stage of the SARA model, often serving as the first source of information that a crime problem has emerged. Mapping becomes extremely useful in the analysis stage in identifying the underlying causes of crime problems. Such analyses help guide officers in developing an effective response that addresses the underlying cause of the crime problem. Finally, the SDPD uses mapping in the assessment stage to determine the response's impact and identify any possible displacement that may have occurred.

The San Diego Police Department has recognized the importance of open communication among crime analysts, officers and the community for effective problem solving. There is a constant interaction between the people in the field and the people creating the maps. On a daily basis, officers, investigators and community members request maps and analysis for specific problems. Often, the map requested has never been made or the data are not currently in the system; analysts employ creative methods to fulfill these requests.

Chicago Police Department. The Chicago Police Department has a long history of working closely with the community. This is reflected in the ways that information is made available to officers and the community. Chicago was the first department in the country to decentralize crime mapping by putting crime maps in the hands of all officers with the Information Collection for Automated Mapping (ICAM) system. This system is designed to be easy to use by those with very limited computer knowledge. ICAM enables an officer to sit down at a computer, press a few buttons and produce a map showing robberies (or other crimes) on his or her beat for the last week.

In addition to enabling officers to produce their own crime maps, the Chicago Police Department makes maps available to residents and community groups. To facilitate community policing, problem-oriented policing, partnerships, and shared problem-solving efforts, it is vitally important that police agencies share their data. In Chicago, officers use ICAM to produce maps for meeting with neighborhood associations in an effort to improve communication, collaboration and cooperation. Community members who are familiar with the nature of the crime problems in their neighborhoods are better able to work with the department and participate in two-way information sharing.

Baltimore County Police Department. The Baltimore County Police Department uses GIS for creative tactical analyses, searching for series and crime patterns on a daily basis. Specific crimes are mapped daily and weekly to help determine whether there is a particular perpetrator, trend or pattern associated with a particular crime problem. To better accomplish this task, Baltimore County began to share information with neighboring agencies. In 1994, the Baltimore County Police Department recognized that there were many criminal incidents occurring within the county, specifically within the city of Baltimore, about which they did not have access to information. Subsequently, the department established a consortium of 13 agencies to create the Regional Crime Analysis System (RCAS). These agencies, representing several counties, now share a common offense and suspect database that enables the agencies to analyze and map data across jurisdictional boundaries. Baltimore County police are now leading the implementation of a new regional system called Regional Crime Analysis GIS (RCAGIS), which is being developed by the U.S. Department of Justice Criminal Division.

Redlands Police Department. The Redlands Police Department is a smaller agency in Southern California that is actively involved in mapping nontraditional data such as risk and protective factors. Chief Jim Bueermann is one of the more progressive people in the field of crime mapping. As a captain, Bueermann wanted to see what data, in addition to crime data, could be incorporated into crime mapping to assist in analyzing and addressing underlying problems and developing long-term prevention strategies. This effort involved examining risk factors to see how they can affect many of the problems faced in community policing. To achieve this, analysts map data collected through a survey of high school students designed to measure their involvement in delinquent behavior and their perceptions of the extent to which their parents and neighbors care about such behavior. Redlands represents a unique collegial working relationship between the police department and the school system, and has forged an environment of cooperation and coordination necessary to implement effective long-term prevention strategies.

GIS and Problem Solving

As mentioned briefly above in reference to SDPD's use of mapping, GIS is a helpful tool at every stage of a problem-solving effort. The first step in the SARA model, scanning, is the identification of a problem. Digital maps can be used to identify problems by grouping specific types of crimes together (e.g., all violent crimes) and looking for distinctive elements present in more than one incident. GIS offers the capability of breaking incidents down to identify a specific problem, trend or pattern. For instance, after isolating homicides, it is possible to further distinguish between nighttime and daytime homicides, or homicides in which a gun or knife has been used.

Analyzing the problem, the second stage of problem solving, involves considering the different layers of data included in the GIS or displayed on a map to better understand the problem. Before it is possible to efficiently respond to a problem, all aspects of it must be understood. As mentioned earlier, to facilitate analysis, GIS offers the capability for spatial querying. For instance, a query can make it possible to use red symbols to plot all the burglaries where the point of entry was the front door, and blue symbols for those burglaries with the chimney as the point of entry. This isolation of data enables the identification of patterns, a specific modus operandi, or a specific time of day or week. The extent to which GIS can help with a query is limited only by the available data. All the information that is included in crime and arrest reports can be coded and put into a GIS. Although it can be time consuming to fill in all the information on the reports, all these data are helpful to the crime analysts and, ultimately, to the patrol officer engaged in problem solving.

GIS can also facilitate assessment of efforts and aid in response evaluation. Not only can a GIS quickly show how much the problem has increased or decreased, but it can illustrate crime displacement as well. Plotting changes in drug markets is a popular example of illustrating displacement. There may be certain neighborhood areas that are known locations of drug problems— whether it's a house, apartment, motel, or open-air drug market. Responses may include educating citizens, increasing enforcement, increasing patrol, passing out fliers, or working with businesses. When the problem is studied three or six months later by observing the location of the dots representing drug problems or arrests, it is possible to note any changes in the location or number of the dots. Have the dots become less clustered, have they moved a mile away or five miles away, or have the dots completely disappeared?

Crime Mapping: Successful Case Studies

Thus far, this chapter has explored the basics of GIS, how it has been applied generally in various law enforcement agencies, and specific applications for problem-oriented policing. The best examples, however, come from the field, and therefore this chapter now turns to a discussion of specific cases in which mapping was used to support problem solving. The following six case studies are taken from the book *Crime Mapping Case Studies: Successes in the Field* (1998), a joint venture between PERF (Police Executive Research Forum) and NIJ (National Institute of Justice). Case studies for the book were chosen and deemed successful if they met one of the following criteria: the mapping (1) assisted in the problem-solving process, (2) aided in catching the perpetrator,

(3) helped in the prosecution of the offender, or (4) improved police operations in some manner. The examples discussed here were chosen for their link to problem-oriented policing.

Overland Park, Kansas. The Overland Park, Kan., Police Department's approach to garage burglaries (also referred to as garage shopping) is an excellent example of problem solving. The Overland Park Police Department responded to a rash of these garage shopping incidents by using crime mapping to identify the neighborhood that had been hit the hardest. Once this neighborhood was identified, the police began a public relations campaign and worked closely with residents. The police disseminated leaflets and talked to citizens to provide them with crime prevention tips and encourage them to take appropriate precautions. Because mapping enabled the police to home in on the area that had been hardest hit with these burglaries, the public relations effort was successful. In addition, the Overland Park police utilized crime mapping to assess the impact of their response. In May, there had been 10 garage shopping incidents in this neighborhood. In September, the number of incidents declined to one.

Nottingham, England. The case study from Nottingham, England, was the result of an analyst's attempt to discern how officers' perceptions of crime hotspots differed from the actual locations of crime. In many cases, officers may not be fully aware of what occurs on the beat during hours outside their shifts. Crime mapping provides the department with a collective knowledge that may not be known otherwise. The analyst found that officers' perceptions of hotspots in Nottingham were slightly skewed and determined that this was due to a policy of taking certain crime reports, including auto thefts, over the phone. Removing officers from the report-taking process and reducing their dispatches to crime scenes meant that their mental maps of crimes occurring on the beat were not as accurate. This case study has direct implications for problem-solving efforts; without the aid of crime maps, officers may be inaccurately scanning crime problems that are not as severe or differ in character from what they perceive.

Hartford Police Department. Many agencies are now sharing digital maps with community members to enlist their help in problem-solving efforts. As mentioned earlier, Chicago is unique in the practice of providing line officers with map data to conduct their own mapping and analyses. The Hartford, Conn., Police Department, however, is the first example of giving hands-on crime mapping capabilities to community residents. An NIJ grant supported the design of a user-friendly crime mapping interface (see Figure 7), which was installed on a number of workstations located in neighborhood association offices. This allows residents and neighborhood associations to produce their own maps using police data and to identify where crimes are taking place. Shortly after this program was implemented, the Blue Hills Civic Association began to produce crime maps. After mapping calls for service for drug-related incidents, the association was confused about why a location that they all recognized as a problem area was not shown on the map as a hotspot. Discussions with the Hartford police revealed that the citizens had witnessed problems at this location for such an extended period of time that they had stopped calling the police about it. The police were unaware that the area was a hotspot. Now, instead of making a standard 911 call when there are drug problems in the neighborhood, the citizens contact their neighborhood community policing officer directly.

Baltimore County. The Baltimore County Police Department incorporates other technology in the problem-solving process in addition to crime mapping. In this case study, after using crime mapping to identify a neighborhood with a high rate of garage burglaries, the police used telemarketing software called the "autodialer" to inform and warn residents of the crime rash. The dialer can be programmed with any message, including crime alerts such as "You should be aware that there have been a high number of garage burglaries in your neighborhood." This phone system allows the police department to program a message that can then be sent out to everyone in the city or in a particular area. The messages can be directed to a specific target popula-

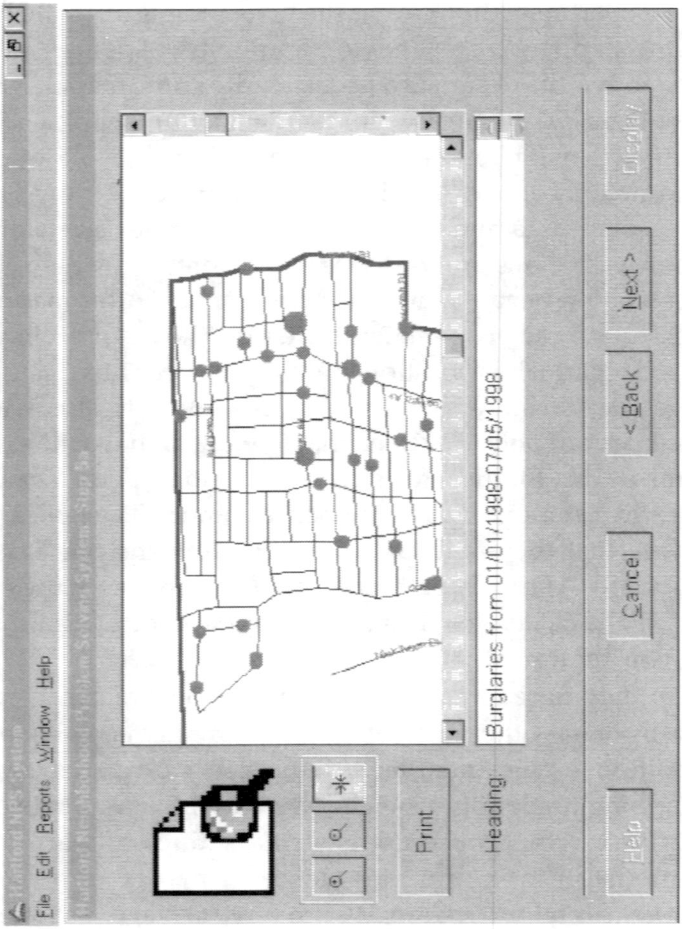

Figure 7. View of a Computer Screen Depicting the Crime Mapping Program Made Available to Hartford, Conn., Community Members

tion by connecting the autodialer to a GIS. Therefore, instead of calling the entire city, the police department can target hotspots for specific crimes—in this example, garage burglaries of single-family homes. Within a few days of the notification being sent out, the Baltimore County police received a call from someone who had received the message. He notified the police of a suspicious person walking down the street with gardening tools and a lawn mower. As it turns out, the suspicious person was the burglary perpetrator. They arrested the individual and the problem was solved.

Detroit Police Department. The final case study chronicles the Detroit Police Department's efforts to reduce arson on Devil's Night (the night before Halloween). The department was perplexed because the arsons were increasing in number and intensity each year. One course of action was to map the arson fires. The department mapped not only where the arson fires were occurring, but how they were associated with the types of buildings or property in or on which they were occurring. As it turned out, the majority of arson fires were occurring in abandoned houses. Based on this information, the department enlisted the community's help in the form of citizens' patrols, and officers were sent to the hotspots. Instead of generalizing resource allocation, the police used GIS to deploy both officer and volunteer patrols to specific neighborhoods with either a history of the worst fires or the highest concentration of abandoned housing. Although Detroit still experiences arson fires, they have eliminated or greatly reduced most of the hotspots, and any fires that are set are now more sporadic in nature.

NIJ Crime Mapping Research Center

An excellent resource for those new to crime mapping as well as those who want to share crime mapping knowledge, the Crime Mapping Research Center (CMRC) was developed to advance applied and basic research involving the analytic mapping of crime. The CMRC is based in the Office of Research and Evaluation as part of the National Institute of Justice, U.S. Department of Justice, in Washington, D.C. The Center has a staff of approximately 10 people with varied backgrounds, including crime analysis, criminology, geography, and anthropology. In addition to staff, the CMRC sponsors visiting fellows who work for a specified time period. The Center coordinates with a variety of agencies and organizations within the Department of Justice (the COPS Office and the Bureau of Justice Assistance), and with outside agencies such as the International Association of Crime Analysts and the Police Executive Research Forum (PERF).

The CMRC's mission and purpose can be divided into four primary functions: research, evaluation, development, and dissemination. The goal of research is to more extensively explore analytical crime mapping methods through a fellowship program, in-house research and a grants program. Fellowships are awarded to individuals who are interested in crime mapping, have an expertise in that area, and would like to spend time in Washington, D.C., doing research and sharing knowledge with the Center staff. This is one way to develop an interdisciplinary knowledge base.

One example of the Center's in-house research is an evaluation of various methods of identifying hotspots. Crime data were obtained from a specified geographic region and distributed to different researchers in the mapping field to identify hotspots. Each researcher employed a different method; a total of 12 methods for identifying hotspots were evaluated, ranging from very simple to quite complex. One method used was simply printing out large maps, giving them to a crime analyst, and asking her to circle the hotspots. CMRC is currently in the process of integrating all this information and comparing the maps from the different methods, and should have some results shortly.

The CMRC has more than 30 active grants in the area of crime mapping. These grants are awarded to organizations or individuals in the field to conduct crime mapping research ranging from software development to the use of mapping as an evaluation tool. Four new grants have been awarded for work with GIS and predictive modeling. Predictive modeling, which is employed using spatial econometrics, spatial modeling and neural network analysis, is useful for strategic planning and triage. The CMRC has focused on software development as an area of grant priority in response to the frustration that the research community is voicing over obstacles preventing more sophisticated spatial analyses. Consequently, the City University of New York has received a grant to work with NYPD to develop analysis support methods for the CompStat process. Ned Levine and Associates received a grant to develop more sophisticated spatial statistical tools that can be used within a user-friendly, Windows-based software program. The Environmental Systems Research Institute, Inc. (ESRI), also through a grant from CMRC, has been developing a crime analysis extension that will serve as an interface to their Arcview GIS software. The interface obscures complex details of the mapping program and allows individuals to perform simple, common queries. The crime analysis extension also includes a number of different tools. An electronic beat book will enable patrol officers to include data from field interviews or contacts with community members in the maps they produce.

The CMRC evaluates the field of crime mapping using instruments such as the survey mentioned in the introduction. This survey of 2,700 law enforcement agencies had a response rate of more than 70 percent. The results indicated that only 13.5 percent of the respondents were doing computerized crime mapping. The survey helped determine what agencies were doing in the way of computerized mapping, what they would like to be doing, and what is preventing them from achieving their goal, whether resources, training or technical assistance. Based on this information, the CMRC is better able to tailor its resources to meet the needs of agencies across the country.

The Center's development goal is to expand and advance the practice of crime mapping. CMRC supports analytic software development. It also promotes the use of crime mapping in a variety of criminal justice applications. Most mapping that is being done now is in the area of law enforcement. The CMRC is currently working to promote the use of mapping for probation, parole and corrections services. This would allow for partnerships between the police and other criminal justice agencies. A grant was recently awarded to the Phoenix Police Department and the Maricopa County Probation Department to enable them to develop a joint database using GIS to analyze crimes in relation to the location of probationers. In addition, training is being developed to assist researchers and practitioners. To accomplish this goal, a training resource group of police officers, analysts, geographers, and criminal justice researchers with diverse expertise is creating six training modules that incorporate classroom and hands-on training. These modules are as follows:

1. What is Crime Mapping?
2. Mapping for Community Policing and Problem Solving
3. Mapping for Managers
4. Integrating GIS in an Organization
5. Introductory Analysis
6. Intermediate Analysis

For further information on the training classes or other CMRC resources, contact us at the following address:

> **Crime Mapping Research Center**
> National Institute of Justice
> 810 7th St. NW
> Washington, DC 20531
> Phone (202) 514-3431
> Fax (202) 616-0275
> Email: cmrc@ojp.usdoj.gov
> Web Site: www.ojp.usdoj.gov/cmrc

Questions and Comments from the Audience

Audience Member: If an agency were interested in beginning to implement crime mapping, what type of software would you suggest they invest in?

Response: The first thing you should do is research what else is being done in your jurisdiction in the field of mapping.

Chances are that the planning department or public works department will have a lot of valuable information that they can share with you. If possible, choose a software product that is compatible with the system that they are using. If choosing a compatible system is not a consideration, ensure that the software you purchase is comprehensive and will meet the agency's current and projected needs. At this time, there is not one type of software that I would recommend over another. Based on the surveys that we sent out, we do know that most agencies are primarily using one of two products: MapInfo or Arcview. Both MapInfo and Arcview are Windows-based programs that are relatively straightforward to use but not simplistic. Arcview, specifically, is designed for people who are doing mapping day in and day out; people with a master's degree, or at least a bachelor's, in geography; and people who have the time to really master the system.

Audience Member: Do you envision using GPS satellites in conjunction with GIS?

Response: Actually, the use of satellites to identify the exact x,y coordinates of a location identified by GIS is already being done. In addition, we recently awarded a grant to Keith Harries to work with the Baltimore County Police Department on the use of orthophotography in conjunction with GIS and GPS. Orthophotography produces digitized aerial photographs that present a picture of the actual landscape on the computer to provide a better understanding of where crime is concentrated in relation to other physical characteristics. GIS and GPS may provide you with a specific location of a hotspot for auto thefts, but do not necessarily provide any indication of why there are so many in the one area. Orthophotography, by providing actual photos, may reveal that the location is, in fact, a commuter parking lot.

Audience Member: Our department [Nottingham, England] attempted to reduce domestic burglaries by locating burglary hotspots and then looking for nearby markets for stolen goods. Initially, the hotspots were defined by police beats. Over a three-year period, we mapped the occurrence of domestic burglaries. Using pinpoint analysis, we identified a relatively large cluster of burglaries that straddled two separate towns in areas that were amalgams of crime. By superimposing the police beats on this map, we were able to determine that the large hotspot actually comprised five separate beats. If we had chosen police beats, an administrative boundary, as our only unit of analysis, we would have been misled. Police beats encompassing larger areas and subsequently experiencing more crime will dwarf smaller beats that may have more burglaries per area.

Response: That reminds me of a recent example from Philadelphia. According to one of their crime analysts, the Philadelphia Police Department has not changed the police beat boundaries for about 10 years, and some have not been changed for 30 years. When crimes were analyzed and mapped, it was found that they were clustered along the borders delineating the patrol beats. One of the largest crime clusters was situated in an area where three to five patrol beats intersected. Officers were unclear of who was responsible for enforcing these intersection areas and the result was reduced enforcement.

CHAPTER 13

HERMAN GOLDSTEIN AWARD FOR EXCELLENCE IN PROBLEM-ORIENTED POLICING

Commentary by Ronald V. Clarke
Chair of the Award Selection Committee

The Herman Goldstein Award for Excellence in Problem-Oriented Policing was established in 1993 to honor Professor Herman Goldstein, who conceived and developed the theory of problem-oriented policing. The award recognizes innovative and effective problem-oriented policing (POP) projects that have achieved measurable success in reducing specific crime, disorder or public safety problems.

Selection Process

In order to recognize a high level of excellence in the award winners, the selection process is designed to be both fair and rigorous. The 1998 award selection committee was composed of seven practitioners or academics (in some cases both) with detailed knowledge of problem-oriented policing. They were Ronald Clarke (Rutgers University), Gary Cordner (Eastern Kentucky University), Ron Glensor (Reno Police Department), Nancy La Vigne (National Institute of Justice), Greg Saville (Florida State University), Mike Scott (management consultant and former police chief), and Rana Sampson (public safety director, University of San Diego).

In 1998, the committee received 82 award submissions. Although this number was slightly lower than in previous years, the overall quality of the submissions was higher than ever. Clearer guidelines regarding eligibility and expectations resulted in submission of fewer unsuitable projects. Once received, all submissions were sent to the committee chair and one other member (someone different each year) for a preliminary screening. This initial screening evaluated each submission using a standardized rating instrument to assess all four steps of the SARA problem-solving model. This scoring was conducted independently and submitted to a committee coordinator at the Police Executive Research Forum (PERF), who compared the two scoring lists for consistency. Any project that was ranked within the top 15 by both preliminary screeners was included among the finalists. In addition, any project that received high marks from one judge but not the other was also included among the finalists.

In 1998, 17 of the 82 award submissions were chosen as finalists. These 17 submissions were then sent to the remaining five committee members to be scored using the same rating instrument as for the preliminary screening. Committee members were required to declare any conflicts of interest that would disqualify them from scoring a particular submission. Once again, the scoring was conducted independently, without consultation with other committee members. Scores from all seven committee members were summed and an average score calculated by PERF. From these results, a winner and six honorable mentions were identified. The winner of the 1998 Herman Goldstein Award For Excellence in Problem-Oriented Policing was the Boston Police Department with their project Operation Cease Fire.

Operation Cease Fire, Boston Police Department

Operation Cease Fire is a well-known and widely acclaimed project. Not only do police professionals recognize it as an outstanding example of problem-oriented policing, but the associated research, conducted by David Kennedy and his team from the Kennedy School of Government at Harvard University, has been widely praised by academics. In short, this was a carefully designed, brilliantly conceived and successfully implemented project that resulted in many lives being saved. It was a worthy winner of the Goldstein Award and is destined to become a classic problem-oriented policing project. The features of Operation Cease Fire that most impressed the selection committee were as follows:

1. The problem addressed—youth firearm violence in connection with gang activities—is of utmost importance. If this problem is successfully addressed, many lives can potentially be saved.
2. Not only was the problem important, but it was clearly defined and tightly focused. These are two vital requirements for a successful problem-oriented project. Success is much harder to attain when the problem is broad and diffuse (e.g., violent crime, gang violence or even youth homicide in general).
3. This problem was analyzed using a comprehensive collection of quantitative data, which permitted
   - mapping of youth firearm homicides to identify hotspots,
   - identification of more than 60 separate gangs and the mapping of their activities,
   - analysis of the characteristics of homicide victims and offenders,
   - collation and analysis of nonfatal injuries reported to hospitals, and
   - analysis of the characteristics of guns recovered by the police from those aged less than 21, to determine gun origins in other states.
4. In addition to this cornucopia of quantitative data, interviews were conducted with front-line practitioners to tap their knowledge about gangs and the contribution of gang conflict to the city's youth homicide problem.
5. The analysis of this problem led to a clearer understanding of several fundamental questions: Who was involved in the gun violence? In which neighborhoods and in which gangs were they involved? Why did these youths carry guns and how did they obtain them?
6. The resulting response was carefully crafted to address the nature of the problem. The response was composed of two primary components: the education of gang members about the consequences of their violence, and a crack-

down on illicit gun trafficking in Boston. Gang member education was achieved through a systematic program of regular meetings with the gangs. These meetings were held to inform gang members that any future violence they committed would be met by a heavy crackdown on the entire gang, and involve the city's coordinated resources. In turn, this would result in certain and severe punishments. The crackdown on illicit gun trafficking in the city was instituted through the use of information about traffickers obtained from gun tracing data and from "debriefing" gang members arrested for serious offenses.

7. The response, as well as being carefully conceived, was innovative. Delivering clear and specific warnings to individual gangs and gang members, and then reinforcing those warnings with swift, coordinated action and severe punishment when necessary, was a new concept.

8. Later assessment indicated that the response had been successful. According to Boston crime statistics, following the implementation of Operation Cease Fire, there was a 60 percent decline in youth firearm homicides. In addition, surveys of the public demonstrated a much-improved level of confidence in the police.

Final Note

It is important to note that undertaking an exemplary problem-oriented policing project does not necessarily depend on federal grants or help from institutions, such as Harvard, that were utilized in Operation Cease Fire. This is evidenced by the strength of the award submissions that received honorable mention.

The appendix is devoted to descriptions of Operation Cease Fire, and the six submissions that received honorable mentions.

APPENDIX

HERMAN GOLDSTEIN AWARD WINNER, HONORABLE MENTIONS

Goldstein Award Winner:
- Boston Police Department
  Operation Cease Fire

Honorable Mentions:
- Nassau County, New York, Police Department
  Fraud Schemes Targeted at Senior Citizens

- San Diego Police Department
  Mission Valley River Preserve—Restoration of a Region of the San Diego River Bed

- Newport News, Virginia, Police Department
  Police Response to Incidents of Domestic Emergencies (PRIDE)

- San Diego Police Department
  San Ysidro International Border

- San Diego Police Department
  Operation "Hot Pipe/Smoky Haze/Rehab"

- Fontana, California, Police Department
  Transient Enrichment Network

OPERATION CEASE FIRE
BOSTON POLICE DEPARTMENT

Scanning

In Boston in 1987, there were 22 victims of youth homicide (victims ages 24 and under). By 1990, that figure had increased 230 percent to 73 victims. Youth homicide remained high even after the peak of the epidemic—Boston averaged 43 youth homicides per year between 1991 and 1995. The police were simply overwhelmed.

"We were responding to six, seven shootings every night," said Lt. Gary French, now the commander of the Boston Police Department's (BPD) Youth Violence Strike Force. "You just ran from crime scene to crime scene." While 1990 marked the peak, the problems persisted. "I think there was a real question in people's minds about whether Boston would remain a viable city," said BPD Commissioner Paul Evans.

For many of Boston's young people, the city had become a dangerous, complicated place. In a 1993 Centers for Disease Control survey, 15 percent of the junior high school student sample said they had avoided school in the last month because they were scared: the highest such response rate in the 10 cities surveyed (Kann et al. 1995). Youths interviewed in Boston portrayed themselves as choosing between living an ordinary life—including having friends and going out at night—with attendant risks of gun violence, or isolating themselves from friends and community to avoid those risks. A young probationer interviewed in 1995 said he did his best to avoid his peers in an effort to prevent being dragged into dangerous conflicts. "I stay home, or go over to my cousin's," he said. "It's too dangerous to go out, or have a lot of friends."

Another young probationer, more active on the streets, said that navigating their dangers required constant, demanding attention. "It's like a video game," he said. "You master one level, and they bump you up a level, and things get harder, and you keep on going until you just can't do it any more. That's what the streets have gotten to be like."

A gun project working group was explicitly designed to draw on the knowledge and ideas of front-line practitioners and to incorporate their views into the framing of project research and any subsequent operations. From the beginning of the working group, police, probation officers and streetworkers described a world in which a relatively small number of frightening youths profoundly affected the nature of community life and the behavior of other youths. Indeed, police gang officers and probation officers said flatly at the project's outset that they essentially knew all those youths who had killed with, or were killed by, gun violence. Probation officers said it was rare to lose a kid to gun violence who previously had not been on probation, and gang officers joked darkly about whether it would be ethical to take out life insurance on certain kids. Their experience was that youths tended to cite self-defense to explain their gun acquisitions. Boston police gang officers spoke of the recent phenomenon of young men "with a gun in one pocket and a scholarship in the other."

The working group's line-level personnel had a very particular view of what was going on in the city. They were convinced the gun violence problem was a gang problem, because

- the worst offenders in the cycle of fear, gun acquisition and gun use were gang members;
- most victims and offenders were gang members, known to authorities and formally court-involved, sometimes—but not usually—on gun charges;
- most violence was not about drugs and drug-market issues or turf but was more "personal";
- acts of violence involving members of different gangs often sparked vendetta-like "beefs" that were assumed by both (or several) gangs and could continue for years independent of the original incident;
- most of the youths involved were not "bad" or inherently dangerous, and many were participating because gang

membership had become a means of self-protection (albeit with its own serious risks); and

- only a tenth or so of gang members were consistently dangerous and frightening, and they set the tone of street life both for the other members of their gangs and, to a lesser but significant extent, for the community as a whole.

It's worth noting that these views were quite contrary to those usually expressed in Boston about the youth violence problem. Those views tended to focus on such larger issues as troubled neighborhoods, the influence of television violence and other cultural issues, and drug trafficking.

Agencies in Boston had responded to the youth violence problem by pursuing a high-arrest strategy aimed at gang members, combined with prevention and diversion programs aimed at drawing youths away from gangs and providing them with alternatives. Probation officers had launched an innovative street probation program, aimed at high-risk youths, called "Night Light," in which probation officers and BPD gang unit officers performed house checks at night. The streetworker program focused on providing high-risk youths with services and mediating disputes. A high degree of cooperation evolved at the line level among Boston agencies involved in youth violence, but working group participants felt strongly that their efforts were not dealing effectively with the problem.

Analysis

The Harvard team, which took primary responsibility for project research and analysis, framed these issues in gun market terms. Gun trafficking and other routes to the illicit acquisition of firearms represented the supply side. Fear and/or other factors that might be driving illicit gun acquisition and use represented the demand side. The researchers employed a variety of research techniques. Youth homicides were mapped geographically, gun markets were analyzed using BPD/Bureau of Alcohol, Tobacco and Firearms (ATF) gun recovery and tracing data, the criminal histories of youth homicide victims and offenders were collected and analyzed, and hospital emergency room data were collected to shed light on nonfatal injuries. In addition to these techniques using formal agency data, innovative qualitative techniques were used in which front-line practitioners systematically contributed their knowledge about such matters as the number and size of gangs in the city, their turf and antagonistic/alliance relationships, and the contribution of gangs and gang conflict to the city's youth homicide problem. These qualitative exercises, which collected information unavailable from formal agency sources, turned out to be among the most valuable contributions to the problem-solving process.

Key findings included the following:

- Most youth (age 21 and under) gun and knife homicides occurred in the three neighborhoods of Roxbury, Dorchester and Mattapan. Most gun and knife woundings also occurred in these neighborhoods. Of 155 gun and knife homicides that occurred in the city from 1990 to 1994, 88 percent of victims were male, 12 percent female; 78 percent were black, 16 percent white, 2.6 percent Asian, and 2.6 percent of other races. Firearms accounted for 84 percent of the victimizations, knives for 16 percent.

- Of the 1,550 firearms recovered by BPD from those age 21 and under between January 1991 and May 1995, 52.1 percent were semiautomatic pistols, 30 percent were revolvers, 8.5 percent were rifles, and 9.4 percent were shotguns.

- While the assumption had been that, due to tight Massachusetts gun laws, any gun trafficking to youths was through trafficking from Southern states, trace analysis showed that 34 percent of traceable firearms recovered from those age 21 and under by the Boston Police Department were first sold at retail establishments in Massachusetts. No other state reached double digits on a percentage basis; the next highest source state was Georgia, with 8 percent. All Southern states combined—

Georgia, Florida, Virginia, Alabama, North Carolina, Mississippi, South Carolina, West Virginia, and Maryland—added up to 31.5 percent.

- While the assumption had been that youths were stealing guns, of all traceable guns recovered from those age 21 and under, 26 percent were less than two years old when recovered by police and thus almost certainly trafficked rather than stolen. Of semiautomatic pistols, 41 percent were less than two years old. Of all traceable guns less than two years old, 84 percent were semiautomatic pistols.
- Nearly 20 percent of all guns recovered from those age 21 and under had obliterated serial numbers, suggesting that these guns were relatively new "trafficked" guns rather than guns that had been, for instance, stolen from houses or cars.
- Guns recovered from those age 30 and older were less likely to be semiautomatic pistols, less likely to have obliterated serial numbers, more likely to have been first sold at retail establishments in Massachusetts, and more likely to be older.
- Of the 155 youth gun and knife homicide victims, before their murders, 75 percent had been arraigned for at least one offense in Massachusetts courts, 19 percent had been committed to the Department of Youth Services (DYS), 42 percent had been on probation, and 14 percent were on probation at the time of their murder.
- Of the 125 cleared youth offenders associated with those homicides, 77 percent had been arraigned for at least one offense in Massachusetts courts, 26 percent had been committed to DYS, 54 percent had been on probation, and 26 percent were on probation at the time they committed their homicide.
- Of the 117 homicide victims with at least one arraignment, the average number of arraignments was 9.5, and 44 percent had 10 or more arraignments. Of the 96 of-

fenders with at least one arraignment, the average number of arraignments was 9.7, and 41 percent had 10 or more arraignments. For both victims and offenders, arraignments for property offenses, armed violent offenses and disorder offenses outnumbered drug offenses. For offenders, unarmed violent offenses also outnumbered drug offenses.

- Boston had roughly 61 gangs with 1,300 members in the high-risk neighborhoods of Roxbury, Dorchester and Mattapan, plus surrounding areas. This represented less than 3 percent of the youth ages 14 to 24 in these neighborhoods. These gangs were responsible for at least 60 percent of Boston's youth homicides. The primary driver of youth violence was a network of standing antagonisms among gangs, which were identified and mapped through work with front-line practitioners familiar with these "beefs."

- Gang members were at extremely high risk for violent victimization. Statistically, if one assumes an average nine-year gang membership (for example, from age 16 to 24), gang members had a one-in-seven chance of dying by gunshot and an even higher chance of being wounded by gunshot. It was thus reasonable, and supported by interviews with Boston youths in Boston, that fear and the desire for self-defense were fueling both gun acquisition and gang formation in the city. It was also reasonable to think that reducing the risk of violence would have a large impact on gun acquisition and other high-risk behavior.

Response

The working group framed two main responses to these findings; together, they make up what is now called the "Cease Fire" strategy. One was to mount a direct law enforcement attack, driven primarily by the BPD and ATF, on illicit gun trafficking. One avenue for this response was to utilize trace information, matched with BPD information, to identify those who were

trafficking guns (particularly to actively violent gangs), and investigate and prosecute them. Another avenue was to systematically
debrief gang offenders facing serious charges for violent, drug and
other crimes regarding who might be selling guns in their neighborhoods. Follow-up on these strategies by the BPD, ATF and prosecutors resulted in a substantial increase in trafficking cases.

The second main response, and probably the most important part of Cease Fire, was a unique approach to creating a very
powerful deterrent to gang-related violence. The "pulling levers"
strategy the gun project working group designed was built on a
simple, but crucially important, realization: chronic offending
made these youths, and the gangs they formed, extremely vulnerable. Authorities had a large and varied menu of ways they
could impose costs on these gangs—"levers to pull," as the group
came to say. They could disrupt street drug activity, focus police
attention on low-level street crimes like trespassing and public
drinking, serve outstanding warrants, cultivate confidential informants for investigations of gang activities, deliver strict probation
and parole enforcement, seize drug proceeds and other assets, ensure stiffer plea bargains and sterner prosecutorial attention, request
stronger bail terms (and actually enforce them), and even focus
potentially very severe federal investigative and prosecutorial attention on, for instance, gang-related drug activity.

This was, of course, not news to the line-level personnel.
The problem was that it was impossible to give all the gangs this
kind of heightened attention all the time, and that occasional
crackdowns, while useful in the short term, had little long-term
impact. The ability to deliver overwhelming crackdowns, however, was not in doubt. The working group's innovation—again,
simple but important—was to make it clear to gangs that future
violence would draw such crackdowns, and then to continue to
communicate with gangs as the resulting strategy unfolded. An
essential part of the Cease Fire strategy was thus a systematic
communications campaign, carried out in part through formal
meetings, or "forums," in which the working group presented
the Cease Fire antiviolence strategy to gang members.

This changed the game rather dramatically. From a world in which the cost to a gang of committing a homicide was, perhaps, that a gang member would be caught and prosecuted (while the gang as a whole accrued "street" benefits such as a reputation for toughness), the cost soared to that original risk, plus everything else the authorities could bring to bear: cash-flow problems caused by street drug market disruption, arrests from outstanding warrants, the humiliation of strict probation enforcement, even the possibility of the severe sanctions brought by federal involvement. The costs were borne by the whole gang, not just the shooter. As long as the authorities were confident they knew what gangs were involved in a particular act of violence, as they usually were, these penalties were certain; the working group always could figure out ways to reach out and touch particular gangs. They were also swift; drug market disruption, heavy disorder enforcement, warrant service, probation attention and the like could be deployed within days of a violent event. Rather than the response to violence being uncertain, slow, and often not very severe, it became, with Cease Fire, certain, rapid and of whatever range of severity the working group felt appropriate.

Talking regularly to the gangs served a number of purposes. Originally, the working group wanted to make sure gangs knew about this new policy, so they could comply if they wished, and also wanted to tell other gangs when a gang was being punished for violence. It also wanted to make clear to gangs that while violence would bring strong attention, refraining from violence would not win them a "pass" to deal drugs or do other crimes; this was, in language the working group used explicitly in the gang meetings, "a promise, not a deal."

Other purposes emerged as the strategy was implemented. One was to make cause and effect clear—to explain to the city's gangs that a particular drug raid, for instance, was but a means to an end and was not about drugs as such, but a penalty being imposed for violence. One was to bolster the working group's own credibility—to be able to say to gangs, in effect, "we said it, we meant it, and here's proof of that: here's what they did, here's what we did, here's how you steer clear." Another was to give gangs that appeared to be on the verge of trouble a dose of what the working group came to think of as "retail deterrence"—to reach out to them and make clear that actual violence would bring a strong response.

Most important, however, was that the working group came to realize that communication allowed the creation of a fundamentally different balance of power between the authorities and the streets. The working group could deploy, at best, only a few severe crackdowns at a time. But like a sheriff facing down a band of desperadoes with one bullet in his gun, direct communication with gangs allowed the working group to say, we're ready, we're watching, we're waiting—who wants to be next?

The Cease Fire strategy was fully implemented by mid-May 1996, the time at which the first gang-specific crackdown, on Dorchester's Vamp Hill Kings, was completed and the gang meetings commenced. Handbills explaining that operation and "advertising" authorities' other gang-violence-focused operations were handed out widely to gang members. While the strategy had already been quietly briefed to key community leaders, the city also formally announced its new policies at this time. In late August 1996, the Intervale Posse, widely viewed as the city's toughest crack-era gang, was largely dismantled in a Cease Fire operation carried out with the DEA's help.

These operations were carried out in parallel with prevention activities spearheaded by the streetworkers, activist black clergy and other community groups who supported the "stop it" message to the gangs; offered gang members services, jobs and other opportunities; and attempted to mediate disputes. More meetings and one-on-one communication with gang members by BPD gang officers, probation officers and streetworkers drove home the message that the Intervale operation had been prompted by the gang's violence, the city would repeat if necessary, and gangs wishing to avoid such attention need only refrain from hurting people.

The Cease Fire strategy was implemented primarily with resources already available to participating agencies, and for the most part utilized activities already within their repertoire (for instance, drug enforcement, warrant service and probation supervision). Partway through implementation, the city was awarded a COPS gang grant, which helped fund BPD gang officers' overtime activity.

Assessment

The Cease Fire strategy was designed to reduce homicide victimization and other serious violence by and among Boston's gang youths. The project generally regards this as a population age 24 and under (rather than the 21 and under framework with which the project began). In the project's first two years, homicide victimization among those age 24 and under fell roughly 70 percent from the mean of the years 1991 to 1995. A detailed examination of gun assaults involving those age 24 and under in Roxbury, the city's most active neighborhood, showed comparable reductions. While the Harvard team is conducting a formal evaluation utilizing advanced statistical techniques, these declines are substantially larger than other cities have seen over the same period, and are not explicable on the basis of demographics or the disappearance of gangs or drug markets (both of which remain, though both in lower-profile ways than before Cease Fire).

Perhaps most gratifying, it has not been necessary to continuously sanction gangs; no further operation of the Intervale scale has been necessary. Working group participants believe that as gang vendettas were interrupted and the "temperature" on the streets went down, the self-sustaining cycle of violence, fear, "self-defense" behavior, and more violence was interrupted. Perhaps most remarkably, gang members have themselves quietly reached out to the working group and pointed fingers at gangs threatening to disturb the peace.

Other information supports the belief that the Cease Fire strategy has made a meaningful impact. Both adults and young people in Roxbury, Dorchester and Mattapan show an increased willingness to use public spaces; Joseph Chery, an anti-violence activist, reports that adults in his neighborhood are no longer afraid of young people and are once again exerting adult influence in the streets. The BPD recently completed a telephone survey of 3,000 Boston households to measure citizen opinion in a wide array of areas. Key findings included the following:

- Approximately 50 to 60 percent of residents in Roxbury, Dorchester and Mattapan felt the BPD does all that can reasonably be expected to reduce crime in their neighborhoods.
- More than one-third of Roxbury, Dorchester and Mattapan residents had a great deal of confidence in the BPD's ability to prevent crime, compared with 8 to 12 percent in 1995.
- Citywide, 76 percent of residents felt safe out alone in their neighborhoods at night, compared with only 55 percent in 1995.
- Eighty-eight percent of residents said they would be willing to work with each other and police to reduce and prevent crime.

Other parties have found the process that generated Cease Fire, and the Cease Fire intervention itself, promising. The Clinton Administration has modeled its 27-city Youth Crime Gun Interdiction Initiative on Cease Fire's gun trafficking component.

A wide variety of jurisdictions have begun operations akin to Cease Fire, with Lowell, Mass., and Minneapolis already reporting positive results (Clark 1997). Planning efforts are underway in Chicago; Los Angeles; Detroit; Rochester and Syracuse, N.Y.; Baltimore; Stockton, Calif.; and a number of other cities. The Justice Department has just commenced a five-city initiative modeled on the gun project, with sites addressing crime concerns ranging from youth violence to sexual assault. All the agencies involved in Cease Fire spend a great deal of time fielding inquiries and advising other jurisdictions.

The basic Boston partnership continues to adapt and evolve. A substantial jobs program has been launched, focused on active (at least previously) gang offenders; in a remarkable development, the program was launched with the leadership of Don Stern, the U.S. Attorney. Prevention and diversion activities, through the streetworkers and others, are being enhanced. Based on its leadership in Cease Fire, the BPD has recently been given lead responsibility for shaping a citywide anti-truancy effort. Nobody in Boston is declaring victory; but something substantial has been accomplished, and continues to be.

FRAUD SCHEMES TARGETED AT SENIOR CITIZENS
NASSAU COUNTY, N.Y., POLICE DEPARTMENT

Scanning

In 1995, the Fifth Precinct Problem-Oriented Policing (POP) Team recognized a pattern of crimes involving scams, cons and frauds targeting senior citizens in Nassau County. In September 1995, the POP officers attended a training seminar in Maryland, and during that conference they learned how senior citizens are victimized by con artists who perpetrate scams and cons against them, often resulting in the loss of their life savings, security and dignity.

After this session, the officers decided to conduct some research to determine whether these types of crimes occur in Nassau County. The use of scams, cons and frauds is common knowledge, but it is not well documented or understood. The POP Team's interviews of patrol officers and the detective division revealed that officers were aware that con artist activity increases in the spring and fall, but officers could not identify the particular types of scams.

There was a wide assortment of opinions regarding the classification of these crimes. Patrol officers and the POP Team did not recall responding to any telemarketing or mail fraud crimes.

The majority of fraud crimes they encountered involved people who promised large rewards if the victim could put up "good faith" money (commonly known as the "pigeon drop"), home-repair scams with large down payments up front and no work performed, or the recommendation of unnecessary repairs.

One of the most prevalent fraud crimes against seniors was the impostor burglar. These criminals impersonate utility workers or government workers, and, by using a ruse, gain access to the victim's home. Once inside, the victim is distracted by one con artist while a second or third burglarizes the home. The POP Team decided to look into this problem further because of its repetitive nature and the often devastating effects it has on its victims.

Analysis

Nassau County is a community of 1.25 million people, 21 percent of whom are senior citizens. It has been identified as one of the most desirable and affluent places to live and work in the country. A wealthy senior citizen population makes this area an excellent choice for con artists; there is a large victim base from which to choose.

Seniors are targeted for these types of crimes for several reasons. Many seniors have cash readily available either at home or in the bank. They are retired and at home during the day. They are a generation of people who are trusting, polite and will hesitate to say no to someone who offers to help them. Some are lonely and welcome the chance to talk with someone, a fact the con artist exploits. They can be intimidated with fear or danger. Once seniors achieve retirement, they survive off pensions, Social Security and maybe some savings and investments. The con artist's offer seems to be a way to increase their nest egg or provide a larger inheritance to children or grandchildren.

The savvy con artist knows seniors make good victims because they may not have the best eyesight or memory, thereby eliminating a good description of the criminal. Also, the criminals know senior citizens can be either intimidated or scared into going along with the scam through hard-sell pressure tactics, such as the emergency home repair.

To determine to what extent Nassau County senior citizens had been victimized by these types of crimes, the POP Team attempted to access the police department's computerized Case Offense System (CHIEF). This proved to be an impossible task—our computer program did not capture these data. The FBI Uniform Crime Reporting System does not include a classification for crimes committed by fraud.

Each precinct within the Nassau County Police Department has a crime analyst who tracks crimes that occur within the precinct for daily review. Fortunately, the Fifth Precinct crime analyst had compiled statistics of scams, cons and frauds committed in the Fifth Precinct since 1992. More than 60 incidents had been reported, and the average victim was 78 years old, with a median loss of $8,600 and a mean loss of $2,500. Only 5 to 8 percent of these crimes are actually reported to the police. This indicates that many more than those 60 reported incidents occurred.

The POP Team interviewed senior citizen groups within the Fifth Precinct and learned that this type of crime is often underreported by seniors because of embarrassment, fear that the perpetrator would harm them if they reported the crime, and fear that their children would ridicule them or force them to stop living on their own.

When the victim is a senior, the obvious financial hardship, loss of confidence, and disruption to his or her style of living can be devastating. The loss of freedom and independence can undermine the senior's ability to remain an active and productive citizen. The victim's family may be forced to provide support for the parent, thereby creating additional financial hardships for them. This creates a second set of victims.

The family may also feel a loss of security for the elderly parent. It is not unusual for family members to ask or order the victim to move into their home (or to a safer, controlled environment, such as a nursing home or assisted living center) where the con artist cannot get to him or her.

County and town agencies often believed scams, cons and frauds were a police problem, but the police considered them civil problems, or bad business deals. By interviewing patrol and investigative personnel, the team discovered the department also lacked a consistently effective and uniform department response to patterns of fraud crime. The police department's Community Project Bureau was contacted for information about educating senior citizens about the dangers of scams, cons and frauds. While it did not keep any statistics, the bureau did provide crime prevention lectures to senior groups when requested. The Nassau County Department of Senior Affairs, the Nassau County District Attorney's Office, Enterprise Crime Bureau, the Town of Hempstead Services for the Aging, and the Town of Hempstead Department of Public Safety were contacted for any information they could provide regarding senior victimization and scams. None of these agencies track any crimes affecting seniors. They did offer an array of support services, which the POP Team incorporated into the response.

The POP Team contacted the American Association of Retired Persons (AARP) and National Association of Bunco Investigators (NABI). Both organizations had conducted surveys regarding crimes and senior citizens. The FBI and United States Postal Inspection Service Operations, which focuses on fraudulent operations, provided information that assisted in the analysis.

The POP Team then focused on the business community. Because banks were to play a key role in the response part of the problem-solving model, the team needed to gather information from them and gain their support. There are 29 separate banking institutions doing business at hundreds of locations in the county. To facilitate meeting with all of them, the team attended meetings of the Long Island Fraud and Forgery Association (LIFFA), which is made up of executive security and investigative personnel from each bank. This group provided information on the types of scams being perpetrated in Nassau County.

The banks do not track these types of crimes, but the expertise of the investigators and supervisory personnel was an important component in developing an efficient and effective lesson plan that met the needs of the banks and police department. Customer service representatives (CSRs) and security personnel from the public utilities companies were interviewed, because con artists posing as utility workers was one of the problems identified.

The Long Island Lighting Company, Bell Atlantic Telephone, Cablevision, and the Long Island Water Conference, which represents the 42 separate water districts in Nassau County, were interviewed about impostor utility workers. Each utility knew of occurrences in which someone impersonated one of its employees. Through interviews conducted with CSRs, we learned that occasionally they would tell the customer to call the police, sometimes the CSR would call the police, and most times no one called the police.

In Nassau County, there were several high-profile house robberies in which the offenders impersonated utility workers to gain entry. While the utility companies were concerned about the image problems that accompany this activity, none of the companies had any procedure in place to deal with it. It was apparent the employees needed training, and a procedure needed to be developed to address this problem effectively. All the companies agreed to work with the police department to accomplish this goal.

The analysis revealed con artists committing these types of scams in Nassau County made little effort, faced minimal risks and received large rewards. When officers attended a meeting of one of the local senior citizen groups to talk with them about scam crimes, the group of approximately 100 seniors began talking with each other about incidents that either they experienced or situations they knew about involving their friends. Additionally, senior groups from various communities around Nassau County were surveyed, and the results were the same.

The nature and extent of the problem was not fully recognized by the police department, county or town agencies because of a lack of a coordinated effort. In the past, the attitude of those agencies had been, "the victims should not have done that—they are greedy," and "I can't believe they fell for that." This attitude only provided a more secure place for the con artists to ply their trade. The transient nature of the con artist and lack of tracking also aided the con artist in committing these crimes—times of occurrence and location varied tremendously.

To incorporate a more proactive approach into our response, we needed to find out more about the con artists themselves— where they come from, where they stay when they are in Nassau County and why they choose the type of scam they perpetrate. Police personnel needed to be trained and made aware of the unique skills required to interview senior victims effectively. Lighting, location, oral skills, and body-language recognition had to be fine-tuned. The vast array of services from organizations available to assist victims and their families had to be made readily accessible and incorporated into the response to create an effective program.

Response

The POP Team's response was multifaceted and required the cooperation of the public and private sectors to attack all aspects of the problem. The team wanted to create as many roadblocks for the con artist as possible, thus increasing the effort and risk, while reducing the rewards for committing these crimes.

The POP Team wrote six lesson plans to educate and create awareness about the issue. The first is geared to command-level training, the second to in-service training, the third is now incorporated in the recruit curriculum, the fourth is for the training of the banking industry, the fifth for all public utility personnel, and the sixth for senior citizens.

The police department training was designed to raise patrol officers' awareness of the problem, ensure accurate reporting and crime classification, and inform officers of the multiagency support and resources available to them. The officers were taught that a proactive approach is most effective. Officers learned to use local laws and consumer affairs regulations not normally associated with the police department for enforcement purposes. A liaison at the Nassau County Department of Consumer Affairs allowed officers to confirm the license and insurance of contractors doing business in Nassau County. The officers also had access to previous complaints or problems with any contractor.

To provide a way to track these crimes, the department Information Systems Bureau created an MO code to be put on all reports identified as scams, cons or frauds. Now reports in the Case Offense System can be singled out based on this criteria.

The training for bank personnel suggested a way for tellers and customer service representatives to intervene in possible scam activities. Time is the enemy of the con artist, so if the bank employee can slow down the transaction by handing the customer a cash withdrawal alert form informing him or her of the latest scams in use, this may help the potential victim recognize his or her situation and terminate the transaction. Research revealed senior citizens often go to the bank to withdraw cash to complete the scam. Training of bank tellers required educating them about scams, cons and frauds; teaching discreet interview techniques; paying attention to the senior citizen's past banking history; and providing the customer with information about the danger of large cash withdrawals. A teller may suggest a certified or bank check, money order or wire transfer in lieu of a large cash withdrawal. Banks were encouraged to take a proactive approach and involve the police in situations where fraud was suspected.

POP officers in uniform trained bank personnel, which emphasized the police commitment to combat crimes against the elderly. For those banks that conducted in-house training, the POP team provided a lesson plan.

The POP Team recognized the need to incorporate public utilities in the response. Impostor burglars posing as utility workers were one of the most frequently used scams, and the utilities did not have a system in place to recognize fraudulent workers. The POP Team recommended a customer call the utility customer service representative and attempt to confirm the identity of the person at their front door. If a CSR cannot verify the identity of the worker through telephone contact with the customer, a police-designed procedure is initiated.

The utility company employee instructs the customer to call the police, and then the employee also calls, ensuring a police response. First, the CSR prepares a physical description/suspicious incident form that the POP Team designed. The form's purpose is to gather as much information from the customer as possible and initiate an informed police response. If the responding police officer does not locate the subject at the scene, the form provides enough information to begin an investigation and possibly identify an MO. The forms are then forwarded to the Special Investigation Squad to develop patterns and assist in the investigation.

All utilities were encouraged to provide informational literature to their customers through billing statements. The literature informs the customer how to verify the employee's identity and provides the customer with a contact number in the event of a potential impostor utility worker. The utilities' ability to distribute this information provided the police department with a vehicle for informing as many potential victims as possible.

When the POP Team conducted surveys of senior citizens, it became apparent they were well-schooled in telemarketing and mail fraud. This was verified through the local postal inspector, who had no reported cases of mail fraud. Unfortunately, they were not well-versed in home improvement scams, good faith cons and identifying impostor utility employees. The POP Team used a variety of county agencies and senior citizen groups to construct a comprehensive and dynamic educational program. Senior citizens receive enough information so they are able to discern the difference between legitimate and illegitimate people. Resource telephone numbers, contact people and a list of supporting agencies are supplied for the seniors' use, and seniors are encouraged to provide feedback in an attempt to modify and improve the educational program.

The Nassau County District Attorney's Office agreed to request that subjects be remanded to the county jail until positive identifications are obtained, and that high bail be requested to ensure their return to court. The Nassau County Department of Consumer Affairs agreed to post the licensing requirements necessary to do business in the county at home improvement centers, lumber yards and commercial building supply warehouses.

The POP Team developed a newsletter to solidify the lines of communication among all interested parties. The newsletter provides information on current scams, cons and frauds, provides helpful telephone numbers, and recognizes participating agencies for their good work and suggestions, and, most important, for their intervention and assistance. Additionally, the newsletter helps the POP Team maintain a heightened awareness among all interested parties concerned about crimes against the elderly.

Assessment
The Problem-Oriented Policing Team developed a comprehensive, proactive approach to combat the victimization of senior citizens through scams, cons and frauds. Analysis revealed a tremendous lack of training and awareness on the part of all parties involved in the prevention of these crimes.

By creating a training program for the police, the team increased officer awareness and improved proper response and documentation. Officers now take a proactive approach in dealing with unlicensed home improvement contractors, who are identified and issued appearance tickets in accordance with consumer affair laws. As a result, the contractor either complies with the law and gets a license, or searches for a new jurisdiction with less stringent laws and less aggressive enforcement.

The development of the computerized tracking code, the guidelines for its utilization, and the training of police officers and detectives is now part of the operating policy for police personnel. Training provided to senior citizens' groups sponsored by town, county or church groups has increased knowledge and awareness greatly among the largest possible victim base for these types of crimes.

A key factor in the plan was the involvement of the banking institutions. To date, POP officers have trained more than 300 bank personnel to recognize a potential scam in progress and what steps to take to prevent the completion of the crime. Several banks that conduct in-house training have adopted this lesson plan and were able to extend the training to even more bank personnel. All bank branch personnel participated in bank training. Employees of bank branches in the neighboring counties also received training, which gave the added benefit of covering a larger geographical area with trained personnel than originally planned.

The additional eyes, ears and experience of these employees is a tremendous asset to the program. They not only utilize the training while at work with their customers, but pass the information along to family and friends, which creates another set of eyes and ears on the street and in homes.

Including the utility companies in the program addressed the problem of impostor scams. More than 400 public utility employees have been trained. In addition to training customer service representatives, most utilities also train field technicians and crews. Because of the training, there has been an increased number of calls to police reporting suspicious people. The civilian personnel trained to recognize these scams have become an integral part of uncovering new scams and cons perpetrated by health care workers, friends and relatives who violate and abuse their fiduciary responsibilities. This has led to additional training regarding the financial exploitation of senior citizens.

The Nassau County Department of Senior Affairs provides investigators who review scams and frauds, and forward the information to the police department and district attorney's office for possible prosecution. The original goal to reduce the number of scams, cons and frauds against the elderly is being achieved. During the first half of 1997, 28 of these crimes were reported, while only 11 were reported during the first five months of 1998. An increase in reporting was expected for the fall in response to the increased training and awareness.

The proactive approach used in this program fosters communication and exchange of information among all participants. Adjoining jurisdictions are aware of the program (it was necessary to alert them because the customer base of the utilities and banks reaches into those areas). Displacement is difficult to study because of the lack of crime report coding in other jurisdictions (this is currently being discussed). This approach can be instituted in any jurisdiction that has these types of crimes. This program demonstrates a beneficial and permanent partnership between the public and private sector.

MISSION VALLEY RIVER PRESERVE— RESTORING A REGION OF THE SAN DIEGO RIVER BED SAN DIEGO POLICE DEPARTMENT

Scanning

The lower San Diego River stretches from Sefton Park—a Little League baseball field to the east—to Interstate 5 to the west, and is bordered by Interstate 8 to the south and Friars Road to the north. It covers approximately 10 acres. The Western Division Police Station is on the north side of the river at the intersection of Napa Street and Friars Road. The San Diego Metropolitan Transit District built a trolley station across the street from the police station. The trolley travels over the river on raised tracks. These tracks traverse the river and offer beautiful views of the area.

Despite being one of the more scenic spots in Mission Valley, the public avoided this section of the river. There was a lack of legal, well-defined access points and trails, and numerous transient people lived illegally in the river bottom—many engaged in criminal activities, which undoubtedly contributed to the public's avoidance. This same illegal camping periodically led to a buildup of unsightly trash, a proliferation of trails through sensitive habitat, pollution of the river banks and water from toxic byproducts of illegal recycling, and other illegal activities. This led to a steady degradation of the area's vegetation.

The area required a disproportionate allocation of police resources from the nearby Western Police Division. Those occupying the river bed were frequently arrested for a variety of criminal violations. These ranged from misdemeanor crimes—such as illegal lodging—to felony crimes, including possession of controlled substances and burglary. Police found hundreds of bicycles—suspected to be stolen property—during inspections of this area. One camp site had huge piles of bicycles, both assembled and in parts.

From July 1994 to July 1996, police documented the following:
- 88 arrests for crimes, including assault with a deadly weapon, drug offenses and trespassing;
- 147 criminal citations for misdemeanor violations, loitering and violations of city ordinances; and
- 205 field interviews, in which officers contacted those suspected of illegal activity.

These numbers are more impressive when it is considered that no routine police patrol was done at the river during that time.

Along with these criminal acts, the individuals caused damage to the environment. Most of the illegal inhabitants raised money by recycling various materials. They somehow acquired hundreds of feet of electrical wiring. This wire must have the insulation removed before recycling, and they accomplished this by burning it. The fire department regularly responded to these blazes, which often overran the crude fire pits made by the individuals responsible. The noxious odors and poisonous chemicals released by this activity caused damage to the river and were hazardous to the fire fighters. The trespassers also brought in a variety of chemicals (paints, solvents, batteries, etc.). Once these items were used, they were dumped in the river or on its banks.

These problems had always been addressed with "sweeps." Law enforcement, working alone or teaming with environmental services (the city agency responsible for waste management), swept the river. Trespassers were asked to leave or were arrested.

The area then was cleaned up. This tactic only worked in the short term. After the police left the area, the violators always returned.

Analysis

In June 1996, Officers Patrick Vinson, Theresa Kinney and Robb McCracken began their analysis of this problem. They were assisting Code Compliance Officers L.C. Wright and Mark Wedenhoff during a clean-up/sweep. Code compliance officers are the enforcement branch of the environmental services department. One of the responsibilities of environmental services is refuse collection.

During June 1996, 100 tons of trash were removed from this section of the river. An additional three tons were removed each week thereafter. The dumping fee alone for this amount of refuse was $4,200. This does not include the cost of worker salaries or equipment use.

Police and code compliance officers brainstormed about what could be done to stop the repetitive and unproductive cycle of these clean-up projects. Officers McCracken and Kinney noted the area's wildlife and history were significant. Officer Vinson already had done preliminary historical research, revealing that the river played an important role in San Diego's past and had a direct impact on the city's present. From a biological and historical perspective, it was obvious this river was perfectly suited to become a preserve.

The officers next analyzed why the river was suffering from so many problems. It was agreed that the river presented criminals these primary benefits:

- **Concealment.** The dense brush and vegetation provided privacy for any acts committed there. Visibility was only a problem when the camp became so big that it was seen from the bridges, streets or freeways.
- **Lack of Access.** Police had a difficult time entering the area. There were no roads or maintained paths. The public did not use the area.

- **Location.** The area is centrally located. Businesses and residences are all within a short distance.

The officers knew they had to eliminate the first two benefits to solve the current problem. The third benefit would work in their favor.

Another major problem identified was that no one seemed to have an interest in the river. Despite the fact that the river is surrounded by condominiums and a thriving commercial area, the concealment provided by the brush mostly kept the activity from the attention of residents and business owners. There was only the occasional complaint. The officers knew they had to make the identification of stakeholders a priority. The surrounding area offered many possibilities.

The University of San Diego is a highly respected private college located about one-half mile away from the river. Dr. Michael Mayer, professor of biology, had been interested in the San Diego River for some time. He had harvested plant samples from the river, but had limited his trips due to his concern about the criminal element that he had observed there. Dr. Mayer felt the river would provide a wonderful opportunity for his students to get hands-on experience in the restoration of urban river water systems. Dr. Mayer introduced the officers to Dr. Hugh Ellis, the head of the biology department. Dr. Ellis also was enthusiastic about the river's future and the role it could serve in education.

The Presidio Museum is another neighbor of the river. The Presidio is a circa–1920s replica of the original mission built by Spaniards on their discovery of San Diego. It is on a hill overlooking the river, just across Interstate 8. The museum is operated by the San Diego Historical Society and is the centerpiece of Presidio Park. The park has active archeological digs that search for and reveal the original foundations of adobes built and lived in by people 200 to 300 years ago.

At the base of the hill is Old Town, the original site of San Diego. The park has an ongoing program operated in conjunction with San Diego city schools. Every fourth-grade student in the city public school system spends two school weeks at the park studying the history and cultures of the people that inhabited the area. Presidio Park historically was connected to the river, and the educational programs at the Presidio could easily factor the river into the curriculum.

The river originally flowed into what is now Mission Bay and San Diego Harbor. The original inhabitants of the Presidio used this section of the river for water and irrigation. The mission was moved east to the Mission Gorge area because this section of river sometimes became a dry, sandy riverbed with no flowing water. In 1769, Spanish explorers noted that the river was inhabited by 35 to 40 Indians. The vegetation noted in this report consisted of poplar, willow and alder trees.

A photo from 1880 shows a view looking south from what is probably the area of 5200 Friars Road. The photo shows Presidio Hill. In the foreground is a riverbed with no trees or vegetation. An 1874 view shows Mission Valley looking east from Presidio Hill. It shows sparse vegetation.

Early inhabitants of Presidio Hill and Old Town relied on this section of river for their water. When the river was dry, residents sank wood buckets or crates into the sand to extract the water. Residents also dug wells in the riverbed. What is now Palm Canyon (located directly behind the museum) was once a large water works facility, supplying water to Old Town and New Town.

In 1852, the United States military was becoming concerned about the river. Sand flowing from the river had rendered what is now Mission Bay completely useless as a port for seagoing vessels. The river's course also was depositing sand into San Diego Bay. The fear was if the river was not turned, San Diego Bay also would be rendered useless.

George Derby, lieutenant with the topographical engineers, was assigned the task of surveying the river and building a levee to change its course. Excerpts from his report to the 33rd Congress (1853–4) are quoted as follows:

> The entire bed of the river from source to mouth,
> with the exception of two points, is of light drift-
> ing sand. . .the banks are low, alluvial bottoms,
> varying in width from one to five miles, and
> mostly destitute of forests or shrubbery.

Lt. Derby noted that at the time of the Presidio's founding, the valley was covered with a dense forest of sycamore, willow and cottonwood, with an undergrowth of various kinds of shrubbery, among which the wild grape was the most abundant. At this time the river ran through the most northern part of the plain, skirting the hills represented on the plan, and emptied into False Bay. This course continued until 1811, when, by the continued deposit of sand, its bed was so much elevated that it altered its channel to the southwest, still however emptying into False Bay, until 1825, when a great freshet occurred. It overflowed its bank, destroying many gardens and much property, and formed a new channel discharging into the harbor of San Diego. From the continued accumulation of sand, its course has some-what fluctuated, but has never been essentially altered since that period.

Lt. Derby recommended that the river be permanently di-rected into False Bay (currently called Mission Bay). He proposed building a bulkhead or levee that would run from Presidio Hill to the larger sloughs. This levee would be eight feet high to en-sure the river would not overrun it. Lt. Derby described this work as of "much importance, preserving from utter destruction one of the finest harbors of the Pacific coast." He submitted several versions of his plan, each slightly different. This offered a range of costs that the government could select from.

The levee was built and became known as "Derby's Dike." However, due to a lack of funding, the dike was not built to the highest standards outlined by Lt. Derby. Construction began in 1853. It was washed out by heavy rains in 1855, but was rebuilt.

The preceding story illustrates the rich historical value of this land. Had the military not taken an interest in preserving the harbor, where would San Diego be today? This educational and historical theme would draw schools and others into a properly restored river park.

Officer McCracken had worked with Senior Park Ranger Tracey Walker on an earlier project. Ranger Walker was responsible for the Tecolote Nature Center and Preserve. Tecolote is a canyon preserve located about a mile-and-a half north of the river.

The officers went to Ranger Walker not only for his expert opinion on plants and wildlife, but also to consult on how to turn this river preserve into a reality. Ranger Walker is highly respected regarding both native plant and wildlife preservation as well as the restoration and management of public-use preserves.

Ranger Walker agreed that the perfect use of the river would be as a preserve. The native species restoration would benefit the area ecology, and the preserve would be an asset and complement to the city's existing preserve system. Ranger Walker explained there were native plant and animal species in the river, but these species were threatened by the growing expansion of non-native species, specifically a bamboo-like grass named *Arundo Donax*. *Arundo* is a rapid, aggressive grower that is difficult to eliminate. It must be cut down, and the remaining stump must be sprayed with poison or it will regroup.

The illegal lodgers used *Arundo* to build their shelters. Its thick and tall growth patterns also made it the primary source of concealment for illegal activity. Elimination of the Arundo would be ecologically sound and necessary, and would greatly decrease the area's appeal as a criminal base of operations.

Among the animal species inhabiting the river is the Least Bell Viros, a small migratory bird. The Viros is an endangered species.

The officers consulted the police department's Crime Analysis Unit. The river presented specific analysis problems. The river has no streets. The only reference points were streets running along its boundaries. It did not exist as a park or public place so it had no common name or location that could be used. This resulted in no single address being used to document the area's activity.

Analyst Ann Carter discussed these problems and came on a "walk along" at the site. This gave her firsthand knowledge of the area and its problems. During her visit, officers arrested one of the river's chronic offenders for possession of stolen property. This suspect not only was uncooperative, but actively resisted being taken into custody. This incident gave Carter insight on not only the crime problems, but the logistical and geographical problems faced in taking enforcement action along the river. The suspect, though not seriously hurt, had to be carried over rough, brush-covered terrain to reach paramedics on Friars Road.

To overcome the data problem, Carter advised the problem-solving team to encourage all officers to use the common address of 5200 Friars Road for the river. Carter compiled statistics from existing data relating to arrests and crime along the river. After researching the river's educational, historical and environmental qualities, the officers approached their lieutenant, Ron Newman. Lt. Newman encouraged the effort by suggesting that they contact the area's council member, Valerie Stallings. Newman said that a group called the Riverbed Task Force was already assigned to solve the river's problems. After contacting Stallings, the officers were invited to give a presentation of our analysis and research at the next task force meeting.

Response

A meeting was organized to bring together representatives from the existing Riverbed Task Force and those identified as probable stakeholder leaders for the proposed river preserve. This meeting took place July 16, 1996, at the Tecoclote Nature Center. The attendance list included city officials, university biologists, environmentalists, and representatives from the environmental services and parks departments.

The officers gave the first presentation of their analysis and proposal to this group. All in attendance supported turning this section of the river into a preserve. On July 26, the officers were invited to attend and give a presentation to a meeting of the Riverbed Task Force. During this meeting, officers learned that the existing task force had tried to help those illegally lodging at the river. The Salvation Army, the city homeless services, St. Vincent De Paul Village, and the county mental health services all had offered their services to those individuals.

Of the individuals contacted by representatives of these groups, none took advantage of the services offered. This further illustrated the extent of the problem and the individuals involved in criminal activity. Even when services and offers of help were brought to them at the river, they declined those offers. This proved that the task force was not dealing with a "homeless/displaced" problem; the people living by the river were not there because of economic or societal problems beyond their control—they were there by their own choice.

The task force discussed the proposal of turning the river into a nature preserve. Though everyone agreed the preserve idea had its merits, there would be problems to overcome. The challenges included the following:

- **Land ownership.** Who actually owned the river property?
- **Preserve boundaries.** What area was being discussed?
- **Cost.** Who would pay for the development?
- **Coastal wetlands.** Was it legal to do anything at all in this area?
- **Protected species, both plant and animal.** Again, was it legal to do anything in this area?

These were complicated problems and issues. Answering these questions and clearing other hurdles that might later arise would take many meetings and discussions with staff from local, state and federal government agencies.

Councilmember Stallings embraced the concept of turning the river into a preserve. The preserve idea paralleled her own vision for the area. It was agreed that further study into the proposal would be needed, but that no problem was too great to overcome. Stallings' aide, Marilyn Mirrasoul, was charged with coordinating future meetings. Agencies responsible for coastal and species protection were contacted for the necessary approvals.

Mike Kelly, from the Native Plant Society, had firsthand experience turning neglected areas—such as this section of the river—into preserves. He also is involved with the Rancho Penasquitos Preserve, a canyon preserve located about 20 miles north of the river. It is open to the public for recreation activity and education. Kelly's experience and dedication to seeing this project completed proved to be invaluable. He knew not only the legal and regulatory rules involving protected native plants and animals, but had solid, practical experience in these matters. Mike Mayer's knowledge of area plants and his role as professor at the University of San Diego added the strong educational theme required for the project's success.

Fifteen city, private and federal agencies were identified as stakeholders, each with a defined area of responsibility. Before the preserve could be brought to the public, these groups would have to work out solutions to the identified initial problems. Only after the initial problems were solved would the group be able to bring this to the public and answer the public's questions about the preserve.

Throughout 1996 and 1997, meetings were held to solve the identified problems. Participants also met at the river. Mike Mayer and Mike Kelly used Global Positioning Satellite technology to map out the river and enter the location of the different plant species. These data created a map that was used at ensuing meetings. Non-native plants were identified, including eucalyptus and palm trees, castor bean, Brazilian Pepper trees, and the previously noted *Arundo.*

The group learned about "mitigation credits." Mitigation is a process required of any party building in a sensitive area. In exchange for a building permit, the party must rehabilitate the area with native species. In the case of this project, the Metropolitan Transit District Board (MTDB) had been assigned mitigation because of its trolley extension through the river. This mitigation included the replanting and irrigation of native willow and the elimination of *Arundo.*

The Army Corps of Engineers and U.S. Fish and Wildlife Service had concerns about constructing trails or opening the area for general recreation. They feared public access would be detrimental to native animal and plant species. Kelly and Mayer were instrumental in solving this problem. They pointed out that more than enough trails already existed from the illegal activity that had been occurring for years at the river. Rather than creating trails, this project would identify trails that would not interfere with the species, but would still allow public use. Trails detrimental to wildlife would be blocked off by native plantings. Recreation would not be an issue. The area would be clearly designated as a preserve—there would be no lawn area or sports sections developed.

The preserve would enhance, not interfere with the native species. This enhancement would come about through the education and involvement of concerned citizens. Other preserves in the city park system have citizen volunteer groups that identify and restore native plant species while removing non-native invaders. They enhance and preserve the area for protected animal species. A volunteer group would be formed for this new preserve. Don Steele of the Parks and Recreation Department was appointed project director. He coordinated the transfer of the property from the City Open Spaces Division of Real Estate Assets to Parks and Recreation Department control. He obtained a kiosk and had it installed at the intersection of Napa Street and Friars Road, marking public access to the preserve. It is posted with information regarding native plants and animals.

The police department implemented regular patrol of the area to prevent the criminal element from re-establishing a hold in the area. During past efforts, the police would not revisit the area for months after the initial sweep. This allowed the criminals time to build massive camps and virtually establish a criminal society along the river. This enforcement was coordinated with the environmental services department. Camps and trash were taken away on a regular basis so they could not build up. Officers noticed a marked decline in the number of people illegally living along the river. Large camps full of stolen property no longer existed.

Assessment

Through the diligent efforts of all those involved, the Mission Valley Preserve was created. On May 23, 1998, the opening ceremonies were held in the front lot of the Western Police Station. Councilmember Stallings officiated the event. Media representatives, parks and recreation personnel, police personnel, and most important, community members attended the event.

Following the brief ceremonies, those in attendance went on guided tours of the preserve. Mike Kelly pointed out native and non-native plant species. Volunteers then grabbed tools and trash bags for the first clean-up of the area by citizen volunteers.

This project accomplished its goals:

- All three originally identified core problems were resolved.
- A neglected, but valuable, resource was identified and promoted.
- The area was taken from a thriving criminal community and turned into an asset to the city.
- The huge, illegal campsites no longer exist.
- The preserve plans include use as an education resource for elementary and college-level classes.
- The preserve is now recognized for its previously ignored historical relevance.
- The community now has an acknowledged and vested interest in the preserve.
- The community can now participate in the area's restoration.
- Transient activity in the surrounding area has markedly decreased.

New partnerships were formed that will continue into the future. The preserve will be a never-ending project. Work is now in progress to form a "Friends of the Preserve" group. This group will be modeled after the successful citizen volunteer groups already active in other city preserves.

The next preserve event will be a kids' day at the Mission Valley Preserve. Children will be given tours of the preserve, and taught about the native plants, how the river and plants were used by both native inhabitants and the Europeans that followed, and how the river affected the course of local history.

Police service to the preserve will remain at the same level as at other city parks and preserves. Cost issues were addressed by simply moving forward. The formation of this preserve had no funded budget. Meetings took place during city employees' normal work hours. Those attending meetings during nonwork hours or spending time researching or writing out proposals did so on a volunteer basis. The kiosk was donated by the Natural History Museum of San Diego. Further funding issues will be addressed by the Parks and Recreation Department. Due to the ecological concerns, there are many grant opportunities being researched.

One eventual goal is to have a city park ranger assigned to this preserve. This ranger would be a wetlands specialist for this preserve and other nearby wetland areas.

This project demonstrates that officers can and should become involved in what, in the past, may have been considered nontraditional projects. When problem solving, officers should use their imagination and all their skills, not only skills acquired and honed as police officers.

Creativity and citizen involvement are the key to solving the core reasons problems exist and thrive. By bringing together concerned, responsible citizens with experts in specialties outside law enforcement, a chronic, unsolvable problem was solved.

POLICE RESPONSE TO INCIDENTS OF DOMESTIC EMERGENCIES (PRIDE)
NEWPORT NEWS, VA., POLICE DEPARTMENT

In 1984, the Newport News, Va., Police Department (NNPD), in conjunction with the Police Executive Research Forum and the

National Institute of Justice, attempted to develop a more effective means of analyzing and responding to a wide variety of problems facing police. A Crime Analysis Task Force was selected to work on this project.

As a detective with the Homicide Division, Marvin Evans requested assignment to the task force; he wanted to find a means of reducing the number of homicides occurring in Newport News. He initially speculated the homicides were related to economic and social conditions existing in the predominantly African-American southeast community. This area had a low median income, a high number of female heads of households, a high drop-out rate, high unemployment, and a high concentration of subsidized housing. While these elements certainly contributed to the problem, it still was difficult to pinpoint the cause of the homicides. He reviewed 174 homicide cases occurring in Newport News between 1976 and 1984. His review indicated domestic violence was the single most significant force—causing 48 percent of the killings.

To accurately determine the extent to which domestic violence was a problem, the NNPD examined calls for service recorded for the addresses where a domestic homicide had occurred and in the city in general. Records showed more than 8,000 calls for service each year, reflecting the following trends:

- Many calls for service were repeat calls—police had responded to the address on more than one occasion.
- Few calls resulted in an arrest. Most were "Handled by Officer."
- Nearly all arrests for domestic violence resulted when the victims obtained warrants.
- Victims requested that the vast majority of victim-initiated warrants be dropped at first arraignment, resulting in a congested docket and wasted effort on the part of the prosecuting attorney's office and the police.
- Nearly all of the domestic homicides had calls for service recorded before the death, and more than half the homicide cases had six or more calls recorded.

Officers typically responded to these calls by issuing a warning or threatening arrest. Domestic calls frequently frustrated officers because the victims did not follow through with the case once a warrant was obtained. Most officers merely threatened to make an arrest if the problem continued. Unfortunately, more often than not, those threats were never carried out. There was little in the way of standardized training on domestic violence and officers were left to their own discretion about how to respond.

Victims and abusers were interviewed. The lack of follow-through was directly related to the cycle of violence. By the time the matter came up in court, the crisis event had passed and the parties were in the "honeymoon stage," the time in an abusive relationship when the abuser is apologetic and the victim has forgiven him or her. In some of the cases, fear of reprisals and future beatings played a part in the failure to prosecute. Also, fear that a breadwinner might be sent to jail, eliminating the family income, caused some victims to drop warrants. The root cause of the problems that precipitated the violence went unabated. Prosecutors, knowing they had reluctant witnesses, most often would not advance the prosecution of the warrant, and the matter was dropped.

To expand the field of information, representatives from the battered women's shelter, mental health providers, courts, commonwealth's attorney, law enforcement, military, and the news media formed an advisory committee to initiate a collective dialogue about domestic violence. The problem tremendously affected many organizations in the area, but each organization attempted to address the problem in its own isolated environment, each focusing on a single element of the problem.

Evans consulted with psychologists, psychiatrists, social workers, and other law enforcement agencies. He continued interviewing victims and abusers, and reviewed several studies that indicated arrest was an effective deterrent to domestic violence. However, research indicated a need to go beyond temporarily deterring the violence by developing a mechanism to assist the parties in resolving the underlying problems.

As a result of this problem analysis, a multidisciplined response was developed that involved organizations actively working on the problem of domestic violence. The response would better coordinate the organizations' efforts and achieve a positive and long-term effect. The major elements of the response included the following:

- NNPD officers were to strictly enforce the law and not issue idle arrest threats. Officers would investigate and document acts of domestic violence as aggressively as they would acts of violence committed by strangers. Police officers would obtain warrants, based on probable cause, to reduce the threats, intimidation and other factors that previously resulted in warrants being dropped before prosecution.
- The prosecutor's office agreed to prosecute domestic violence cases in lieu of having the victim simply testify against the abuser.
- The courts would not allow arbitrary withdrawal of warrants obtained by the victims before any effective intervention took place.
- Mental health agencies agreed to provide evaluation and counseling to dissuade abusers' violent behavior.
- The battered women's shelter agreed to provide a victims' advocate to the victim for court appearances and to provide services to victims and their children.
- The news media agreed to keep domestic violence in the public's attention.

The most significant obstacle to implementing the response was changing officers' attitudes. Many officers viewed domestic violence as a situation they could not control. They felt victims contributed to the problems and should leave the abusive relationship. There was little understanding of "learned helplessness" or the cycle of violence.

The NNPD enlisted the help of professionals from outside the law enforcement community and developed training to help officers fully understand the dynamics of domestic violence, see victims as victims and see abusers as criminals. Younger officers adapted much more readily than veteran officers, but they, too, eventually came to realize the plan's positive potential.

Domestic violence training was also provided to all supervisors, from sergeant to chief. It was important that supervisors understand and support this approach, which was a radical change from the nonintervention approach most commonly used previously.

Once the training was completed, community support secured and service providers committed, the department implemented Police Response to Incidents of Domestic Emergencies (PRIDE). The local newspaper provided public awareness with an extensive report on domestic violence and the PRIDE program in a Sunday edition. Shortly thereafter, articles and reports about PRIDE began appearing in newspapers, on radio, on television, and in magazines.

A formal policy and procedure was approved and distributed to all police personnel and the community agencies involved in the program. While the police department's role was investigating complaints and taking enforcement action, followed by detailed reporting and collection of evidence and statements, the majority of the effort was performed by the prosecutors, courts, mental health professionals, and the battered women's shelter. The police coordinated the groups and facilitated a team response to the problem.

Implementation of the PRIDE response resulted in NNPD officers better understanding the state's domestic violence laws. It also identified inadequacies in the existing laws on protective orders and enforcement of those orders. Those associated with PRIDE were instrumental in successfully having state laws amended to provide for an immediate arrest of people violating a protective order.

Today, a number of state laws exist that require reporting of domestic violence, mandatory arrest, victim assistance, and stronger protective orders. Many of these laws were proposed by agencies associated with the PRIDE program. NNPD officers have testified before the Attorney General's Task Force on Domestic Violence to bring about change.

This program's objective was to reduce the number of domestic violence-related homicides. From 1976 to 1984, the NNPD investigated 174 homicides, of which 84 (48%) were domestic violence-related. PRIDE was implemented in 1985. From 1985 to 1989, the department recorded 78 homicides, of which 21 (27%) were domestic-related. From 1990 to 1997, of 199 homicides, 23 (11.5%) were domestic-related. In 1992, police investigated 33 homicides and none were attributed to domestic violence.

Program evaluation was based on the frequency of domestic violence-related homicides compared with the total number of homicides. In 1996, six of the 27 homicides in Newport News were domestic-related. However, this included a single event in which a distraught husband killed his wife, his two children, and then himself.

Since 1985, even though the frequency of homicide has fluctuated, domestic-related homicides have been on the decline. PRIDE has resulted in a measurable reduction in domestic homicides that has continued over the years. The NNPD did see a significant increase in the number of domestic-related calls for service for the first several years of the program, attributed to the frequent media coverage of PRIDE and increased public awareness of domestic violence. Another unexpected benefit of PRIDE was a significant reduction in the number of assaults on police officers responding to domestic calls.

Following the media attention given to PRIDE, hundreds of law enforcement agencies across the United States, England, Canada, France, and Israel have contacted the department for information on the program. The Victim Service Agency of New York prepared a videotape titled "Agents of Change," featuring two exceptional domestic violence programs: one in Rye, N.Y., and PRIDE.

Since PRIDE was implemented, the only additional funding obtained was a grant for informational pamphlets and posters. No funds—beyond the department's operational budget—were required to implement this program.

SAN YSIDRO INTERNATIONAL BORDER
SAN DIEGO POLICE DEPARTMENT

Scanning

There were five primary types of problems occurring in the area
of 700 East San Ysidro Boulevard:

- **Illegal solicitation and transportation (Wildcatting).** Men
  and women illegally solicit passing pedestrians, then arrange for another person to provide illegal transportation out of San Diego County. These wildcatters are
  generally unlicensed, uninsured and drive unsafe vehicles. The unsuspecting travelers are bullied or tricked
  into using these illegal carriers and then frequently become victims of more serious crimes at the hands of the
  drivers. These crimes have included rape, robbery and
  assault.

- **Car prowls and auto thefts.** Local and transient criminals
  prey on vehicles parked on secluded local streets and in
  parking lots by visitors or tourists who enter Mexico. Officers take many vehicle crime reports for this small area.

- **Commercial vehicle and pedestrian traffic problems.** 700
  East San Ysidro Boulevard was designed with 1970s traffic patterns in mind. Now, on a daily basis, this narrow
  one-way road handles an average of 30,000 pedestrians
  and 3,000 commercial/civilian vehicles, and the San Diego Trolley brings more than 7,000 passengers daily to
  and from the border area. The pedestrians often disregard the many directional signs. The trolleys arriving and
  leaving the area every 15 minutes force many pedestrians and vehicles to wait longer for lights. Large entities
  such as CAL-TRANS, the City of San Diego Traffic Engineering Division and the Metropolitan Transit Development Board have neglected this area for other priorities.
  Communication and language barriers create confusion
  about the area's lights and signs.

Cruising taxicabs cause an unusual amount of traffic and associated code violations in the area. The area had only two taxi stands—one held three cabs and one held two. Both stands were a distance from the main U.S. Customs exit, the place where pedestrians from Mexico would look for a taxi. The cabs, fearing loss of business to illegal solicitors, would constantly drive around the small, looping, narrow road, stopping anywhere they could to pick up a fare. The cabs would stop in red zones, no stopping anytime zones, bus loading zones, fire lanes, and in the middle of intersections with complete contempt for local ordinances.

Additionally, this two-block area is home to three large bus companies and more than 10 van transportation companies. These companies carry travelers throughout California and the United States. All companies have offices within the area and conduct business on the street. These vehicles have to negotiate the narrow roadways, constricting them to a standstill. Competition between companies is fierce, and occasionally turns violent. Many of these companies use unsafe vehicles and unlicensed drivers. The businesses often conduct illegal advertising, illegal solicitation and illegal ticket sales practices.

To add to the problem, several small stores line the street and require the delivery of goods via large semi-tractor trailers. The large trucks and transportation companies compete for street space.

- **911 pay phone calls.** Confusion and lack of education about the 911 emergency system in the United States has many travelers accidentally dialing 911 to make an international call rather than the international 011 prefix. Additionally, local criminals use the 911 system to get police to respond to a specific area, while the criminals move to another area to conduct illegal activities.

- **Extensive officer service time.** Beat officers spend an enormous number of hours handling calls in the 700 East

San Ysidro Boulevard area. It wastes valuable officer time to have separate, unfamiliar officers handle similar, repeated radio calls.

In 1994, the first meetings were held among the local police, federal agencies and community members. In 1996, the San Diego Police Department's (SDPD) Crime Analysis Division produced serious statistical evidence consistently ranking 700 East San Ysidro first in San Diego for out-of-service time and calls for service. The police department met with federal, state and local agencies again. The community and businesses had, with the SDPD's aid, formed groups that demanded the problems be addressed. The local media publicized the area's problems.

Analysis

Local community and business members said the problems at 700 East San Ysidro had been around for 30 years. The enforcement posture before this project was completely reactive—officers responded when needed. Officers handled the problem at hand, then left the area before they could be flagged down to handle another problem. While the types of problems experienced in this area remained the same for years, the number of incidents escalated.

Crime analysis officers compiled crime statistics, arrest numbers, calls-for-service numbers, and out-of-service time. The SDPD took informal surveys of the business and community members at community meetings. Officers and supervisors from U.S. Customs' Immigration and Border Patrol who had worked the area; the California Highway Patrol; the California Public Utilities Commission; the Metropolitan Transit Development Board; the Code Compliance Enforcement Units; and many departments and divisions in the city of San Diego and the SDPD were asked for input. The discussions and surveys resulted in a detailed profile of the many different offenders, victims and stakeholders.

The offenders included local gang members, local drug addicts, visitors from out of the county who committed various crimes of opportunity, undocumented immigrants passing through, unemployed manual laborers, and employed males and females who illegally solicited and carried passengers out of San Ysidro.

The victims included local residents and business members, tourists visiting San Ysidro and Mexico, local insurance companies, local hotels and restaurants, passengers traveling out of San Diego County, and local federal, state and city government agencies.

Conservative estimates put the loss of annual revenues to the transportation companies alone at nearly $500,000. Local citizens who might have wanted to visit the area were afraid and complained they could not visit. In 1996, more than 1,000 vehicles were taken from Southern Division and more than 20 auto burglary reports were taken by officers every month. It cost more than $1 million for officers to respond to the nonemergency 911 calls received from that area during 1997. The associated out-of-service time cost even more. Court time and costs to prosecute all associated crimes and the follow-up probation were enormous.

Response

The first step in finding the appropriate response was to form a special team of officers. In 1993, the two-officer team was known as the Border Area Special Enforcement (BASE) team. In 1994, the team was expanded to four officers and obtained the assistance of the South Bay Municipal Court system and the San Diego County District Attorney's Office. In May 1997, the Southern Division command staff added additional officers and a supervisor to the team, bringing it up to eight officers and a supervisor. The team's name also was changed to the Border Crime Suppression Team (BCST). This new larger team now could cover the area seven days a week from 6 a.m. to 11 p.m. each day.

The goals of the SDPD and the BCST were to address community and business safety issues, address criminal business practices, reduce the fear of crime, decrease police officers' wasted time, and lower the need for police intervention.

The primary difficulty encountered when formulating responses was how to properly deal with the massive amount of interagency and interdepartmental communication, and how to use the correct protocol. With so many government agencies involved with the responses, each with its own rules and regulations, this project had several hurdles and pitfalls that were previously unknown in the problem-oriented policing field.

Illegal solicitation and illegal transportation (Wildcatting). This problem was so large and costly to the legitimate businesses that a first-of-its-kind task force—the San Diego Wildcat Task Force—was formed in 1994. The unit included members of the U.S. Customs and Immigration Service, U.S. Border Patrol, California Public Utilities Commission, California Highway Patrol, San Diego District Attorney's Office, the Metropolitan Transit Development Board, and the San Diego Police Department. Enforcement began vigorously in 1996. BCST officers worked with border patrol agents to develop strategies, and adjusted their hours to conduct undercover operations. The district attorney's office developed a geographic probation program to keep repeat offenders out of the area. Judges and members of the business community were given specialized training on citizen's arrest for open solicitation by wildcatters. The arrested wildcatters had their vehicles impounded and thoroughly inspected for vehicle safety. Jail time and large fines were levied against the most serious repeat offenders.

Local media and a BCST newsletter continue to educate the mainly Mexican travelers that use the unsafe and illegal wildcatters. Also, the border team assisted the legal transportation carriers in forming the Border Transportation Council. This group has gained local political clout, and its members have agreed to conduct legal business practices along the border.

Car prowls and auto thefts. This problem is not a new one for heavily traveled areas. Crime prevention through environmental design (CPTED) was used in many locations, and victims and stakeholders were educated. Many tourists would park their vehicles on a secluded street with limited vehicle travel, and enter Mexico. Posted signs warned of the possibility of theft and told people not to leave valuables in their vehicles. These signs cut down on the losses, but the broken windows, damaged locks and stolen vehicles continued. Finally, the curbs were painted red and signs were posted prohibiting parking anytime.

Police met with owners of parking lots around the area and suggested improvements and changes that could slow or stop crime on their lots. Some of the lots hired roving security guards and installed increased lighting. Police used bike patrols to cover the secluded areas, and plainclothes officers in unmarked police vehicles conducted operations in the parking lots during high-volume parking nights. With the combination of painted curbs, signs and increased lot security, the car prowls almost completely stopped.

Working with U.S. Customs and the California Highway Patrol, traffic officers also conducted "Operation Buckstop." This operation stopped many of the stolen vehicles from leaving the Unites States.

Commercial and pedestrian traffic. Many meetings with CAL-TRANS, city engineering and MTDB were held at 700 East San Ysidro Boulevard. These meetings resulted in new traffic light patterns and the removal and modification of some stoplights. Crime prevention through environmental design also was used in this area. Curb markings and fences along the curbs were changed and added to improve the pedestrian problem substantially. Timed parking zones were implemented to move traffic in and out of the worst problem areas.

The SDPD trained the transportation companies on the local code compliance laws. This aided in their understanding of proper business practices. The owners and employees were trained on the large number of laws that had been violated previously, and how they could prevent them from being violated in the future. Selective enforcement methods were also used.

The business owners requiring delivery of goods were educated on the massive traffic problems and many voluntarily changed their delivery schedules. The SDPD also suggested ways of limiting delivery time for drivers of the large semi-trucks.

The owners of the 25 buses from six Mexican companies that carry tourists into Mexico met and, with the aid of police, came up with a working schedule to allow only one bus at a time into the narrow area to pick up passengers. This schedule has cut the bus traffic by 85 percent.

The 10 van and three large bus companies that carry passengers into Northern California and the United States met and voluntarily decided not to park in the area until they actually were loading or unloading. If they had to park in the area, they agreed to park in private parking lots—not on the streets. A transportation center is being designed and developed to house all the companies in one location. This will be a one-stop terminal for all travelers leaving the area.

Random inspections were also conducted to inspect vans and buses. The California Public Utilities Commission, the California Highway Patrol and the California Department of Motor Vehicles assisted members of the BCST in these ongoing inspections. As a result, many of the unsafe buses and unlicensed drivers are now both safe and licensed.

By far, the largest people-movers in and out of the two-block area are the taxis and jitneys. Jitneys are vans designed to carry 20 to 25 people. They carry shoppers on a predesignated route. The owner/drivers were easy to deal with and without hesitation agreed to a staging area one block away. This reduced the number of cruising vans to zero. They park, load and, as they drive by the staging area, honk the horn, which alerts the next driver to move up and load. With that staging area working well, the focus turned to the largest number of commercial carriers at 700 East San Ysidro—more than 50 taxis.

This group was the hardest to deal with, as the drivers were ethnically diverse and did not trust police. However, after several meetings, drivers agreed to the first self-enforced staging system for taxis. The staging area was designed by the BCST officers and is policed mainly by the senior cab drivers with the aid of officers working the area. It works much like the mandatory system at the San Diego International Airport. Up to 40 cabs can stage/wait on a nearby bridge. Parking space was provided, safety lines painted on the roadway and safe hit pilons installed for the drivers' safety. A taxi stand was placed in front of the Customs pedestrian exit. The waiting/staging drivers now wait approximately two blocks away. When a driver at the pedestrian exit has a fare they signal the waiting area for another cab to move up. Taxi traffic around the two-block area has fallen dramatically. Drivers are delighted because they don't have to drive around the street all day and night, and now enforcement officials are not "always after" them. Many of the drivers now even trust the officers and their intentions.

Currently, laws are being drafted by the BCST, the South Bay District Attorney's Office, and the city attorney's office. These laws will create a defined crime prevention zone within the 700 East San Ysidro area for a transportation district. One of these laws would make it mandatory for taxis to use the new staging system.

911 pay phone hang ups. One of the largest out-of-service time producers was the many accidental 911 hang-up calls. Officers met with the three individual phone company owners or their representatives. Statistics were shared and all agreed to post signs in English and Spanish that would state it is a crime to dial 911 when there is no emergency. The signs would also have the SDPD nonemergency phone number on them. However, accidental callers had to be dealt with differently.

A dialing delay system was considered, but the cost of placing a two- to three-second delay with a Spanish language message was more than $1 million, and liability in the event of a real emergency was tremendous. Recorded messages at the location of the individual phones were considered, but the cost to the phone companies was too great. Many other possible solutions were thought of, but all had some problem with implementation. BCST members came up with an idea that was cost effective (almost free) and safe for real emergencies.

The number "9" on each of the 36 phones in the two-block area was painted bright red. The bright red button cut down the accidental 911 calls tremendously. A local company donated paint, and BCST officers completed the actual painting. This solution was unique and shows promise for other areas with similar problems.

Officer out-of-service time. Officers of the Southern Division handled calls at 700 East San Ysidro Boulevard in different ways. With the formation of the BCST, a standard policy was adopted and put into effect. The team officers took on the two-block area as if it were a new service area. The police communications division received instructions to send BCST officers to all calls at 700 East San Ysidro Boulevard. To improve visibility and presence, BCST officers acquired and modified a trailer to use as a storefront. Now, with seven days of coverage each week, the out-of-service time has been cut dramatically, and the beat officers can concentrate on other police problems.

The BCST also developed a community-based police newsletter, The Border View, and formed a Border Interagency Information Network. The newsletter increases information sharing with the community, and the network has increased the dialogue among the law enforcement community in the small border area.

Assessment

The results seen so far for this project are fantastic for the businesses and community members. Crime analysis staff used two full years of statistics to evaluate progress, and showed a 43 percent decrease in wildcatting. Auto thefts and car prowls decreased by 53 percent during the eight months after environmental design changes were made in the area. The accidental 911 pay phone calls also declined. After the signs were posted and the "9" keys painted, the calls fell by 43 percent. This decrease has dramatically cut wasted time by officers having to check them. Also, over a one-year period, arrests fell 13 percent and crime cases fell by 46 percent.

Many of the problems addressed have existed for nearly 30 years. While monitoring continues to ensure the area doesn't return to its prior state, most of the changes and ideas are self-sustained and require no further monitoring. For the BCST officers, the results were positive and motivated them to continue to improve the systems at 700 East San Ysidro. The team has gained valuable partnerships and continues to build on its good reputation.

OPERATION "HOT PIPE/SMOKY HAZE/REHAB"
SAN DIEGO POLICE DEPARTMENT

Scanning

University Avenue is a business community bordered by apartment complexes in one of the most densely populated areas of San Diego. Beyond the first few blocks of medium-sized apartment complexes are established single-family homes of residents who have lived in the neighborhood for decades. The apartment dwellers are transient, ethnically diverse, low-income renters. Students at the local middle school speak 33 primary or secondary languages. Low rents attract Section 8 and welfare recipients, as well as undocumented immigrants. Area businesses are a mixture of thrift, pawn or secondhand stores alongside ethnic restaurants, automobile shops, liquor stores, and storefront churches.

A few community groups and civic organizations played an important role in the scanning of this problem. The University Avenue Business Improvement Association (UBIA) has, in the past, been at odds with police over how to handle crime problems. It has also been at odds with the local governing organization—which had been much more moderate and supportive of the police, although they did not hesitate to apply pressure when it suited their cause.

Police also formed a group, primarily composed of long-term residents and business owners, designed to guide police identification and prioritization of problems. The Weekly Problem-Solving Group meets at a local church to give information and feedback to the police. They lamented especially vocally about drug trafficking problems on University Avenue. In fact, all three groups unanimously disdained the drug problems.

Officers surveyed the community to verify that drug dealing was a top priority for City Heights residents. The survey showed that 82 percent of residents and business owners viewed narcotics dealing as the top problem facing their neighborhood.

The survey results allowed supervisors and officers to refine their focus from "quality-of-life" issues, which scored relatively low in the survey, to more substantial issues tearing apart the neighborhood's fabric.

To gain consensus among community leaders, officers interviewed them to determine the extent of the narcotics problem and verify its importance to each group. Community leaders and business owners did not know why the problem existed in the City Heights area, but wanted the problem to go away.

Shortly thereafter, interviews were conducted with residents and business owners who had a long-term perspective on the problem. They tended to believe the "entrenched" problem was businesses who were friendly to drug dealers. Three businesses were known to be coconspirators with drug organizations, while others tolerated the criminals because they contributed to increased merchandise sales.

The stakeholders in this problem, identified by their level of involvement on University Avenue and their sphere of influence over the dynamics controlling this problem, were business owners and merchants, the University Avenue Business Improvement Association, property owners, consumers, local residents, police, city government, drug rehabilitation centers, and the users themselves.

Analysis

Officers reviewed current research on street-level drug dealing, interviewed recovering offenders and current users, surveyed the community about the problem, and researched how marketing affects a product and what factors attract or repel customers. They also researched street sales of narcotics through the Internet and telephone contact with researchers.

Team members tapped into the National Institute of Justice Web page and found three studies of note. The one of the greatest value was *Crack's Decline: Some Surprises Across U.S. Cities* by Andrew Lang Golub and Bruce Johnson. Golub and Johnson, among others, treated crack cocaine as an epidemic. Like epi-

demics, which tend to follow a natural course, crack or rock cocaine was on a cycle of decline. Epidemics tend to be localized in
popularity and severity. When a drug appears in the established
user population, it is a key signal an epidemic is coming. From
there it expands to youths and gains a foothold.

The research identified four distinct phases in a drug's popularity over the course of an epidemic: incubation, expansion, pla-
teau and decline. The researchers noted, "each phase can be
distinguished by the proportion of hard drug users (such as previous users of cocaine or heroin) at any location who use crack."

Early in their analysis, officers realized they were witnessing a full-blown rock cocaine epidemic on University Avenue.
Ethnographic reports of growth and development of the epidemic were very useful. Early pioneers of rock cocaine told other
acquaintances about the drug, and word-of-mouth marketing
rapidly expanded the drug's popularity. Rock cocaine has been
a stable commodity on University Avenue since the early 1990s,
when gangsters primarily sold the drug. While its overall popularity has declined, "the corridor" has remained an entrenched
location and is stabilized by word-of-mouth marketing. University Avenue was heavily populated with seasoned and hard-core
drug users. Based on field interviews, officers learned most University Avenue smokers were established criminals with a long
history of addiction. Most had used other drugs. These people
were a small piece of the epidemic puzzle—the visible part of
the problem.

A second study focused on causal factors associated with
crime. The study concluded that offenders increase or decrease
specific criminal behaviors depending on which life circumstance
was undergoing change. The powerful nature of rock cocaine as
an addictive drug caused people to undergo rapid change, especially when binging. Drug addicts, like the ones located along
University Avenue, were 54 percent more likely to commit a property offense, and the odds of committing an assault increased by
more than 100 percent. Overall, illegal drug use increased the
odds of committing a crime sixfold.

This information caused grave concern, because individuals going through life-changing experiences were constantly arriving on University Avenue ready to continue cyclic crime waves because of a life-changing drug. Jeremy Travis, director of the National Institute of Justice (NIJ), was quoted in the *San Diego Union Tribune* as saying, "There is no single drug problem; there are many local drug problems." The article also stated that 16 percent of San Diego's crack users lived on the streets.

One last source of literature was critical to understanding the problem. In the October 1996 issue of *Subject to Debate*, a PERF newsletter, Malcolm Gladwell wrote an article called "The Tipping Point." He stated, "When it comes to fighting epidemics, small changes can have huge effects. And large changes can have small effects." Gladwell was referring to a threshold at which an epidemic spreads uncontrollably, and police need to learn to bring the problem to the safe side of that threshold. Small changes can accomplish this if police understand where the threshold lies.

The second phase of review was to make telephone contact with relevant researchers and other resource people. Officers talked to Susan Pennel of the San Diego Association of Governments, Dennis Kenney of PERF, Anthony Braga of Harvard University, Loraine Green of the University of Cincinnati, John Eck of the University of Maryland and the Baltimore High-Intensity Drug Trafficking Area (HIDTA), Bruce Johnson of the National Development and Research Insititutes, and Moses Sullivan of Rutgers University.

Based on information gathered from researchers, six critical principles were established to guide our local research:

1. **Evaluate "the health of the beat."** Determine if neighborhood disrepair exacerbates the problem. The character of the neighborhood can act as a crime catalyst.
2. **Determine the sellers' role.** In street drug dealing, the seller and the user are often the same person.
3. **Identify the type of drug.** This determines the sales method. For example, Meth is sold through a closed network and rock cocaine is dealt in an open market.

4. **Determine the type of rehabilitation to be encouraged.** Court-imposed rehabilitation vs. volunteer participation can determine a rehab program's effectiveness.

5. **Employ the small change theory.** Small changes can have a major impact on drug trafficking, but large changes can have a relatively small one.

6. **Expand the time to buy.** Expanding the time it takes to purchase increases the risk to both parties.

Basic marketing principles became important when researchers asked police how sellers and users know where to go to engage in illegal enterprise. Kevin Stuck, vice president of marketing for a local firm, compared the illicit drug market to any retail chain. He identified six reasons why people choose to shop, on which stores base their marketing plans. Some highlight one reason; however, most try to perfect several qualities and create a market niche.

Shoppers' motivations include

1. **convenience**—the ease with which the buyer can access the product;

2. **safety**—a greater degree of physical and emotional security will increase sales directly;

3. **environment**—the level of comfort the customer feels while deciding to purchase;

4. **quality/price**—the product quality and value in relationship to cost;

5. **customer service**—the level at which the customer can depend on the retailer to provide top-notch consistent service; and

6. **need or desire**—the extent to which the customer believes he or she has to have the product. How much adversity will a person endure to obtain the product?

To determine why the rock cocaine trade was concentrated on University Avenue, patrol officers interviewed drug users. A volunteer, Bill Arnsparger, interviewed users at a drug rehab facility.

Both those in rehab and in the field were willing to answer questions as long as they were not about specific dealers or their own criminality. Ninety percent had purchased other drugs in the past. Seventy-eight percent of users came to University Avenue because of its history as a drug location. Safety was an important factor to 75 percent of current and former users, and 72 percent identified drug sales locations by watching transient people hanging out on the street. Seventy-two percent identified access to product as very important, and 66 percent said University Avenue was close to home. Sixty-one percent said the condition of the neighborhood was important to them. Other important factors included the time it takes to buy, the time it takes to get the drug to a safe spot to smoke and the presence of facilitators.

Ninety-six percent of current and former users were with a friend when they purchased rock cocaine for the first time, and 86 percent heard where to purchase through word-of-mouth marketing. Seventy percent identified a friend as the source of knowledge. The sellers' tactics were important to 68 percent of the current and former users when they identified their source.

The Retired Senior Volunteers in Patrol (RSVP) surveyed residents and local businesses and learned that 68 percent of local residents would rather shop for legitimate gods elsewhere— most cited safety concerns—and that fear increased with the respondent's age and length of time he or she had lived or worked in the neighborhood. Fifty percent reluctantly shopped on University Avenue, and 90 percent said they did so because it was close to home.

Citizens and criminals viewed the area as a high-intensity drug area where criminals were comfortable and citizens absent. This image was accentuated by lax business practices and a narcotic enterprise that relied on neighborhood deterioration and word-of-mouth marketing by transient crack addicts.

Response

University Avenue did not belong to smokers and drug dealers, but to the area residents who vastly outnumbered criminals. Police and community stakeholders attempted to "sell" the area through their own joint marketing campaign. The police marketed to criminals—especially the smoker-facilitators—that University Avenue is the last place in the world they wanted to be. The businesses marketed to residents that University Avenue is a convenient, safe and great place to shop. The response was divided into three stages: Operation Hot Pipe, Operation Smoky Haze and Operation Rehab.

Operation Hot Pipe's goal was to destroy the perceived safe and suitable environment that attracted cocaine smokers to this location. Officers created a University Avenue High Intensity Zone (HIZ) and diligently told smokers that they would be arrested for any and all crimes committed in this zone. A concentrated marketing campaign began telling user-facilitators what officers were going to accomplish.

Several squads of officers began a systematic campaign of arresting drug users who loitered on University Avenue and acted as facilitators. Early in the response, officers recognized three types of cocaine consumers: habitual smoker-facilitators, who were the biggest portion of the problem; binge users, who lived on the street smoking rock and scamming for robbery opportunities to get more cocaine; and partiers, who came to buy cocaine and then went home—they most often had jobs and homes, but used the drug.

The bingers and partiers identified where to buy by looking for habitual smoker-facilitators. With that group out of the picture, the bingers and partiers would be lost and would have to look elsewhere. Officers spoke with store owners and used personal knowledge to identify and arrest the facilitators. Officers told offenders they would be a focus of enforcement as long as they were in the HIZ, and gave the facilitators fliers that marketed University Avenue as off-limits to cocaine smokers.

At first, the users did not believe officers, but it did not take long before the user-facilitators began offering information to get out of arrests. Officers arrested them anyway. One smoker walked into jail and was handed a flier, and as the officers left, the prisoner was reading the flier to the rest of the inmates. Fliers also were posted on store fronts, electrical boxes, planters, windows, bus stops, and almost any place identified as a place to buy cocaine or facilitate sales. Each person contacted was told to tell his or her friends that University Avenue was too hot to hang out.

Operation Smoky Haze's goal was to destroy the drug market's convenience and safety by confusing the buyers and facilitators who operated on University Avenue. Officers used three tactics to achieve this goal. First, they used an undercover, reverse sting operation. In this operation, officers posed as sellers working University Avenue. When people approached in search of narcotics, they were arrested for solicitation. Buyers were confused and became leery of fresh faces selling on University. Officers used informants to spread the word that the operation was continuing, even though it had to be scrapped.

With the second tactic, officers casually leaked information to smokers about pending drug-user sweeps. After the first leak, officers followed through with a large sweep. On subsequent leaks, no sweep was planned, but the information was spread via smokers at field interviews. Officers also spread word of drug dealers ripping off buyers. During field interviews, officers asked users for information concerning rip-offs and robberies, or information on phantom suspects. The resulting confusion made buying inconvenient and risky.

The third tactic involved referring people to a newly formed drug court. Those who applied and were eligible were put on drug court probation. Under the supervision of the court and a full-time police officer, the smokers were interviewed at home when they were suspected of being on University Avenue. Many of the initial responders were subsequently arrested and jailed for dirty urine tests, even though they were not on University Avenue at the time. This response compelled users to attend sessions at CRASH, a drug rehabilitation group.

The constant marketing of the CRASH program was vital to the project. Every flier handed out mentioned the program, and every arrestee was told to call CRASH for help. Every person admitted to the drug court was mandated to attend CRASH. All of those referred finished the program or were sent to jail to serve the maximum length of their sentence.

The goal of Operation Rehab was to change the perception of the area from that of a drug corridor to that of a strong business community. Tom Dizzino and Associates, a private marketing firm, volunteered to assist in developing a marketing plan for businesses. The plan was designed to attract local residents back to the "Global Village." The University Avenue merchants were receptive to using a free marketing plan, but were reluctant to spend money to attract more customers. The police officers, however, believed it was vital to fill the void created by heavy enforcement with residents who would add to the quality of the "Global Village."

Assessment

Officers administered a survey to business owners and held informal interviews with transient cocaine smokers to test the newly created environment. Forty-five percent of business owners reported a rise in business during the six months before the survey. Of those surveyed, 86 percent said the increase in business came from local resident traffic, 50 percent said the drug users had become less obvious, and 36 percent thought the drug users had left the area entirely. Eighty-one percent of owners said they are safer on University Avenue and most reported seeing more families and shoppers walking on the street.

The user-facilitators said they were aware of increased enforcement on University Avenue, and all of them knew of a person who was arrested on the street. All the users reported seeing—or tearing down—marketing fliers, and all stated cocaine was more difficult to find.

The police determined that the HIZ enforcement area reduced the number of street robberies on University Avenue. Officers also identified 20 user-facilitators as having left the area, and complaints about rock cocaine sales on University Avenue disappeared from the Weekly Problem-Solving Group meetings.

TRANSIENT ENRICHMENT NETWORK
FONTANA, CALIF., POLICE DEPARTMENT

Scanning
Fontana, Calif., is a city of approximately 108,000 people located 50 miles east of Los Angeles. The city covers 38 square miles and has two major state highways running through it. The largest single industry in the city is trucking. For several years, Fontana experienced significant problems involving large homeless and transient populations. The police department received an average of three calls a month from irate business owners complaining about crimes caused by homeless people or the negative impact that homeless people were having on their businesses. Citizens often felt intimidated by aggressive panhandlers and felt they detracted from the community's aesthetics.

In some areas of town where large numbers of homeless people were known to live or panhandle, thefts from businesses and public facilities of easily sellable items, such as tools and scrap metals, were becoming epidemic. The police department was also responding to an average of more than 55 calls for service per month directly attributable to homeless people.

The Fontana Police Department has had an extremely active community policing program since the early 1990s. As part of that program, all patrol officers are required to become involved in problem-solving projects in their assigned patrol areas. When a business owner or private citizen complained about a continual homeless problem in or around a specific location, the beat officer frequently would be assigned to deal with the problem. Officers became extremely proficient at developing strategies that would cause homeless people to relocate. Unfortunately most of those strategies simply resulted in displacing the homeless to another location in the city. The homeless person would simply relocate, and new business owners would complain. Officers would then start the process over again.

The Fontana Police Department routinely holds meetings with community and business groups throughout the city. Residents generally rated problems caused by homelessness as the number-two priority for the police department. Businesses routinely rated problems caused by homelessness as the top police issue.

By early 1996, any person driving down a major street in Fontana was likely to see large numbers of obviously homeless people sitting on the sidewalks, walking down the streets or panhandling. Both the city council and business community were concerned this was affecting not only existing businesses, but the city's ability to attract other new business projects to the city.

In April 1996, department staff decided to re-evaluate how they were handling problems related to homeless people. They decided to develop a citywide strategy that would actually reduce the number of homeless people on the street. One of the department's sector coordinators, who is responsible for coordinating community policing in a specific area of the city, was assigned to use the SARA model to develop a citywide strategy for addressing the homeless problem.

Analysis

The police department contacted homeless people and several local social service groups that provide services to that population. They discovered Fontana actually had a significantly greater problem with homeless people than any other city in the area. There were several community factors contributing to the problem. There is a large railroad switching yard located just outside the city limits, and several major rail lines run through the city. These rail lines and the two major freeways running through the city give homeless and transient people easy access to the area. The area's large trucking industry also furnished transportation for homeless people and provided part-time work that attracted some homeless and transient people. A number of groups, mostly churches, were supplying meals and clothing to the homeless. By helping them, these groups inadvertently were making Fontana a more attractive place for that population. No other city in the area had the amount of resources devoted to helping people living on the street.

Officers talked with several homeless people who kept a list of locations in Fontana where they could go every single day of the week to receive a free meal. Despite all these resources, there was not one single homeless shelter or program devoted to helping get homeless people off the street.

The department's goal was to come up with a strategy that ultimately would reduce the number of homeless and transient people in Fontana. They hoped to increase the quality of life for all citizens, and reduce the amount of police resources being spent on problems related to homelessness. Of all the factors contributing to the homeless problem, police felt they could have the greatest impact on those community organizations that were inadvertently contributing to the problem.

In late April 1996, the police department corporal assigned to the project chaired a meeting to address the problem. It was attended by several community business and church leaders. That group agreed to form the Transient Enrichment Network for Fontana (TEN-4). The members agreed on seven goals:

- to recognize and deal with continuing problems of homelessness in Fontana;
- to develop a plan to improve the condition of homeless people through the joining of resources by the city of Fontana, Fontana Police Department and community service groups;
- to design and develop a facility to serve as a temporary processing center equipped to feed, bathe, clothe, and find housing for homeless people;
- to design and implement a program to rehabilitate homeless people and integrate them back into society through training provided by local rehabilitation centers and churches;
- to determine a convenient location site for the facility in an area affected by problems related to homelessness;

- to establish a committee to develop guidelines and procedures for implementing and promoting this program; and
- to serve as a liaison to assist homeless people in entering existing programs.

At the first meeting, everyone agreed to meet weekly until a solution and specific strategy could be worked out. By the third meeting, members had developed a program, methodology and implementation strategy that appeared to offer the best chance of meeting all the group's goals.

Response

Neither the city nor any of the groups involved in the TEN-4 project had budgeted any money for the program. The lack of resources required that all groups involved be extremely creative and use existing resources to deal with homeless problems. A number of organizations offered housing services, rehabilitation programs and free medical care to qualified homeless people. A number of local business groups were willing to supply money and services to assist the homeless if they were given an effective outlet. The plan that was developed called for opening an office where homeless people could be counseled and processed for entry into various public and private programs. A homeless person entering the TEN-4 program would be interviewed and given a meal, shower, clean clothes, and medical care, if required. He or she would then be transported to either some type of long-term care or rehabilitation facility, or some short-term housing solution until he or she could be admitted into a long-term program.

Because the TEN-4 program originally had no money budgeted, members of the group led by Fontana Police Department personnel went to businesses, community groups and individuals who were most affected by the homeless problem. They solicited donations of time, materials and money. An office location was found in a strip mall in an area of the city heavily impacted for many years by problems caused by homelessness. The city worked out a creative financing plan, allowing for the strip mall owner to receive a significant discount on sewer fees in exchange for 18 months free rent.

The building needed significant repairs. Volunteers agreed to do a major renovation. Four thousand dollars in cash and construction material were donated by more than 20 local businesses and community service groups, and 40 individuals. Volunteers—mostly supplied by local churches—staffed the facility. Several local public service agencies, including the California State Employment Development Department and Veterans' Administration, agreed to supply trained personnel. One trained counselor with extensive experience dealing with the mentally ill also volunteered.

Transportation from the facility to various shelters and rehabilitation programs would be supplied largely by police department volunteers using vehicles dedicated to police volunteer use. Whenever a police patrol officer contacts a homeless or transient person, they volunteer to transport that person to the TEN-4 facility. When church or community service agencies that supply free food and other benefits contact homeless people, they also try to talk those people into entering the TEN-4 program. Many of the churches that supplied services to help the homeless have cut back or eliminated those services and instead refer people to TEN-4.

The department and TEN-4 volunteers are constantly re-evaluating how TEN-4 supplies services. When the program originally opened, group members thought the main focus would be on placing people in other organizations' rehabilitation programs, with little emphasis on job counseling and placement. Since the program has been operating, they found there are large numbers of not only organizations, but individuals in the community who want to provide job opportunities. The best example of this is Lewis Homes, one of the largest land developers in the area, which has hired several TEN-4 clients and has a standing offer to employ any qualified candidate referred to them. In addition, numerous other local companies supplied permanent jobs. A local trucking company, a local rental company and a local kennel have all supplied part-time jobs for numerous TEN-4 clients involved in rehabilitation programs. As a result, the program increased emphasis on job placement.

The TEN-4 program is not a stand-alone solution to the homeless problem in Fontana. All Fontana police officers were advised of the program and encouraged to refer clients to TEN-4. Officers who in the past had been reluctant to issue citations for minor infractions to obviously homeless people became more aggressive once they knew that any homeless person on Fontana's streets could find a place to stay and a job simply by entering the TEN-4 program. All individuals who have agreed to enter the TEN-4 program have had lodging that same day. Officers became more aggressive in enforcing nuisance laws against sleeping on sidewalks, in parks and on private property without permission; panhandling; and drinking in public. Many aggressive panhandlers, some of whom were only pretending to be homeless, have found it easier to work in other cities.

In October 1996—less than six months after the initial meeting to discuss the problems—the TEN-4 program opened its doors. While one of the department's corporals was assigned to develop the original strategy, all of the department's patrol and bicycle units were involved in contacting and referring homeless people to the program. City staff were involved when the city manager approved the sewer financing agreement that helped pay the facility's rent for the first 18 months. All city fees were waived and building inspections conducted free of charge.

There were some problems early in the program. It was originally intended that volunteers rotate staffing of the TEN-4 facility. Early in the program, it became necessary to have at least one volunteer who was extremely knowledgeable in dealing with homeless people at the facility at all times. Two local ministers were willing to take the program on and agreed that one of them would be on the site whenever the facility was open.

Initially, there was a great deal of resistance from the other businesses in the shopping complex where the TEN-4 facility was being placed. They were concerned that their homeless problem—which was already severe—would get even worse. Police department personnel and TEN-4 volunteers talked with each of the business owners and assured them program participants would not be dropped off at the TEN-4 facility unless they agreed to enter the program. Any subject taken to the facility for evaluation who did not agree to enter the program would be given a ride away from the area by the person who brought them. It also was agreed that homeless people who did not enter the TEN-4 program would not receive any food or clothing, or be able to use any of the TEN-4 facilities. These simple rules satisfied business owners. They are now the biggest supporters of the TEN-4 program. Several area business owners, including all of the other occupants of the mini-mall where the TEN-4 facility is located, have spoken in support of the TEN-4 program when it was evaluated by outside groups.

Assessment

Between the opening of TEN-4 on October 2, 1996, and June 1, 1998, 510 people entered the program. All but 13 have been successfully rehabilitated or are still in a rehabilitation or housing program. To be considered successfully rehabilitated, a participant must be in permanent housing, be self-supporting, or have returned to his or her family. All TEN-4 participants are tracked until they are in permanent housing, unless they have returned to live with family members out of state. More than 53 percent of TEN-4's clients are currently in permanent housing. More than 16 percent of all TEN-4 clients have permanent jobs. All the other subjects that have entered the TEN-4 program, with the exception of the 13 that have dropped out, are in some type of rehabilitation program or shelter.

Before the start of the TEN-4 program, the city had no census of the number of homeless people actually on the streets. The fact that more than 500 homeless people are no longer on the streets in a city of 108,000 people has had a significant impact. Department and city staff estimate the total number of homeless people actually living in Fontana has been reduced by more than 90 percent. It is now not only possible, but normal, for a person to drive through Fontana without seeing a single homeless person.

In 1997, the department received only one complaint from a business owner about homeless people. So far in 1998, there have been no complaints. Issues involving homeless people are no longer important to the Fontana business community.

The police department has no way of tracking crimes specifically committed by homeless people. Prior to instituting the TEN-4 program, they felt that a significant number of crimes, especially property crimes in the city were related to homelessness. In 1997, the first full year after the TEN-4 program was implemented, Fontana had a 15.6 percent decrease in Part 1 crimes. Fontana had the largest decrease in Part 1 crimes of any city of more than 100,000 population in the state of California. Police feel the program was a significant factor in this reduction.

While it is impossible to determine how many total calls per service were indirectly related to homelessness, it is possible to track the number of calls that were directly related to homeless people. As soon as the TEN-4 program opened, the number of calls directly related to homeless people started going down. Several months after the program opened, calls for service related to homelessness actually went up. This was likely caused by the increased publicity on homeless issues created by the opening of the TEN-4 program. During the program's first year, calls for service fluctuated when compared with the year before opening TEN-4, but were still reduced to an average of 48 per month. Since October 1997, calls for service for homeless people are averaging 25 a month—less than half what they were the year before the opening of TEN-4. While the city has no way of specifically tracking quality of life for its residents, police feel confident there has been a significant improvement. The aesthetics of the city have definitely and noticeably been improved by the lack of obviously homeless and destitute individuals camping on city streets.

All of the initial goals established by both the police department and the TEN-4 Task Force have been accomplished. The homeless population has not been displaced to other communities—the overwhelming majority of the people who have entered the TEN-4 program are off the streets permanently.

TEN-4 has been, and continues to be, funded without the use of additional city money. One of the problems that the TEN-4 program has encountered in recent months has been generating funds from local churches and businesses to continue to support the program. Most business and community members no longer perceive the city as having a homeless problem, so they tend to be more reluctant to donate money for a problem they cannot see.

The TEN-4 program and other police responses associated with it have been so successful that the TEN-4 facility has had to adapt and change the services it supplies. Initially the largest number of referrals was by city police officers. Most of the referrals the TEN-4 program is receiving now are coming from San Bernadino County Welfare and Social Service offices. Many of the people being referred have lost their jobs or welfare benefits and are in imminent danger of being evicted or being forced to live with friends to stay off the streets. TEN-4 provides these people with housing referrals and job placement services to help them stay off of the streets, thus eliminating homeless issues before they occur.

The department intends to continue monitoring both calls for service and other problems related to homelessness and homeless people within the city. They also intend to continue using the TEN-4 program, as it has evolved into a more general social service organization for the city. The community relationships developed through the TEN-4 program have been extremely useful and police have used many of these relationships with community businesses, and especially with area churches, to assist in developing strategies and responses to other community problems.

REFERENCES

Clark, J.R. 1997. LEN Salutes Its 1997 People of the Year: The Boston Gun Project Working Group. *Law Enforcement News* 22(480). 31 December.

Kann, L et al. 1995. Youth Risk Behavior Surveillance—United States, 1993. *CDC Surveillance Summaries* 44(SS-1):1–56. 24 March.

ABOUT THE AUTHORS

Tracy Allan, at the time this book was being developed, was working as a Police Executive Research Forum (PERF) research associate. During her tenure with PERF, Allan worked on a variety of projects, gaining experience in areas such as research design and methodology, survey development and administration, and data analysis. Allan has since left PERF and is now living in Canada, working as a contractor on a variety of criminal justice projects. She holds a master's in forensic science (MFS) from The George Washington University.

Daniel Brookoff is a physician actively involved in patient care and teaching residents and medical students. Brookoff is the associate director of medical education at Methodist Hospitals of Memphis, and clinical associate professor of medicine and preventive medicine at the University of Tennessee College of Medicine. Since 1992, he has been working with the Memphis Police Department on research projects that combine aspects of health care and law enforcement. Brookoff is also a reserve officer with the department (still waiting for his first promotion). He is active in community groups involved in preventing drug abuse (board member of Drug Watch International, vice chairman of the International Drug Strategy Institute), and family violence (board member of the Exchange Club Family Center). Brookoff attended medical school and completed his residency and fellowship training at the University of Pennsylvania.

Ronald Clarke is a professor at the School of Criminal Justice, Rutgers, the State University of New Jersey. Formerly the director of the British government's criminological research department (The Home Office Research and Planning Unit), Clarke had a significant role in the development of situational crime prevention. He also helped to establish the Home Office Crime Prevention Unit and the now regularly repeated British Crime Survey. Clarke is the editor of *Crime Prevention Studies* and the author of some 150 publications, including *Designing Out Crime* (1980), *The Reasoning Criminal* (1986), and *Situational Crime Prevention: Successful Case Studies* (1997). Trained as a psychologist, he holds a master's degree (1965) and a Ph.D. (1968) from the University of London.

Charles Cook is an inspector and precinct commander in the Memphis Police Department. He has been involved in several research projects on the relationship between drug use and crime and is responsible for starting the "drugged driving detection" program, which has been running for more than five years in Memphis. He is a Navy veteran and has B.S. and M.A. degrees from the University of Memphis.

Colleen Cosgrove works as a consultant for the Police Executive Research Forum. Cosgrove has more than 20 years of experience in designing and directing both qualitative and quantitative research. She has conducted numerous studies examining a variety of policing issues, including resource allocation, precinct management, stress among police officers, productivity of detectives, and community policing. She was the director of field research for the NIJ-sponsored evaluation of the Community Patrol Officer Project in New York City, and coauthored a book based on that research, *Community Policing: The CPOP in New York*. Cosgrove has a Ph.D. in criminal justice from the School of Criminal Justice, State University of New York at Albany.

Walter Crews is deputy chief of investigative services for the Memphis Police Department. He started the Memphis Police Department's Crisis Intervention Team Program and the Intervention Team for Domestic Assailants, both of which have become national models. Under his auspices, the Memphis Police

Department has conducted on-scene drug testing of intoxicated drivers for the past four years, the first program of its kind in the United States. He is the author of several publications focusing on crisis intervention, and has conducted extensive research on hostage-taking incidents. During his 30-year career, Crews has held two lateral deputy chief positions. Before becoming chief of detectives, he was chief of special operations for the Memphis Police Department. He is a graduate of the University of Memphis Graduate School of Counseling, and the FBI Law Enforcement Executive Development School.

David Curry is an associate professor of criminology and criminal justice at the University of Missouri-St. Louis. Curry conducts basic and evaluation research on gang-related violence under his broader research interest in organized violence. This general interest developed out of Curry's service as a captain with Army Counterintelligence in Vietnam. Curry has authored two books: *Sunshine Patriots: Punishment and the Vietnam Offender* and *Confronting Gangs: Crime and Community* (coauthored with Scott H. Decker), in addition to numerous book chapters, journal articles and research reports. He has a Ph.D. in sociology from the University of Chicago, and completed additional postdoctoral study at the University of Chicago in quantitative methods of evaluation research and psychometrics.

John Eck is an associate professor of criminal justice at the University of Cincinnati. He has been the evaluation coordinator for the Washington/Baltimore High Intensity Drug Trafficking Area, where he developed procedures for understanding the nature of regional drug trafficking. Eck was previously the director of research for the Police Executive Research Forum, where he helped pioneer the development and testing of problem-oriented policing. His interests are in police effectiveness, the origins of crime problems and patterns, the study of crime places and hotspots, drug dealing, and problem analysis techniques. He has served as a consultant to the Office of Community Oriented Policing Services, the National Institute of Justice, the Police Foundation, the Police Executive Research Forum, the Royal Canadian Mounted Police, and the London Metropolitan Police. Eck earned his Ph.D. from the department of criminology at the University of Maryland. He also has a master's of public policy from the University of Michigan. He lives in Cincinnati with his wife, daughter, and corgi.

Nancy La Vigne is the founder and director of the Crime Mapping Research Center at the National Institute of Justice, U.S. Department of Justice. Her research areas include the geographic analysis of crime, situational crime prevention and community policing. Her previous work experience includes consulting for the Police Executive Research Forum, the National Council on Crime and Delinquency, and the National Development and Research Institute. She also served as research director for the Texas Punishment Standards Commission from 1991 to 1993. La Vigne is a member of the Joint DOJ/Office of the Vice President Crime Mapping Task Force and chairs the task force's subcommittee on training and technical assistance. She is also the Department of Justice delegate to the Federal Geographic Data Committee and an active member of the Department of Justice's GIS Working Group. La Vigne is the author of more than a dozen publications in journals, edited volumes and technical reports in the areas of crime prevention, policing and spatial analysis. She pursued her undergraduate studies at Smith College in Massachusetts, earned her master's degree at the LBJ School of Public Affairs at the University of Texas at Austin, and her Ph.D. at the School of Criminal Justice at Rutgers University.

William F. McDonald is a professor of sociology and the deputy director at the Institute of Criminal Law and Procedure, Georgetown University. He has published research on many aspects of American criminal justice including victimology, the police, prosecution, defense, and sentencing. He has been a National Institute of Justice Visiting Fellow. His current work focuses on the police and immigration, and on the emerging structures of transnational law enforcement. His most recent edited book is titled *Crime and Law Enforcement in the Global Village* (1997). He holds a D. Crim., University of California, Berkeley, 1970; M.Ed., Boston College, 1965; and A.B., University of Notre Dame, 1964.

Andy Mills is a sergeant with the San Diego Police Department's Mid-City Division. Mills is a frequent lecturer and trainer at conferences, police departments and universities. He teaches on a variety of topics from police supervision, management and problem solving to ethics in government. Mills was a member of a select team who helped transition the San Diego Police Department into a community policing agency. He was part of the team that developed the transition plan, provided training and sold the idea to what is now recognized as one of the leading community policing agencies in the world. Mills works with the National Institute of Justice, Police Executive Research Forum and the Law Enforcement Assistance Network to deliver effective training and management consulting. He has also helped several foreign governments transition to community policing through problem solving. He is a graduate of Grand Rapids Bible College with studies in church administration and theology.

Gregory Saville is on the faculty of the School of Criminology and Criminal Justice at Florida State University. He is also an associate director of the Florida Police Corps Academy. He spent nine years as a police officer before moving to British Columbia, where he became codirector of an urban planning firm that specialized in crime prevention through environmental design (CPTED), the first of its kind in Canada. In 1996 Saville founded the International CPTED Association, an organization he currently chairs. He teaches and consults around the world on safe urban design and CPTED, and has just returned from Australia, where he instructed designers of the Sydney 2000 Olympic site in CPTED principles.

Jacqueline L. Schneider is a research fellow with the Crime Control Policy Center at the Hudson Institute. She has worked on several large-scale research projects, including evaluating police departments' response to juvenile gangs, analyzing gang organizations and gang leaders' criminal behavior, and restorative justice conferencing. Schneider is currently developing a project to investigate the use of Internet technology to further criminal behavior. She has practical experience as a narcotics agent and in the administration of justice, and is the author of several research articles, monographs and professional papers. Schneider has also been featured in national news discussion programs and on the local news. She holds a master's in public policy and administration (1987) from The Ohio State University and a doctorate in sociology with an emphasis in criminal justice (1995) from the University of Cincinnati.

Lawrence Sherman is professor and chair of the department of criminology and criminal justice, University of Maryland at College Park. He joined the New York City Police Department in 1971 as a civilian research analyst and has worked with more than 30 police departments in the United States and other countries to find more effective ways to fight crime. Since earning his Ph.D. at Yale University in 1976, he has written four books and more than 100 research articles on police policy matters, including domestic violence, drug raids, community policing, hotspots of crimes, police crackdowns, and gun crime. He is currently working with the Australian Federal Police on a project to reduce juvenile delinquency, and is serving as president of the Scientific Commission of the International Society of Criminology in Paris. In 1994–95 he served as chief criminologist of the Indianapolis Police Department, and previously served as a criminologist with the Kansas City, Milwaukee and Minneapolis Police Departments. As the director of the Kansas City Gun Experiment, he has frequently appeared on national television, lectured at the FBI Academy, been cited in the U.S. Supreme Court and other decisions, and testified in courts in more than 15 states. In 1996, he cohosted the Governor's Summit on Gun Enforcement at the College Park campus, a gathering of law enforcement leaders from across Maryland to discuss the major issues affecting law enforcement today.

Corina Solé Brito, a Police Executive Research Forum (PERF) research associate, has more than eight years experience in criminal justice and public health research, training and technical assistance. Solé Brito has experience in survey development and administration, focus group administration and training coordination. Currently, she serves as PERF's coordinator at the Community Policing Consortium. Before joining PERF, Solé Brito worked with the Pacific Institute for Research and Evaluation. She has an M.A. in criminology from the University of Maryland at College Park.

John Stedman worked as a senior research associate with the Police Executive Research Forum (PERF) from 1986 to 1999. At the time this book was being developed, he was the project director for PERF's NIJ-funded project *Reducing Repeat Victimization of Residential Burglary*, the COPS Office *Problem-Solving Partnerships Cross-Site Evaluation Project*, and BJA's *National Guns First Training Program*, *Comprehensive Gang Initiative*, and *Documentation and Assessment of BJA-Funded Firearms Projects*. Before joining PERF, Stedman spent 16 years with the Alexandria, Va., Police Department, beginning as a patrol officer and holding the positions of police investigator, sergeant and lieutenant. During his time in Alexandria, he served as the commander of the Personnel and Training Division, Patrol Division, Special Investigations Division, and the Operational Support Division. Stedman holds a B.A. in sociology from Bowling Green State University in Ohio, and an M.A. in psychology from George Mason University in Virginia.

Mike Sutton is senior research officer in the British Home Office Policing and Reducing Crime Unit. He has published British government reports in diverse areas including fines enforcement, evaluating crime prevention programs, multi-agency partner-ships and stolen goods markets. Sutton has worked on and pub-lished findings from numerous large-scale government projects, including an impact evaluation of the Safer Cities crime preven-tion program. He has published in academic journals on stolen goods markets and crime on the Internet. Sutton's publications include *Supply by Theft: Does the Market for Stolen Goods Play a Role in Keeping Crime Figures High* (1995); *Implementing Crime Pre-vention Schemes in a Multi-agency Setting: Aspects of the Process in the Safer Cities Programme* (1996); *Safer Cities and Domestic Bur-glary* (1996); *Handling Stolen Goods and Theft: A Market Reduction Approach* (1998); and *NetCrime: More Change in the Organisation of Thieving* (1998). He holds a first degree in law (1983) and a Ph.D. in criminology (1987) from the University of Central Lancashire.

Terry Thompson is a patrol officer with the Memphis Police De-partment. He has been very active in community policing and was the first police officer assigned to the domestic violence project in Memphis. He developed the "Stockholm syndrome" questionnaire, a survey tool that has been very useful for rap-idly assessing the judgment capabilities of battered women at the scene of a police call for domestic violence.

Nick Tilley is a professor of sociology at the Nottingham Trent University in England, where he was until recently director of the Crime and Social Research Unit. He has also been attached to the Home Office since 1992, where he is currently helping full-time with the development and evaluation of the government's new Crime Reduction Program. His research in-terests lie in crime prevention, policing and program evaluation methodology. He has recently completed a study of attempts to implement problem-oriented policing in Britain, and an evalua-tion of a demonstration project aiming to reduce crime against small businesses in two areas of Leicester. He has produced more than a dozen reports published by the Home Office. He is coau-thor of *Realistic Evaluation* (Sage, 1997).

Samuel Walker is Kiewit Professor of Criminal Justice at the University of Nebraska at Omaha. He is the author of nine books on criminal justice, policing and civil liberties. These include *The Color of Justice: Race and Crime In America* (1996); *Sense and Nonsense About Crime* (fourth edition, forthcoming); *Hate Speech: The History of an American Controversy* (1994); and *In Defense of American Liberties: A History of the ACLU* (1990). The third edition of *The Police in America* was published in the fall of 1998. Professor Walker held a fellowship from the Open Society Institute in 1997–1998 for research on citizen review of complaints against the police. His work to date includes a national survey of citizen review agencies, the *Citizen Review Resource Manual*, and several articles. The fellowship will support a book on citizen complaints and police accountability. Along with Eileen Luna, Professor Walker completed an evaluation of the citizen oversight mechanism for the Albuquerque, N.M., Police Department in 1997. He has also been a consultant to the Charlotte, N.C., Police Department regarding its citizen complaint procedure, and is working with the Buffalo, N.Y., Police Department on a project related to police officer stress.

Julie Wartell is a senior research and technology associate with the Institute for Law and Justice. Wartell is currently working on several projects related to information technology and community policing. She recently completed a fellowship at the National Institute of Justice Crime Mapping Research Center, where she coordinated the development of a series of crime mapping training modules and coedited a book about successful crime mapping case studies. Wartell spent more than five years as a crime analyst at the San Diego Police Department, and one year as a field researcher for the Police Executive Research Forum. Her responsibilities for the police department and PERF included research and analysis of major crime problems; serving as a liaison to patrol, investigations and administration; and working on the departmentwide strategic planning effort. Wartell has done extensive training and presentations for officers and analysts around the country on topics relating to crime analysis and problem-oriented policing. She has a master's in public administration with an emphasis in criminal justice administration.

Deborah Lamm Weisel, at the time of this writing, was a senior researcher with the Police Executive Research Forum (PERF). Weisel joined PERF in 1987. She has conducted numerous studies on policing, including case studies of decision making in municipal law enforcement agencies, a national study of the various forms of community policing, an assessment of alternative drug enforcement tactics used by police agencies, and extensive work on safety and security in public housing environments. Weisel has conducted extensive research on gangs, including a study for the National Institute of Justice to determine if gangs evolve into more highly organized groups over time. She recently began an NIJ-funded examination of police responses to gang problems in a community policing context in two cities. Weisel has been principal investigator in a study to develop a problem-solving model to address gang problems as part of the Comprehensive Communities program funded by the Bureau of Justice Assistance. In addition, she is currently conducting an examination of the nature and extent of repeat victimization for residential burglary in Dallas, San Diego and Baltimore, with funding from the National Institute of Justice. Currently, Weisel is on the faculty of the Department of Political Science and Public Administration at North Carolina State University, where she serves as director of police research. Weisel holds a bachelor's degree from the University of North Carolina at Chapel Hill, a master's of public affairs from North Carolina State University, and a doctorate in public policy analysis from the University of Illinois at Chicago.

ABOUT PERF

The Police Executive Research Forum (PERF) is a national professional association of chief executives of large city, county and state law enforcement agencies. PERF's objective is to improve the delivery of police services and the effectiveness of crime control through several means:

1. the exercise of strong national leadership,
2. the public debate of police and criminal justice issues,
3. the development of research and policy, and
4. the provision of vital management and leadership services to police agencies.

PERF members are selected on the basis of their commitment to PERF's objectives and principles. PERF operates under the following tenets:

1. Research, experimentation and exchange of ideas through public discussion and debate are paths for the development of a comprehensive body of knowledge about policing.
2. Substantial and purposeful academic study is a prerequisite for acquiring, understanding and adding to that body of knowledge.
3. Maintenance of the highest standards of ethics and integrity is imperative in the improvement of policing.
4. The police must, within the limits of the law, be responsible and accountable to citizens as the ultimate source of police authority.
5. The principles embodied in the Constitution are the foundation of policing.

RELATED TITLES

The following publications also address issues related to problem solving and community policing. PERF also offers a free publications catalog. To request a free catalog or order PERF publications, call the toll-free PERF publications line at **1-888-202-4563**. A full listing of PERF's publications can also be found at www.policeforum.org.

> (To qualify for the PERF membership discount, you must be active on membership dues. Please note that membership is by individual, not agency. You can request a membership application with your publications order.)

Problem-Oriented Policing:
Crime-Specific Problems, Critical Issues and Making POP Work,
Volume I
(Tara O'Connor Shelley and Anne C. Grant, eds., 1998)
442 pp., Product #831
ISBN #: 1-878734-60-1
Member Price: $26
Nonmember Price: $29
This publication reflects the latest knowledge about problem-oriented policing. It is the first in a series that highlights information shared at previous annual POP Conferences by practitioners and academicians with expertise in three areas: crime-specific problems, critical issues and practices, and the challenges of making problem solving work. Authors include such national experts as Scott Decker, Malcolm Klein, Sam Walker, Jack Greene, Ron Clarke and Gary Cordner.

Crime in the Schools:
Reducing Fear and Disorder with Student Problem Solving
(Dennis J. Kenney and T. Steuart Watson, 1998)
236 pp., Product #830
ISBN #: 1-878734-58-x
Member Price: $20
Nonmember Price: $23.95
More metal detectors, school security personnel and other target-hardening approaches alone fail to make our schools safer. *Crime in the Schools* provides a student-oriented response that builds on the success of police problem-solving efforts. The authors outline a tested curriculum that empowers students to make creative uses of school, student, faculty and police resources to combat the fear and disorder problems many experience during the school day. The School Safety Program applies the police problem-solving model, used successfully in community policing efforts nationwide, to school situations.

How to Recognize Good Policing
(Jean-Paul Brodeur, ed., 1998)
272 pp., Product #833
ISBN #: 0-7619-1614-8
Member/Nonmember Price: $27.95
Copublished with SAGE publications, this book is divided into four parts. Part I provides a general overview of community and problem-oriented policing. Part II is comprised of five chapters that specifically address issues in the assessment of police performance that include: the assessment of individual police performance; the problems raised by making an evaluation; the role of the public in community policing through participation in beat meetings, neighborhood watch schemes, and public surveys to determine satisfaction levels. Part III of this book addresses organizational change and its assessment. It also includes a portion devoted to a summary of exchanges that occurred between chapter authors, police professionals and others involved in the

areas of security. This book concludes with future perspectives on increasing roles for private security agencies, hybrid agencies and community involvement in civil policing.

Neighborhood Team Policing:
Organizational Opportunities and Obstacles
(Richard DeParis, 1997)
60 pp., Product #822
ISBN #: 1-878734-51-2
Member Price: $6
Nonmember Price: $6.50
In *Neighborhood Team Policing*—another addition to the "Research and Evaluation" series—then–San Diego Lieutenant Richard DeParis examined the factors that contribute to or detract from the success of neighborhood police teams. After conducting an extensive survey of neighborhood police teams in California and analyzing the data collected, DeParis concluded that most ineffective teams failed not because of the officers' deficiencies, but because of organizational obstacles that prevented them from effectively fulfilling their mission. DeParis outlines the various organizational factors that influence team success, and makes policy recommendations for police agencies that wish to avoid or overcome obstacles.

Why Police Organizations Change:
A Study of Community-Oriented Policing
(Jihong Zhao, 1996)
140 pp., Product #811
ISBN #: 1-878734-45-8
Member Price: $16.95
Nonmember Price: $18.50
Why do police organizations change? What prompts them to make the shift to community-oriented policing? In *Why Police Organizations Change,* Jihong Zhao addresses the various factors in both the internal and external environment that prompt a police organization to adopt innovative approaches

to policing. Such factors range from managerial tenure and personnel diversity to local political culture and community characteristics.

The Nature of Community Policing Innovations:
Do the Ends Justify the Means?
(Jihong Zhao and Quint Thurman, 1996)
24 pp., Product #810
ISBN #: 1-878734-46-6
Member Price: $5.95
Nonmember Price: $6.50
In *The Nature of Community Policing Innovations,* authors Jihong Zhao and Quint Thurman use James Thompson's theory of organizational change as a theoretical framework to investigate the core mission of American policing. They first examine the prioritization of police functions and go on to address the relationship between those priorities and the means used to achieve them, particularly as they relate to community policing.

Themes and Variations in Community Policing:
Case Studies in Community Policing
(PERF, 1996)
92 pp., Product #809
ISBN #: 1-878734-42-3
Member Price: $14.95
Nonmember Price: $16.50
Supported through a grant from the National Institute of Justice, *Themes and Variations in Community Policing* offers six examples of how community policing has been developed and applied by police agencies throughout North America. Each case study provides the historical context in which community policing has emerged, the specific steps the police agency has taken to implement it, and frank insights from police personnel, city officials and citizens regarding this modern approach to policing.

Managing Innovation in Policing:
The Untapped Potential of the Middle Manager
(William A. Geller and Guy Swanger, 1995)
204 pp., Product #803
ISBN #: 1-878734-41-5
Member Price: $24.95
Nonmember Price: $27.50
The conventional wisdom holds that middle managers are almost inevitably obstacles to strategic innovation, including community policing. In *Managing Innovation in Policing,* however, authors Geller and Swanger argue that, when properly motivated and supported, police middle managers have been and can be key players in policing reform. This book includes case studies of successful middle managers and suggestions for how police senior leaders, city officials and others can help position middle managers to voluntarily, proactively and effectively help implement community policing. *Managing Innovation in Policing* has become a popular text for community policing training courses.

Dispute Resolution and Policing:
A Collaborative Approach Toward Effective Problem Solving
(Ron Glensor and Alissa Stern, 1995)
16 pp., Product #007
Member Price: $5
Nonmember Price: $5.50
Today's police are called upon to handle an increasingly diverse array of community problems, some of which they lack the authority or expertise to resolve. Consequently, some law enforcement agencies have turned to dispute resolution as a means for working with professionals from other fields to develop new problem-solving strategies. In *Dispute Resolution and Policing,* authors Glensor and Stern discuss dispute resolution techniques and use case studies to illustrate how some agencies have successfully used dispute resolution to address recurring problems.

Quality Policing: The Madison Experience
(David C. Couper and Sabine H. Lobitz, 1991)
101 pp., Product #200
ISBN #: 1-878734-22-9
Member Price: $10
Nonmember Price: $11
This discussion paper chronicles the experiences of the Madison, Wis., Police Department in using quality improvement methods to implement a problem-solving approach to community policing. *Quality Policing* is a detailed diary of the obstacles and achievements experienced by that department over a nine-year period as it moved toward a style of leadership conducive to formulating long-term solutions to the chronic, underlying causes of crime and disorder. The account details how department personnel worked together to establish advisory councils, mission statements and neighborhood police districts in their quest to improve the department.